19.95

The One Year® Devos for Teens

Tyndale House Publishers, Inc., Carol Stream, Illinois

DEVOS

for teens

usie Shellenberger

Visit Tyndale online at www.tyndale.com.

The One Year Devos for Teens

Designed by Jacqueline L. Nuñez

Edited by Karin Stock Buursma

Published in association with the literary agency of Alive Literary Agency, 7680 Goddard St., Suite 200, Colorado Springs, CO 80920.

The Library of Congress has cataloged the first edition as follows:
Shellenberger, Susie
One year devos for teens / Susie Shellenberger.
p. cm.
ISBN 978-0-8423-6202-3 Vol. 1 (pbk)
ISBN 978-1-4143-0181-5 Vol. 2 (pbk)
1. Teenagers—Prayer-books and devotions—English. 2. Devotional calendars. I. Title.
BV4850 .S47 2002
242′.63—dc21 2002011517

Printed in the United States of America

21 20 19 18 17 16 15
16 15 14 13 12 11 10

Dedication

Dedicated to the staff of *Brio* magazine. Your desire to see teens grow intimately close to their heavenly Father enthuses, inspires, and motivates me. One of the greatest blessings in my life is the privilege of working with you every day. Marty Kasza, Krishana Kraft, Kathy Gowler, Lexie Rhodes, and Michelle McCorkle . . . I love you!

Details Matter

Most of us don't like to get bogged down with the fine print. We enjoy seeing the big picture but don't want to take the time on the small details. Take a peek at the result of overlooking some of the finer details (such as word placement and spelling) in the following church bulletin announcements.

- Bertha Belch, a missionary from Africa, will be speaking tonight at Calvary Memorial Church. Come tonight and hear Bertha Belch all the way from Africa.
- The cost for attending the Fasting and Prayer conference includes meals.
- The peacemaking meeting scheduled for today has been canceled due to a conflict.
- Don't let worry kill you—let the church help.
- At the evening service tonight, the sermon topic will be "What Is Hell?" Come early and listen to our choir practice.
- Scouts are saving aluminum cans, bottles, and other items to be recycled. Proceeds will be used to cripple children.
- This evening at 7 P.M. there will be a hymn sing in the park across from the church. Bring a blanket and come prepared to sin.

When it comes to establishing an intimate, growing relationship with Jesus Christ, it's important to pay attention to the details. God knows how busy you are. He's not interested in burdening you with so many details you become spiritually frustrated and give up.

In fact, I've discovered only two really important details he wants us to focus on:

1. Being committed to God requires 100 percent.
2. Being committed to God requires meeting with him daily.

So let's take the next year to develop these two details. In fact, go ahead and make this part of your New Year's resolution, okay? If you'll stick with it—meet right here every single day for a year—next year at this time, you'll not only have a solid handle on how to grow closer to Christ . . . you'll already *be* closer to Christ.

Wow! Think about it: In one year, you could be closer to God than you've ever been before! Ready? Let's go!

If you're willing to take the plunge, sign up:

Know It!

God loves you and wants to empower you to become spiritually victorious.

Read It!

1 Chronicles 22:19; Colossians 4:2

Pray It!

Father, I commit this year to you. I really want to know you better and to become all you want me to be. So with your help, I pledge to meet with you every single day. I'll trust you to develop my spiritual muscles and mold me into solid spiritual shape.

____

Sign Here

Ignoring the Details

Know It!
God wants to be in charge of your life. This is a detail you can't afford to overlook.

Read It!
2 Kings 9

Pray It!
Confess to God your tendency to try to do things on your own. Ask him to help you wait on his guidance so you can become all he dreams for you to be.

His name was Jehu (Jay-who?), and his story is found in 2 Kings 9-10. His bio starts out great—he loved God and wanted to wipe out idol worship. He was particularly focused on eliminating a specific idol—Baal. Thousands of people in Israel worshiped Baal, and Jehu wanted them to worship the one true God—Jehovah. So he decided to force them.

You can already see the bad beginning to develop with the good, can't you? Common sense tells you we can't force anyone to follow God. Jehu started out with a wonderful desire—we applaud him for wanting to bring his entire country to God—but his plan quickly soured when he took matters into his own hands.

God doesn't want to share control with you. "For I, the Lord your God, am a jealous God" (Exodus 20:5). He is God; you are not. He wants total control over your life—decisions about dating, your future plans, your activities, your friends.

The world is filled with people doing good things in their own power, without involving God. Guess what? A million good things accomplished in human power are only temporary at best. Jehu devised a scheme to wipe out Baal worship from the entire country of Israel. That would be like you creating a plan to wipe out all evil from your school! Mind-boggling, huh? With a task of this magnitude, wouldn't common sense tell you that God's help and intervention (and control) would be a necessity?

Jehu's plan went down fast and furious. I'll save the gory details for your own personal reading, but it's safe to say if his life were a movie, it would be rated R for violence. Eventually, with a lot of bloodshed and zeal, Jehu eliminated Baal worship from Israel. A good thing! But he did it with deceit and gross violence—a bad thing!

We often try to rationalize, don't we? *But this is really a good thing I'm doing*, we think. Yet if we're going about it the wrong way, in our own power, "unanointed and unappointed," we've forgotten some details that could eventually mean spiritual death.

Details That Cost

Jehu was obsessively focused on one goal: removing Baal worship from Israel.

God wants you to have goals and strategy. Without them you won't be able to accomplish anything that really matters in life. Can you imagine this conversation between a coach and his football team?

"Go get 'em, guys!"

"Yeah! We're fired up, Coach. What's the strategy?"

"Strategy? Ah, we don't need a strategy. Just go win."

"But what about specific plays?"

"Uh, I never got around to that. Just do the best you can."

That's crazy, isn't it? Just as an athletic team can't be successful without goals and strategy, neither can you be spiritually successful without them. But God doesn't want you to become so focused on the goal that you can't tell if the strategy (the way you accomplish your goal) is good or bad.

Jehu's goal was wonderful. His strategy reeked. But he couldn't see that, because he was too obsessed with the goal. When we become obsessed with anything other than Jesus Christ, we're obsessed with the wrong thing—even if it's a good thing!

Jehu deceived a large gathering of Baal worshipers into believing a huge Baal rally would be held at their facility. But when they turned out for the festivity, Jehu locked them inside their own sanctuary and had all of them brutally slaughtered. Check out the result in 2 Kings 10:28: "So Jehu destroyed Baal worship in Israel."

Wow! That's an incredible feat. But Jehu's victory was short-lived. Why? Because he overlooked a really important detail: Being committed to God requires 100 percent of our attention. Sneak a peak at 2 Kings 10:29: "However, he did not turn away from . . . the worship of the golden calves at Bethel and Dan." Then check out 2 Kings 10:31: "Yet Jehu was not careful to keep the law of the Lord, the God of Israel, with all his heart."

Jehu did a ton of good—he wiped out Baal worship in Israel! But there was one area of his heart that simply wasn't in God's control. And now the sad ending begins to take shape: "At about that time the Lord began to whittle down the size of Israel" (2 Kings 10:32, TLB). Shortly afterward, Jehu died.

Don't be a Jehu—committed in outward appearance but overlooking the important detail that being committed to God requires 100 percent.

Know It!
We serve a jealous God. He wants to give you life abundantly, but it requires 100 percent submission to his authority.

Read It!
2 Kings 10

Pray It!
Ask God to help you not become so obsessed with your own goals that you can't see his will. Tell him you want his goals and strategy for your life; you want to give him 100 percent.

Seems Weird

Know It!
Being committed to God requires 100 percent.

Read It!
John 3:19-21;
Ephesians 3:20;
1 Timothy 3:1

Pray It!
Ask God to help you keep focused on him alone—not on other people who might make fun of you. Pray that others will see the positive difference Jesus is making in your life.

When you decide to live a life that's 100-percent committed to Jesus Christ, others will notice.

Those who don't share your faith may interpret your actions and your commitment to God as something really weird. That's okay. The Bible is very clear on the fact that it won't be easy to live a holy lifestyle. Check this out: "It is quite true that the way to live a godly life is not an easy matter. But the answer lies in Christ" (1 Timothy 3:16, TLB).

What behavior of a 100-percent-committed Christian would appear weird to nonbelievers? (Circle all that apply.)

a. Refusing to attend a party where alcohol will be served.
b. Walking out of the theater in the middle of a PG-13 movie that's filled with four-letter words.
c. Abstaining from sexual intimacy outside of marriage.
d. Reaching out to the campus dweeb.

The truth is, if you really are committed 100 percent to Christ, your entire lifestyle may seem weird to friends who don't share your faith.

Here's an example: Sixteen-year-old Britni was determined to serve God with a 100-percent commitment. But each day she had lunch with the same group of girls, who bragged about their sexual escapades and hassled Britni for her "prudishness."

One day, she'd had it. Britni looked the girls in the eye and said, "Anytime I want to, I can become just like you. But you'll never be able to regain what you've lost. You can never go back and reclaim what I still have."

Guess what! They never made fun of her again.

Your friends won't understand your godly convictions. They won't relate to your standards and your morality. But . . . what did the Scripture say? "The answer lies in Christ."

If you'll maintain a strong, intimate, growing relationship with Jesus, others will eventually respect the peace that's shining through your life. They'll notice your calm spirit, your confidence, your deep satisfaction in something (and Someone) much more powerful than a weekend party. And who knows? Eventually . . . they may even ask you how they can get what you have!

On-fire Christians may seem weird to the world. That's okay. Expect it. Know that people won't understand. That's not the issue. The issue is remaining focused on God.

I Need a Little Help

The Bible doesn't give us his name, so let's just call him Brandon. His story is tucked away in the second chapter of Mark. We begin the story with good news and bad news. The bad news? Brandon was paralyzed. He couldn't walk. The good news? He had some incredible friends!

His friends had heard that Jesus was teaching in someone's home. They'd also heard that Jesus of Nazareth had healed blind men. *Hey! If he can make someone see, maybe he can make Brandon walk,* they thought.

Imagine for a second that you're Brandon. You've heard about the miracles, and you know Jesus will soon be in your town. You desperately want to be where he is . . . but you can't get there. Even though it's just down the street, it's still too far for you, because you can only go where someone carries you.

Wouldn't it be heartbreaking to be so close to healing, yet not be able to do anything about it? Sometimes there are things we simply can't do on our own.

Enter Brandon's friends. They were just as excited as he was about the possibility of getting him to Jesus! They truly cared about Brandon. They wanted to see him walk. So they decided to intervene and help Brandon do what he couldn't do for himself—get to Jesus.

Problem: The house where Jesus was speaking was completely full. Hundreds of people swarmed outside the walls. No one dared surrender an inch of space—not even for someone on a stretcher.

Solution: "Let's go where no one else has gone!" Jeremy said.

"Look around, dufus. They're everywhere!" Ryan responded.

"Oh yeah? No one's on the roof!" Jeremy stated.

Teen guys. Aren't they great? Daring, brave, persistent . . . Brandon's friends cared enough about him to break through the roof and lower their buddy through the ceiling with ropes.

Jesus smiled at their faith. He loves it when we go the extra mile for our friends in need. Without hesitation, Jesus healed Brandon.

Is there something in your life that seems so big you're afraid to tackle it on your own? Turn to your Christian friends. Ask them to pray *with* you. Ecclesiastes 4:9-10 talks about the importance of having a friend. Memorize it. And don't be afraid to ask someone for help when you need it.

Know It!

Jesus never intended for you to go it alone. He values godly friendships. It's not only okay to ask for help; it's wise.

Read It!

Ecclesiastes 4:9-10; Mark 2:1-12

Pray It!

Does your pride prevent you from seeking the help you need? Confess that to God and ask him to make you willing to ask for help from godly friends when you need it.

Excuses

Know It!
Jesus doesn't expect you to be perfect. He *does* expect you to be honest about your mistakes and admit you need help.

Read It!
Proverbs 20:27; 21:2; 2 Corinthians 8:10

Pray It!
Ask God's forgiveness for your habit of justifying your shortcomings. Tell him you want to be honest and learn from your mistakes.

Jason was always late, and his friends were fed up with him. Whenever they made plans to do something or go somewhere, they automatically told Jason to arrive 15 minutes earlier than anyone else—thinking he'd be late and arrive at the time they were actually leaving.

But it didn't work. Jason was *still* late.

He always had an excuse. And that was part of the frustration. Jason rationalized everything. "My alarm didn't go off." "Traffic was unbelievable!" "I couldn't find a clean shirt."

He was a master at justifying his actions.

Deana was convinced her teachers were out to get her—every single one of them! "Mrs. Woodard gives me detention at least twice a week," Deana complained. "And Mr. Hoskins gave me a zero on that history project. Can you believe it?"

It didn't matter that Mrs. Woodard gave Deana detention because she was continually late for class, or that Mr. Hoskins had given her an extra week to complete her history project and still never received anything.

It's easy to rationalize our actions, isn't it? We can justify why we did this or didn't do that. But God doesn't listen to excuses. He's interested in something much deeper . . . our hearts. He focuses on our motives. Our intentions.

Where do you stand? Has it become easy for you to justify something in your life that's not right? Do you find yourself making excuses?

You've known about your science report for three weeks. It's due tomorrow. You . . .

a. ask your teacher for an extension, naming the many reasons it's been impossible for you to complete it on time.
b. complain that Mr. Nelson never gives anyone enough time to do a decent job.
c. quickly pull something together and hand it in—even though you know it won't be worth much.
d. admit you procrastinated and learn from your mistake.

God can do a lot with an honest heart! He knows we make mistakes, and he's willing to help us learn and grow from them. But if we continue to justify wrong actions and refuse to admit we have a problem, we'll never become all he dreams for us.

"We've been studying prayer in youth group for three weeks now," Eric said, "and I don't get it. The Bible clearly says that we can ask for anything using Jesus' name and we'll get it."

"So what'd you ask for—a zillion dollars?" Kayla teased.

"No. I *did* ask for a new Porsche. But nothing's happened."

"You're not supposed to ask for stupid stuff, Eric!" Sheree said.

"A brand-new Porsche is *not* stupid," Brian added.

"So we're not supposed to take the Bible at its word?" Eric asked.

"No," Sheree said. "I mean, yes."

"Well, which is it?" Kayla asked. "Either the Bible really is true, or it's not."

While the Bible is true, we often need to look a little more carefully at Jesus' teachings so we understand them better. Jesus did tell his disciples they could ask for anything using his name, and he would do it. But he went on to say he'd accomplish it *because of the glory it would bring to God.*

So before we start making a list of material demands, we first need to ask ourselves if our requests will glorify our heavenly Father. Maybe we should also take a look at what it means to "pray in Jesus' name."

I'll never forget the date I had to the big Valentine banquet my junior year of high school. Mom handed me her credit card with permission to purchase a new dress and sign her name to the statement. I knew, though, that when I signed Mom's name I'd be signing *for* her. That meant I needed to buy something she would approve of. If the dress was too short, too tight, or too low, I couldn't in good conscience sign Mom's name to the statement.

I understood that when I shopped, I was "shopping in her name." I was in essence saying, "This is something Mom will like. This is what she would have bought for me if she had done the shopping."

It works the same with prayer. When we pray "in Jesus' name," we're praying as we think Jesus would actually pray himself. In other words, we're saying, "God, I believe this is what Jesus would have said if he were praying for me."

It's not a magic phrase to get what we want. It's a way to focus intently on how he wants us to pray and what he wants us to pray for.

Know It!
When you pray, think carefully about what Jesus would want you to pray about. Pray according to his will—which means you don't pray for things that go against his character.

Read It!
Psalm 4:1;
Proverbs 15:8;
Matthew 21:22;
Acts 1:14

Pray It!
Ask God to teach you to pray according to his will. Pray that you will not look at prayer as a way to get things but will see it as genuine communication with God.

Our Father

Know It!
God longs to hear his children pray. Don't think of the Lord's Prayer as a specific formula. But let it teach you how to get into the proper mind-set for approaching God.

Read It!
Matthew 6:9-13; 2 Chronicles 7:14; Psalm 32:6

Pray It!
Tell God you realize he's in charge, and you want to learn how to communicate more effectively with him. Ask him to teach you how to pray from the heart.

Jesus lived 33 years, and only his last three years were devoted to public ministry. Since time with his disciples was so limited, he had to prioritize what he would teach them. We might think he'd cram in a few of the following:

- Creating a buffet for 5,000 with just a few fish.
- Providing 20/20 vision without contact lenses or laser surgery.
- Building the world's largest church with only 12 members.

But instead of spending time on what may have *seemed* important, Jesus got right to the basics: He taught his followers how to pray. He modeled his own prayer life for them and instructed them to follow his example. We refer to this specific prayer as "the Lord's Prayer." Over the next few days we'll take a closer look at this prayer as it appears in the New King James Version (see Matthew 6:9-13).

Jesus begins with *Our Father in heaven.*

Why did Jesus begin with this? Did he need to remind himself whom he was talking to? No. But he *did* want to remind us right off the bat who's in authority. We tend to think of a father figure being the head of the family, or the one who's in charge. Jesus wanted his followers to remember that God, as their heavenly Father, is in control. He is God; we are not.

And why did he bother praying "in heaven"? Heaven is a perfect place—God's kingdom—and it symbolizes everything that's perfect. Jesus wants to remind us that we're praying to a perfect Father in a perfect place.

Our Father: The Perfect One who's in absolute control and cares for our well-being. By admitting that he's in control, we also recognize we're under his authority.

In heaven: The perfect kingdom of the Almighty. No other gods dwell in this kingdom. It is eternal, and the only way we can receive entrance is through the Son of God the Father.

Think about *your* prayers for a second, and answer this question:

When I pray,

a. my prayers are usually filled with gimmes.
b. my prayers are . . . well, I really don't pray that much.
c. I talk with God about everything, but sometimes I forget that he's the authority in my life.
d. I try to say stuff I think God wants to hear.

It's almost impossible to turn on the TV and not hear someone using God's name. It's frequently used as a punch line or to express emotion. In fact, most of us don't even think twice when we hear someone say, "Oh, my God!"

Guess what? God wants our stomach to twist in knots whenever we hear his name being misused. And unless the name of GOD is being used in prayer or in talking about him, it's being misused.

When Jesus taught his disciples how to pray, he said to his Father, *Hallowed be Your name.* In other words, "I give the utmost respect and honor to your name, Almighty God."

What does this mean? First, we recognize that God is our Father. He is in authority over us and reigns in a perfect kingdom that will someday be our home if we follow him. Then we recognize that his very name is holy. When we approach God with this mind-set, we're laying out the proper ingredients for genuine communication.

In Leviticus 22:2, God tells Moses to instruct Aaron and his sons (who were the priests) how to treat the sacred offerings with respect, "so they will not profane my holy name." And in Deuteronomy 28:58, the Israelites are told if they don't revere God's name, they'll suffer fearful plagues, prolonged disasters, and sickness that will seem to hang on forever. Malachi 4:2 talks about the rewards of revering God's name.

*How can **you** revere the name of God? (Circle all that apply.)*

a. Hit anyone who misuses God's name.
b. Leave the room when someone takes God's name in vain.
c. Ask the person misusing God's name if he realizes what he's doing.
d. Start a "Revere God's Name" club on your campus.
e. Make sure whenever you use his name, it's always done with respect, honor, and reverence.
f. Share your thoughts on honoring his name with some of your friends. Discuss it. Pray about it.

While you can't rewrite movie scripts, you *can* ask God for a tender heart so that when you hear something you shouldn't, you'll wince. Or walk away. Or write a letter. Or make your thoughts known. After all, if someone used your mother's name or even your name in a derogatory way, you'd probably take a stand. Will you do the same for God's name?

Know It!

God never wants you to become comfortable hearing his name taken in vain, used as a punch line, or spoken in negative terms. If it doesn't bother you, it needs to!

Read It!

Matthew 6:9-13; Psalm 33:8; 89:7; Ezekiel 36:23

Pray It!

Are you often not even aware of God's holy name being used in vain? Confess that to him. Ask him to give you a sensitive heart and teach you how to revere his holy name with your words and actions.

Your Kingdom Come

Know It!

You don't have to wish for God's will. You can actually live in it each day of your life. You have the power to make that choice. And you can ask God to fill you with his Holy Spirit to live out God's will through your thoughts, actions, and attitudes.

Read It!

Matthew 6:9-13; Psalm 40:8; 143:10; Matthew 26:42

Pray It!

Tell God you want to live in his perfect kingdom, and ask him to establish his kingdom within your heart so you will do his will.

It's hard to imagine a perfect world, isn't it? Our minds often drift to fairy tales when we think about a perfect kingdom. But God assures us that heaven is no fairy tale. It's an actual place that truly exists—God's perfect kingdom—and we can live there eternally with him if we accept him as our Lord and Savior.

Are there days you long to be in God's perfect kingdom? When you're faced with a pop history quiz, when you've been rejected by someone you care deeply about, when your heart is torn in two, do you find yourself longing for heaven—for a time and a place where there will be no more hurt, no more illness, no more death, and no more tears?

Jesus knows exactly how you feel! As he faced persecution, rebuke, and rejection from those he loved, he too longed for God's perfect kingdom. In praying *Your kingdom come*, we can imagine Jesus lifting that portion of his prayer as a plea to his heavenly Father. "Come quickly, Lord! Remove the sin and injustice from the world and let your kingdom reign."

Your will be done on earth as it is in heaven. We've already recognized that heaven is a perfect place where God's perfect will is constantly in effect. But wouldn't it be incredible if that happened on earth as well? Can you even imagine going to a school where everyone loves one another? A place where no one cheats, lies, or puts anyone down? Can you visualize being employed in an office where honesty reigns and the other person always comes first? Imagine playing sports against a team that actually cared about your physical well-being and never intentionally fouled other players or spoke negatively about them. It's almost impossible to imagine a godly environment here on earth.

Though the entire earth is not a godly place, you can ask God to help you create a holy environment where you live and work and interact with others. What if everywhere you went, people saw God's perfect kingdom being lived out through your life? Talk about a powerful influence!

Yes, we know God's will is being done in heaven. But he wants you to yearn for his will to be accomplished right now . . . on earth . . . *through your life*!

Daily Bread?

Isn't it exciting to know you serve a God who is extremely focused on meeting your needs?

A missionary once told the story of a poor widow living in Mexico. She had two small children and was down to her last few cents. But she believed God would meet the needs of her little family. So she spent three hours in prayer seeking the Lord's direction as to how she should spend her last few cents.

Eventually she sensed God directing her to a large market in a nearby village. She had never been there before, and when she arrived at the market, she was overwhelmed with its enormity. There were 122 checkout lanes!

She entered the building and sensed God telling her to get a shopping cart and fill it with a three months' supply of groceries! When her cart was overflowing with the essentials for her little family, she approached the checkout lanes and sensed God directing her to lane number seven.

There was only one man in front of her. When the clerk was finished with him, she pulled a chain across the lane and said, "Sorry. It's my lunchtime. You'll have to go to another lane."

The widow looked the clerk in the eyes and calmly said, "No. My Father told me to come here. I'll wait."

An hour later, the clerk returned to find the widow standing patiently beside her cart of groceries. Together, they unloaded the items onto the conveyor belt. The widow's heart was pounding as the bill began to mount. She nervously fingered the 22 cents in her worn purse.

When the next-to-the-last item was being rung up, the noise of the supermarket was interrupted by the sound of the manager's voice through the intercom. "Attention, shoppers!" he announced. "Today is our seventh-year anniversary. Whoever is being checked out right now in lane number seven will receive all groceries absolutely free—compliments of our market."

When Jesus prayed, *Give us this day our daily bread*, he knew his Father was in the business of provision. Even before we were born, God was already working to meet our needs—creating oil in the ground so we would have fuel; filling lakes, rivers, and streams with water to quench our thirst. Let this portion of the Lord's Prayer be a constant reminder that God has promised to take care of his children.

Know It!

You can trust the creator of the universe to take care of you. If he cares for the animal kingdom, the plant life, and all of nature, think how much more he'll care for you!

Read It!

Matthew 6:9-13;
Psalm 37:25;
Hebrews 13:5;
Revelation 7:16

Pray It!

Thank God for caring for your deepest needs. Ask him to help you remember that he will always provide for your physical and spiritual needs.

JANUARY 12

Forgiving Our Debtors

Know It!

You'll never be all God intends for you to be until you allow him to help you forgive those who have hurt you. *So if I say I forgive someone, does that mean the hurt automatically goes away?* No. Your wounds may require time to heal. *Yeah, but what if I don't feel like I'm actually forgiving someone?* Forgiveness is a decision. Tell God you consciously choose to forgive, and trust him to make your feelings eventually match your decisions.

Read It!

Daniel 9:9;
Matthew 6:9-15;
Ephesians 4:32

Pray It!

Are there people you don't even want to forgive? Tell that to God, and ask him to change your heart. Choose to forgive instead of holding a grudge, and trust him to do the rest.

"I can't believe Ryan!" Brent yelled. "He told Coach Andrews I failed the math test, and now the coach is talking about suspending me until I can bring my grades up. I'll never forgive Ryan for that!"

"Ugh!" Katie groaned. "I knew I shouldn't have trusted Julie with my secret. Now she's told the entire zip code that I'm planning on breaking it off with Matt. How could she do this to me? I'll never forgive her for this!"

You understand, don't you? When someone hurts you, disappoints you, or breaks a trust, it's often hard to forgive. Your emotions take over, and because you're angry, you decide to hold a grudge. After all . . . the person had no right to treat you that way!

But for you to fully experience the forgiveness of God, Jesus teaches that you must also forgive those who have wronged you. Read carefully this line in his prayer: *And forgive us our debts as we forgive our debtors.*

That little two-letter word "as" really connects the process, doesn't it? It works like an equation. We forgive, and we're forgiven. But if we hate, hold grudges, and let bitterness fester in our lives because of the wrong we've suffered from someone else, how can we expect to experience forgiveness from God, whom we ourselves have wronged and hurt?

When God forgave us of our sin, he made the ultimate choice. We were the ones who crucified his Son. Think about it: His only Son died for our sins—us, the ones who have failed, tuned him out, and walked away. Do we deserve his forgiveness? No. Do we need his forgiveness? Yes.

Maybe you feel as though the people who have hurt you don't deserve to be forgiven. It doesn't matter. You don't deserve it either. But because God chose to forgive *you*, it's essential that you choose to forgive others. And when you do, God's freedom is unleashed in your life. There's absolutely nothing in the world more freeing than forgiving someone.

Make that choice. Decide right now to forgive. Go ahead. Let it go.

"Hey, Matt! How's it goin'?" Paul yelled across the parking lot. He sprinted to catch up with his friend.

"Okay."

"You don't sound too convincing. And you sure didn't seem like yourself at practice today."

"Yeah . . . well. I guess I'm just going through a tough time right now."

"Come on, Matt. What gives?"

"Paul, God's just really giving me a work-over this week."

"Whaddya talking about, Matt?"

"Everywhere I turn, I'm being blasted in the face with temptation."

"So?" Paul prodded. "All of us are tempted; you know that. Why do you think Pastor Steve talks about it so much in youth group?"

"Nah. This is different. I think God's trying to see if I can handle being tempted. He keeps tripping me up."

"Whoa, Matt. Wait a sec. God isn't out to trip you up. Remember what Pastor Steve said last week? God is on *your* side, Bro! No way does he want you to fail."

"We got a new computer at our house last week."

"Uh-oh," Paul said. "I know what that means."

"Yep. You guessed it. I mean . . . I don't even know where this stuff comes from, but I'm getting all kinds of porn e-mails and junk that shows up! I accidentally opened one."

"Then what?"

"I quickly deleted it, but it's still hanging on my mind."

"You did the right thing in deleting it. But Matt, it's not God's fault you're being flooded with junk like that."

"Yeah? I think he's bringing all this stuff on me to see how I'll handle it."

"Look, Matt. First thing you gotta do is get your parents to get one of those protector devices put on the computer. That'll block most of the junk."

"I just can't figure out why God threw that stuff right in my face—especially when I was tired and vulnerable. He keeps tempting me, and I can't stand it!"

"Hey, Matt, you need to talk to Pastor Steve. I think you're confused about some stuff. Remember that line in the Lord's Prayer: *And do not lead us into temptation*? I don't think God's tempting you. Hey, Steve and I are gonna shoot hoops tomorrow after school. Why don't you meet us at the gym, and we can both talk to him?"

"I guess it couldn't hurt. Deal."

Know It!

God never tempts us! The only one who tempts us is Satan. God equals holiness, goodness, and purity. Satan equals deceit, hate, and evil. Bottom line: Satan will never do anything good, and God will never do anything evil.

When you're tempted, don't blame God. It's not his fault. He's here to bring you *through* temptation. Satan, on the other hand, is out to tempt you, trip you, and hate you.

Read It!

Matthew 6:9-13; Mark 1:13; Luke 4:1-15; James 1:13-16

Pray It!

Ask Jesus to cleanse your mind and purify your heart so you'll be disgusted with sin. Thank him for wanting to help you be victorious over sin.

Deliver Us from Evil

Know It!
God will not put you in a vacuum and exempt you from temptation. But he will provide a way out. Every single time. Your job? When you're tempted, run! And while you're running, pray!

Read It!
Matthew 6:9-13;
1 Corinthians 10:13;
Hebrews 2:18; 4:15

Pray It!
Ask God for the strength to help you run the opposite direction from temptation.

"Not bad, Steve . . . for an old guy!" Paul teased after a quick game of basketball.

"Yeah," Matt joked. "Let's see if you can eat like you can dribble."

"Oh, I get it! You guys ask me to shoot hoops just so you'll have someone to stick the pizza bill with."

"Yeah!" Matt said. "Seriously . . . I wanna talk about some stuff."

"Well, what are we waiting for? We've got a double-pepperoni to order!" Steve said. "I'll call it in now."

Steve dialed the pizza place from his cell phone, then sat down on the bleachers.

"So, what's going on, Matt?"

"Well, you know all that temptation stuff you've been talking about in youth group?"

"Yeah. We're all tempted. No one's exempt."

"Especially me, Steve! I'm constantly barraged with temptation. It's only a matter of time before I'm afraid I'll give in."

"Okay, Matt. First of all, you *do* know who's behind the temptation, right?"

"I've been thinking that God was tempting me—just to see how I'd hold up."

"You can sit on that for good, pal. God never tempts us!"

Matt told Steve about the new family computer and the pornographic mail he was getting. "I asked my parents last night to get some kind of block for the computer, and Dad's looking into it today."

"Good move, Matt," Steve said. "And until that block is installed, stay away from the computer."

"Yeah, but . . . how can I resist the temptation if I don't have it in front of me to say no to? Don't you think the way we resist temptation is to stand up against it?"

"No, I don't, Matt. God never once told anyone to handle temptation by facing it."

"Then how are we supposed to resist?" Paul asked.

"By running away from it," Steve explained. "You see, God knows you can't escape being tempted. After all, you live in the *world.* But he wants you to stay as far away from temptation as possible."

"So when I'm being tempted, I should run the opposite direction?" Matt pressed.

"Exactly," Steve said. "And the cool thing is that God will *deliver* you from Satan's grasp. Remember the Lord's Prayer? Jesus prayed, *And do not lead us into temptation, but deliver us from the evil one.* God wants to give you victory OVER temptation."

It's hard for our human minds to understand that God never had to be created. He's always been in existence; he was never born. There's no beginning with him, because he *is* the beginning. Absolutely nothing—zero—existed before he did.

We're human, so we want to create a beginning for him, because that's how we understand life. Our lives had a beginning, and our lives will have an end. So we naturally want to put God in that same box.

But know it: He is the beginning and the end. God is all-powerful, all-knowing, and everywhere at once, and yet he is also able to be intimately involved in every area of our lives. He created the smallest ant, and he created the mammoth grizzly. He designed the Appalachian Mountains, and he designed the Sahara Desert.

He invented music, color, rhyme, motion, laughter, surprise, adventure, and mystery. He masterminded the intricacies of the human body, all of plant life, and even snowflakes.

He called into being the vastness of the Grand Canyon, the strength of Niagara Falls, and the wonder of the ocean waves. He alone decided why donkeys are stubborn, when water would freeze, and how the earth rotates.

God IS. And he is above ALL. He's wonder and miracles and clarity and purpose. He's the definition of good and holy and absolute truth. He is Genesis, and he is Revelation. He is now, and he is eternal.

God is the Supreme Being and has authority over everything. There has never existed—nor will there ever be—anyone or anything greater, more powerful, more holy, or more mighty than he is.

God is the Father of time, the Father of the universe, and the Father of humanity. He is eternal glory and righteousness. His faithfulness will never end.

No human has eternal life without him, and every human will bow in allegiance to his holy name. He will judge, he will forgive, and he will punish. He is grace, and he is wrath. He is perfect and beyond our finite understanding.

Man cannot escape God's sight. No rocket or submarine can propel a person beyond or beneath God's creation. His all-seeing eyes know exactly where each life on the planet lives and breathes.

He IS. Above all things, he IS. And he is forever.

For Yours is the kingdom and the power and the glory forever. Amen.

Know It!

You can't outsmart or outgive God Almighty. He's the reason you live, and he wants to fill your life with incredible meaning. Make time to think about his vast goodness. Praise him for his holiness. Ponder his faithfulness.

Read It!

Matthew 6:9-13;
John 1:1-14;
Romans 8:35-39;
Revelation 1:8; 21:6

Pray It!

Praise God for his power and faithfulness, and thank him for reminding you that there is no one above him. Ask for his help so you will think about his holiness and awesomeness more often.

Quiz Time

Know It!
God not only wants you to pray consistently, he wants you to understand why and how Jesus taught his disciples to pray.

Read It!
2 Chronicles 6:39; Psalms 40:1; 50:15; 118:5; Matthew 6:9-13

Pray It!
Ask God to help you make the Lord's Prayer part of your lifestyle.

Prayer is a **direct line** to heaven. Think about it: **God's line is never busy.** He doesn't have "call waiting." When you call, he answers. Every time.

Let's recap what we've talked about the past few days on prayer. Ready for a quiz? In each question, circle all answers that apply.

Jesus begins his prayer by addressing God as Our Father. What are some of the other names God is called throughout Scripture?

a. Alpha and Omega (Beginning and End)
b. The Big Guy in the Sky
c. Jehovah
d. Supreme Being

When we ask that ***God's will be done*** *on earth as it is in heaven, we're saying*

a. "What will be, will be."
b. "If it's gonna happen, it's gonna happen; there's nothing we can do about it."
c. "God, I know you're in charge. Turn the hearts of our people to you."

When Jesus asked God to ***give us food*** *again today as usual, he*

a. was afraid God would forget supper.
b. was hungry.
c. wanted to remind the disciples that we are not our own providers; we trust our heavenly Father to meet our needs.

When Jesus asked God to ***forgive our sins,*** *it served as a reminder*

a. that God actually can forgive our sins.
b. that we should forgive others, because God forgives us.
c. that we only have to forgive immediate family members and close relatives.

Jesus asked our heavenly Father to ***deliver us from temptation.*** *This serves as a great reminder*

a. to do our homework.
b. that God really can save us from being defeated through temptation.
c. that every Christian in the world is tempted.
d. that even though we're tempted, God can help us flee from temptation.

Using Your Hand as a Prayer Guide

Prayer is the most powerful and effective tool God has given us. But sometimes it's hard to know who to pray for. Today, concentrate on praying using your hand in the following guide.

1. Your thumb is nearest to you. So begin your prayers by praying for those closest to you—close friends and family. They're the easiest to remember. To pray for our loved ones is, as C. S. Lewis once said, "a sweet duty."
2. The next finger is the pointing finger. Pray for those who teach, instruct, and heal. This includes teachers, doctors, and ministers. They need support and wisdom to point others in the right direction. Keep them in your prayers.
3. The next finger is the tallest finger. It reminds us of our leaders. Pray for the president, leaders in business and industry, and administrators. These people shape our nation and guide public opinion. They need God's guidance.
4. The fourth finger is our ring finger. Many people are surprised that this is our weakest finger, as any piano teacher will tell us. It should remind us to pray for those who are weak, in trouble, or in pain. They need your prayers day and night. You can never pray too much for them.
5. And lastly comes our little finger; the smallest finger of all . . . which is where we should place ourselves in relation to God and others. As the Bible says, "He who is least among you all will be great" (Luke 9:48, NKJV). Let your pinkie remind you to pray for yourself. By the time you have prayed for the other four groups, your own needs will be put into perspective, and you'll be able to pray for yourself more effectively.

Know It!

God loves to hear us pray. He never grows tired of hearing our voices, drying our tears, rejoicing with us, and meeting our needs.

Read It!

Philippians 2:1-8;
1 Thessalonians 4:1-2; 5:23-25

Pray It!

Thank God for the incredible privilege of talking with him. Ask him to help you take advantage of this wonderful communication line you have with him.

Don't Worry . . . Be Happy

Dear Diary:

Okay, I admit, I'm not a diary-writing person. In fact, this is my first time. But hey, I got this thing for my birthday from Aunt Rosie, and I have to try it out, because I know the next time I see her she's gonna ask me if I've used the diary.

So here goes.

Hmmm.

I'm not even sure what to put in a diary!

Guess I could just write about my day, huh?

Okay. So today reeked. I was so worried about track team tryouts, I bombed my speech for class treasurer. And I was so worried about my speech, I couldn't eat lunch. And I was so worried about being seen with this huge zit on my face when I walked into school, I didn't even look up when Katie said hi. Now she thinks I'm mad at her.

Sigh.

Why is life so hard?

Now that I'm home, I'm worried I won't get my homework done before I have to go to work this evening. And I'm worried my boss is going to yell at me when I do get to work. He's always in such a bad mood. Guess I'm still worried about what happened yesterday. It was an honest mistake. I gave a customer change for $10 when he really gave me $20. He came back later and complained to my boss. I apologized and told him I thought he'd given me $10. Now I'm worried my boss is gonna think I'm trying to rip off the customers.

And I'm worried about the basketball game tomorrow. I'm really not ready for it. I need to work on my jump shot for about three hours straight. But how can I when I have homework and my job?

And I'm worried people are gonna laugh at me tomorrow cuz I've still got this Mt. Everest-sized zit exploding on my face.

Sigh.

Life is reallyreallyreally hard.

Know It!

God doesn't want you burdened with worry. He wants you to love life and experience the joy he offers. Do you realize that every time you worry about something, you're robbing yourself of God's joy?

Worry is different than concern. It's okay to be concerned—even burdened—about your non-Christian friends, your grandmother who's in the hospital, or the fact that your dad was recently laid off from his job. But to worry obsessively about things over which you have no control goes against God's best for you. Worry keeps you from experiencing God's peace.

Read It!

Proverbs 3:6; Matthew 6:25-34; 10:19-20; Philippians 4:6-7

Pray It!

Thank God that he's concerned about everything that concerns you, and ask his forgiveness for forgetting that and worrying. Trust him so you can experience his joy and peace.

Nehemiah's Construction Company

You probably remember where you were, what you were doing, and maybe even what you were wearing when you heard the devastating news on September 11, 2001, that two planes had crashed into the World Trade Towers in New York City.

I remember where I was and what I was doing when I heard the news that the Alfred E. Murrow building in Oklahoma City had been bombed. Though I was living in Colorado Springs, Colorado, my family was in Oklahoma City, and I immediately wanted to find out if they were okay.

Nehemiah was in a similar situation. He was away from his hometown of Jerusalem when he received the news that the wall surrounding the city had been torn down. If he were alive today, he could probably tell us exactly what he was doing when he got the news. Nehemiah immediately thought of his family and friends still back in Jerusalem. He yearned to help, so he asked his boss (the king) if he could have some time off to go home.

Nehemiah was a man of integrity and a hard worker. He kept his word. If he said he'd be on time, he was. When he worked at the palace, he gave 100 percent. He was dependable. The king trusted Nehemiah and granted his request to return home.

It may not sound as though a *wall* is really that important. After all, a wall is just a pile of bricks and stones, right? Well, yes and no. This was a *physical wall of protection* that surrounded the city of Jerusalem, but it was also a *spiritual wall of morality* that encompassed the city.

A physical wall protected the citizens from neighboring enemies, war, and terror. When the physical wall was torn down, the spiritual atmosphere was also damaged. It gave immoral people from other cities a chance to invade Jerusalem. Nehemiah cared about his people too much to let them be influenced by wickedness inside Jerusalem's city limits.

So he headed home to begin reconstruction on the city wall. A big task? Yes. A bigger God? Definitely.

Know It!

God will sometimes ask you to step out in faith and complete a big task. Know this: He will never ask you to do something without equipping you with everything you need!

Think about your own life right now. Do you have a spiritual wall of protection around yourself? Have you established accountability with other Christians? Or are you leaving yourself wide open to the attacks from Satan, your enemy?

Read It!

Nehemiah 1–3;
1 Peter 5:8-9

Pray It!

Confess that you often leave your spiritual wall in shambles. Ask God's help in making time to build a strong spiritual wall around your life by reading the Bible daily and developing an intimate prayer life with him.

Nehemiah's Building Crew

Know It!

God is calling you to build a strong, spiritual wall of righteousness around your own life. How do you do that? First you lay a solid spiritual foundation in Jesus Christ—you make sure you've trusted him for your salvation. Then you lay spiritual brick upon spiritual brick upon spiritual brick—by reading your Bible and praying daily.

Read It!

Nehemiah 4–6;
Proverbs 4:25;
Isaiah 40:31

Pray It!

Ask God to help you build a spiritual wall around your life to protect your relationship with him.

Nehemiah arrived home and immediately began recruiting a construction crew. Imagine the excitement of the Jerusalem citizens when they saw Acme Brick Company's trucks pull onto the work site. Next came the concrete mixers, the building supplies, and the youth group across the street that had set up a hot-dog stand to earn money for next summer's missions trip.

Nehemiah and his building crew got right to work. They built with purpose and determination. They were extremely focused on this all-important task. That is . . . until Sanballat and Tobiah tried to get in on the action.

Sanballat and Tobiah were officials in nearby cities. They didn't want Jerusalem's wall rebuilt, because that meant they'd no longer be able to influence the people of God's city with their wicked ways.

So Sanballat flew into a rage and began to mock, insult, and laugh at Nehemiah and his crew. When that didn't stop the construction process, Tobiah and *his* cohorts joined in. (Who knows? With names like Sanballat and Tobiah, these two probably suffered major inferiority complexes!)

Nehemiah's instructions were direct: "Keep working!" He reminded his crew that nothing was more important than doing God's work. Sanballat and Tobiah then launched into Plan B: They began physically attacking the construction crew. Nehemiah merely paused long enough to put half his crew on guard against the attacks and instructed the other half to continue their work.

Time for Plan C: Sanballat and Tobiah sent a prestigious message to Nehemiah inviting him to an elegant meeting with important officials. God enabled Nehemiah to see through their evil plot (they actually planned to kill him), and he continued building the wall.

Finally, just 52 days after they'd started construction, the wall was complete! Amazing!

Question: How in the world were they able to accomplish such an incredible task in such a short amount of time? *Answer:* Nehemiah refused to be sidetracked! Despite all that was going on around him, he determined to keep intensely focused on his goal. What was his goal? Doing God's work. And what was God's work? Building the wall that would guard the city.

Imagine the shock (and disappointment) of Sanballat and Tobiah when Nehemiah's building crew completed the entire wall surrounding the city of Jerusalem in just 52 days! They were boiling mad. They'd tried to stop the construction through mockery, physical attack, emotional abuse, and intimidation. But nothing worked.

Know this: When you're dead-center in God's will, others will try to lead you astray. Remember, Satan *hates* you, and he'll stop at nothing to discourage you and tempt you to throw in the towel. He'll use people to make fun of you, gossip about you, lie about you, and laugh at you. Don't give up! There is absolutely nothing more important than being smack-dab in the center of God's will doing what God is calling you to do.

And just what is he calling you to do?

1. Lay a strong spiritual foundation on Jesus Christ as your Lord and Savior.
2. With the help of the Holy Spirit, build a strong wall of righteousness around your life. Allow the Holy Spirit to help you set up defenses against things that could knock holes in your spiritual wall.
3. Reach out and help others lay a strong spiritual foundation on Jesus Christ.
4. Aid others in building a wall of righteousness around their lives.

Nehemiah was not only physically successful in rebuilding the wall, he was also spiritually victorious! How?

He realized the importance of the individual. (Reread Nehemiah 6:3.) He knew that what he was doing mattered! Do you really know that? What you do for God matters! It may seem insignificant to you, but your spiritual activity is important to the Almighty! So, what specifically are you doing for God right now?

Nehemiah knew how to protect himself from attacks. At one point, he paused long enough to put half his crew on guard while the other half continued to build. What are you doing to protect yourself spiritually? Do you take time daily to clothe yourself with spiritual armor? What are you doing to protect yourself against movies, music, relationships, and activities that go against God's will?

Know It!

God's plan for your life will involve a variety of things through the years. But his immediate plan for you is for you to develop a solid, intimate, growing relationship with him and to guard that relationship (wall) with your life!

Read It!

Nehemiah 7–13; Jude 1:24-25

Pray It!

Tell the Lord that you want to be more consistent in reading the Bible, and that you want a tight prayer life with him. Ask for his help to realize that what you do matters and to say no to the stuff that's harmful to your relationship with him.

Cool, Cooler, Coolest

Jacob limped because his hip was sore.
God was sore because Jacob was trying to be hip without him.
Today we think we must be hip to soar.
And we're sore at those who are not hip.
Yet God's message remains the same–
If we're truly hip to him, we soar.
If not, we become sore from trying to be hip without him.

(See Genesis 32 for the entire story.)

Know It!

God made you in his image, and he wants you to have a healthy, positive self-esteem. He also wants you to remember, though, that everything you have and are and will be is a gift from him. When you dare to think you've got it made in your own strength, you're in danger.

Read It!

Romans 12:3;
1 Corinthians 4:20;
2 Corinthians 5:16;
Philippians 2:3-8

Pray It!

Ask God's forgiveness for times you get caught up in accolades and forget that he is the reason you're good at the things you excel in. Keep him as Lord of your life.

Making Good out of Bad

Good things really can come from past mistakes! Take a quick peek at the following people who refused to allow their failures to dictate their future.

- One April Fool's Day, Jimmy Carter ditched school and went to a movie with friends. The principal punished him by spanking him and refusing Carter his right to graduate as class valedictorian. Jimmy Carter married another class valedictorian, Rosalynn Smith, and became Georgia's governor in 1970. In 1976, he was elected the 39th president of the United States.
- Christopher Columbus miscalculated the size of the globe and the width of the Atlantic Ocean and ended up discovering the island of San Salvador in the Bahamas (which he thought was in the Indies), Cuba (which he thought was in China), and the Dominican Republic (which he miscalculated to be in the Far East). Talk about being off! But he later made three more voyages to the New World and finally discovered Central and South America.
- In 1975, Bill Gates dropped out of Harvard University. Later that same year, he established Microsoft Corporation. He then designed software to run personal computers and became the richest man in the world!
- Orville Wright was expelled from the sixth grade for misbehaving at school. In 1903, he (and his brother, Wilbur) invented the world's first power-driven airplane.
- Thomas Monaghan knew all about going in circles. He spent many of his younger years in an orphanage. He was later placed in a variety of foster homes. He eventually enrolled in college but dropped out. He enrolled in a Catholic seminary and dropped out. He also spent a few years serving in the Marines. In 1960 he borrowed $500 and purchased a failing pizza parlor in Ypsilanti, Michigan, with his brother James. A year later, Thomas traded a VW Beetle for his brother's half of the company. That company became Domino's Pizza, which now boasts more than 5,200 restaurants.

So does this give us permission not to take life seriously? No. But we do serve a God who has the power and desire to make good things happen from our mistakes and failures.

Know It!

God not only wants to celebrate your victories, he also wants to share your failures. When you blow it, are you tempted to simply give up? Or do you take your mistakes to God and ask him to work *in spite of them?*

Read It!

Deuteronomy 20:3;
Joshua 1:5-9;
John 18:25-27; 21:15-19

Pray It!

Rather than getting down when you blow it, ask God to use your failures to bring glory to his name.

So How's It Goin'?

Know It!

God takes resolutions seriously, and he wants you to take *yours* seriously. Several people in the Bible made important resolutions. Let's take a look at some biblical resolutions right now.

Read It!

Psalm 17:3; Daniel 1:8; 1 Corinthians 2:2

Pray It!

Ask God's forgiveness for not taking your resolutions seriously. Realize that you can't keep these promises by yourself, and ask for his help.

Okay, we're approaching the end of January. So this is a great time to ask, "How are you doing with your New Year's resolutions?" You were challenged on January 1 to make some resolutions. Maybe you did; maybe you didn't. If you haven't made a resolution, it's never too late. You can do it right now.

If you've already made some resolutions, how are you doing at keeping them? Wouldn't it be great if there was some kind of strategy to help you keep your resolutions? Let's create a strategy right now, and spend the next few days zeroing in on living it out.

We'll use the alphabet to focus on an A-to-Z plan for keeping those resolutions. Ready? Let's dive in!

A: **Accountability**. Make yourself accountable. There's always power in numbers.

B: **Bring** your friends into your resolution. For instance: Want to lose weight? Get a friend to exercise with you. Trying to stop watching so much TV? Do something with a friend during TV time.

C: **Call**. Be willing to call for help. A change in lifestyle isn't always easy. It's okay to ask for help.

D: **Discipline**. Change requires discipline. And discipline isn't fun. It's also hard work. That's why you need accountability.

E: **Exclude** temptations from your life. If you have a problem looking at pornographic magazines, don't hang out by a magazine stand. If you're trying to lessen your sugar intake, remove the stash of candy that's left over from Christmas.

F: **Find** others who are willing to make the very same resolution you're making. Again, there's strength in numbers. Encourage each other. Of course, this requires being open and a bit vulnerable—which brings us back to accountability.

G: **Give** your resolution to God. Go ahead and admit you can't do it on your own. You need a supernatural power to help you keep this resolution. God wants to empower you with his strength.

Still Resolved?

Let's keep plowing ahead with our A-to-Z strategy on how to keep our New Year's resolutions. Remember, God doesn't expect you to forge ahead on your own. He wants to work *with* you. Aren't you glad he's not saying, "I'll check on you next year at this time to see how you did"? But rather, he's saying, "I'm proud of you for making some important resolutions. Let me help you keep them. I want to strengthen and empower you."

H: **Hold on!** There's an old saying, "When you've come to the end of your rope, tie a knot and hang on." Guess what! There's a lot of wisdom in that. No one said making this lifestyle change would be easy . . . or even fun. When it gets tough, simply hold on tighter to the promises God has given you in his Word.

I: **Iron** sharpens iron . . . which brings us back to accountability. Don't dismiss the power of allowing someone to hold you accountable with your new resolution.

J: **Just do it!** (Yep, this one's taken from an old Nike commercial.) Quit thinking about it. Stop talking about it. Just DO it!

K: **Kvetch.** What in the world is *that*? It's actually in the dictionary, and it means "to complain habitually." Don't do it! If you're going to whine and complain about how hard it is to keep your resolution, you've got bigger problems than keeping your resolution.

L: **Live it!** Make your resolution a part of your lifestyle—not simply a promise you hope you can keep on your good days. Live it out!

M: **Mean it.** Don't make a resolution just to make a resolution. Mean what you say and say what you mean! Back your words with action. Make a lifestyle change.

N: **Never give up!** You may blow it. That's okay. That doesn't mean you have to stop and wait till next year to try again. If your resolution is to exercise consistently, and you miss a day, don't beat yourself up. Talk with your accountability partner and keep going.

Know It!

The most powerful resolutions you can make are ones that glorify your heavenly Father. An incredible resolution King David made is found in Psalm 101:3. What specific changes in your life will you need to implement in order to make King David's resolution your own?

Read It!

Psalms 1; 101:3; John 21:15-17

Pray It!

Thank Jesus for never giving up on you, even when you fall short. Ask for his help to carry on instead of getting discouraged.

Keep Your Resolutions!

Know It!

Not everyone will applaud your determination to keep your resolutions. Some of your friends may get angry because you're not doing the same stuff with them any longer. Expect flak, and continue to draw strength from your growing relationship with Christ.

Read It!

1 Peter 4:1-3;
2 Peter 3:18;
1 John 5:1-4

Pray It!

It hurts when others give you a hard time about your standards. Ask Jesus to help you toughen your spiritual skin and guide you to the point where you care more about what he thinks than what your friends think.

Any goal worth reaching requires a strategy. All great athletes have a strategy. Imagine Tiger Woods as a child aimlessly hitting golf balls across the green. Didn't happen that way, did it? His dad created specific plans to help his son learn the required skills and follow-through needed to be a successful golfer. Whenever his dad took him to a golf course, they went with a strategy.

It works the same with resolutions. Anyone can aimlessly make a halfhearted pledge. But God wants his disciples to solidify their pledges into resolutions that equal lifestyle changes. So let's keep on keeping on with our A-to-Z strategy on maintaining your resolutions.

O: **Optimistic**. Always remain optimistic, even when you feel you can't go on. How can you do this? Memorize a Scripture verse that will help! Start with this one from *The Living Bible*: "We are pressed on every side by troubles, but not crushed and broken. We are perplexed because we don't know why things happen as they do, but we don't give up and quit. We are hunted down, but God never abandons us. We get knocked down, but we get up again and keep going" (2 Corinthians 4:8-9).

P: **Pray** daily about your resolution. God is even more concerned about it than you are. That's right! He wants you to be victorious. So keep your resolution right at the top of your prayer list, and pray daily.

Q: **Quit** doing things that hinder your ability to keep your resolution. For instance, if you've resolved to make better grades this year, quit leaving your books in your locker. Quit putting off your homework. Quit talking during class. Quit anything that's holding you back from being successful with your resolution.

R: **Repeat** progress. If getting up at 5 A.M. works in helping you get your jogging done, do it! If you can memorize Scripture better in the afternoon, do it then. Whatever works, repeat it!

S: **Surround** yourself with positive people who can cheer you on to victory. If you've resolved not to attend any more R-rated movies, terrific! But it would be wise to surround yourself with people who have similar morals. Why continue to hang out with friends who will tempt you?

When Michael Jordan was a high school sophomore, he tried out for the varsity basketball team and was cut. But he made a resolution that he'd make the varsity squad the following year. He took that resolution seriously and practiced hour upon hour every single day.

You know the rest of the story. He not only made his high school varsity basketball team, but also went to college on a basketball scholarship, played pro, and is still known as the world's greatest player.

It's not enough simply to make a resolution; we've gotta follow through. And to follow through, we need a strategy. So let's get back to our A-to-Z strategy on keeping your resolutions.

T: **Track** your progress. If you've resolved to read the Bible through in one year, mark off the chapters as you read them. Or if you're exercising, create a chart that you can put stickers on. Any kind of graph or progress report can serve as motivation to continue your success.

U: **Understand** you're not perfect. You'll probably mess up. You'll skip a day of Bible reading; you'll eat that second piece of cake; you'll watch too much TV; you'll forget to do your homework. Understand it's okay to fail—as long as you commit that failure to Christ. He doesn't want you to stay down. He wants to pick you up and get you back on track. Let him.

V: **Visualize** victory! Imagine how great you'll feel next year at this time when you've brought your science grade up from a D to a B-. Imagine how good it will feel to say you read the whole Bible through in one year. Or you read those 28 novels. Or you brought five friends to church. Or you led three teens to Christ. Visualize your victory and success in one year.

W: **Write** it down. Make time to actually write out your New Year's resolutions. Don't just think about it. Write it out. Then copy it the following day. By writing the same thing over and over and over again, you're pounding your goal into your mind and your thoughts. Write it down and hang it on the wall, stick it on your mirror, stuff it inside your wallet, or post it inside your locker. But write it down!

Know It!
Like Michael Jordan's, your resolution may require daily work. And that will mean making some sacrifices. Are you willing to make sacrifices if necessary? What, specifically, will you need to deny yourself in order to reach your goal and keep your resolution?

Read It!
1 Corinthians 9:24-27; 15:58; 2 Corinthians 4:16-18

Pray It!
Admit to God that it's tough for you to deny yourself some of the things you need to give up to keep your resolution. It's hard to take a step back from some of your friends who don't share your faith. Tell the Lord you realize he has a high calling on your life, and you want to answer his call.

Keeping Your Strategy

Know It!
Yes, God wants to make you a winner with your resolutions, but he also dreams much bigger for you! That's why total surrender to him is so important.

Read It!
Isaiah 43:19; Ephesians 3:20-21; 1 Timothy 1:18-19

Pray It!
Ask Jesus to show you daily how you can grow deeper in your relationship with him. Ask him to remind you that he knows best and that you can trust him in all situations.

Actor Buddy Ebsen (who became famous as Jed Clampett in the TV series *The Beverly Hillbillies* and later starred in TV's *Barnaby Jones*) was originally cast to play the role of the Tin Man in *The Wizard of Oz*. He had to give up the role, however, because he experienced an allergic reaction to the aluminum dust that was used to powder his face as part of his Tin Man costume. (The role was then given to Jack Haley.)

Imagine how difficult it must have been for Buddy Ebsen to walk away from such a great role—a fun part in a movie that families could enjoy together. He gave it up but later received incredible praise, fame, and accolades for other roles.

Sometimes we too have to give up something we desperately want in order to get something better. As we wind down with our A-to-Z strategy for keeping your resolutions, ask God if there's anything you need to give him in order to make your resolution stick. It may be hard to give up what you want now, but God has something much better in store for you!

X: **Xenophile**. Yep, it really *is* in the dictionary. It means "One attracted to foreign things." Don't allow yourself to be attracted to the things of this world. This is merely a temporary dwelling place. Your real home is not of this world. Set your sights—as well as your resolution—on something that's eternal . . . the power of Jesus Christ.

Y: **Yield** every single area of your life to the authority of Jesus Christ. Not just the area you want to change—but yield your will to his will. That means you put what you want for your life behind what he wants for your life. Ask him to help you live in total obedience to him.

Z: **Zealously** attack your resolution. That means to go after it wholeheartedly. Don't make any halfhearted, weak-kneed promises. Be zealous about your decision, and it will show up in your results.

Paid in Full

(Author unknown)
A young man was getting ready to graduate from college. For many months he had admired a beautiful sports car in a dealer's showroom, and knowing his father could easily afford it, he told his dad that was all he wanted.

As graduation day approached, the young man awaited signs that his father had purchased the car. Finally, on the morning of his graduation, his father called him into his private study. His father told him how proud he was to have such a fine son, and how much he loved him. He handed his son a beautifully wrapped gift box.

Curious and somewhat disappointed, the young man opened the box and found a lovely, leather-bound Bible, with the young man's name embossed in gold.

Angrily, he rose and said to his father, "With all your money, you give me a Bible?" And he stormed out of the house.

Many years passed, and the young man became very successful in business. He had a beautiful home and wonderful family, but he knew his father was very old and thought perhaps he should go visit him. He had not seen him since that graduation day years earlier.

Before he could make arrangements, he received a telegram telling him his father had passed away and had willed all of his possessions to his son. The son needed to come home immediately and take care of things.

When the man arrived at his father's house, sudden sadness and regret filled his heart. He began to search through his father's important papers and saw the still gift-wrapped Bible just as he had left it years ago. With tears running down his face, he opened the Bible and began to turn the pages. His father had carefully underlined a verse of Scripture: "If you, then, though you are evil, know how to give good gifts to your children, how much more will your Father in heaven give good gifts to those who ask him!" (Matthew 7:11).

As he read those words, a car key dropped from the back of the Bible. It had a tag with the dealer's name—the same dealer who had the sports car he had desired. On the tag was the date of his graduation and the words "Paid in Full."

How many times do we miss God's blessings because we can't see past our own desires?

Know It!
God, as your loving, heavenly Father, wants to bless you. He loves to give gifts to his children. Can you trust him to know your needs and desires even better than you do?

Read It!
Deuteronomy 7:13;
Psalm 72:15;
Ezekiel 34:26;
Acts 20:35

Pray It!
Tell God you want to follow his path—not just to get blessings, but because you love him and trust that he knows what's best for your life.

God's Peace

Know It!

Jesus *does* want you to "get it" spiritually. He wants you to understand his Word and his plan. But he won't come down on you when you're confused. Instead, he offers incredible peace. In the midst of *your* doubt and confusion and fear, he offers peace!

Read It!

John 14:27; 16:33;
Romans 8:6;
1 Corinthians 14:33;
Ephesians 2:14;
2 Thessalonians 3:16

Pray It!

Do you desperately need God's peace right now? Ask him to fill you!

Jesus' disciples had spent three years in his company. They'd seen him move with intense purpose and obedience to God's leading. They were amazed when he opened the ears of a deaf person and gave sight to a man blind from birth. They had witnessed Jesus bringing dead people back to life!

The disciples had learned to pray from Jesus. They had cried together, laughed together, and talked of his approaching Kingdom.

Though Jesus talked about his approaching death—and even predicted his crucifixion—his disciples still didn't get it. They thought his Kingdom was going to be set up on earth. They all looked forward to ruling *with* him as he freed his people from Roman law.

So when Jesus was arrested, they ran like scared rabbits. *Hey, this wasn't part of the plan,* they thought. *What about the kingdom? He said he'd set us free! What's happening?*

When their Lord was crucified, the disciples were devastated. *We've given up everything to follow him! We left our careers, our friends, our homes. Now what? He's dead!*

Imagine the doubt and confusion. Imagine the turmoil, the huge knots in their stomachs. Imagine the fear—*If the government crucified him . . . they may come after us, too!*

Picture it: They're all huddled together somewhere in a little upstairs room. And into the confusion . . . right in the midst of the despair and fear and hopelessness . . . into the center of doubt . . . walks Jesus Christ. In the flesh!

We can imagine he might say, "You guys just don't get it, do you? I told you over and over again that I was going to die. But I also told you I'd conquer death and rise out of the grave after three days. Why didn't you believe me?

"And about the Kingdom thing—we went over it again and again. My Kingdom is not of this earth. When I talked about setting you free, I wasn't talking about freedom from Roman law. I was talking about something much deeper and more confining. I was talking about sin! Do you get it now? Is it starting to sink in?"

Jesus didn't say anything close to that. Instead, he simply spoke words of peace. Imagine how that must have comforted the hearts of his followers!

What kind of **peace** *does Jesus give? (Circle all that apply.)*
a. A piece of this, a piece of that.
b. Everlasting.
c. Deep.
d. The expensive kind.
e. Peace like a river, or an ocean, or a fountain, or something big and bubbly like that.
f. Genuine.

Behind locked doors*, in the midst of fear and confusion, Jesus appeared offering peace. This tells me that*
a. Jesus understands me way better than I can imagine.
b. When my world is falling apart, he can put it back together.
c. There's no emotion I experience that he doesn't know about and understand.
d. That's just like my Jesus—showing up in the most unlikely of places.

How did Jesus handle Thomas' ***doubts****?*
a. With anger.
b. Gently.
c. By giving him the evidence Thomas needed.
d. By ignoring him.

When you ***struggle*** *with spiritual doubts, what helps?*
a. Friends who understand.
b. Talking to Jesus.
c. Running or other physical activity.
d. Spending time alone and thinking things through.
e. Talking with adults you trust spiritually (parents, youth leader, pastor, Sunday school teacher, etc.).
f. Reading the Bible.
g. Thinking back and remembering God's faithfulness in the past.
h. Journaling.

Know It!
When you're insecure, angry, confused, or filled with doubts, Jesus wants to walk right through every single one of your emotions and stand with you! How does that make you feel? When your world caves in, ask for a fresh touch of his peace.

Read It!
Numbers 6:24-26; Psalm 29:11; 34:14; 37:11; 119:165; 2 Thessalonians 1:2

Pray It!
When you feel as though your world is falling apart, ask Jesus to remind you of his great faithfulness in the past and teach you how to live and cultivate peace.

The Gift of the Garbage Man (Part 1)

by Carolyn McInnes
Have you ever stopped to think of all the garbage man does for you?

It's a clear blue day. I suck in the pure air like a hungry vacuum cleaner. First, I inhale sweet dogwood. Then pine, rich and earthy. . . . Everything smells like freedom. As I stroll through the parking lot to the mailbox, I'm intoxicated with life.

What glorious scent will the next breath bring? I draw in the air slowly, with great anticipation. And then . . .

My throat suddenly constricts. My stomach lurches up and down wildly, and I think I might lose my lunch right there. The air has changed, and I'm strangled by a combination of the most offensive smells known to man. As I round the corner, holding my breath, I see the garbage truck.

I only glance at the garbage man on the tailgate as I hurry by. From the corner of my eye, I can just make out his stained blue work jumper and a greasy ponytail. I feel his eyes following me, and my pace quickens.

"Hey, wait!"

So I freeze. The parking lot is empty, and the garbage man is obviously calling out to me.

As he approaches, the putrid scent intensifies. He smells like all of the things he's been surrounded by. Sour milk. Dirty diapers. Rancid meat. Rotten fruit. His work suit is smeared with the remains of all of these items and more. I think I might pass out.

"Hi!" he grins and brushes away a wisp of his long hair with a filthy glove. "We're running a little behind schedule. I was wondering if I could use your phone."

I stare at him. "In my apartment?" I ask. This must be a joke. I think of the vanilla scent that hangs in the air of my immaculate home. Then, cringing, I envision his steel-toed boots tracking unidentified waste across my ivory carpet.

"No offense," I say, still trying not to breathe any more than necessary, "but I just cleaned my house. And you . . . well, you don't smell so great."

The garbage man doesn't appear insulted. "No offense," he responds matter-of-factly, "but if I didn't pick up your garbage every day, your house would always smell the way I smell."

I don't understand his point. I just want to get away from this weirdo. I want to breathe the fresh air again.

"I appreciate that you pick up my garbage," I say. "Now, if you'll excuse me . . ."

"Do you really appreciate it?" he asks. "How often do you actually say to someone, 'I sure am thankful that the sanitation engineer picks up my trash every day'? I've seen you out here before. You never once thanked me."

"I wave sometimes," I answer defensively. "Besides, why are you acting so noble? This is your job!"

The garbage man chuckles a little. "You think this is how I make a living?" he asks, a knowing smile dancing on his lips. "You don't recognize me, do you?"

Know It!
God wants you to thank and praise him consistently.

Read It!
Psalms 62:1-2; 115:1; Proverbs 18:10; Hebrews 13:1-2

Pray It!
Ask God to give you his eyes to help you see clearly the things you take for granted.

The Gift of the Garbage Man (Part 2)

Know It!
God can help you see beyond outward appearances. He can give you spiritual insight that will help you discern a person's character.

Read It!
James 1:19-27; 2:1-7; 2 Peter 1:3; 2 John 1:3

Pray It!
As you spend time in prayer today, ask God to give you a discerning spirit to see godly character in those around you.

by Carolyn McInnes

I look him over carefully now. Even peering past the grime, I just see a strong man with gentle green eyes. Unfamiliar. Nondescript. And really smelly.

"What, are you an actor or something?" I ask. "Is this one of those deals where you're going to play a garbage man in a movie, so you're trying to learn about the part firsthand?"

"Well," he smiles, "I guess you *could* say I'm doing it so I can understand people better. You can learn a lot by going through a person's garbage, you know."

"You go through our garbage?" I'm seized by an eerie, violated feeling. What have I thrown away that he might have seen?

"I know all about you, Carolyn." I gasp as he calls me by name. "I know you use tons of tissues because of your allergies. I read the letters you toss, the receipts telling how you spend your money. I see the thoughts you write down and throw away because they're so private, you can't even keep them in a journal. I know you better than you know yourself."

I just stand there, petrified and naked before the garbage man. I want to flee from this lunatic, but he already knows too much. Running now might provoke him to do something drastic.

"Why do you do this?" My voice is pinched and small.

"Because I love you," he replies simply.

I can't help it now: My feet are in motion. But before I can escape, I'm caught by his dirty hand. He holds my arm.

"Don't worry. I'm not some stalker or freak. I love *people.* Your neighbor in 302 is Mr. Donaldson. Sweet old man. Had a leg injury that kept him from playing pro football back in the '50s, but he's still a volunteer coach at the youth center. Did you know that?" I shook my head. "And the Hansons upstairs, with that spunky three-year-old—I love them, too! I remember when little Bradley got into some cleaning chemicals and nearly died last year. What a rough time for them."

I watch his eyes as he speaks. They're deep and clear, and they glisten like sunlight on water. My fear is transforming into fascination.

"I even know the lady in 310 you call Crabby Cakes. She got lonely after her husband passed away, so she decided to visit elderly people once a week." He chuckled to himself. "You should see how excited they get on Tuesdays waiting for her! See, even she has some good inside. Everyone does."

He holds out his hands, as though laying understanding before me. "That's why I'm a garbage man."

The Gift of the Garbage Man (Part 3)

by Carolyn McInnes

"I still don't get it," I say. "If you're not a stalker, not a blackmailer, what could possibly be good about sifting through our trash?"

Then, I see the most amazing glow envelop his face. It's that look of blissful satisfaction someone gets when he's quietly accomplishing his wildest dream.

"I get to take it away," he says. "I destroy it, so no one else will ever have to see it. I wade through this filth so that your life will be clean. Take this letter. . . ." he pauses, his gloved hands retrieving a wadded package from the back of his truck. He flashes it before me, just long enough for me to see my handwriting and recognize the document. It's my draft of a letter to a friend, full of gossip and hate toward a mutual acquaintance.

"I shouldn't have written that," I stammer, red-faced.

"Imagine what your house would look like if it were filled with all the letters you've ever written," he says. "What if the words you spoke could stain the walls, and your actions were slimy heaps of debris on the carpet? What if each of your bad thoughts hung in the air like an odor? Would you really want to live in that place?"

Now I'm speechless. I want to ask, "Who are you?" But I think I already know.

"Thanks to me, you don't have to live like that," he continues, waving the letter. "By tonight, this will be gone forever. I won't even remember it tomorrow. Believe me, my memory about this stuff is horrible!"

Once again, I notice a putrid stench. But I suddenly realize it isn't coming from him at all. It's me. I hang my head in embarrassment, but he just smiles.

"So what do you say? Can I use your phone?"

I nod. There are no words left, only tears.

And right there in the parking lot, the garbage man puts his arms around me. Some guy driving to the next building turns to stare. His jaw is on the floorboard.

But it doesn't matter what anyone thinks. The garbage man's arms are warm, and immediately the stench is gone.

The air smells fresh and sweet again.

It's the scent of freedom.

Know It!

When God forgives you from sin, he chooses to remember it no longer. The Bible tells us he casts our sin as far as the East is from the West. There's no way to measure dimensions from the East to the West as there is from the North Pole to the South Pole. So God casts your sins so far from his mind, they simply don't exist any longer.

Read It!

Psalm 103:12; Luke 5:21; Acts 10:43; Colossians 2:13

Pray It!

Spend time thanking God for taking your garbage—your sin, your rotten attitudes—and not only forgiving you, but choosing to forget as well.

How's Your Swing?

Know It!
Yes, you may be pretty good right now. You may even feel as though you're on top of the world. But your "good" is nothing next to God's "amazing." Will you give him the authority to do more with you than you can even imagine? It will require being broken. But God never leaves his children broken for long. And when *he* puts the pieces back together, you can rest assured that his creation always shines brighter!

Read It!
Romans 12:1-2; Ephesians 1:19; 3:20; 4:18

Pray It!
Tell God you're willing to be broken and reshaped in his image.

In 1997, Tiger Woods became the first African-American to win the famed Master's Golf Tournament. Later that same year, he went on to win two other major tournaments, giving him $2,000,000 in winnings. On top of that were his endorsements, which brought in an additional $60,000! Not bad for one year, was it?

After such an incredible year, Tiger surprised the world when he announced to his coach that he wanted to change his golf swing. Many were thinking, *You're crazy! Why mess with a good thing? You're on top right now!*

But Tiger was determined not to settle, and he had a nagging feeling that if he changed his swing, he would actually play an even better game. So he studied videotapes of himself, memorizing every move he put into his swing and making mental notes on how he would change it.

During the next 19 months, he only won one tournament. But after that, he won 10 out of the next 14 tournaments—6 of them in a row!

You may think you're pretty good spiritually . . . but guess what? You're nothing compared to what you *can* be! Will you dare to allow God to stop you completely in your tracks in order to change and improve you? Yes, it will slow you down at first. And yes, people may wonder why you're not "on top" any more. But in time, God will be able to do far more with you, in you, and through you than he's doing right now.

The difference? Allowing God to completely break you. Then giving him the authority to pick up the pieces and remold you . . . reshape you in his image. The best singers are those who sing from a broken—yet healed—heart. The best speakers are those who speak from joy born of despair. The best artists are those who are able to paint hope because they've known hopelessness. The winning athletes are those who are secure enough to climb out of the spotlight for a while to improve themselves while losing.

As Tiger Woods made time to improve his golf swing, you can take time to improve your "spiritual swing." Let's take a closer look at what that involves.

1. Be open to God's power. He's able to do things in your life, with your life, and through your life that are beyond your wildest imagination! You may think there's no way you could teach a Sunday school class, sing a solo, or speak in public. And maybe in your own strength, you can't. But guess what? God's mighty power is way past your boundaries. He's dreaming of things for you that you haven't even thought of yet!

Contemporary Christian artist Scott Krippayne sings a song called "Wild Imagination" that reminds the listener of God's wonderful creativity and dreams. Grab the CD (also named *Wild Imagination*) and plug in your headphones. You, too, will be reminded of all that God wants to do for you beyond what you could dream of yourself!

2. Open your heart to God's grace. We toss the word *grace* around quite a bit, but do you truly know the definition? Grace is God giving you what you need instead of what you deserve. And he can give you the ability, the power, and the desire to make the changes in your "swing" (or your life) that you can't make on your own.

Perhaps you've tried to make positive changes in your own strength. And maybe they've lasted for a few weeks or a couple of months. God is able to go far beyond that. He's able to make changes in your life that will last for eternity!

3. Open your life to God's love. God is crazy about you! He loves you beyond human comprehension. Whatever changes he prompts in your life—even though you may initially not understand them—are for your good and his glory.

You were created by God for a relationship with God, and until you really understand that, life won't make sense. Can you open yourself to his power? Can you trust yourself to his grace? Can you commit yourself to his love? If you can, and if you will, he'll make a masterpiece out of your life!

Know It!
When you walk with the creator of the universe, you're in for an exciting ride!

Read It!
Romans 3:22; 5:1-2; 1 Corinthians 6:13; Ephesians 2:8; James 4:6-8

Pray It!
Tell God you're ready to trust him with all of your life—including the changes he wants to make.

Coca-Cola Around the World

Know It!
God is counting on *you* to be his advertisement. Think about it: You personally know the King of kings. Tell someone! The creator of the universe calls you by name. Talk about him!

Read It!
1 Corinthians 2:1-5;
Ephesians 3:7;
Colossians 3:17;
2 Timothy 1:6-8

Pray It!
If you're sometimes afraid to talk to others about God, ask him to fill you with his boldness. Ask him to help you remember that he'll give you the right words to say at the right time.

I've traveled to every continent in the world—except Antarctica—and I've found Coca-Cola in every country I've visited.

Even in remote villages without electricity, I've found bottled Coca-Cola. People can't read or write in many of these villages, but they drink Coke. Plumbing is unheard of, clean water is a rare privilege, and homes are simply huts made of grass, clay, and animal dung. But look closer, and you'll notice the villagers are drinking Coca-Cola.

Amazing, isn't it? Even though Pepsi, Mountain Dew, Sprite, and a ton of other drinks are popular, Coca-Cola rules worldwide.

In Jayapura, Irian Jaya, no one had even heard of root beer, but they proudly displayed Coca-Cola along the side of the road. I wasn't able to get a 7-Up in the mountains of Bolivia, but I saw row after row of Cokes. In the Philippines; Ethiopia; Australia; Chiang Mai, Thailand; Tahiti; on a safari in Kenya, East Africa; Calcutta, India; Tokyo; Beijing; Singapore; Guam; and a plethora of other sites I've been, I couldn't always find a Squirt, Pepsi Light, or Mellow Yellow. But I've never been without a Coke. No matter how remote . . . no matter what language . . . no matter what culture . . . Coca-Cola is there!

The marketing and advertising groups at the Coca-Cola headquarters have really done their job, haven't they? They've made Coca-Cola the most popular and well-known soft drink around the world.

What if Christ were marketed the same way? Think about it: In every language, every culture, every remote area of the world, wouldn't it be exciting if everyone could tap into Christ as easily as they can get a Coke? Well, they could . . . if they knew. Hmmm. If only God could come up with an advertising committee as good as Coca-Cola's.

Guess what—God *does* have an advertising committee. And it's a lot more powerful than even Coke's prestigious team. His marketing crew consists of you. And me. And every single Christian around the world.

So why aren't you busy advertising Jesus?

Every single day of your life, you advertise something. A sweet spirit, a rotten attitude, coarse language, forgiveness, kind words, affirmation. Your very lifestyle is a walking advertisement.

What . . . or whom . . . have you advertised today?

Coca-Cola . . . The Real Thing?

I should probably tell you that I really like Coca-Cola. It's my favorite soft drink. In fact, I collect Cokes from around the world—cans and bottles still full of the sugary brown liquid, with *Coca-Cola* written across the side in a foreign language. I even have a working 1950s Coca-Cola machine in my basement so I always have plenty of "the real thing" to offer my guests. (And me.)

Some have even gone as far as to say I'm *obsessed* with Coca-Cola. I have Coca-Cola pencils, pens, notepads, clocks, yo-yos, lapel pins, T-shirts, pants, jackets, skirts, bath mats, towels, socks, and even dishes and silverware.

I also have a working Coca-Cola telephone, board game, framed puzzle, table and chairs, light-switch plate, and watch. Should I even mention the napkins, salt and pepper shakers, stickers, and place mats?

Okay, I admit . . . I have Coca-Cola lamps and Christmas ornaments. Yep, even blankets, books, and wallpaper that all sport the Coca-Cola logo. Ever seen Coca-Cola marbles, cameras, and key chains? You would if you came to my house.

I guess you could say I'm saturated with Coca-Cola and Coca-Cola stuff.

As much as I enjoy the sugary brown soft drink, I love Jesus Christ a whole lot more. He's definitely "the real thing"! He gave his *life* for me. And he wants to be much more than a hobby to us.

Jesus wants us to be saturated with *him.* He doesn't want to be number one in your life. He wants to *be* your life! You see, he knows that whatever we place in the number one spot will eventually get shoved to the number two position. God doesn't want to settle for a spot or a position. He wants to saturate you. He doesn't want to simply live in your heart; he wants to take up residence inside your head as well. He wants to rearrange your thinking and affect your actions and reactions.

He wants to possess your thinking. Not to control you like a puppet—God doesn't work that way. But he wants to possess your thinking in such a way that whatever breaks *his* heart will begin to break *your* heart. He wants you to be focused on becoming all he calls you to be.

Know It!

You may have a great collection of "Jesus stuff." Perhaps you have more than one Bible, some Christian posters, contemporary Christian music CDs, and several Christian books. Jesus wants to move you far beyond being a "Christian collector." He doesn't want to be your hobby; he wants to be your *life.*

Read It!

Psalms 74:13-17; 77:18-20; 81:9-14

Pray It!

If you start to fall into the trap of merely "collecting" things that resemble God, ask him to wake you up with a strong but gentle reminder that he and he alone is the real thing!

Crusty Facts about Coca-Cola

Know It!
God wants you to be "the real thing!" Acting one way but *being* another is phony. Let your lifestyle reflect your inner commitment to Christ.

Read It!
Psalms 139:23-24; 141:1-4; Proverbs 28:13; Romans 2:5-9

Pray It!
Tell God you definitely want to be "the real thing," and ask him to show you anything in your life that's not pleasing to him so you can commit that to him.

As refreshing as an ice-cold Coca-Cola can be at the end of the day, it's not *all* good. Check out these weird but true facts about the world's favorite soft drink.

- In many states, highway patrol cars carry two gallons of Coke in the trunk to remove blood from the highway after a car accident.
- If you can put a T-bone steak in a bowl of Coke, the steak will be gone in two days.
- To clean a toilet: Pour a can of Coke into the toilet bowl. Let "the real thing" sit for one hour, then flush clean.
- To remove rust spots from chrome car bumpers: Rub the bumper with a crumpled-up piece of aluminum foil dipped in Coca-Cola.
- To loosen a rusted bolt: Apply a cloth soaked in Coca-Cola to the rusted bolt for several minutes.
- To remove grease from clothes: Empty a can of Coke into a load of greasy clothes. Add detergent and run through a regular cycle. The Coca-Cola will help loosen the grease stains. It will also clean road haze from your windshield.
- The active ingredient in Coke is phosphoric acid. Its pH is 2.8. It will dissolve a nail in about four days.
- To carry Coca-Cola syrup (the concentrate), a commercial truck must use the "hazardous material" place cards reserved for highly corrosive materials.
- The distributors of Coke have been using it to clean the engines of their trucks for more than 20 years.

Though Coca-Cola looks good on the outside, the facts tell us there are some extremely strong ingredients on the inside. Used in moderation, it's not harmful to most people. But used in the above situations or in obsessive amounts, it can be unhealthy.

As Christians, it's easy for us to look good on the outside. We learn how to appear and sound spiritually attractive. But if we're harboring negative influences on the inside, we're spiritually unhealthy. Acting nice to someone in your class but secretly hating him inside can be spiritually deadly. Allow God to match outward actions and your inner commitment to him.

Talk about Impulsive!

In Old Testament times there was a pretty cool family tradition floating around. (Well, it was cool for the oldest son. If you were a daughter or a son anywhere else in the birth order, it wasn't so great.) The oldest son in each family was entitled to the "birthright." That meant, simply because he was the oldest male, he was in line for the family goods. At some point, all the family owned would become his—the farm, the animals, the house, the four-wheel-drive SUV, everything!

But what happened if the oldest boy was a *twin*? Enter Esau and Jacob. Since Esau was the firstborn twin, he was the one in line for the birthright. How do you think that settled with Jacob? How would *you* feel if your twin beat you into the world by maybe a minute or so?

So Jacob began scheming . . . and cooking. You see, Esau loved to hunt, fish, and trap, while Jacob loved to stay home and cook. And one day he created a recipe for goat stew that had his bro's eyes rolling backward. Esau *loved* that stew! Couldn't get enough of it.

Near the end of hunting season, Esau returned home starving. Jacob had been waiting for this very moment. He pulled his famous stew out of the fridge, popped it in the microwave, and sat it on the kitchen counter.

"Wow! Is that your goat stew?" Esau asked.

"Sure is, Bro. I'll bet you're hungry after that long hunting trip, huh?"

"Yeah! Where's the spoon?"

"Not so fast. I was planning on eating this myself."

"Ah, come on, Jacob! I'm starving!"

"Wanna trade me for it?"

"Sure. Anything. Just give me the stew. Hey! That's homemade bread! Yeah, anything you want."

"I want your birthright."

"Take it. Just give me the stew and the bread."

That's all it took. Esau acted on an impulse, and his decision caused a split between the brothers that reverberated for many years.

It's easy to act on impulse. Have you ever purchased something without thinking it through and regretted it later? Or made a rash promise you wished you could take back? If so, you know what it's like to act impulsively. It's almost always followed by regret, sorrow, bitterness, or anger.

Know It!

God wants you to think things through before you act. He wants to help you with your decisions. Our choices can have long-term consequences. Don't put your needs and desires before God's plan for your life.

Read It!

Genesis 25:21-34; 27; Proverbs 13:18; Hebrews 12:11

Pray It!

Confess to God that you often act impulsively. Ask his help to develop the discipline he wants you to have.

The Grabber

Know It!
Jacob became a man who held on so tightly to God that he wasn't willing to move ahead without God's approval. That's exactly where God wants you to be. He wants your grip on him to become so tight that you'll seek his guidance in all you do.

Read It!
Genesis 28–29; Romans 9:11-13

Pray It!
Thank God for grabbing on to you! Pledge to grab on to him and hold tightly forever.

Jake is a pretty cool name . . . today. But it may not have *always* been cool. Jacob and Esau were twin brothers born to Isaac and Rebekah. Esau was born first, and Jacob followed with his hand grabbing the heel of his twin brother. Mom and Dad named him "Heelgrabber"—or Jacob. Imagine signing up for Little League as "Heelgrabber." They eventually shortened it to "Grabber." But we can assume other kids made fun of him. He eventually began to lie, cheat . . . and grab.

Later in life, he grabbed Esau's birthright. (See yesterday's devotional.) In his adult life, he grabbed two wives and several farm animals from his Uncle Laban. And finally, he grabbed onto the most important thing worth grabbing in life—God Almighty. The best part of this story, though, is that God grabbed on to Jacob . . . and wouldn't let go.

He wants to grab you, too, and show you how to make the most out of your life. God doesn't only use people who seem to have it all together. He has a knack for grabbing the ordinary and helping them accomplish the extraordinary.

If you're aware of your weaknesses, you're in good company. Jacob had plenty of shortcomings! He was selfish. He became extremely wealthy but didn't want to share. When his back was against a wall, he tried to figure things out on his own instead of turning to God.

But God kept holding on. And eventually God began to change Jacob and develop in him a true godliness. You see, God saw potential in the "Grabber." God knew what Jacob could become. He didn't overlook Jake's weaknesses, but he focused his attention on developing Jacob into a man of God.

God won't overlook your shortcomings, either. In fact, if you ignore your weaknesses, he'll bring them to your attention. He wants to help you deal with failure, because he loves you too much to let you stay the way you are.

When we grab onto God, he's able to use us in spite of ourselves. What about you? Ready to become a God-grabber?

Where's Your Heart?

God spoke a lot about a man's heart.
Know it by heart . . .
When you break someone's heart
He'll want a heart-to-heart with you.
David was a man after God's own heart
But he soon had a heavy heart
After breaking God's heart.
From the bottom of his heart
He had a change of heart.
David crossed his heart
That he would follow God's heart
With all of his heart.
He did.
And God still refers to him as a man after his own heart.
Cool how God finds it in his heart to forgive, forget, and restore!

Know It!

God not only wants *control* of your heart, he wants to *shape* your heart. And when you give your heart 100 percent to him, he'll pour his very self into your heart of hearts.

Read It!

Joshua 22:5;
1 Chronicles 28:9;
Psalm 9:1-2; 44:21;
Romans 10:1

Pray It!

Seek God's forgiveness for the times you've broken his heart. Tell him you want to serve him with all of your heart.

Name Change

Know It!
God won't force you to give him total control. But it's only when you do that he begins to complete the life-changing work he wants to do in and through you.

Read It!
Genesis 32:28; Acts 9; Philippians 1:21-22

Pray It!
If you want to commit yourself to God, consider praying this prayer: *Jesus, I admit my failure to you. Will you forgive me for ______________? I accept your forgiveness, and I commit everything I am to you. Lord, change my life, my actions—even the way I see myself. I want to be putty in your hands.*

After Jacob grabbed on to God with everything he had, God changed the Grabber's name to *Israel.* At that point, things really started happening! Israel (the man) became the father of the 12 tribes of Israel (the country). He also became one of the most significant people in the Old Testament—not on his own strength, but because God fulfilled his plan in spite of Israel's weaknesses.

The Bible is filled with folks just like Jake—and just like you—ordinary people failing, confused, and frustrated who become victorious, confident, and strong simply because they finally give God 100 percent. You see, when we give God everything, things start happening! That's when he looks past our humanness and begins to work in supernatural ways to accomplish his will.

God's plan will not be thwarted by your humanity. He has the power to make wonderful things happen out of mistakes.

There's another name change in the Bible that made history. The apostle Paul wasn't always Paul. He started out as *Saul*—and was dedicated to killing as many Christians as he could. But on the road to Damascus, he was confronted by God Almighty. Convinced that Jesus Christ actually was who he claimed to be, Saul gave God 100 percent. God then changed his name to Paul—and things started happening!

He wrote letters to several new churches, and these letters became part of the New Testament. He preached the gospel throughout the Roman Empire on three mission trips. He discipled Timothy and was instrumental in helping the Gentiles become Christians. Paul was filled with God's strength, and because of that, he was never afraid to face confrontation head-on.

God has a knack for taking our weaknesses and turning them into his strengths. But there's a catch: We have to admit and commit. Once we admit our failure and commit everything to him, he's able to work *through* our past and develop his character within us.

Are you willing to allow God to make the changes he needs to make in your life? What if he wants to change your name—or how you perceive yourself? He may want to change your reputation—how you're known and perceived by others. Are you willing to allow him total control?

New York City had a tough time between 1804 and 1918. The following epidemics ran rampant during those years:

- Yellow fever (three outbreaks resulting in 445 deaths)
- Typhoid fever (one outbreak equaling 200 deaths)
- Influenza (one outbreak causing 12,562 deaths)
- Smallpox (two outbreaks resulting in 7,044 deaths)
- Cholera (six outbreaks equaling 13,210 deaths)

Imagine if there was an outbreak of Christian teenagers truly being, doing, and saying exactly what God directed them to! The news might read something like this:

- Following God to the mission field (52 outbreaks resulting in 15,000 new Christians)
- Witnessing to friends at school (1,000 outbreaks equaling 5,000 spiritual conversions)
- Refusing to participate in drinking, drugs, or premarital sex (20,000 outbreaks causing 13,659 nonbelievers to visit church)
- Speaking up in class against evolution, abortion, and New Age (638 outbreaks resulting in 9,220 students researching what they believe and why they believe it)

What if . . . just what *if* you decided to start an outbreak for Christ? Would your class notice the difference? Would your school be the same? Would fellow employees at your part-time job take notice? Would your unsaved family members try to sneak a peek at your Bible?

We can rest assured that your friends, family, fellow employees, city, and school would never be the same if you started and consistently participated in an outbreak for Jesus. How could you do such a thing?

Well, you could start a Bible club at your school before or after hours (yes, it's legal!); carry your Bible to school; invite non-churched friends to church and youth group; participate on a missions trip and recruit others to join you; share with those who don't know God the difference he's made and is continuing to make in your life; call 20 people and ask how you can pray for them—no strings attached; initiate a support group to raise money for the persecuted church.

There are a number of things you can do . . . if you're serious about causing an outbreak for Christ. The best place to start is with your heavenly Father. Ask him for specific direction. Plead for his guidance. And when he speaks, be willing to obey!

Know It!

You're on a first-name basis with the Lord of lords. So tell someone! Don't be selfish with the Good News; spread it around! Talk it, live it, be it, do it—and things around you will never be the same.

Read It!

Acts 1:8; 2:14-47; 3:12-26; 4:1-4

Pray It!

Tell God you don't want to be a couch-potato Christian who simply sits through a relationship with him. Ask God to use you to make a difference, and ask him to show you specific ways you can begin an outbreak for him!

Giving Your Heart Away

Know It!

Love isn't always easy. Jesus loved, and it cost him his life. Are you willing to pay the price to love as Jesus loved? If so, you may not be loved in return. But there's not a better idea in the world than to give your heart away. Not just today . . . but every day for the rest of your life. That's right—make loving others part of your lifestyle.

Read It!

1 Corinthians 13

Pray It!

Tell the Lord how thankful you are that he gave his life and still continues to give. Ask his help getting past your own wants and focusing on the needs of others.

Chad was the most awkward kid in his entire third-grade class. He was skinny and shy and didn't know quite how to make friends. But with Valentine's Day approaching, he announced an idea to his mom. "It's only three days away," he said. "And I want to make a valentine for every kid in my class."

His mom's heart sank, because she was afraid Chad would put everything he had into this project and not get much in return. But she didn't want to drain her son of his newfound excitement, so she took him to the store. Chad bought bright red construction paper, colored glitter, paste, markers, stickers, and huge envelopes.

During the next couple of days, he spent nearly every waking hour creating big, beautiful, and personalized valentines for every student in his class. Finally the big day arrived. He was too excited to eat breakfast. He gathered his stash under his arms and headed off to school.

Around 2:30 P.M., his mom decided to bake fresh peanut butter cookies—Chad's favorite—and have them ready and warm when he arrived home from school. *He's worked so hard on these valentines, and he'll probably only get a handful in return,* she thought. *His heart will be broken.*

At 2:50 P.M., she looked out the kitchen window and saw five third-grade boys laughing and showing their valentines to each other as they walked home. About a hundred yards behind walked Chad. Alone. His head was down, and his hand clutched one crumpled valentine.

His head's down, he's walking faster than normal, and he's about to cry, his mom thought.

She opened the front door, and Chad ran right past her. "Mom!" he screamed.

"Honey, I'm right here."

"Mom," he said, trying to catch his breath as he spun around. "Mom, there were 32 kids in our class—not counting me—and I made 32 valentines. I had a valentine for every single kid. I didn't forget anyone, Mom!"

She glanced at his hand and noticed his only valentine was a duplicate the teacher had made for the entire class. Chad was so focused on making sure everyone around him got a piece of his heart, he hadn't even noticed he wasn't loved in return.

Tears fell down his mom's face as she prayed, "Oh, Father! Make me more concerned with others' needs than my own."

If the Number Two pencil is really the most popular, why is it still number two?

Why is there Braille on the drive-through ATM machines?

If you try to fail, and succeed at failing, which have you done?

If all the world's a stage, where's the audience sitting?

There's a story in the Gospel of John that includes what seems like a stupid question. John 5:1-18 tells of a man who had been paralyzed for many years. Jesus found him in Jerusalem at Bethesda—a pool of water that was rumored to be stirred by angels. Legend stated that the first person into the water after it had been stirred would be healed.

This pool was probably a hot spring or sulfur water that bubbled up from the ground. This particular man had waited by the pool for 38 years, hoping someday to be the first to touch the water's surface after it stirred in its mysterious way.

Jesus saw the man lying by the pool and approached him. "Do you want to get well?" he asked.

Do I want to get well? the paralyzed man may have thought. *What kind of question is that? Why else would I have spent almost four decades lying beside a pool of water?*

At first glance, it might seem as though Jesus asked a stupid question. After all, Jesus *is* God. He knows everything. He knew exactly how long the man had lain by the pool's edge, and he knew why. Yet he still approached the paralytic with the question, "Do you want to get well?" Since we know that Jesus is the source of all wisdom, there must be more to the question than we first see.

People don't understand the ways of God. Noah probably thought it was a stupid idea to build an ark. Up to that point in history, rain hadn't existed. The earth was watered by a daily dew. Only after the flood did God choose to water the earth with rain.

So, never having heard of rain, Noah may have thought it was a stupid idea to build a boat big enough to hold his entire family and two of each creature that roamed the earth. And why was he building this boat? To save himself, his loved ones, and the animals from huge torrents of "rain" he couldn't even imagine. But he trusted, and he obeyed.

Know It!

God's infinite ways are beyond your finite thinking. When God's plan seems stupid on the surface, know there's much more behind it that could be life-changing.

Read It!

Genesis 6–8; John 5:1-18

Pray It!

Admit to God that you sometimes ignore him when you don't understand his ways. Ask his forgiveness and his help in obeying him no matter what.

Focused on H_2O

Know It!

God wants you so tuned in to him that when he needs your attention, he automatically has it. When you're faced with problems, don't think of God as your last resort. Turn to him first. After all, he's standing right next to you just waiting to help.

Read It!

2 Chronicles 16:9; Lamentations 3:22-26; John 5:1-18

Pray It!

When you're faced with a problem, it sometimes seems easier to go to a friend or look somewhere besides God for the answer. Ask him to remind you that he's ready and willing to share his wisdom with you when you turn to him.

Jesus was on his way to Jerusalem for a special feast—the Feast of the Jews—when he found the paralytic at Bethesda. Jesus would have passed merchants selling fish, lamb, and other food in the open-air market. He would have noticed children playing in the streets and heard the haggling of shopkeepers trying to earn a day's living. He would have seen women selling brightly colored shawls and fabric and would have smelled freshly baked bread warming over an open grill. Though hundreds of activities and people could have distracted him, he walked straight to the paralytic at Bethesda.

Jesus walks straight to you as well. Yes, he has famines to end, new stars to hang, tortured Christians calling his name, diseases to tend to, and planets to rotate, but he still sees *you* in the midst of your need and walks straight to you.

It's interesting to note that the paralytic was so intensely focused on the water's surface, he didn't even notice who was in his presence. *The creator of the universe standing next to me? Hmmm. Wouldn't know about that. I don't want to take my eyes off the water.*

How often are you so focused on your own problems that you fail to notice the King of kings is standing next to you waiting to meet your needs? We get so busy looking to other sources for answers that we forget to notice Jesus *is* the answer!

Yes, Jesus asked the paralytic what seemed a silly question. But he had to get the man's attention. What does he have to do to get your attention? He'll go to great lengths to get it. His death and resurrection should be enough to capture your attention.

Eventually he'll command the attention of everyone in the world when they'll bow and confess that he is Lord on the Day of Judgment. Are there things or people you're so focused on right now that they're interfering with your full attention to Jesus Christ?

Here are a few excuses given to teachers to explain a student's absence from school:

- This note is to excuse Johnny from being absent on January 29, 30, 31, 32, and 33.
- Sheila wasn't feeling well, so we had her shot.
- Please excuse David for being. It was his father's fault.

Speaking of excuses . . . so Jesus asked the paralytic lying by the water's edge a question the man would never forget. "Do you want to be well?"

We might assume the man would seize the incredible opportunity to walk again. "Yes!" we expect him to say. "Oh, Jesus, I've been waiting for you for 38 years! Now you're here, and I can become whole!"

If you've read the Scripture, you know that wasn't his response. Check it out in John 5:7: " 'Sir,' the invalid replied, 'I have no one to help me into the pool when the water is stirred. While I am trying to get in, someone else goes down ahead of me.' "

He didn't really answer Jesus' question, did he? Sound familiar?

"Did you do your homework?"

"My dog is sick. I had to work last night. I think I'm getting the flu. I lost my textbook. I ran out of gas. My date stood me up. I was up late last night. My dad lost his job. I forgot to set my alarm. I didn't know we had school today. I never knew the S.A.T. wasn't an open-book test. I can't remember where I put my notebook."

It's a yes/no question! Why give excuses? When someone asks, "Did you do your homework?" all you need to say is yes or no. Nothing else really matters.

When Jesus asked, "Do you want to be well?" all the man needed to do was respond with a yes or a no. Instead, he made an excuse: "There's no one here to help me." (What about the creator of the universe standing right next to you?)

"Someone else always beats me to the water." The question wasn't, "Why haven't you made it to the pool?" The question was simply, "Do you want to be well?"

What kind of excuses do you give the creator of the universe? When he asks a specific question, give him a specific answer. Don't mess around with excuses.

Know It!
When God asks a specific question, he wants a specific and honest answer. He knows all our thoughts and motives anyway, so there's no reason to give excuses.

Read It!
John 5:1-18; 14:15-23

Pray It!
Have you gotten into the habit of making excuses? Tell the Lord you want to be open and honest with him, and ask his help in being specific and truthful when you pray.

God's Intensive Care Unit

Know It!
If God makes you spiritually whole, things will have to change. Are you willing to let go of a relationship, a friendship, a specific environment, your identity?

Read It!
Matthew 15:29-31; Luke 17:19; John 5:1-18; 1 Thessalonians 5:23-24

Pray It!
Tell the Lord you do want to be whole and you're willing to make the changes necessary for him to do everything he desires in your life.

When Jesus asked the paralyzed man, "Do you want to be well?" it was the wisest question he could have asked.

Think about it: The paralytic had stayed by the pool for 38 years. If he truly wanted to get well, why didn't he recruit some friends? "Hey, guys! I need a little help," he could have said. "See, when the water is stirred, I gotta be the first one in the pool. And well . . . it's obvious I can't do that on my own."

After 38 years, couldn't he have come up with *something*? Or had he become comfortable in his sickness? Maybe he'd become cozy by the pool. Perhaps he made friends with the other sick people at the water's edge.

If Jesus were to make him well, things would have to change. First of all, his *identity* would change. He was probably known as "Paralyzed Pool Guy." He would no longer be PPG; he'd be a new man with a new identity.

Next, his *environment* would change. If Jesus made PPG whole, he'd leave the pool. He would no longer hang out with the same friends at the same place. Could it be that PPG really didn't want to change?

It's easy to become comfortable in our "sick" surroundings. You may not deal with physical illness, but you might have a comfortable, sinful environment you hate to leave behind. It's tough to think about change—walking away from friends, giving up old habits.

"Do you want to be well?" was an extremely wise question, wasn't it?

Jesus is referred to in a variety of ways throughout Scripture, and one title is "the Great Physician." Let's picture the pool of Bethesda as God's intensive care unit. He showed up ready and willing to do "surgery" on someone who desperately needed a physical touch.

God's I.C.U. isn't limited to a pool. In fact, it could be your bedroom, your car, or wherever you talk with him. The Great Physician is here, and he's ready and willing to make you whole. What kind of spiritual surgery do you need? He's asking you the same question he asked PPG: "Do you want to be well?" If so, you'll be willing to allow him to touch you in a way that will necessitate change.

Even though PPG made excuses, Jesus saw right through them. He knew deep inside the man wanted to be well. Perhaps fear kept him at the pool for 38 years. Or maybe he saw others worse off than he was, and he didn't want to keep them from experiencing the water's healing touch. Whatever the reason for his excuses, Jesus broke through the barrier.

Note the first thing Christ instructed PPG to do: "Get up!" We might think since PPG had just given an excuse instead of answering Christ's direct question, he might give another excuse: "I can't 'get up.' I'm paralyzed! Why do you think I'm lying here by the pool?"

But he didn't. He simply obeyed. No arguments. No questions. No resistance. He just did as Jesus said. He got up.

Jesus asked PPG to do the impossible. It's crazy to think a man who's been paralyzed for 38 years could get up and walk. But the Great Physician holds all power and is definitely in the miracle business. With God, all things are possible!

There will be times when Jesus will ask you to do what seems to be impossible. How will you respond? With excuses or with obedience?

Jeremiah was only a teenager when God called him to be a prophet and speak his holy Word. Jeremiah's response was, "I can't do that! I'm too young!" But God reminded Jeremiah that he would put his very words in Jeremiah's mouth. All Jeremiah needed to do was simply obey.

God will never ask you to do something without giving you everything you need to complete the task. If he says, "Get up!" know that he'll provide the strength you need to do so.

When PPG heard the command, "Get up!" he knew right away it would mean action on his part. Are you willing to put forth the action and do whatever God asks of you to become whole?

Know It!

Instead of questioning God's ways, you need to respond in obedient faith. What's impossible for humans is always possible for the Great Physician.

Read It!

Jeremiah 1:5-10;
John 5:1-18; 14:12-14

Pray It!

Do you wonder how much more God could do in and through your life if you'd simply obey him instead of question him? Ask him to strengthen your faith so you can obey him in every area of your life.

Identify Your Bags

Know It!

It's scary to identify your baggage, isn't it? But you're not alone. The Great Physician stands with you. He's ready to take the luggage that's been crippling you.

Read It!

Isaiah 49:13; 57:18-19; John 5:1-18

Pray It!

Dear Lord, as of today, I will no longer place the blame for the hurt in my life on other people. Yes, at times I've been a victim. But I'm tired of wallowing in the pain. I identify my baggage, and I give it to you. Please make me whole.

After Jesus healed the paralyzed man, he told him to pick up his bedroll. "Grab your bag. Get your stuff. Identify your luggage."

When you check your bag at the airport, you label it so you'll be able to identify it quickly when your flight has landed. You've been there, haven't you—waiting by the carousel at baggage claim, carefully watching for your bag. When your luggage glides through, you reach out and claim it. Basically, you're saying, "This is my baggage. It has my name on it. I'm identifying it as mine."

Jesus was asking the paralyzed man to identify his baggage. No more excuses. Stop blaming others. Just go ahead and admit, "This is mine."

Jesus wants you to do the same: Identify your baggage. Go ahead. Admit it. "This is my eating disorder. I'm naming it."

"This is my problem with lust. I'm identifying it."

"This is my battle with alcohol. I admit it."

"This is my addiction to porn. My name is on this baggage."

Whatever your baggage consists of, stop blaming others and admit it's yours. "Sleeping with my boyfriend. I'm not going to blame him any more for pressuring me. It was my decision, and I need to deal with it."

"Cutting myself. I've always said it's because of the hurt she caused. But I'm through blaming. I accept this baggage as my problem. I want to deal with it."

After you've identified your baggage, give it to the Great Physician. He died for your baggage. Why hold on to it?

The days of lying around the pool are over. God is here to make you whole. *So get up!* Yes, that requires faith in him to do the impossible.

Pick up your mat. First you'll have to identify it. "Yes, this is my baggage." Then you'll need to get rid of it. You don't need it any longer. Give it up. "Here, Jesus. I place this in your hands."

And walk. Get on with your life. Allow God to take your past, your illness, your failure, and make something beautiful out of it.

Emotionally Crippled?

While the paralyzed man was staring at the water, Jesus walked right into his crippled environment offering hope and healing. To the world it seemed impossible . . . that a man paralyzed for 38 years could somehow, someday walk again. But with God, the One who made life from dirt and created order from chaos, anything is possible.

You may not be physically paralyzed, like the guy in our story. But there's more than one way to be crippled. Are you spiritually paralyzed? Has it been years since you've really grown spiritually?

Could you be emotionally crippled? Yes, it hurt when Dad walked out, when the uncle you loved abused you, when others made fun of you, when you were left alone. But the King of kings is standing next to you, and he asks the same question he asked the man by the pool: "Do you want to get well?"

If you really do, he's here to help, and you'll respond.

If you've become comfortable in your crippled state, however, you'll never hear him ask the question.

If you truly want to become whole, things will have to change. You won't be able to sit comfortably by the pool any longer. You'll need to actually get up and walk away.

We've talked about identifying your baggage and giving it to God. Releasing it to his authority means giving it up for good. Are you willing to do that?

I interviewed a girl with an eating disorder so severe, she had been admitted to a treatment facility. This was actually her second time around. When I asked her about getting well, I was impressed with her honesty.

"I *say* I want to get well . . . but at the same time, I'm scared to let go. Back home I'm known as 'the girl with the eating disorder.' My identity is wrapped up in this. If I become well, I'm afraid I won't know who I am." She had allowed an eating disorder to paralyze her awareness of who she was.

What paralyzes you? A habit you can't break, a relationship that's drawing you away from God, your past? Whatever is crippling you, the Great Physician is here . . . and he wants to do some spiritual surgery in your life right now. Will you let him?

Know It!

God created you and knows you better than anyone. He also *loves* you more than anyone. He understands your uncertainty and fear. Be honest with him about where you are spiritually right now.

Read It!

Isaiah 42:5-7; 43:1-2; 58:11; John 5:1-18

Pray It!

Are you afraid of the spiritual surgery Jesus can give you? Admit that fear of change. Ask him to help you trust him completely and hand over your baggage to him.

Quiz Time

Know It!

There *will* come a day when we'll run out of excuses. This is known as Judgment Day. God wants to use you to reach your friends for him before it's too late.

Read It!

Joel 3:12; Micah 4:3; John 5:1-18, 27

Pray It!

Ask God to bring to your mind the names of friends he wants to influence through you. Ask him for courage to talk to them.

In each question, circle all that apply.

*The **question** Jesus asked the paralytic by the pool seemed to be*

a. multiple choice.
b. a stupid question.
c. frightening.

*Jesus asked a **direct** question, and the man*

a. didn't really answer the question.
b. asked Jesus for his autograph.
c. pulled out a banjo and began playing country music.
d. made excuses.
e. ignored the creator of the universe.

*How long had the **sick man** been waiting by the pool?*

a. too long to count
b. a couple of days
c. 38 years
d. four hours
e. no one knows for sure
f. he had just arrived by ambulance

*Write about a time in your own life when you wanted something but others kept **getting in front** of you.*

____

____

____

*"Later Jesus found him at the temple and said to him, 'See, you are well again. Stop sinning or something worse may happen to you.' " List **worse** things (physically, spiritually, and eternally) that could happen to the man.*

____

____

____

*What are some **excuses** your non-Christian friends make when it comes to giving their lives to God? How about excuses you or your Christian friends make when it comes to giving up everything to God?*

____

____

____

Kindness: A Thing of the Past?

Dear Diary:

I'm really not a journal-writing type of person . . . but I'm bored so I decided to jot some thoughts down.

I've heard it a million times: "Be kind to one another." And I've read it over and over again in the Bible. But this morning, during my quiet time, I read it once again, and it hit me like a ton of bricks.

Am I kind?

I mean . . . what specifically have I done to show kindness to someone in the past week? Month? Okay . . . year?

Pretty pathetic, huh, Diary? I'm self-centered and rarely take time to think of others.

But I'm not gonna stay this way! I'm asking God to help me become more deliberate in my actions. I want to be kind.

So I'm gonna start now . . . by listing some easy stuff I can do during the next few weeks to show kindness to others. Then I'll check each one off after I do it.

- Write Mom and Dad a note and tell them how much I love them.
- Pick up leaves in Mrs. Tucker's yard.
- Take a doggie treat to the Saint Bernard down the street.
- Send an appreciation card to my youth leader.
- Say something nice to one of my teachers.
- Find someone who doesn't have many friends and talk to him or her.
- Smile at someone I don't know.
- Clean the house without being asked.
- Cook dinner for my family one evening.
- Call someone who hasn't been to church or youth group in a few weeks and tell her she is missed.

Know It!

Non-Christians will notice something positive and different about you if you treat those around you kindly. Decide right now to become someone who develops a lifestyle of kindness.

Read It!

Psalm 86:5;
Proverbs 14:31; 19:17;
Ephesians 4:32;
1 Thessalonians 5:15

Pray It!

Tell God you don't want to just talk about kindness and love, you want to live it! Ask him to help you think of specific ways to be kind.

How Come?

Know It!
You're kidding yourself if you think you can live the Christian life without making Bible reading a consistent part of your life.

Read It!
2 Timothy 2:19, 22;
2 Timothy 3:16-17;
Hebrews 4:12-13

Pray It!
Confess to God that you don't read the Bible as much as you should. Ask him to give you a hunger for his Word, plus the discipline to pray and read the Bible every day.

How come male gorillas beat their chests? If you've been to the zoo, you've probably seen this. A gorilla actually does it for a number of reasons: when a rival approaches and threatens his affections for a female gorilla; in order to establish his dominance within the group; when approached by people; when he's excited; when he's alarmed; to mark his territory when approached by another troop of gorillas; and as a location signal—often when one gorilla beats his chest, he's answered by another gorilla. This can be a way to keep the group together.

How come we never see anyone riding a zebra? Zebras aren't very friendly toward humans. They're known as mean animals, and they're close to impossible to train. They tend to kick and bite when restrained, and they're extremely unpredictable and dangerous.

How come crackers are filled with little holes? They're not thick enough to bake evenly throughout, so the holes provide a way for the heat to move consistently through the entire cracker. Without the holes, the middle of a cracker would stay soft.

How come it's so important for Christians to read the Bible? The Bible, God's holy Word, teaches us how to live as Christ wants us to live. We learn about our spiritual heritage through the Bible. We're given the history of Jesus and the biography of his life. The Bible provides wisdom, insight, and answers. We learn to know ourselves better by reading the letter from the One who created us. We're taught how to live victoriously and how to forgive. We're warned about the end times and motivated to share our faith with others.

The Bible is more than simply a good book; it's our guide for living. The Bible contains the answer for any problem we'll ever encounter. It may not mention specific words regarding a particular issue we face, but it does provide the answer for the situation. For instance, the Bible doesn't say, "Don't look at pornography." But it's filled with instructions on keeping our minds and thoughts pure. And the Bible doesn't say, "Don't walk in front of a moving train," but it *does* talk a lot about common sense, wisdom, and not behaving foolishly.

"Hey, Matt! Whatcha listenin' to?" asked Jeremy as he caught up to his friend after school.

"It's an old Usher CD—*My Way.*"

"Yeah, I used to have all his stuff," Jeremy said. "But last year I got really serious about my relationship with God, so I started to think twice about the stuff I was listening to."

"I've been a Christian for three years," Matt said. "But what's that got to do with the music I listen to?"

"A lot. I finally began to realize that the more I listened to junk that went against God's character, the more it began to affect me in a negative way."

"Ah, Usher's not that bad," Matt said.

"Hey, in that one album alone, he boasts to another man that he's having sex with his woman, he advocates playing with guns and using cocaine, and he even rationalizes rape."

"Okay, okay. I get your point. But he's not as bad as Limp Biskit or Korn or—"

"That's like saying stealing's not as bad as murder. Sin is sin."

"I never thought about it that way," Matt admitted.

"Hey, I can tell you firsthand that since I stopped listening to junk God doesn't want in my head, I've seen an incredible difference in my life!"

"Yeah?" Matt said. "How?"

"Well, I'm not so negative any more. Or angry. And my relationship with Christ has skyrocketed."

"Yeah, but . . . I love music. If I give this up, what am I gonna listen to—my parents' collection?"

"That's what worried me too, at first," Jeremy said. "But, Matt, I've found that every single sound I loved in secular music is also available with Christian lyrics."

"You're kidding. It can't sound as good!"

"I'm *not* kidding! And a lot of it sounds even better!"

"I don't know any of those groups. I don't even know what to shop for."

"I've got an hour before I have to get to work. Let's stop by the Christian bookstore."

"Yeah, but CDs are expensive. I don't want to plop down $15 on some group I might not like."

"The bookstore has a play station. You can actually listen to a CD before you buy it. That way you don't end up with something you don't like."

"What are we waiting for?" Matt said. "Let's go!"

Know It!

God wants you to fill your mind with things that reflect his holy character. Ever heard the saying, "Garbage in/garbage out"? It's true. Whatever you put into your head will eventually come out in your lifestyle.

If you need some ideas about good Christian music groups, check out www.pluggedinmag.com

Read It!

Philippians 4:8;
Colossians 3:17;
1 Thessalonians 4:1-5;
5:22-24

Pray It!

If you don't always think seriously about what you listen to, tell the Lord you're sorry. Commit to filling your mind with things that help you draw closer to him, and ask him to make you willing to change your listening habits the way he wants you to.

In Just One Day

Betcha didn't know that in the United States, in just one day . . .

- 25,000 people realize lice have made a home in their hair.
- 69,000 gallons of mouthwash are gargled by people wanting fresher breath.
- People buy 190,000 wristwatches.
- 364,000 wild animals are brought into America.
- $1,000,000 is spent on tuxedo rentals.
- Chairs, sofas, beds, and mattresses are the cause of 1,200 people being injured.
- People eat 6.5 million gallons of popcorn.
- 275,000 pounds of yarn are purchased.
- 25 children are involved in accidents with coins.
- Lots of children stay home from school due to a head cold–164,000 of them, to be exact. And 137,000 adults miss work using the same excuse.
- People spend $12,000 on dental floss.
- Enough soft drinks are consumed to fill a 530-foot Coke bottle. (That's 23,000,000 gallons of soft drinks!)
- Ten tons of colored aquarium gravel is purchased.
- People take 21,000,000 photographs.
- 5,000 pounds of candy is consumed.
- Golfers make 110 holes-in-one at golf courses around the nation.
- Teeth are brushed with 550,000 pounds of toothpaste.
- 75 acres of pizza is eaten–enough food to stretch across 60 football fields.

And . . . betcha didn't know that if you'll read three chapters of the Bible every single day and read five chapters every Sunday, you will have read the entire Bible in just one year!

Know It!

God wants his holy Word to saturate your life. Don't allow your Bible to collect dust or simply be used as a bookend. Pledge to read it consistently! Carry it with you wherever you go. When you have a few spare minutes, read a couple of verses—and maybe even try to memorize them. Wouldn't it feel great to have read the entire Bible? It's not impossible. You can do it! Start today.

Read It!

Psalm 119:105;
Matthew 22:29;
Luke 8:16;
1 Timothy 4:13;
2 Timothy 3:16

Pray It!

Ask God to help you understand his Word, to speak to you through it, and to help you memorize Scripture so you can share it with others who need him.

You're Not Alone

Jamie tossed her backpack on the kitchen counter and flipped on the computer. *Hope Ashley is online,* she thought. *I need a good buddy chat right now.*

Jamie enjoyed chatting with her cousin and hearing stories about college life in her dorm. *Can't wait till I'm out of high school and on a college campus,* she mused.

Jamie17: Hey, Ash! How's it goin'?
20ash: Two finals today. Did great in biology. Not sure about trig. What's up?
Jamie17: Sigh. Another so-so day. Hate high school. I feel totally alone.
20ash: In a school of 2,100?
Jamie17: I don't know any other Christians there. Pretty sure I'm the only one on campus.
20ash: Reminds me of someone in the Bible who felt alone: Elijah.
Jamie17: The guy who murdered all the prophets of Baal. Yeah. We talked about him in youth group last month.
20ash: Did you talk about the fact that even though he was convinced he was the only follower of God on earth, there were actually several thousand other godly people in Israel?
Jamie17: Don't remember that part.
20ash: Jamie, I know it must be frustrating to feel as though you're the only Christian on your campus, but it may not be true.
Jamie17: Well, I don't know any other Christians.
20ash: So? That doesn't mean they're not there.
Jamie17: What am I supposed to do? Wear a sandwich sign that says, "Looking for a Christian friend"?
20ash: Try starting a Bible club. Make it a point to participate at the annual "See You at the Pole" event in September. That's a great way to find out real fast who the other Christians are.
Jamie17: Yeah. I forgot about that.
20ash: One more thing, Jamie. Pray specifically for Christian friends. Ask God to show you who the Christians are. And don't be afraid to take the initiative.
Jamie17: Whaddya mean?
20ash: Carry your Bible to school. Another Christian student may notice that and approach you. Keep your eyes open for anyone who's carrying his Bible, wearing a piece of Christian jewelry, or praying over her lunch in the cafeteria.
Jamie17: I hadn't thought of that! I will, Ash! Thanks a lot.

Know It!

You may feel alone, but you're really not. God has promised never to forsake you. He's with you every second of every minute of every hour of every day. Lean on him. Plus, there may be Christians around you whom you don't even know! Look for opportunities to meet others who believe the way you do.

Read It!

1 Kings 19:11-18;
Isaiah 55:6;
Philippians 2:1-2;
Hebrews 13:5

Pray It!

Ask God to help you identify the Christians at your school, and pray for the courage to be identified as his child.

A Real Hero

Know It!
God wants you to speak out for him, but he also wants to use your lifestyle. Do your actions reflect him?

Read It!
Acts 6:3–8:2

Pray It!
Before you can give your life for the Lord's sake, you must first live your life for his sake. Ask God to strengthen you and give you the courage to live for him . . . and, if necessary, to die for him.

Stephen was the first martyr of the Christian faith. (A martyr is someone who dies for his or her faith. Many people have labeled Cassie Bernall and Rachel Scott—of the Colombine High School massacre in Littleton, Colorado—as modern-day martyrs.)

All most Christians remember about the story of Stephen is that he was stoned to death. He was also a good administrator and a powerful orator. And it was his speech that invited his death. Stephen knew Jesus Christ was who he claimed to be—the Messiah, the Son of God. And he just couldn't keep quiet about it. He desperately wanted those around him to experience forgiveness for their sins, as he had. He was burdened for his community and his people. He wanted them to know the true joy that only God can give.

So he talked about Jesus. A lot. In fact, he talked so much, he made his listeners angry. You see, he didn't just talk fluff. He called sin by its rightful name: Sin. And he accused them of murdering Jesus, the Messiah. The high council of priests panicked at the thought of their evil deeds being exposed. So they had him stoned.

Can you imagine dying by having people throw sharp stones and rocks at you? It was an excruciating death. Yet, as Stephen was dying, he prayed that God would forgive those who stoned him. Even in his last moments of life, he was concerned about the needs of others.

And to those who knew him, that was no surprise. Stephen made it a habit to help those in need. He was one of seven leaders chosen to supervise distribution of food to the poor, and he took his responsibilities seriously. Because Stephen had fulfilled small assignments with excellence, he was prepared for the bigger assignment—that of giving his life for the gospel.

What kind of risks have you taken to be a follower of Christ? Are you willing to die for him? How about living for him . . . day by day by day?

Have you ever wondered why we have leap years? The year, which we define as the time it takes the earth to completely rotate around the sun, isn't an exact number of days . . . it's about 365¼ days. By adding an extra day into our calendar every four years, we can make sure that the year doesn't gradually become out of step with the seasons.

Sounds as if we're trying to control time, doesn't it? The exciting (and frightening) thing about time is the fact that it's continually moving forward. We can't recall it. Once you've spent time doing something, you can't change your mind and undo the time you've already spent.

That makes *time* the most precious gift you can ever give. Think about it. When you give someone your time, you're giving him something that can never be replaced, given back, or exchanged. Time is a precious commodity. Whether you're in a leap year or a non-leap year, the time you spend on this particular day you'll never get back.

Millions of people around the world ask God for some of his time. His followers pray for healing, wisdom, relationships, deeper faith, protection, and a multitude of other things. And he hears all of them! God created time, so he's not constrained by it like we are. He doesn't have to choose which thing he's going to do at a given moment; he can do millions of things at once. So when *you* ask God for some of his time, he gives it to you! Right then. Exactly when you need it. At the precise moment you ask. What an incredible gift from the Father!

How are you using the precious gift of time? Are you being productive with the minutes and hours God has given you?

Know It!

Because God gives *you* time, he wants you to give others time. Has it become too easy to put off seeing your grandparents? Or dropping your uncle a note? Or offering to help Mom with the dishes?

Read It!

Proverbs 2:6-10; 16:3; Ecclesiastes 3:1-8

Pray It!

Ask God to help you use your time well—in a way that glorifies him.

A God-Sized Void

Back in the 1800s, the Winchester rifle was the weapon of choice among cowboys, lawmen, and outlaws. Because of the widespread use of the weapon, the Winchester family became quite wealthy. Mrs. Sarah Winchester dabbled in the occult, and a psychic she consulted informed her that the ghosts of those killed by her family's rifles would seek to do her harm.

Mrs. Winchester desperately wanted to escape the curse. *If I can confuse the ghosts,* she thought, *I'll be safe.*

So she hired a construction crew to work on her house every single day until she died. She had builders make doors open into walls, create secret passageways, and construct stairs that led to nowhere. This house going nowhere ended up with 40 staircases, 10,000 windows, 47 fireplaces, and 2,000 doorways.

Have you ever felt as though your life resembled the Winchester mansion? Are you simply going in circles? Living in a confusing maze? *Okay, I'm on the right track now,* you may think . . . until your hallway leads you right into a wall. *Ah, finally! This is the staircase that will take me where I want to go,* you muse . . . until it takes you to a dead end.

You're not alone. Every human being in the world is looking for direction, answers, and meaning. Nothing wrong with that. In fact, it's normal. You see, each one of us was created with a void in our soul. It's a big hole that needs to be filled before we'll truly be complete. The problem is that most of us are looking in the wrong places. You probably know people who are trying just about anything to fill the void in their lives, but that's as futile as walking through a maze that leads nowhere.

"I thought a fast car would make me happy," Alan says. "And I guess it did for a month or so. But after the newness wore off, I was still empty inside."

Brianna says, "I just wanted to be loved. I thought by giving myself to Eric, I'd feel complete. But now I feel used, and I'm still missing something."

"I went through elementary school with very few friends," Charlie recalls. "So when my family moved and I had a chance to start over, I decided to do whatever it took to be popular in high school. Know what? It definitely wasn't worth it. I feel so guilty because of the stuff I've done just to get attention from those around me."

Know It!

Each of us was created with a God-shaped void in our lives. That means the only One who can fill the emptiness is God himself. Drugs, sex, possessions—nothing else fills the hole except God. He's the only One who fits exactly inside that void. Has he filled the void in *your* life?

Read It!

Exodus 15:2;
2 Samuel 22:3;
Psalms 13:5; 118:14;
Isaiah 12:2

Pray It!

Thank God that he can fill the emptiness in your life when he takes charge of it.

Hard to Imagine

Know It!
God wants you in heaven so much that he sent his only Son to die for you. The death and resurrection of Christ is your entrance to eternity with God.

Read It!
James 2:5; 1 Peter 1:3; Revelation 21:6

Pray It!
Tell God how thankful you are that Jesus died in your place on the cross! Ask him to help you live a life of gratitude.

How can you earn more money and fame—by being an athlete or by being a brain? Well, let's look at the stats:

Basketball pro Michael Jordan "retired" with $40 million in endorsements and still makes $178,100 a day . . . whether he's working or not. (This was before he started playing again for the Washington Wizards.) If Michael sleeps seven hours one night, he makes $52,000. If he goes to see a movie, it may cost him $8, but he'll make $18,550 while he's there.

Michael makes $7,415 an hour more than minimum wage. He'll make $3,710 while watching his favorite 30-minute television sitcom. If he wanted to save for a new Acura NSX ($90,000), it would take him a whole 12 hours.

If someone were to hand him his salary and endorsement money, they'd have to do it at the rate of two dollars every second.

If you were given a penny for every $10 Michael Jordan made, you'd be living comfortably at $65,000 a year. This year, he'll make more than twice as much as all United States past presidents for all of their terms combined.

Amazing, isn't it?

However . . . if Jordan saves 100 percent of his income for the next 500 years, he'll still have less than Bill Gates has at this very moment.

And if Bill Gates saves 100 percent of his income for the next 500 years, it still won't buy even one minute of eternity in heaven with Christ.

Whoa! As hard as it is to comprehend how much money Michael Jordan and Bill Gates have, it's even tougher to understand eternity. Because we're human, we want to place a beginning and an end on everything. But eternity *never* ends. It simply goes on and on and on and on and on and on and on and on and on and on and on with no period at the end of the sentence because there *is* no end to eternity EVER.

Hmmm. Guess it's pretty important that we know where we're going to spend eternity . . . since it has no end. The Bible is clear that each one of us has two choices: heaven or hell. No in-between. No multiple choice. Every single person who has ever lived will spend forever in heaven or hell. Do you know where *you'll* be?

Shake It Off!

One spring day, Farmer Green's donkey fell into a well. The animal brayed loudly as Mr. Green tried to figure out a solution. He finally decided that since the animal was old, and the well needed to be covered up anyway, it just wasn't worth it to rescue the donkey.

He recruited his neighbors to help, and together they all grabbed shovels and began to toss dirt into the well. At first the donkey realized what was happening and wailed louder. After several minutes, however, he quieted down. The neighbors were amazed at how calm the animal had become.

Farmer Green finally looked down the well and was astonished at what he saw. With every shovel of dirt that hit the donkey's back, the animal did something incredible. He shook the dirt off and took a step up.

As Farmer Green's neighbors continued to shovel dirt on top of the animal, the donkey continued to shake it off and step up. It wasn't long until the donkey was able to step up over the edge of the well and simply trot off!

We can't go through life without having some dirt tossed on us. Every single one of us will experience trials and loneliness. When life tosses dirt in your path, you have a choice: Let it bury you alive, or shake it off and step forward. Try to view your problems as stepping stones. If you so choose, you can actually learn from your trials.

Know It!

You can't escape troubles. But you *can* become stronger through each one. The next time you're faced with a problem, go straight to God. Stop focusing on the *why* and start looking for the lesson.

Read It!

2 Corinthians 4:8-9;
James 1:1-4;
1 Peter 1:6-7

Pray It!

When you're dealing with a problem, ask God to help you see how to learn from it, move ahead, and trust him more.

That's Expensive!

Know It!
It's easy to become focused only on ourselves and what we want. But God wants to help you see life clearly—through his perspective.

Read It!
1 Kings 19:11-18; Proverbs 13:20; 21:22; Luke 9:52-56

Pray It!
Ask God to help you see things from his perfect perspective.

We often complain about the rising costs of gasoline. But let's put it in perspective with other liquid items we regularly purchase.

- Lipton iced tea: 16 ounces for $1.19 = $9.52 per gallon
- Diet Snapple: 16 ounces for $1.29 = $10.32 per gallon
- Gatorade: 20 ounces for $1.59 = $10.18 per gallon
- Ocean Spray cranberry juice: 16 ounces for $1.25 = $10 per gallon
- STP brake fluid: 12 ounces for $3.15 = $33.60 per gallon
- Vick's NyQuil: 6 ounces for $8.35 = $178.13 per gallon
- Pepto-Bismol: 4 ounces for $3.85 = $123.20 per gallon
- Scope: 1.5 ounces for $.99 = $84.48 per gallon
- Evian water: 9 ounces for $1.49 = $21.19 per gallon

Next time you're filling your vehicle, be grateful your car doesn't run on NyQuil, Scope, or even water!

As much as we complain about gasoline prices, when compared with purchasing gallons of any of the above liquid items, gasoline suddenly doesn't seem that expensive, does it? That's because we've put it in perspective. Cool things happen when we're able to put life's events into perspective. Things suddenly don't seem so bad. That person really isn't out to get us; the homework assignment didn't actually kill us.

On February 27 we talked briefly about the prophet Elijah. He *felt* as though he was the only follower of God left on the earth. He really wasn't. He simply needed a perspective adjustment. When he allowed God to shift his perspective, he realized there were actually several thousand godly people around him!

Do you need a perspective adjustment? If so, you're not alone! At times even the disciples needed help with their perspective. Luke 9:54 shows us that James and John wanted to pray fire down from heaven to nuke an entire town! Thankfully, Jesus helped them with perspective. It truly *can* make all the difference.

It seems like the Old Testament prophets were always asking God questions. It's important to know that God doesn't mind our questions, as long as we learn to listen for his answers.

Habakkuk the prophet and Habakkuk the book are both full of questions . . . and answers. Habakkuk was fed up! You can read the list of complaints in the first chapter of his book. He's unloading on God: "I don't like what I see! Bad people are rich, and the good people are suffering. How long must I call for help? God, it feels as though you're not listening."

Have you ever felt like that? Did you know you can tell God exactly how you feel? He wants your honesty. We often think he only wants to hear the good stuff—praise, worship, thanksgiving. But God wants to hear your heart. All of it. The disappointment, confusion, frustration, hurt, loneliness. He wants to hear your prayers filled with honesty.

Think about it. Are you telling God what you think he wants to hear? Or are you being honest with him?

Habakkuk has a whole chapter of "Why, God?" But here's the key: After he asked the questions and presented his case to God, he *waited* for God's response. And he waited *expectantly.* (See Habakkuk 2:1.) Too often, we bombard God with questions, then walk out the door. We don't want to wait.

Habakkuk waited. And waited. And waited. God doesn't always promise a fast answer. He does promise perfect timing. (See Habakkuk 2:3.) According to an old saying, he's never early, yet he's never late.

God's delays in your life are not denials. There's a huge difference between "No" and "Not yet." When you realize God isn't saying "no," but neither has he given you a green light, then his answer is more than likely, "Not yet." When you receive a "not yet" from God, use that as a time of preparation, meditation, and cooperation. Let him prepare you during the "not yet" for the time when he'll say, "Yes, now."

Know It!

God always answers your prayers. It's not always with a yes, and it's not always the answer you want, but he always answers. So remember to pray with honesty. It's okay to bombard God with questions—as Habakkuk did—as long as you're willing to wait expectantly for the answers and accept them when they come.

Read It!

Habakkuk 1; 2:1-6; James 1:5-8

Pray It!

Ask God to teach you to wait for his perfect timing.

Lessons from Habakkuk

Know It!
God wants to strengthen your faith. Sometimes he chooses to use the trials in your life to accomplish that. Instead of grumbling because you don't understand, keep praying and trust his wisdom.

Read It!
Habakkuk 2:7-20; Job 1; 42:16-17; James 5:9

Pray It!
Ask God to use your trials to teach you patience, perseverance, and a deeper faith.

The Old Testament prophet Habakkuk bombarded God with lots of questions, and he complained about the injustice around him. But it's important to note there's a difference in complaining to God and being a grumbler. James warns against grumbling. You've heard the expression, "Rise and shine"? Unfortunately, many Christians have turned that into "Rise and whine."

Again, God wants your honesty. It's okay to give him your complaints. But don't forget to thank him for his blessings as well. If you simply focus on the bad without making time to acknowledge the good, you're whining.

God wants to teach his children perseverance. That means he wants you to "keep on keeping on" in the *midst* of injustice and trials. Habakkuk learned that lesson. So did Job. In just two 24-hour periods, Job experienced death in his family, disease, and the murder of servants and cattle. His "friends" came to mourn with him. You'd think that would be a good thing, wouldn't you? They sat in silence with him for three days, then began berating him and accusing him of sin in his life. But if you read Job 1 you'll see that it wasn't sin—it was spiritual warfare!

How would *you* respond if what happened to Job happened to you? Job responded in praise. He maintained his faith. He said to his friends, "I came into the world naked, and I'll leave naked." In other words, he recognized he didn't have anything when he was born and he wouldn't be able to take anything with him when he died.

Through it all, Job learned to persevere. He, too, questioned God with an honest heart, but he waited expectantly for the answers. God honored Job's perseverance and blessed him with more than he had before his trials began.

You have a choice. When life doesn't turn out as you expect, you can grumble, whine, become angry at God, and walk away from your faith. Or you can give God your complaints—as well as acknowledge his blessings—and wait expectantly for his answers. Know what else you can do? During the time of waiting, you can ask him to teach you perseverance.

*When we **pray***
a. God doesn't always answer.
b. he answers exactly how we want him to, if we have enough faith.
c. he always answers but sometimes not in the way we want him to.

*When we pray with an **honest heart***
a. it means we can ask God to zap the people we don't like with diseases.
b. it means we'll probably complain a little, question some, and also thank God for his blessings.
c. it means we can expect God to answer right away with the response we desire.

*When God **delays** in giving us an answer*
a. we have permission to walk away from our faith.
b. we can assume he never heard our prayer.
c. we should use that time of waiting to develop perseverance and deeper faith.

*During the **midst of a problem**, we can assume*
a. God didn't give us the problem, but he wants to help us through it.
b. God placed the problem in our path to see how mad we'd get.
c. God no longer loves us.

*Trials can **develop***
a. great material for stand-up comedy.
b. stronger faith and more dependence on God.
c. into punishment for not understanding God's ways.

*During Job's trials, **he lost***
a. his mind.
b. his patience.
c. his children, servants, livestock, and health.

*Through his trials, Job **gained***
a. national coverage on CNN.
b. more than he had before the trials began.
c. a new Porsche.

*Habakkuk asked God **lots of questions** and*
a. that ticked God off!
b. waited expectantly for his answers.
c. left the scene before God had a chance to answer him.

Know It!
God wants to hear our honest prayers, and he always answers—in his own time.

Read It!
Job 42:10;
Isaiah 45:18-19;
Habakkuk 3

Pray It!
Tell God how thankful you are that he cares about everything in your life.

I Don't Get It!

Know It!

God understands everything you feel—in spite of whether you understand it or not. And he wants you to experience his joy. That doesn't mean you'll always feel happy, but you'll have peace because you know he's with you and understands you.

Read It!

Psalms 9:10-12; 34:18; 43:5

Pray It!

Tell God thank you for knowing you better than you know yourself.

"Natalie, wanna grab a Coke after school today?"

"Nah."

"What gives, Nat? You didn't come to Allison's slumber party last Friday, you haven't been to youth group in forever, and you've started eating alone during lunch time. I miss you!"

"Megan, I . . . well . . . I don't know. I'm just not happy anymore," Natalie said. "I can't figure it out. Maybe I'm depressed."

"I know what you mean! I was really depressed when I made a C on my math test."

"No, Meg. I think it's more than that."

"Yeah, I'm hearing you. I get totally depressed when I don't have anything new to wear, or when Jason's a jerk to me, and when I forget something important–like what we're supposed to read in literature."

"I don't even think you're hearing what I'm saying."

"Sure I am, Natalie! You're bummed. You're down."

"No, Megan. I honestly think it's more than that."

"I'm not following you."

"Obviously."

"Well, don't cut me off. I can't help you if I don't know what you're talking about. Explain what you mean, Natalie."

"Megan, it's more than being a little down. I can't seem to get happy."

"But . . . why?"

"That's just it! I don't know why!"

"Do you think you should talk with Pastor Steve?"

"Yeah. But I'm so down . . . I don't want to talk to anyone. Or be with anyone. I just wanna run home and crawl in bed, pull the covers over my head, and sleep. Forever. I just wanna be alone and sort of withdraw from everyone . . . and everything."

"Look, Natalie. I don't understand what you're going through, but I care. And I'm going to call Pastor Steve and ask him to come get you for a Coke tomorrow after school."

"But, Meg–"

"No excuses, Nat. You need to talk with someone. I'm calling Steve."

"Thanks, Megan. You really are a good friend. I don't think I'd ever make the call myself. And I don't know . . . I'm kinda scared about talking with him."

"Want me to go with you?"

"Would you, Megan?"

"That's what friends are for, Girl!"

"Hi, Natalie! We've missed you in youth group the past few weeks."

"Yeah. Well . . . stuff came up."

"Thanks for taking us out for a Coke, Pastor Steve," Megan said.

"No prob. I'll spring for root-beer floats too!"

"Oooh," Megan said, gazing at the menu. "Can we talk you into some onion rings to go along *with* a root-beer float?"

"Sure," Pastor Steve laughed. Natalie smiled as he placed the order. She really liked Pastor Steve, but she wondered if even he could help her through the feelings of hopelessness she was experiencing.

"Hey, Nat," Pastor Steve said. "You seem as though you're in a different world."

"Yeah. I guess that's how I'm feeling right now."

"What do you mean?"

"I don't know . . . exactly. I'm just not happy. And even though I appreciate you and Megan being here with me, I don't really want to be with people."

"Feeling like you just want to withdraw? Crawl into a hole and stay there forever?"

"Exactly!" Natalie said. "How'd you know?"

"I've been in that hole," Pastor Steve said. "Let me ask you a few more questions, Natalie. Have your sleeping habits changed?"

"Yeah! I just want to sleep all the time. I can't really say I'm that tired . . . I just want to stay in bed."

"And what about your eating habits?"

"I'm not eating as much as I used to. I don't know why."

"And how about your friendships?" Pastor Steve continued. "Are you maintaining them?"

"Not really. I kinda stopped doing things with my friends. Nothing seems like fun anymore."

"You could be depressed, Natalie," Pastor Steve said.

"I've been wondering that. But it's not like before—when I've gotten down because I didn't do well on a test or when I couldn't catch the attention of a guy I liked. This is deeper."

"Depression is often misunderstood because we use the term incorrectly," Pastor Steve said. "We tend to say stuff like, 'I'm so depressed; there's nothing to do!' Or 'Mom won't let me buy that new sweater, and I'm totally depressed.' But depression is much more than being disappointed, bummed, or a little down. It can be caused by external things such as losing a loved one or internal things such as a chemical imbalance."

Know It!
God created you. He understands depression. And if you're battling it, he wants to help you through it.

Read It!
Psalms 34:1-10; 37:7-8; 43:5

Pray It!
Ask God to help you be sensitive to any friends who might be experiencing depression.

Understanding Depression

Know It!
Battling tough issues doesn't mean God has left us.

Read It!
Deuteronomy 31:6; Joshua 1:5; Psalms 27:10; 37:5; Hebrews 13:5

Pray It!
Tell God what a comfort it is to know he'll never forsake you—no matter how confused or desperate you feel.

"Pastor Steve, why do you know so much about depression?"

"I've been through it, Natalie."

"I don't get it," Megan said. "You're our youth pastor! How could you have been depressed?"

Pastor Steve smiled as he reached for some onion rings. "Depression has nothing to do with being a Christian, Megan. It isn't a spiritual thing. You get the flu, don't you? Does that mean you're not a Christian?"

"No."

"Then why would depression mean you're not a Christian?"

"Well . . . I just think if Jesus is really Lord of our lives, we won't get depressed," Megan said.

"Depression is an illness, Megan. Anyone can experience it–whether she's a Christian or not. The advantage of having Christ in our lives, though, is that he understands depression and wants to help us through it."

"But I can't figure out *why* I'm depressed, Pastor Steve! No one in my family has died. I have a good life. My parents love me. I have terrific friends."

"Natalie, depression isn't always due to outward situations. Sometimes it's because of a chemical imbalance in the brain."

"Does that mean I'm crazy?" she asked.

Pastor Steve chuckled. "No, Nat. But sometimes the chemicals in our brains can get a little off-whack. And when that happens, we can become depressed."

"So am I gonna feel this desperate for the rest of my life?"

"I don't think so. The good news is that depression is treatable," Pastor Steve explained. "I encourage you to talk to your parents first. Then see your family doctor and tell him what you're feeling. A doctor can prescribe antidepressants, if he feels they're needed, and he can put you in touch with a Christian counselor. You'll be amazed at the difference that will make in how you feel."

"And God won't be mad at me?" Natalie said.

"No way!" Pastor Steve continued. "God loves you, Natalie. He wants to help you through this. And he often uses people to do that. Sometimes he even works through medication. You really need to make an appointment with your family physician."

"I'll do it, Pastor Steve. Anything to quit feeling so desperate and hopeless. You know what? In a way, I'm relieved. I was beginning to think I was loony, because I didn't know what was happening. But now that we've labeled it, and I know God is still with me, I feel better!"

Did you know?

The shortest chapter in the Bible is Psalm 117.

The longest chapter in the Bible in Psalm 119.

The very center of the Bible is marked with Psalm 118.

There are 594 chapters before Psalm 118.

There are 594 chapters after Psalm 118.

Add these numbers and you get 1,188.

What is the center verse in the Bible? Psalm 118:8. "It is better to take refuge in the Lord than to trust in man."

This verse says something very significant about God's perfect will for our lives. We're told to trust in him rather than people. If we do that, we'll find it much easier to stay in the center of his will.

When are you tempted to place your trust in people rather than Christ? We often tend to trust what we can see and feel. Placing our trust in God when we can't see him is where faith comes in.

Many times we can't see or feel the sun. But we don't doubt its existence simply because it's hidden behind the clouds. And there are times we can't feel the wind. Do you still believe that the air exists even when you can't feel or hear it? To stay in the center of God's will requires faith, and faith is trusting without seeing.

The next time someone says he'd like to find God's perfect will for his life . . . or that he wants to be in the center of God's will, just send him to the center of God's Word!

Isn't it odd how this works out . . . or could God be in the center of it?

Know It!

What often seems a coincidence to us is divine provision from God Almighty. Allow him to help you stay grounded in the center of his will.

Read It!

Psalm 118:8;
Luke 18:1-8;
Ephesians 6:10;
2 Thessalonians 3:5;
Hebrews 11:1

Pray It!

Ask forgiveness for the times you stray from God's will, and ask him to give you the discipline you need to stay grounded in his Word.

God's Voice

Know It!

If you think God never speaks to you, you're mistaken. He's speaking . . . but it could be that you simply haven't learned the sound of his voice. We'll talk more tomorrow about how to recognize God's voice.

Read It!

Deuteronomy 30:19-20;
1 Samuel 15:22;
1 Kings 19:11-13

Pray It!

Tell God you want to be tuned in to him, and ask him to teach you the sound of his voice.

James Alexander Langteaux knows God's voice. He often talks about the "road trips" God directs him to take. And during these road trips, God speaks to him very clearly about specific areas in his life that need attention. You can read about his adventures in the two books he's written: *God.com* and *God.net.*

Someone else knew God's voice extremely well. You can read his story in 1 Kings 18 and 19. After Elijah defeated 450 prophets of Baal, he fled his enemies and ran to the mountains. While waiting for God to speak to him on Mount Sinai, a lot began to happen around him. He experienced a tornado, an earthquake, and a fire.

Elijah had gone to the mountains specifically to hear God's voice. We tend to think that when God speaks his voice thunders through something big . . . such as thunder or fire or a stormy blast of wind. But Elijah sat through all those natural disasters and didn't hear God's voice at all. As he continued to wait for God to speak, he finally heard the faint rumblings of a *whisper.* The Bible tells us when Elijah heard that whisper, he knew it was the voice of God.

We often wish God would speak to us through a heavenly e-mail or phone call. But most of the time when he speaks, his voice comes in a still, small whisper from within.

Chances are, when your mom calls you, she doesn't have to identify herself. "Honey, this is your mother calling. Remember me? I'm short with dark hair. . . ."

You probably recognize her voice as soon as you hear the first syllable of her first word on the other end of the phone line. Guess what! God wants you to know *his* voice that well, too! He wants you to be so tuned in to him that if you're caught in the middle of downtown traffic amid the blaring of horns and screeching of tires, you'll still hear his whisper if he chooses to speak.

If God speaks to you at school, right in the middle of shuffling feet, hallway clatter, and campus chit-chat, will you be so tuned in to his whisper that you'll hear his voice?

Elijah was. James Langteaux is. And you can be, too.

Recognizing God's Voice

How can you learn to decipher God's voice? How do you learn anything? It's a process. The more time you spend with him, the better you know his voice.

Think of your relationship with God as a friendship. Yes, it's much more than that, but let's focus on a few qualities that make your earthly friendships special and apply them to your relationship with your heavenly Father. First, imagine that you and Derrick have just become friends. The first few times you call each other on the phone, you may need to identify yourselves.

But the more you hear Derrick's voice, the faster you recognize him when he speaks to you. After a few weeks, he sees you walking down the hall and calls your name from behind. Before you even turn around to face him, you know it's Derrick, because you've learned the sound of his voice. You know his inflections, his accent, and his pitch.

During the week, the two of you exchange e-mails. And when he spends the summer at his grandparents' house in Canada, Derrick sends you postcards and letters.

When the two of you graduate from high school, you part ways and attend different universities. Several years pass before you hear from Derrick. When the phone rings, he may need to reintroduce himself to you. Perhaps his voice is deeper than it used to be. He may have a cold, or you may have forgotten his vocal inflections because of the time you've spent apart.

Apply those same principles to your relationship with God. The more time you spend together, the better you get to know him. And the more you talk to him and listen to his voice, the faster you learn to *recognize* his voice. Just like postcards, letters, and e-mail from a friend can help you get to know her better, reading God's holy Word can help you get to know him better.

But like any friendship, your relationship with God needs consistent care. If you go too long without talking to him and listening to him, you'll have a hard time discerning his voice. How well do you know the voice of God?

Know It!

God wants to teach you about himself, but it takes effort on your part to get to know him. Are you willing to invest time into making your relationship with him the most important friendship in your life?

Read It!

Psalms 29:3; 95:7; Isaiah 30:21; Revelation 3:20

Pray It!

Ask Jesus to help you dive into his holy Word and become saturated with it! Tell him you want your relationship with him to become the most important thing in your life.

Abishag, R.N. on Call

Know It!

God knows all. He sees the good you do, and he never takes your actions for granted. He will reward you in his perfect time. Other people will sometimes use you, but God will never treat you as less than his child.

Read It!

1 Kings 1:1-4; 2:13-25; Proverbs 14:10; Luke 21:1-4; Ephesians 4:31

Pray It!

Do you still harbor a grudge against someone for what they did to you? Are you tired of feeling angry? Admit it to the Lord, give the hurt to him, and ask him to help you forgive the person.

King David had been known as a "man after God's own heart." And as King David grew old, Abishag became known as David's live-in personal nurse. Of course, she had to do without fancy prescriptions, X-ray machines, and heart monitors. So her main responsibility was simply to keep King David warm.

Often times, as one grows older, he develops poor blood circulation and it's easy to be cold much of the time. King David was so cold, nurse Abishag was brought in to help. What a job description: Warm the king!

It's important to know that this was not a sexual relationship. She was simply trying to physically warm up her patient. But only a few months after she accepted the job, King David died. Abishag then became involved in a bitter family battle between the king's sons. Solomon and his brother Adonijah both wanted the throne, and Adonijah tried to use Abishag as a bargaining chip. Solomon saw through his plan.

Imagine how Abishag must have felt! She gave her best to the king–tried to make him comfortable in his final days–and instead of being thanked, she's simply taken for granted and used for someone's selfish means.

Can you identify a time in your life when you felt used? It doesn't feel good when something we do goes unnoticed, or a family member treats us like a piece of dirty laundry, does it? Instead of falling into the trap of feeling sorry for yourself, take comfort in the fact that Jesus knows exactly how you feel. He was used too. But he looked past the fact that people used him and saw their deeper need. Strive to do that yourself. When someone's using you, he or she usually has a much deeper need inside (inferiority, jealousy, anger) that needs to be addressed more than your hurt feelings of being used. By maintaining a growing, intimate relationship with your heavenly Father, you'll be guarding against feelings of bitterness and resentment.

Worry Not!

Americans consume about 97 percent of the world's aspirin. More and more people are having heart problems at earlier ages. Teens are being fitted with pacemakers and are getting ulcers. If you're *not* worried about something, people tend to view you as abnormal.

As far as we know, Jesus never had ulcers. True, he didn't have children or a wife. He didn't have to make car payments and try to figure out how he'd get that term paper done on time while shuffling his part-time job at the gas station. Even though there are lots of differences between his culture and ours, Jesus *did* have pressures. But from what we read in the Gospels, he never seemed to worry.

How did he achieve something most of us can't even imagine—life without worry? Maybe the answer lies in the resources that were available to Jesus. Guess what! Those very same resources are available to you! What are they?

Learn to retreat. There are several times in Scripture we read that Jesus took a step back. He went somewhere and prayed. He spent time alone. This enabled him to maintain his Father's perspective. You can learn to retreat too. Take a few steps back from time to time, and allow the Holy Spirit to recharge your spiritual batteries. Go hiking. Pitch a tent and spend the night in your backyard. If you know a relative or friend who's going to be out of town, ask if you can stay alone in his home for a day.

Don't be afraid of what others think. You probably have friends who are worried about getting a high-paying job so they can look successful when they graduate from college. You may be worried about making an extremely high grade on the S.A.T. We're bombarded with pressure from all sides to succeed. Be the best. Climb the corporate ladder the fastest. Make the highest grades.

Jesus didn't seem very concerned about being a success, did he? Several people acknowledged their disappointment in him: The Pharisees were disappointed he didn't push the law more with his disciples. The disciples were disappointed he didn't start and win a war with Rome. His mother and brothers were disappointed he didn't leave the crowds at one point to come talk with them. But Jesus didn't allow other people's expectations and disappointments to slow him down.

Know It!

Other Christians' opinions can be helpful. Godly people can keep you on the right track and can encourage you when you're confused. But sometimes the opinions of others can cause you to worry unnecessarily. As long as you're living in the center of God's will, he wants to help you block out the opinions of others who cause you worry.

Read It!

Matthew 6:25-34

Pray It!

Ask God to help you stop worrying about others' opinions and keep your focus on him.

Learning Not to Worry

Know It!
God won't take you out of the world to give you freedom from worry. He wants to help you experience his peace in the *midst* of a troubled world.

Read It!
Joshua 1:6-9; Psalm 34:4; Isaiah 35:4; 1 John 4:18

Pray It!
Ask God to help you remember that he's in control.

If Jesus can live a lifetime without worry, you can too! It's important to note the difference between worry and concern. Jesus was concerned with those around him. When he was speaking to the crowd of 5,000, he told his disciples he was concerned with the fact that the people had not eaten all day. He was concerned about the long walk home they would make in the hot sun without nourishment for their physical being. But he wasn't worried about it. What's the difference? He knew who was in charge.

Jesus also wants you to be concerned with those around you. When you see a need, he wants you to be concerned enough to get involved. But he doesn't want you to worry about it. While concern leads to action, worry doesn't bring about anything positive. How can you avoid worry?

Remember who's in charge! Jesus never forgot that his heavenly Father could do anything. People are the creation of God Almighty. Jesus knew his role was to make the gospel known to people, to explain forgiveness for sins, and to sacrifice his life for sinners. But he knew their reaction was *not* his responsibility, and he refused to bear responsibility that wasn't his. He left it in the hands of his Father.

Yes, Jesus sweat great drops of blood, he endured tremendous torture, he was misunderstood, he faced incredible temptations, and he walked with massive burdens. But he refused to forget who was in charge. Jesus never said, "Ah, just forget it. Someway, somehow, everything will work out." He *did* teach us to take our worries and place them in the lap of God . . . and leave them there!

God *is* in control! Even with war, famine, disease, and terrorism, God still rules. The person who can learn to rest in that knowledge is the one who will experience freedom from worry and learn to live life abundantly!

I'd Love to Help

Dear Diary:

Here I am again . . . spilling my thoughts onto your pages. Yeah, I know. February 23 was the last time I wrote anything. But hey, I'm here now.

You know, every now and then, I see those commercials on television with the starving children, and I wish there was something I could do for them. But it's not like I can pack my bags, drop out of school, and head for Ethiopia or some other faraway place.

And today in social studies class, Mr. Gowler talked about the devastation the mud slides in Caracas, Venezuela, caused a few years ago. He showed some shots he'd taken when he went with a relief team to help dig homes out of mud.

Wow. It was unbelievable. Entire homes buried under giant mud slides. I think it's pretty cool that Mr. Gowler spent his spring break to help. . . . But what can I do?

It costs money to travel. And I don't have it. I can't even afford a passport! I wish there was something I could do right here.

I'll never forget several months ago when Pastor Steve challenged our youth group to "feed the hungry and help the poor." I went home and dreamed about being a missionary to a bunch of people living in grass huts. But even if I do become a missionary, I still have to go to school first.

Sigh.

It just seems as though the needs are growing and the resources sit here in North America. I wish I could personally pack up billions of bags of food and give it to the people I see on television who are starving.

Why does helping always have to involve money? Cuz I really don't have it! I mean I really really really really don't have it. I even had to borrow lunch money from Katie last week. And I still owe Carter $10 for that field trip we took with our science class.

Sigh.

I'm so tired of wanting to help and being too young to do anything. Guess I'll go to bed and dream about all the stuff I can do when I'm out of college and finally have some money and resources to make a difference.

G'night, Diary.

Know It!

If you're not concerned with the needs around you, God wants to make your heart more tender. He wants you to be so in tune with him that the things that break *his* heart will also break your heart. And when you begin to hurt over the needs of his children, he'll provide the resources you need to make a difference—so you don't have to feel hopeless.

Read It!

Matthew 25:31-46

Pray It!

Dear Jesus, help me to be bothered by the things that bother you. And show me how to make a positive difference.

You CAN Make a Difference!

Know It!
God wants you to be involved with the needs of others. Don't allow Satan to make you think you have nothing to give. Ask your creative heavenly Father to help you discover a variety of ways to make a difference.

Read It!
Matthew 25:31-46;
1 Corinthians 3:10-15

Pray It!
Tell God how thankful you are that you're able to make a difference with the resources he gives you.

It may seem as though you can't really make a difference in the world, but that's simply not true! Here are a few things you can do to feed the hungry and help the poor.

Downsize your wardrobe. How many pants and shirts are you no longer wearing that are still stacked inside your drawers? Take a few minutes to go through your wardrobe and pull out everything you no longer use. Take it to Goodwill, give it to a homeless shelter, or ask your pastor if your church has a ministry to needy people in your area who need clothing.

Go to jail. Ask your youth leader if your youth group can join a prison ministry in your area. There are several ministries available to inmates, and there are other ministries designed to help ex-convicts following their release. Families of those in prison are often neglected and forgotten. For more information, contact Prison Fellowship, P.O. Box 17434, Washington, D.C. 20041 or Amnesty International, 322 Eighth Avenue, New York, NY 10001.

Consider sponsoring a needy child. Compassion International is an excellent child development ministry that has work around the world. By sponsoring a child for $28 a month, you're providing clothing, one hot meal a day, school supplies, and an education. The best part of the education is that schools sponsored by Compassion International are connected with neighboring churches. So when your child receives an education, he's also hearing the gospel. Perhaps $28 is too expensive for you to fund by yourself. Ask your parents to pray about sponsorship as a family. Or recruit a few of your friends to help you sponsor one child.

Organize a soup kitchen. Most churches have big kitchens that would easily allow them to operate a soup kitchen for the hungry. Of course, you'll need to get permission from your church leaders and will need their support. Once you have that, get creative. Give your soup kitchen an imaginative name: "Dusty's Diner," "Sheila's Soup," "Chow Corner." Place an advertisement in your local newspaper and ask the TV station to film your first open night. Providing a nightly (or even weekly!) nutritious meal is an amazing way to make a difference in the lives of others. If your church is unable to open and maintain a soup kitchen, consider getting involved in an already existing soup kitchen in your city.

But They're So Cute!

You've seen them—adorable chimpanzees dressed in cute clothing, gracing the movie screen or your television set. One glimpse, and it's hard not to fall in love with the furry little guys. Watching them act and react to the people near them, it's easy to give them human characteristics. After all, humans and apes *do* have a lot in common. Both have and show deep emotions, both can walk upright, and both have the ability to learn quickly. Even facial features and body parts are similar—we all have fingers, toes, elbows, and faces that carry common characteristics.

Sound like the perfect pet? What could be more fun than a little chimp trotting around the house in cute clothes, crawling up in your lap to watch TV with you, cuddling beside you in bed, and even playing a game of catch with you in the backyard? Almost too good to be true? It is!

Chimps don't make good pets at all. In fact, in the state of Florida, it's against the law even to have one—they're considered as dangerous as a lion or tiger! Chimps are incredibly dangerous and strong. One punch from a chimpanzee equals the strength of seven men. Chimps also require a great deal of specialized care that most people can't provide.

A baby chimp sells for $50,000. You'll pay about $30,000 for an adult. Yes, the cost is high to *get* one but even higher to *maintain* one. A good cage will cost anywhere from $10,000 to $20,000. And a cage is essential, because chimps are not "free roam" animals. In other words, you can't leave home in the morning and let your pet chimp have the run of the house as you would a dog or a cat. Chimps are known for tearing off wallpaper; climbing on, knocking over, and breaking furniture; and destroying entire homes.

In movies, chimps are diapered, dressed, and ready to make you fall in love with them. But they grow up. And an adult chimpanzee will not wear clothing. Chimps live to be approximately 60 years old, and after their third or fourth birthday, their wild instincts kick in and they're no longer the cute little animals you fell in love with. They're primates—apes—who become extremely angry that they're living in confinement.

Know It!

It can seem impossible that something so cute could be so harmful. Guess what? That's exactly how sin works. We tend to think, *How could that harm me? I'll just be involved for a little while!* The truth is, what we see as harmless can have long-term negative effects on us.

Satan hates you and is out to destroy you. He's a master of disguises. In other words, making evil look harmless is his specialty. Don't fall for it.

Read It!

2 Corinthians 11:14;
1 Peter 5:8-11;
Revelation 12:9

Pray It!

Ask God to teach you discernment so you can recognize sin when you see it.

Dangerous Creatures

Know It!

Sin is often packaged as cute, fun, and alluring. But just like a chimp, it's only a matter of time before we become a prisoner of the very thing we started out to love. Sin will steal your freedom and eventually your life.

Read It!

Romans 8:3-13; Galatians 5:19; 1 Peter 2:11; 1 John 3:8

Pray It!

Are you sometimes drawn in by what looks, feels, and sounds good? Confess that to God and ask his forgiveness. Commit to living your life for him.

Baby chimps may look adorable, but their strength can do serious damage! One monkey owner says, "Bozo had been reaching through the bars of his cage and grabbing my plants and knickknacks and throwing them around the room, so I scooted them away from his reach. He was so angry that he began biting me when I reached inside his cage to feed him. The fight lasted 45 minutes, and I ended up getting 200 stitches."

Chimpanzee owners will tell you that almost anything can set off a chimp's temper. One punch from an adult chimp can kill a man. A full-grown male chimp weighs 200 pounds. These primates are intelligent and have minds of their own. They will constantly challenge your superiority, and the typical owner will always lose. Yet most people don't know this when they decide to get a baby chimp for a pet.

Since primates can't be left alone for more than short periods of time, and since chimps can live up to 60 years of age, the owner ends up having to change her entire lifestyle to care for the animal. In other words, she's no longer free to leave for a weekend (or even a day), she stops having company over because of the ape's volatile temper, and essentially she becomes a prisoner inside her own house. What's even more distressing is that an owner who loves her ape will spend hours and hours inside the house to care for him, but rarely will she be able to even get close to him because of the animal's anger, destructive strength, and hatred toward his owner.

Food bills for a chimpanzee will run a minimum of $100 per week. Vet bills can cost around $1,500 per visit. Any time a chimp is taken to the vet, the veterinarian will always anesthetize him because of the animal's violent nature.

In short, a baby chimp who looks adorable will very soon mature into an animal with the potential of killing its owner. The owner who purchases a chimp because she wants to love and cuddle with it will soon become prisoner to the animal she spends her life caring for.

We've all seen the TV specials each year around Easter depicting the life, death, and resurrection of Jesus Christ. It's easy to become so familiar with the story of his life that we fall into the trap of taking his death for granted. The truth is, however, that Jesus' crucifixion was no simple matter.

As you read the accounts of the Crucifixion and, later, the Resurrection, you may notice that each of the four Gospels tells the story a bit differently. Why? Because each Gospel was written by a different person, using different sources, and with a different audience in mind. Should this make us doubt the accuracy of the Bible? No! Historians and Bible scholars agree that the Gospels are remarkably harmonious, and the evidence is convincing. (Check out *A Case for Christ* by Lee Strobel for more information.)

Jesus spent his last hours before the Crucifixion at various places in Jerusalem. He began the evening in the upper room. While there, he and his disciples shared what is known as the Last Supper. He announced that his body and blood would be given for them.

From the upper room, Jesus went outside the city walls and spent time in prayer at the Garden of Gethsemane. Luke (who wrote the New Testament books of Luke and Acts) was a physician and was extremely interested in accuracy. He mentions in Luke 22:44 that Jesus began to sweat great drops of blood while he was praying in the Garden of Gethsemane. Though skeptics dismiss this as impossible, medical literature explains this phenomenon. It's a rare condition called *hematidrosis*. Under great emotional stress, tiny capillaries in the sweat glands can break, mixing blood with sweat.

Jesus was then approached by Judas—one of his disciples—and an army of soldiers. Judas had told the soldiers that the man he kissed (a common greeting) would be Jesus. Judas betrayed Jesus with a kiss, and the King of kings was then arrested. His disciples fled, and he was led out of the garden. This arrest was illegal. According to the laws of his society, no arrests could be made at night.

He was led away for a trial before the Sanhedrin court and Caiaphas, the High Priest. The Sanhedrin didn't have the authority to instigate charges. This court was only supposed to investigate charges brought before it. Yet in Jesus' trial, the Sanhedrin court itself formulated the charges.

We read in Matthew 26 that it was during this trial that his first physical trauma was inflicted. When Caiaphas asked Jesus if he was the Messiah, he responded, "Yes, it is as you say." The religious leaders then surrounded Jesus, mocking and taunting him as they dared him to identify his assailants as each passed by, spat on him, and struck him in the face.

Know It!

Everything that happened to Jesus in his last days was unfair. He did absolutely nothing to deserve the hate, torture, and humiliation he endured. But he did it for you. He did it *willingly* for you. You can show your gratitude to him by the way you live your life.

Read It!

Matthew 26:17-29;
Luke 22:39-54;
John 18:1-32

Pray It!

Tell Jesus how grateful you are for his sacrifice.

MARCH 22

Jesus' Trial

Know It!

Jesus Christ not only willingly gave his *life* for you; he willingly was beaten, abused, and lied about for you. He loves you more than you can imagine. Show your gratitude to him by giving him 100 percent of your life.

Read It!

Deuteronomy 19:15; Matthew 22:15-21; 26:59-68; 27:1-31; Luke 23:1-25

Pray It!

Oh, dear Jesus! I never thought about all the torture you experienced before you were even hung on the cross. Will you forgive me? It should have been me experiencing the punishment. But you willingly took it upon yourself . . . so I could be free! Thank you, Jesus!

The Sanhedrin court met in the early morning hours and sentenced Jesus to death. (Remember, this particular court had no authority to actually sentence anyone. What's happening is illegal!) And because the Jews were not legally able to carry out an execution but the Romans *were* able to, Jesus—battered, bruised, dehydrated, and worn out from a sleepless night—was led across Jerusalem to the area governed by Pontius Pilate.

At this point, another illegal action took place: The charges against Jesus were changed during the trial! Jesus had initially been charged with blasphemy based on his statement that he could destroy and rebuild the temple of God in three days, as well as his claim to be God's Son. When he stood before Pilate, however, the charge was that Jesus had claimed to be a king and didn't agree with paying taxes to the Romans. (Of course, Jesus had never urged anyone to refrain from paying taxes. In fact, he had encouraged his disciples to pay the government what the government requested—see Matthew 22:21.)

In spite of the charges, Pilate found Jesus to be not guilty and shifted the responsibility to Herod, who ruled over the region of Galilee, where Jesus came from. Jesus stood silent before Herod. Herod, frustrated, sent him back to Pilate.

Pilate called together the religious leaders and the people and tried to convince the mob that he was unable to find any crime Jesus had committed worthy of the death penalty. The mob only became more volatile. Pilate, afraid of losing his popularity with the people, finally announced that a rebel named Barabbas would be released, and Jesus would be crucified.

More illegal happenings occurred: Christ wasn't permitted a defense. Under Jewish law, an exhaustive investigation into the accusations presented by the witnesses should have occurred. Instead, Jesus Christ was condemned to be crucified.

The physical torture he suffered even before his death was horrendous. After Pilate's verdict, Jesus was stripped of his clothing, and his hands were tied to a post above his head, leaving his back entirely exposed. The Romans used a *flagrum*, which was a whip made of leather strands. Small pieces of bone and metal were attached to these strands. This heavy whip was brought down with full force again and again across the shoulders, back, and legs of Jesus.

At first the weighted thongs cut through the skin only. But as the whipping continued, they cut deeper into tissue, exposing a bloody mass of muscle and bone. Extreme blood loss occurred from these beatings. The victims would often lose consciousness. When the centurion in charge pronounced the victim near death, the beating finally ended.

The half-fainting Jesus was untied and slumped to the ground, soaked in his own blood. The Roman soldiers laughed and made a joke out of the fact that he who claimed to be a king couldn't even walk straight. In mockery, they threw a heavy robe across his bare and bleeding shoulders and placed a stick in his hand to symbolize a scepter. Still needing a crown to complete their joke, they grabbed small, flexible branches covered with long thorns (possibly up to two inches in length) and quickly shaped them into a crude crown.

The soldiers then violently jabbed the crown of thorns into Jesus' scalp while continuing to beat him on the head. Each blow drove the thorns deeper into Jesus' scalp and forehead. As the thorns pierced his vascular tissue, Jesus began bleeding profusely from these wounds.

The Roman soldiers finally grew tired of their sadistic joke and ripped the scarlet robe off of Jesus' back. The robe was stuck to the clots of blood and serum in his wounds, and removing it caused excruciating pain. (Think about carelessly ripping off a surgical bandage.) The wounds on his back were now reopened and began to bleed again. Jesus' own clothing was then put back on his body.

Just how severe was the beating Jesus endured? The Bible doesn't detail the entire beating, but the book of Isaiah, which contains prophecies about Jesus' punishment, suggests that the Romans pulled out his beard. It also mentions that Jesus was so severely beaten that his form no longer looked human. People were appalled to look at him.

After he was beaten, the soldiers tied the heavy *patibulum* (wooden beam) of the cross on his bleeding shoulders. The weight of the entire cross has been estimated at 300 pounds. The crossbar Jesus carried probably weighed between 80 and 110 pounds. Jesus, the two thieves who were crucified with him, and the execution squad of Roman soldiers began the slow journey through a narrow street of stone, known today as Via Dolorosa—or "way of suffering"—to be crucified at Golgotha. The total distance has been estimated at 650 yards.

Know It!

Even with the details of Jesus' crucifixion, we still can't even imagine the pain he endured. Can you think of someone who has willingly endured pain for your sake? Even the pain of childbirth doesn't come close to what Jesus experienced. Why not tell him how thankful you are . . . every single day of your life?

Read It!

Genesis 3:17-18;
Isaiah 1:18; 50:6; 52:14;
Matthew 27:27-44

Pray It!

Jesus could have asked an army of angels to rescue him from this torture. But he endured it for you! Thank him for his goodness.

The Crucifixion

Know It!

The crucifixion Jesus experienced wasn't a quick death, nor was it a simple procedure. The creator of the universe experienced horrendous pain so each one of us could be forgiven of our sins.

Read It!

Luke 22:47-71; 23:1-38

Pray It!

Even though we read about Jesus' crucifixion, we'll never comprehend what he endured for us. Thank him. Ask him for the courage to share with those around you his power of forgiveness and what he experienced.

In spite of Jesus' efforts to walk erect, the weight of the heavy wooden beam, together with the loss of blood, was too much. Jesus stumbled and fell. He tried to rise, but his body had been pushed beyond its endurance. An onlooker, Simon of Cyrene, was then selected to carry the beam for Jesus. After reaching Golgotha, Jesus was again stripped of his clothing except for his loincloth.

The crucifixion began.

Jesus was offered a mild pain-relieving mixture—wine mixed with myrrh—but he refused the drink. Simon was ordered to place the crossbar on the ground, and Jesus was quickly thrown backward with his bare and bleeding shoulders against the wood.

The soldier felt for the small, weak area at the front of the wrist and pounded a heavy, square wrought-iron nail through the wrist and deeply into the wood. He quickly moved to the other side and repeated the action, careful not to pull the arms too tightly, but to allow some movement.

The crossbar was then lifted into place at the top of the vertical wooden beam, and the sign reading "Jesus of Nazareth, King of the Jews" was nailed into place.

The left foot was pressed backward against the right foot. With both feet extended, toes down, a nail was driven through the arch of each. This left the knees slightly flexed. Jesus was now crucified.

As the body of Jesus slowly sagged down, it placed more weight on the nails in his wrists. Excruciating, fiery pain shot along his fingers and up his arms, exploding in his brain. The nails in the wrists put pressure on the median nerve—large nerve trunks which travel through the middle wrist and hand. As Jesus pushed himself up to avoid this torment, he had to place his full weight on the nail through his feet. Again, he experienced searing agony as the nail tore through the nerves between the metatarsal bones of his feet.

As his arms grew tired, great waves of cramps swept over the muscles and knotted them in deep, throbbing pain. When these cramps overcame him, Jesus was unable to push himself upward. Since he was hanging by the arms, his pectoral muscles (the large muscles of the chest) were paralyzed. The intercostal muscles (the small muscles between the ribs) were unable to move. Air could be drawn into the lungs but couldn't be exhaled. Jesus fought to raise himself in order to get even one short breath. Finally, the carbon dioxide level increased in his lungs and bloodstream, and the cramps partially subsided.

Very spasmodically Jesus was able to push himself upward to exhale and take in oxygen. It was probably during these periods that he spoke the seven short sentences he uttered while dying on the cross.

The Roman soldiers threw dice for Jesus' seamless robe. The first sentence Jesus spoke from the cross is about them: "Father, forgive them for they do not know what they do."

His next spoken words were to the repentant thief by his side: "I assure you, today you will be with me in paradise."

A while later, Jesus spoke to his mother, Mary: "Woman, behold your son!" Then he looked into the eyes of John, the only disciple who hadn't run away when Jesus was arrested, and said: "Behold your mother!" (John 19:26-27, NKJV).

The next words Jesus spoke were from the beginning of Psalm 22: "My God, my God, why have you forsaken me?"

Jesus suffered hours of unending pain: cycles of twisting, cramps that had engulfed his joints, intermittent partial asphyxiation, and excruciating pain as tissue was continually torn from his lacerated back due to his up-and-down movements against the rough splinters of the wooden cross.

Jesus then experienced incredible chest pain as the sac surrounding his heart slowly filled with serum and began to crush his heart. This fulfilled the prophecy of Psalm 22:14 ("I am poured out like water").

The loss of fluids from Jesus' tissues had reached a critical level. His compressed heart struggled to pump heavy, thick, sluggish blood to the tissues, and his tortured lungs made a frantic effort to inhale small gulps of air. With the end rapidly approaching, Jesus gasped his fifth cry: "I thirst."

A sponge was soaked in cheap, sour wine and lifted to his lips. Jesus felt death exploding through his body and uttered his sixth statement—probably just a whisper—"It is finished."

His mission of dying for the sins of the world—past, present, and future—had almost been completed, and he could now allow his physical body to die. With one last surge of strength, he pressed his mutilated feet against the nail, straightened his legs, took a deeper breath, and spoke his final cry: "Father, into your hands I commit my spirit."

The common way to end a crucifixion was by breaking the bones of the legs. This kept the victim from pushing himself upward. The tension couldn't be relieved from the chest muscles and suffocation quickly occurred. The legs of the two thieves were broken, but when the soldiers approached Jesus, they didn't break his bones because he was already dead.

Just to be sure he was dead, one of the soldiers drove his spear between Jesus' ribs, up through the pericardium and into the heart. The blood and water that escaped proved that Jesus was indeed dead. Why? Because the fluid would have collected around Jesus' lungs and heart only after he had experienced heart failure.

Know It!
Even though Jesus died a tormenting death, he wants you to focus not on his pain, but his victory *over* death!

Read it!
Psalm 22:1-8, 14-18; John 19:25-37

Pray It!
As you approach the Easter season this year, ask God to help you truly focus on the real reason we celebrate.

The Resurrection

Know It!

Don't believe the Resurrection simply because you've heard the story all your life. Know the facts! Do your research. The only way you'll be able to defend your faith is if you know why you believe what you do!

Read It!

Matthew 27:50-66;
Mark 15:46-47;
Luke 23:55;
Hebrews 12:2

Pray It!

Sometimes it's hard to know what to say when others try to disprove Jesus' death and resurrection. Ask God to give you his thoughts and words and to know the facts so you can speak out confidently.

The Crucifixion leaves Christians without hope . . . unless they keep reading the Bible and realize Jesus' death is not the end of the story! Just as Jesus predicted, he rose from the dead three days after he was buried. This is referred to as the Resurrection.

And just as skeptics say that the Crucifixion was a fairy tale, many believe Christ's resurrection was also a hoax. Yet we have documented proof that crucifixion was indeed a common practice in Jesus' day and that Jesus was actually crucified.

If we continue to let history speak for itself, we soon realize Jesus actually did what he promised he'd do: he conquered death! The Resurrection actually happened.

Josh McDowell entered college as an atheist who was challenged by a professor to prove that the claims of Christ were simply lies. As Josh began researching the life, death, and resurrection of Jesus, he soon came to a crossroads: Either Jesus Christ really *is* who he claims to be . . . or he's the greatest liar the world has ever known and has successfully deceived an entire planet.

Josh didn't want to believe, but as he continued trying to disprove Jesus' claims, he was finally convinced—by the facts—that Jesus Christ truly is the Son of God, was crucified for our sins, and rose from the dead three days later.

You, too, can study the facts. Let the evidence speak for itself. For more study, check out Josh McDowell's book *More Evidence That Demands a Verdict.* Another great book that will enhance your research is *The Case for Christ* by Lee Strobel.

Over the years, skeptics have created several theories to try to explain away the Resurrection. One such theory is called "The Wrong Tomb." Skeptics state that the disciples were so distraught at the death of their leader, they didn't pay close enough attention to where he was buried. Therefore, when they arrived at the tomb on Sunday morning and found it empty, they were actually at the wrong tomb!

But Matthew, Mark, and Luke all tell us that Mary, the mother of Jesus, and a few others *watched* Jesus being laid in the tomb. There's no stronger witness than an eyewitness! Jesus' mother knew where his grave was located. Would she suddenly forget? Would the others who were with her suddenly forget as well?

Dead . . . or Just Fainted?

Another theory skeptics have created to disclaim the Resurrection facts is the "Jesus Didn't Really Die; He Just Fainted" theory.

History tells us many victims didn't even survive the Roman beatings, yet we're to believe Jesus flew through *that,* shook off the blood that covered his scalp from two-inch thorns, ignored the open flesh on his back that revealed torn tissue and muscle, was only faking it when he fell under the weight of the wooden cross beam, and simply *fainted* from the excruciating pain caused by the Crucifixion? According to Roman law, a death certificate couldn't be signed by the authorities until they were certain beyond belief that the victim was indeed dead. These Roman soldiers were professional executioners and wouldn't have been fooled easily. Plus, the mixture of blood and water that came from the tissue surrounding his heart was a clear sign that he was dead.

But let's just pretend Jesus fooled everyone and merely fainted. His broken and battered body was wrapped in huge amounts of spices and strips of linen cloth (see John 19:39-40). The embalming ointment alone weighed 75 pounds. He was literally encased in massive bondage. Even if he wasn't dead when he was buried, surely three days inside a dark, damp, cold, wet tomb, receiving no medical attention, would demand his last breath.

But the skeptics say no. So . . . suddenly after being encased in a tomb for three days (in the broken physical condition he was in), Jesus gets his second wind? And he's able (with a crushed heart, punctured lungs, lacerated back, shoulders, scalp, feet, and wrists) to break out of the 75 pounds of wrapping, move the stone away from the tomb's entrance (that weighed close to a ton), and then appear to his disciples, bruised and bleeding, and claim that he had risen himself from the dead?!

To believe *that* takes more faith than simply to believe Jesus is who he has always claimed to be, and that he lived, died, rose from the dead, and lives today!

Know It!

You can depend on Jesus Christ. He is the embodiment of truth. He has never deceived and never *will* deceive. His character is holy and honest and righteous.

Read It!

Luke 24:1-3;
John 19:34, 38-42

Pray It!

You don't have to know how Jesus rose from the dead; you simply need to believe that he did. Tell him you believe!

Stealing the Body

Know It!
Jesus wants you to view Easter as a celebration beyond words! Yes, he died. But that's not the end of the story. He conquered death and rose from the grave!

Read It!
Matthew 27:57-66; 28:1-20

Pray It!
Tell Jesus your hope truly is in him, your living Lord and Savior. Ask for his help in celebrating this Easter season with a deeper, more steadfast faith in him.

Another theory created by skeptics to dismiss the reality of Christ's resurrection is the "Disciples Stole His Body" theory. Proponents of this theory believe that the disciples took Jesus' body out of the tomb and hid it, then spread a rumor that he had been raised from the dead.

What's wrong with this picture? First, we know the disciples were so frightened at Jesus' arrest in the Garden of Gethsemane, they fled! They thought their lives were in danger.

Peter watched the trials from a distance, but when people asked him if he was one of Christ's followers, he denied he even *knew* Jesus . . . three times! Judas hung himself, the others hid, and only John stayed close enough to watch his Lord's crucifixion.

So let's look at the facts we read in the Gospels: The day after Jesus' burial, the chief priests and Pharisees told Pilate of Christ's prediction to come back to life after three days. So Pilate ordered his official government seal to be placed on the stone covering the entrance to the tomb. Pilate also issued guards to watch the tomb.

Pilate's seal on the stone was a big deal! If anyone broke that seal, he would pay for it with his own life. So . . . according to this theory, the skeptics would have us believe that 11 disciples (one who denied he even knew Jesus and nine who had run in fear at his arrest) were able to sneak past an army of soldiers guarding the tomb, quietly move the boulder that weighed close to a ton, tiptoe inside the tomb, lift a dead body encased in 75 pounds of embalming spices, tiptoe past the guards again—this time carrying the body with them—to a different location?!

Remember, the soldiers guarding the tomb knew they'd pay with their lives if anything happened to the body of Jesus. They wouldn't have risked falling asleep on such an important mission. And even if they *had,* 11 clumsy disciples who were scared and shaking would have surely woken them in the process of trying to move a ton-sized stone!

Because the soldiers couldn't explain what happened to Jesus' body, they lied. They *said* the disciples took his body . . . but to this day, no one has ever found the body. One surefire way to disprove the fact that Jesus actually rose from the dead would be simply to produce the body. We know where Stalin, Muhammad, Gandhi, Lenin, Joseph Smith, and Buddha are buried. We have their bodies. But the grave of Jesus Christ is empty, because he is risen!

Jesus did indeed conquer death! He is alive! As Christians, that gives us an incredible reason to celebrate! Let's take a closer look at what happened.

On Sunday morning, Mary Magdalene and some other women approached the tomb and found the stone had been rolled aside. Peering inside the tomb, they saw that the body of Jesus was gone, but his grave clothes were still there, folded neatly where he had once lain.

An angel appeared to them and explained that Jesus had risen from the dead. They informed the disciples, and Peter and John ran to the tomb to discover the same thing: It was empty!

Later that day, Jesus himself appeared to two of his followers as they approached the village of Emmaus. Jesus also appeared to the 10 disciples and proved to them he had actually conquered death. Thomas wasn't with the disciples when Jesus first entered their meeting place, but Jesus appeared later with Thomas among them. He told Thomas to feel the holes in his hands where the nails had been and to place his hand in Jesus' side where he was pierced with the spear.

Thomas fell on his knees and proclaimed that Jesus truly was his Lord. Jesus continued to appear to the disciples and several hundred others during the 40 days after his Crucifixion.

Know It!

Again, there is no stronger witness in a court of law than an eyewitness. Several hundred people were eyewitnesses to Christ's life after his death. The facts speak for themselves: Christ rose from the dead and is alive today! People saw him, talked with him, ate with him, and touched him after his resurrection from the grave. Yes, our hope lies in the fact that Jesus is alive. But even *that* isn't the end of the story! Jesus promised he'd return. He's coming back! And you serve a living Savior who never breaks his Word! What he says he'll do . . . he *will* do!

Read It!

Mark 16:9-20; Luke 24:1-52; John 20; Acts 1:1-9

Pray It!

Thank Jesus that even in your darkest days, your hope remains steadfast and strong . . . as long as your hope is in him!

Reinstating Peter

Know It!
Christ issues the same challenge to you as well. He wants you to spread the gospel and to care for his people. Are you actively doing that right now?

Read It!
Romans 8:35; John 21

Pray It!
Thank Jesus for continuing to dream dreams for you even though you've failed. Tell him you want to be all he dreams for you.

Isn't it comforting to know that Jesus knows you much better than you know yourself? When you feel discouraged, hopeless, and alone, he understands. Peter must have felt pretty low. After all, he boldly bragged at the Last Supper that he'd never desert Jesus—that he'd even die for him. Yet when he was approached by a young girl in the early morning hours following Jesus' arrest, Peter denied ever having known Jesus. He lied!

This was the same man upon whom Jesus had said he would build his church! This is the guy who walked on water and appeared with Jesus at the Mount of Transfiguration (the special place where Moses and Elijah spoke with Jesus). Peter, one of the privileged three who was with Jesus when he raised a girl to life, didn't even admit he knew Jesus when it mattered the most.

Can you imagine how low he must have felt? He failed. He boldly stated he'd follow Jesus to the end, but he blew it. Can you identify? Have you ever felt as though you didn't deserve God's forgiveness?

After the Crucifixion, Peter went back to something familiar—fishing. We often do that, too, don't we? We tend to lean toward our comfort zone when we feel insecure or intimidated. And Peter was certainly at home on the water. It was his business, his *life.*

But Jesus knew exactly where Peter was. (Jesus always knows where *you* are, too. Even in your darkest hour, Jesus knows where you are and how you feel.) And Jesus, knowing Peter would be in his boat, headed toward the beach. It was breakfast time. While Peter was still out on the water, Jesus started a fire and a fish-fry on the shore.

Peter, seeing his Lord (and smelling the fish), quickly rowed to shore and met Jesus on the sand. After they had shared breakfast, Jesus reinstated Peter as a disciple. He wanted Peter to know that even though he had blown it, he still dreamed big dreams for his disciple.

Jesus instructed him to "Feed my sheep." Jesus had to repeat it three times, but Peter finally caught on that Jesus wasn't talking about playing shepherd and chasing after woolly-coated animals. Peter realized that Jesus was referring to his children as his sheep. Peter took the challenge—to feed the flock of God.

Feed My Sheep?

We can't help but wonder why Jesus had to ask Peter the same question three times. It's kind of intimidating when someone keeps repeating the same question to us, isn't it? When a teacher asks, "Are you paying attention?" more than once, we're embarrassed.

When parents ask, "Have you cleaned your room?" over and over again, we're frustrated.

The Bible tells us that Peter was grieved at the way Jesus kept rephrasing his question and repeating it. Why did Peter need to hear it three times? Was it because he just didn't get it at first?

There are times we don't get it as quickly as we'd like. Often we have to be told over and over again to do something. Sometimes we're asked the same questions, only phrased a little differently to make sure we truly understand. Could it be that Peter was on a totally different wavelength than his Savior?

When Jesus told Peter to "feed sheep," maybe Peter took him literally. *What?!? Me? Feed sheep? You've gotta be kidding. I'm a fisherman. I don't do sheep.*

Maybe Peter thought he was above doing what Jesus was asking him to do. *Hey, look at me! I'm used to battling horrendous waves on rough seas. I'm a man's man. I don't prance around the hills watching a bunch of sheep chew grass all day.*

But as Jesus kept rephrasing the question slightly and coating it with, "Do you love me?" Peter began to understand that Jesus was commissioning him to be the hands and feet of God.

What are some specific ways you can do that today? You see, through the years, God's call on our lives hasn't changed. He's still commissioning us to take care of his children—to be the hands and feet of our heavenly Father.

If you were to take that call seriously . . . and truly begin living it out through your actions on a daily basis . . . what would it look like? Would you let someone cut in front of you? Would you go out of your way to help a friend? Would you sit with someone who's totally alone in the school cafeteria? Would you reach out to the campus weirdo? Would you go the second mile for someone who needed you?

Know It!

If you'll ask God for opportunities to feed his sheep, he *will* give them to you! So . . . what are you waiting for?

Read It!

John 21; 1 John 3:11, 18

Pray It!

Tell Jesus you want to take his call on your life seriously. Ask him to help you "feed his sheep" and show you specific things you can do to be his hands and feet to those around you.April 1

Don't Be a Fool!

An atheist was complaining to his new acquaintance in the seat next to him. He'd just discovered his seatmate on the flight to Baltimore was a Christian. "You Christians are lucky," he said. "You have Christmas—a holiday where you can take off work and celebrate."

"Yes, that's one of my favorite holidays," the Christian replied.

"And the Jewish people can celebrate during Hanukkah."

"Yes, that's correct. I have several Jewish friends who celebrate during Hanukkah."

"But we poor atheists don't have a holiday to celebrate."

The man seated behind them couldn't help overhearing their conversation. He leaned forward and said, "There's always April Fool's Day."

Many of us have a lot of fun pulling pranks and setting our friends up with jokes on April Fool's Day. But Christ had some strong things to say about being a fool. He taught that anyone who held on to his life on earth would eventually lose it for eternity. Those who chose to call their own shots, do their own thing, and control their own lives were actually fools; while those who gave their hearts to Christ were making the wisest decision they'd ever make.

Jesus told us he's the Way, the Truth, and the Life. If we truly believe that and follow him, we're wise. If we allow others to deceive us with vain words and shallow philosophies, we're foolish. Those who don't know Jesus Christ personally will say you're a fool for trusting a God you can't see. But to be a "fool" for Christ is actually an extremely intelligent decision. In the past few days, we've looked at the facts concerning the death and resurrection of Jesus. They are historical events that have been proven. To ignore the evidence would be foolish.

You have a choice: You can look stupid in the eyes of the world and be a fool for Jesus. Or you can embrace your culture and its beliefs and be a fool for eternity.

Know It!

You'll never go wrong by trusting God.

Read It!

Proverbs 13:19-20; 14:9; 1 Corinthians 1:18-25; 2:14; 3:19; 4:10

Pray It!

Tell God that you sometimes care too much about what others think. Ask for his help in getting past that simply to concentrate on pleasing him with your entire life.

Quiz Time

Know It!
The death and resurrection of your Savior is no fairy tale. It really happened. Know the facts and be willing to share them with your non-Christian friends.

Read It!
2 Timothy 4:1-5; Titus 3:14; Hebrews 4:2

Pray It!
Thank God for having the ability and the desire to answer all your questions and handle your doubts. Ask him to help you become more and more confident of the facts concerning his death and resurrection.

*During the **Last Supper**, Jesus*
a. asked what the cost was for the room they were renting.
b. rebuked his disciples for eating too much.
c. told his disciples that his body and blood would soon be given for them.

*Jesus was **arrested***
a. with handcuffs and leg shackles.
b. in the Garden of Gethsemane.
c. among thieves and gangsters.

*Pilate released Jesus to the crowd of accusers to be **crucified**, because*
a. Barabbas was a good friend of his, and Pilate wanted to spare his life.
b. he wanted to satisfy the crowd.
c. he had seen Jesus steal money and knew he was guilty of several other crimes as well.

*The path that Jesus took to **Golgotha**, where he was crucified, is known today as*
a. the road to death.
b. the road to Zion.
c. the Via Dolorosa.

*During his remaining time on the cross, Jesus spoke how many **sentences**?*
a. 7
b. 68
c. Too many to count.

*The soldiers broke the legs of the two thieves who died with Jesus, but they **didn't break Jesus' legs** because*
a. his knees were grossly swollen.
b. he was already dead.
c. they felt sorry for him.

*Skeptics who refuse to believe have created some **theories** in an attempt to explain away Christ's resurrection. Some of them are:*
a. The "Dead Man Wasn't Really Jesus" theory
b. The "Wrong Tomb" theory
c. The "Jesus Was Drowned, Not Crucified" theory
d. The "Disciples Stole His Body" theory
e. The "Alien Abduction" theory
f. The "Jesus Never Really Died; He Only Fainted" theory

The Right Signals

The only survivor of a shipwreck was washed up on a small, uninhabited island. He prayed fervently for God to rescue him. For days he scanned the horizon for help, but his situation seemed hopeless. He eventually managed to build a small shelter out of driftwood and leaves to protect him from the wind and rain and to protect the few possessions he had.

Several weeks passed, and one day while he was scavenging for food, he arrived back at the lean-to only to discover it in flames. He fell on the sand and sobbed while watching the smoke rise to the sky. The worst had now happened; he had lost what little he had.

Desperate and filled with anger, he shook his fist and screamed toward heaven, "God! How could you do this to me? I have no hope. Why won't you help me? Now I'll surely die." Exhausted, he fell asleep heavy with grief.

Early the next morning, however, he was awakened by the sound of a ship approaching the island. He began waving his arms frantically, and when he saw the ship lower a small boat, he knew it had come to rescue him.

When he was finally safe and aboard the ship, he asked his rescuers, "How in the world did you know I was here?"

"We saw your smoke signal," they said.

It's easy to get discouraged when things don't go our way, isn't it? We often feel we're at the end of our rope and without hope. But God has promised never to abandon us.

Can you trust the creator of the universe to solve your problems? When things look the worst, God is often at work behind the scenes. All we need to do is trust him.

For all the negative things we say to ourselves, God has a positive response:

We say, "It's impossible."
God says, "All things are possible."
We say, "I'm too tired."
God says, "I will give you rest."
We say, "No one really loves me."
God says, "I love you."
We say, "I can't go on."
God says, "My grace is sufficient."
We say, "I can't figure things out."
God says, "I will direct your steps."

Know It!

The next time your security goes up in smoke, know that it *could* be a signal that's summoning the grace of God.

Read It!

(And match these Scriptures with the quotes in the first column.) Luke 18:27; Matthew 11:28-30; John 3:16; 13:34; 2 Corinthians 12:9; Psalm 91:15; Proverbs 3:5-6

Pray It!

Tell God you want to trust him more—to wait patiently for him to act when things don't go your way.

Who Knew?

Know It!

God never asks you to do something without equipping you with everything you need to do it.

Read It!

Acts 1:8;
1 Corinthians 1:25;
Philippians 4:13

Pray It!

Ask God to help you become more confident in your relationship with him and give you his deep, settled peace if he wants you to go on a missions trip.

Who would have guessed that . . .

- you burn more calories sleeping than you do watching TV.
- oak trees don't produce acorns until they're 50 years of age or older.
- the first product to have a bar code was Wrigley's gum.
- American Airlines saved $40,000 in 1987 by eliminating one olive from each salad served in first class.
- Barbie's full name is Barbara Millicent Roberts.
- all United States presidents have worn glasses. Many just didn't like being seen wearing them in public.
- Venus is the only planet in our solar system that rotates clockwise.
- the plastic things on the ends of shoelaces are called aglets.
- pearls dissolve in vinegar.
- it's possible to lead a cow upstairs, but not downstairs.
- Betsy Ross is the only real person to ever have her head depicted on a Pez dispenser.
- the average life span of a major league baseball is seven pitches.
- a duck's quack doesn't echo.

Who would have guessed all that?

And who would guess that you have a personal, loving, growing relationship with the creator of the universe . . . unless you tell them? Before Jesus physically left the earth, he commanded his disciples to go into all the world and spread the gospel. Note he didn't say, "When you feel ready," or "When you get around to it," or "If it's convenient," or "When you figure out a splashy way to do it." He just said, "Go."

So what are you waiting for? Have you ever "gone"? Short-term mission trips can be life-changing adventures. Would you dare to allow God to stretch you? Would you be willing to get out of your comfort zone? Would you be willing to make the sacrifices necessary to earn and save enough money to fund such a trip?

If so, then you may want to pray about participating with Focus on the Family's *Brio* magazine's annual two-week international missions trip. Each year we take approximately 500 teens out of their comfort zone. And guess what! They come back totally changed, charged, and centered. If you're interested in such an adventure, get more information from the *Brio* Web site: *www.briomag.com.*

Missions: An Eye-Opening Experience

I arrived in Fortalesa, Brazil, with Compassion International on a media trip. I was there to learn about Compassion's work and the incredible difference they're making in the lives of children. One of our stops was to the city dump. Fortalesa's dump doesn't simply fill a city block; it stretches for miles. And there are no restrictions on what can and can't be tossed in the dump. Toxic waste, syringes, sharp pieces of metal—anything someone wants to get rid of.

The smell is atrocious. Vultures hover around the trash hunting for scraps of food. Human waste mixed with rotten edibles tempts one to cover one's nose when walking among the filth. But working feverishly in the garbage are a few thousand people desperately trying to find anything they can salvage and sell to recyclers who come around at the end of each day. Plastic bottles, glass, tin—anything that can be recycled is sold. In a good month, someone can make anywhere from five to 10 dollars.

I'll never forget 14-year-old Alena. As she paused momentarily from gathering trash, I asked her (through an interpreter) how long she had worked at the dump. "I work from dawn till it gets dark," she said. "And around 10 P.M. when trucks come in with new garbage, we often race out here again and work for a couple of hours before getting to sleep. Then we start over again at dawn."

"What do you do for fun?" I asked.

"I don't have fun," she said. Her eyes were dark. There wasn't even a hint of happiness on her face, and I realized Alena couldn't comprehend the luxury of reading a magazine or going swimming. She was living in total misery and couldn't even imagine anything different.

Unless someone tells her, Alena will never know that she can have joy *in the midst* of her garbage-filled world. How will she know that Jesus yearns to work and walk beside her among the trash, and that he offers peace and forgiveness for sin?

Our team was only allowed 10 minutes at this particular site because of the danger involved. Yes, I can pray for Alena and trust God to send someone else along her path to share his Good News. But who will that someone be?

Could it be . . . *you?*

Know It!

God is calling you to share his love with others. Sometimes he'll take you out of your comfort zone to accomplish that, and other times he'll allow you to remain home.

Read It!

Romans 1:16; 15:16-20; 1 Corinthians 9:16

Pray It!

Are you uneasy thinking about sharing God with people you don't know? Confess that to him now, and tell him you want to be willing to go anywhere and do anything he asks.

Missions: A Life-Changing Experience

Know It!
It's often hard to imagine how only one person can make a difference. But God can use *you* in a mighty way to influence changes around you. Again, if you've never been on a short-term missions trip, pray about the possibility.

Read It!
Isaiah 6:8;
Acts 3:24-26; 10:38;
1 Corinthians 2:9-10

Pray It!
Tell God how exciting it is to think that he can use you to make a difference in someone's life. Trust him to open the right doors for ministry.

A few years after my personal trip to Brazil, I took several hundred teens to Rio de Janeiro. One of our first stops was the dump in Rio.

Jenni was so moved by the sights, smells, and sounds she experienced during her time at the dump that she called her mom back in the United States as soon as we arrived back at our home base. "Give it away, Mom," she said during the long-distance phone call. "Everything I haven't worn in the past year, all my childhood toys, anything I don't use on a regular basis. Give it all away to a group or organization that can get it all to people who need it. You won't believe what I experienced today at the dump. Mom, these people are living in cardboard lean-tos. They breathe, sleep, and eat out of the garbage."

Jenni had a life-changing experience.

So did Cara. She entered the dump and was immediately drawn to a naked little 18-month-old girl playing in the trash. Cara bent over and scooped her into her arms and swung her around. As she held the little girl, she couldn't help but feel and notice several huge infections on her small, exposed bottom.

Through an interpreter, she asked the girl's mother what they were. "Oh, those," the mother replied. "Those are bites from the rats that chew on her during the night."

Cara reached into her backpack for wet wipes and cleaned the little girl's bottom as best as she could. And motioning for the interpreter again, she asked permission to take the girl to the ministry site several yards away from where they were working. While there, Cara bathed and diapered the girl and decided to sponsor her for $20 a month through the ministry that organized help for those working in the dump. Her money would ensure the little girl would receive food each day and hand-me-down clothing.

Cara headed back to her team and shared her decision with them. Because Cara had been so deeply affected, her passion contagiously touched her teammates. They, too, were moved and decided to sponsor the rest of the mother's nine children.

A short-term missions trip can definitely be a life-changing experience. You'll see, hear, taste, smell, and touch things you've never experienced before.

You can probably imagine how heartbroken our small group of six was as we made our way through the dump, dodging buzzards, covering our noses to help diminish the atrocious stench, and seeing the children with distended tummies due to not having enough to eat.

One person in our group suggested we feed the several hundred people in our area. *Wow! That must have cost a fortune,* you're probably thinking. And at first glance, it would have seemed impossible. After all, how much of a difference could six people make with a group so large?

We purchased bread and butter and gave it to the folks at the ministry site. Guess what! They were able to feed close to 900 people from that purchase. The cost? An amazing $12!

God does unbelievable things when we place our few resources in his hands. He's able to take the little we have and multiply it for his glory. We tend to think our small portion won't be of any significance, but what if the small boy in the crowd of 5,000 had thought that? He unashamedly gave Jesus all he had—even though it was only some small fish and a few pieces of bread. You know the end of the story, don't you? Jesus fed more than 5,000 people because of that little boy's obedience.

Rachel played varsity volleyball for her high school team. She wore her tennis shoes to the dump. But as soon as she witnessed firsthand the dire poverty in front of her, she *had* to react. Approaching a barefooted elderly woman digging through the trash, Rachel untied her shoes without hesitation and placed them in the hands of the old woman. Rachel didn't care that the woman smelled of garbage. She held tightly as the woman hugged her and flashed her toothless grin.

Because of the needles, waste, and dangerous materials that stretched across the ground of the dump, we couldn't allow Rachel to make the long walk back to our van barefooted. Without hesitation, one of her adult sponsors hoisted her around his shoulders and carried her down the hill. Because Rachel had given so freely, Jeff didn't think twice about giving to Rachel.

A little boy gave his food. Rachel gave her shoes. Jeff gave his shoulders. What can *you* give?

Know It!

A short-term missions trip provides incredible opportunities to give your life away. But guess what—you don't have to go on a missions trip to be the hands and feet of Jesus! You can give your life away right where you are. You can make a difference in someone's life without even leaving your hometown. The question is . . . *will* you?

Read It!

John 12:26; Romans 12

Pray It!

Since God freely gave up his life for you, ask him to help you give your life away to those around you by showing you specific ways to be his hands and feet to neighbors, family, classmates, and people you don't even know.

Out of Date?

Know It!
God's holy Word—the Bible—is the most precious possession you can own. Its words are priceless. Its wisdom is abundant. It contains the answers for any problem you'll ever encounter. Make time every single day to devour more of its contents.

Read It!
Proverbs 2:1-6; 4:1-13; 2 Timothy 3:16-17

Pray It!
Realize that God's holy Word is filled with ordinary people—just like you—who failed, repented, and received victory. Ask him to help you understand the Bible as you commit to reading it on a more consistent basis.

"Justin, this is Pastor Steve. How's it goin'?"

"Fine," Justin answered as he balanced the phone on his left shoulder and slapped a piece of bologna between two slices of bread saturated with peanut butter.

"Just calling to let you know we've missed you at youth group."

"Yeweibsy," Justin muttered between bites.

"Justin, I know you're taking a foreign language at school, but I'm not familiar with this one," Pastor Steve said with a chuckle.

"Sorry 'bout that," Justin said. "I just got home from school, and I'm starving. It's peanut butter and bologna time!"

"Ugh!"

"Serious, man. It's great!"

"I'll take your word for it. Can I pick you up for youth group this week?"

"Ah, I don't know," Justin said.

"Okay. Level with me, Justin. What's going on?"

"I don't know. I just don't get into the stuff we've been talking about."

"You mean the series we started last month on people from the Bible?"

"Yeah. It's all so irrelevant. It happened like a zillion years ago. What's any of that got to do with me?"

"Okay. Well let's say this week we tackle something that *is* relevant. Think any of these topics will hit home? Terrorism, unmarried and pregnant, murder, rape, peer pressure, New Age."

"Now you're talking, Pastor Steve! See, that's the real world. Those are the things we face every day—not stuff like chariots and marching around walls and talking donkeys."

"Hey, Justin. That list of topics I just rattled off came right from the Bible! It's all the stuff we're scheduled to take a look at during the next few weeks."

"You're kidding! The Bible talks about all that stuff?"

"Sure does, Justin. Don't ever be deceived that the Bible isn't relevant. It's the most relevant guidebook you'll ever read. Studying it is the beginning of wisdom."

"Well, I can definitely use some wisdom right now! I'm in a jam because of a lie I told Coach Baker."

"I've got just the book for you, Justin!"

"All right. I'll see you in a couple of days."

Hall of Fame for the "Lasts"

Ever thought being last would have a place in history? Betcha didn't know . . .

- the twentieth president of the United States, James Garfield, was the last president born in a log cabin. The year was 1831, and the place was Cuyahoga County, Ohio.
- there are 773,692 words in the King James Bible. The very last word is "Amen." The sentence preceding it? "The grace of our Lord Jesus Christ be with you all" (Revelation 22:21).
- that John Clayton, Jr., Lord Greystoke, was the childhood name of Tarzan.
- Amelia Earhart's last contact with the Coast Guard was on July 3, 1937.
- the last words of Julius Caesar were, "Et tu, Brute?"
- the last United States president to weigh more than 300 pounds was President William Taft, who tipped the scales at 332 pounds.
- the last episode of *The Brady Bunch* was titled "The Hair-Brained Scheme" and was televised on March 8, 1974.
- if Dorothy–of *The Wizard of Oz*–had a last name. She did. Dorothy Gale.
- the last of the Union of Soviet Socialist Republics–known as the U.S.S.R.–happened in 1992 when it broke up into 15 independent countries.
- the last letters added to the English alphabet? J and V.
- the last face carved on Mount Rushmore was Theodore Roosevelt's.
- the last time tug-of-war was an official game in the Olympics: 1920. Great Britain won the gold, Holland won the silver, and Belgium took home the bronze.
- Alice of *Alice's Adventures in Wonderland* didn't have a last name. But the book was written in honor of Lewis Carroll's friend Alice Liddell.
- *Telosphobia:* The fear of being last.

As you can see, sometimes our last words, last names, and last moments can become historic. Have you ever thought of what your last words, last attitude, and last characteristic to be remembered by will be?

Know It!

God wants to help you develop a good reputation and a holy lifestyle. His desire is that you be remembered by his reflection. Wouldn't it be great if the last mental picture your friends and family have of you is one that glorifies Jesus Christ?

Read It!

Proverbs 5:21; 22:1-2;
1 Timothy 3:7; 4:12;
1 Peter 2:17

Pray It!

Ask God to help you invest yourself into being all he wants you to be each day of your life, for as long as you have left. He will teach you how to pour all you have into people, tasks, and your relationship with him.

Getting Through

Know It!
God desires to answer your prayers. But he wants to help his children move away from generalized prayers to specifics.

Read It!
Proverbs 3:6; Matthew 20:29-34

Pray It!
Do you have trouble believing that God really wants to answer your prayers? Confess that to him now. Ask him to deepen your faith and teach you how to pray more specifically.

Jamie rushed home from volleyball practice, tossed her books on the kitchen counter, and flipped on the computer. *Hope Ashley is online,* she thought. *I need to talk to my cousin right now.*

Jamie17: Hey, Ash! Coming home for spring break?
20ash: No can do, Cuz. Our campus Bible group is doing an evangelistic outreach in the Bahamas. So what are your plans?
Jamie17: I'm hangin' at home during spring break, but I'm thinking about doing something special this summer.
20ash: Yeah? Spill it!
Jamie17: Well, . . . I don't know. I've been praying about my summer and telling God I want to use it for him, but I don't have any direction yet.
20ash: How are you praying?
Jamie17: Whaddya mean?
20ash: One thing I'm learning in Bible class is that God wants us to pray specifically. Are you praying in general terms, or are you being specific when you talk with him?
Jamie17: I've just been praying that I'll have a great summer and do stuff for him.
20ash: Okay, Cuz. What would you really like to do this summer? Any specific ideas for ministry?
Jamie17: Yeah, I'd love to go on a missions trip. My friend Katie's church is going to Philadelphia. And I heard about another one to Mexico from our Christian radio station. But the one I'm really interested in is with *Brio* magazine.
20ash: And why that one?
Jamie17: Well, it's just for two weeks. So I'd have a chance to serve, but I could still come back and work until school starts. Plus it's not just a work thing. We'd be doing a little of everything-drama, orphanages, painting, Compassion International Projects, hauling brick, evangelism.
20ash: Sounds great!
Jamie17: But that's not all! There's like 500 who go, and every night we'd have a giant youth rally. They bring some of the top Christian artists with them, and you get challenging messages and small group devotions.
20ash: So have you prayed about it?
Jamie17: Nah. I didn't think it was right to pray for just one thing.
20ash: Hey, Cuz, I encourage you to pray specifically for that trip. Ask God to redirect your desires if it's not his will. Place the responsibility in his lap.
Jamie17: You really think it could work out?
20ash: Absolutely! But when you pray . . . pray specifically.

Calling Out to Jesus

Jesus and his disciples were leaving the city of Jericho, and a large crowd was on their heels. The people had seen the miracles Jesus had performed, many had heard him preach, and several were simply curious. But hundreds were moving down the dusty road toward Jerusalem.

You know how it is in a crowd—especially an anxious and excited crowd! Someone's always stepping on someone else's foot, a few children are always crying, and some are always angry because the crowd isn't moving faster. This crowd wasn't much different—except for the fact that Jesus of Nazareth was in the lead. He has the incredible ability to hear everything at once. And amid the shuffling of hundreds of feet, the laughter, and the three-way conversations, Jesus heard something else: two distinct cries from the side of the road.

These two men weren't part of the crowd. It seemed impossible Jesus would hear them above the roar of those following, but they dared to call his name anyway because they desperately needed his touch.

"Lord, Son of David, have mercy on us!"

The crowd immediately shushed them. "Leave him alone. Be quiet! Jesus has important things to do. He's on a mission."

But the two men shouted even louder, "Lord, Son of David, have mercy on us!"

Jesus must have admired their persistence, because he stopped. He knew the two men were blind, but he still asked the obvious question, "What do you want me to do for you?" (If that seems like a silly question, flip back to the devotions found on February 15-22.)

If we put this scene under a microscope and take an even closer look, we'll find some spiritual principles for our own lives.

#1: These two men sought after Jesus. He loves it when his children actively seek him. Do you casually shoot prayers toward heaven, or are you putting forth effort to communicate with Christ?

#2: Jesus stopped for them. He'll stop for you, too, when you seek him with an honest and expectant heart. Isn't it comforting to know that amid the crowds of people who are calling for the attention of Jesus, he still hears your cry? And he'll always stop . . . just for you!

Know It!

Jesus Christ is crazy about you! Though his agenda is always full, you're right at the top of the list!

Read It!

Matthew 20:29-34; Ephesians 1:19-23; 3:20-21

Pray It!

Tell Jesus how thankful you are that he cares for you the way he does!

Growing with the Specifics

Know It!
Jesus calls you, asks you personal questions, desires specific answers, and cares about your present. He wants to meet your "right now" needs!

Read It!
Matthew 20:29-34; John 14:13; 16:24

Pray It!
Thank God for asking you personal questions and caring about your needs. Tell him you want to respond specifically, honestly, and immediately.

Imagine the excitement of the two blind men when Jesus halted a crowd of hundreds to focus specifically on them! When the King of kings takes time to zero in on our needs, it's exciting!

Let's continue our closer peek at this story so we can gain the spiritual principles Christ wants us to apply in our own relationship with him. A quick recap:

#1: These two men sought after Jesus.

#2: Jesus stopped for them.

#3: Jesus called for them. He calls you, too. It's one thing to talk to Jesus, but it's another thing to know he talks back to us! He recognizes your voice! When you speak his name, he returns your call–immediately! Are you answering his call?

#4: Jesus asked them a specific question. He didn't ask because he was clueless about what they wanted. He wanted them to identify their specific need. When you pray, instead of praying in general terms like, "God bless all the missionaries," pray instead for specific things. Identify your need and the needs of others.

#5: Jesus asked a pointed question. There was no beating around the bush, was there? "Hey, how's it goin'? Comfortable here on the road?" No. Jesus got right to the point. There's nothing more important to him than being intensely focused on your point of need. "What do you want me to do for you?" he asked. That set them up to answer in a specific way, didn't it? There was no need to make small talk; Jesus made it convenient for them to state their exact need. He desires the same from you.

#6: Jesus also asked a personal question. It wasn't "What do your friends need? What does everyone else say you should be doing?" It was directed specifically at them: "What do *you* want me to do for you?" The more you walk with Jesus, the more intimate your relationship with him will become. You'll talk about extremely personal things. This is a sign of spiritual growth.

#7: Jesus asked a "present" question. It was all about *right now; this very moment.* Jesus didn't ask what the men would need next week. Nor did he turn their thoughts to the past. He simply focused on the present–right now!

What Jesus Wants You to Ask Him

Jesus asked the two blind men a specific question: "What do you want me to do for you?" And they responded in a specific manner: "We want our sight." When Jesus asks *you* a question, he wants you to respond in a specific way too.

But Jesus doesn't want to be the only one asking questions. There are also some things he wants *you* to ask *him*! Read through these statements and then check out the Scriptures listed in the next column. They'll back up these questions and give you more information.

#1: He wants you to ask his help in revolving your life around him. He doesn't simply want to reside in your heart. He wants total residence in your entire life. He wants to guide and direct each one of your steps.

#2: He wants you to ask for a hunger and thirst for the things of God. It's not enough to simply know him; he wants to develop a hunger within you to know him better. He also wants you to grow in your desire to be with his people.

#3: He wants you to ask him to help you keep up with the basics in developing a growing relationship with him. Without continuing in a consistent prayer life and in daily Bible reading, your relationship with Christ will slowly fade.

#4: He wants you to ask him to deepen your trust in his Word. He wants you to know—beyond doubt—that he never breaks his promises.

Know It!

You can wholeheartedly trust the creator of the universe. He's never broken his word, and he never will. One of his greatest desires is to strengthen your faith and help you draw ever closer to him.

Read It!

Psalms 42:1; 51:12;
Proverbs 3:6;
Isaiah 43:2;
John 3:16;
Philippians 2:13;
Hebrews 13:5

Pray It!

Ask God to help you ask the right questions and wait for his answers.

What's in a Name?

Know It!

God doesn't simply "wish you luck" at living a godly life. He wants to *empower* you and *enable* you to live a life of holiness.

Read It!

1 Corinthians 4:20; Hebrews 1:10-11; 10:12-17

Pray It!

If you're not sure you've surrendered to God, consider praying this prayer: *Dear Jesus, I've asked you to forgive my sins, but I don't think I've ever totally given you complete control of myself. I'd like to do that right now. I realize I can't live out the definition of your name in my own strength, so I submit to your authority. Will you fill me with the power of your Holy Spirit? Sanctify me wholly, and enable me to glorify your name with my lifestyle.*

Have you ever wondered what your name means? Here are some common names and the meaning behind them. Check the list and see how many friends you have with these names and how many come close to the description.

Alana (bright, mysterious)
Alexander (intelligent, leader)
Amy (educated, calm)
Ben (strong, lovable)
Bradley (sensitive, fun loving)
Carla (independent, outgoing)
Christian (well mannered, honest)
Christy (friendly, cute)
David (handsome, intelligent)
Douglas (handsome, strong)
Drew (attractive, independent, trim)
Jody (delightful, friendly)
Joel (popular, nice, sensitive)
John (intelligent, dependable, well groomed)
Patrick (popular, happy)
Roxanne (feminine, enthusiastic)
Stacy (active, cute)

While the above descriptions may or may not be accurate of you or your friends, it's fun to see how close we come to fitting the meaning.

What if you were given a name at birth and expected to live up to its meaning? If you failed, you would be stripped of your name. Your identity would be taken from you. Our names are special, and to imagine having them taken away from us is unsettling.

Have you ever thought of what it means to carry the name of Christ? When you dedicate your life to him, you take on his name. Are you living up to its meaning? Are you reflecting the nature of Jesus Christ to a watching world?

When we call ourselves a Christian, it's important that we live up to the word's meaning. While the above definitions with common names were simply created by people, God gives us a genuine description of his Son's name in his very character. The word *Christian* means one who follows Jesus Christ; one who adapts his lifestyle to Christ's; one who lives as Christ lived. And under that umbrella we find honesty, integrity, purity, kindness, holiness, a godly lifestyle.

There's no way we can live out the above definition in our own strength. It would take a supernatural power within us to enable us to live that way. Guess what! That supernatural power is available through the Holy Spirit. *In his power,* you can live out the true definition of a Christian.

How does one live in his power? Through total surrender. By completely submitting yourself to the authority of Jesus Christ, you release control of your desires, your will, and your life to his charge.

The Truth about Names

Ever wonder if some of your favorite celebrities and athletes were actually born with the names they have? Some really weren't. For instance, Kareem Abdul-Jabbar was born Ferdinand Lewis Alcindor, Jr. Andre the Giant's real name is Andre Roussinoff. Hulk Hogan's real name is Terry Bodello. And Jason Alexander, who played George Costanza on TV's *Seinfeld,* was born Jay Scott Greenspan.

If you enjoy watching reruns of *I Love Lucy,* you might enjoy knowing Lucille Ball's real name was Dianne Belmont. Nicholas Cage was born Nicholas Coppola, Cher was born Cherilyn Sarkisian, Tom Cruise was born Thomas Cruise Mapother IV, Jodie Foster was born Alicia Christian Foster, Whoopi Goldberg was born Caryn Johnson, and political talk-show host Larry King was born Larry Zeigler.

You've probably heard of Harry Houdini. But you probably haven't heard of his original name, Ehrich Weiss. And you've no doubt heard of Elton John but probably haven't heard of what he started out with: Reginald Kenneth Dwight.

Wolfman Jack probably gets more attention than his original Robert Smith. Madonna is much easier to remember than Madonna Louise Veronica Ciccone, and Marilyn Monroe is easier to recall than Norma Jean Mortenson Baker.

Rudolph Valentino shortened his name from Rudolpho Alphonzo Raffaelo Pierre Filibut Guglielmo di Valentina D'Antonguolla. (What were his parents thinking?!?) And Pauline Esther "Popo" Friedman Phillips shortened her name to Abigail Van Buren ("Dear Abby").

Have you ever wanted to change *your* name? Maybe you've wished you had a different name or have created a nickname for yourself. On the other hand, perhaps you're trying to live down a nickname someone else has given you.

Guess what? No matter what your name is, and no matter how it's been changed or how you'd like to change it, it's important to God. He knows your name, and he calls you by name. When he wants your attention, he doesn't say, "You! The one who failed the history quiz!" He calls you by your name.

We all love to hear our name when it's used in a positive way. And God loves to speak your name enveloped in love, dignity, and pride. Isn't it amazing to know that the creator of the universe knows and speaks your name?

Know It!

God never makes fun of your name. He never laughs at it, never mocks it, and never spreads untrue things about it. He wants to protect your name and add his very character to it. He desires to bring dignity and an all-encompassing love to your name.

Read It!

Isaiah 40:26; 43:1; 45:3-4

Pray It!

Thank Jesus for knowing, speaking, and loving your name. Ask him to help you respond immediately when you hear him call you by name.

The History behind Historical Names

Know It!
He loves your name with his life. He wants to help you protect it. And he wants to help you develop a pure reputation around it.

Read It!
Genesis 12:2;
2 Samuel 7:9;
Psalm 147:4;
Proverbs 3:4; 18:10; 22:1;
Ecclesiastes 7:1

Pray It!
Seek God's forgiveness for any times when you allow your name to embarrass him. Tell him you want your name to bring honor to him, and ask him to help you develop a good reputation with your name.

Names of many figures from the past have a history behind them. For instance, did you know that Johnny Appleseed's real name was John Chapman? Sitting Bull's real name was Tatnaka Iyotake. (Sitting Bull is a lot easier to pronounce, isn't it!) Former U.S. President Gerald Ford was actually born Leslie Lynch King, Jr., but he took the name of his adoptive parents.

Nancy Reagan was born Anne Frances Robbins, and Malcolm X was born Malcolm Little. Tashuna-Uitco later changed his name to Crazy Horse, and Harry Longbaugh changed his name to Sundance Kid.

You probably know the published name of the man who created Alice in Wonderland, Lewis Carroll. But you probably don't know his real name was Charles Lutwidge Dodgeson. You may have read George Orwell's *Animal Farm* in class, but ask your teacher if she's familiar with the author's real name, Eric Arthur Blair.

Have you ever wondered if *your* name had a history behind it? Have you ever asked your parents why you were given the name you carry? No matter what your name is, and regardless of its meaning, God wants to give you a holy history behind your name.

A basketball purchased at Wal-Mart holds no special significance. But if Michael Jordan picked it up, dribbled it a few times, and spun it on his finger, it would suddenly mean something. A tennis racquet found at a garage sale wouldn't mean much. But if Venus or Serena Williams purchased it, it would hold incredible value.

You may think your name is nothing special. But when the King of kings speaks it, he transforms it from ordinary status to an extraordinary level! When Jesus calls you by name, he speaks it with the same authority that placed the stars in the sky, raised the dead, and rotates the earth. Your name definitely means something to him! When he hung on the cross to pay for the sins of the world, *your name* was on his mind! In the midst of horrendous torture and suffering, his heart was hugging your name, your identity, your reputation.

Heaven-Bound 101

"Hey, Chelsea! You goin' to Explosion tonight?" Luke asked as he tossed his backpack on his shoulders.

"Sure want to. But I've got tons of chemistry homework. I'm hoping I can finish it in the library before I head home."

"Exactly where I'm headed," Luke said as he waved to some of his friends across the hall. "Pretty good crowd last night, huh?"

"I couldn't believe it! The church was packed."

"Pastor Steve was right when he said God wanted us to saturate this youth revival with prayer. We've prayed, we've fasted, we've invited kids till we're blue in the face—"

"And God's blessing our efforts," Chelsea finished.

"I really liked what Pastor Steve talked about last night. You know—heaven and stuff."

"Yeah, me too, Luke. He made it sound like we could know for sure if we'll end up there."

"I've been a Christian for almost three years, but I always have these nagging doubts about whether I'll really make it to heaven."

Chelsea smiled. "I know exactly what you mean."

"You, too?"

"Yep. My grandparents are Christians. My parents are Christians. And I became a Christian in the fourth grade. I'll never forget asking Jesus to forgive my sins and make me a new creature in him. But still—"

"You doubt where you'll spend eternity," Luke finished.

"Exactly."

"Sometimes I wish I were Pastor Steve. He seems so confident—spiritually."

Chelsea agreed. "I wanna be that confident, Luke."

"Yeah, me too. That's why I'm going back tonight. I want to make sure I get it, you know?"

"Yeah, I know exactly what you're talking about. So help me with this chemistry homework. I wanna go, too!"

Know It!

When it comes to where you'll spend eternity, you don't have to hope. Neither do you have to guess. Or beg. Or wonder. You can know for sure if you'll spend eternity in heaven with Jesus. And since we don't know how much time we have on earth, it's comforting to know we can be absolutely sure we're ready to meet Christ!

Read It!

John 1:12; 3:16; Romans 10:9; Revelation 3:20

Pray It!

Do you want to know beyond a doubt that you're ready to meet God and that you'll live with him forever in heaven? Ask him to help you find the proof you need from his Word, through his voice, and in his Holy Spirit.

Establishing a Relationship

Know It!
Jesus wants you to invite your friends to youth group, church, and Bible studies. He can use *you* to lead your non-Christian friends into a personal relationship with him.

Read It!
2 Corinthians 4:5;
Colossians 1:28;
2 Timothy 1:8;
1 John 1:1; 4:14

Pray It!
Ask God to give you specific opportunities this week to share your faith with friends who may not be ready to meet him.

"Hey, Chelsea!"

"Hey, I'll catch you later, Luke. I invited some girls from history class, and I just saw them come in."

"Hi, Chelsea! Are we in the right place?"

"Hi, Hannah and Tawni. I'm really glad you guys came. We're giving away some pretty cool prizes each evening."

"Okay, then what?" Hannah asked.

"Our youth pastor, Steve, is talking about heaven tonight—and how you can know if you're ready to meet Jesus," Chelsea said.

"Well, I'm a Christian," Tawni said. "I was baptized when I was a baby."

"Christianity's really more than just being baptized," Chelsea said.

"Hey, let's quit gabbing and get inside so I can win a prize," Hannah said.

Chelsea laughed. "I hope you win a prize, too, Hannah," she said. "But the message about how to get to heaven is really more important than winning a prize."

"I don't even know if I'm a Christian. Does that mean I won't go to heaven? I try to be a good person."

"I know you do, Hannah. But it's more than being a good person. You see, Christianity is all about having a personal, growing relationship with Jesus Christ."

"I don't think I have that," Tawni said. "I know *about* God, because my family goes to church every Christmas and Easter. But I don't really have a *relationship* with him."

"What do you mean, a relationship?" Hannah asked. "Like we can actually *know* God?"

"Exactly," Chelsea confirmed. "We can know God as our best Friend, our Savior, our Sustainer, our everything!"

"But how do you know if you *know* God?" Tawni asked.

"Well . . . how do you know if you know me?" Chelsea said. "Or Hannah?"

"That's simple," Tawni said. "I talk with you guys. We do stuff together."

"It works that way with God, too. You can actually talk with him, and he'll talk back. He'll go everywhere with you. He's promised never to leave us."

"Hey, Chels, I want that," Hannah said. "If you're telling me I can actually talk with and personally know the One who made this entire world, I want that."

"Me, too," Tawni added. "I want a personal relationship with Jesus."

"Cool! I can pray with you guys right now. I'll say a prayer, and you can repeat it after me. We're gonna ask God to forgive your sins and commit your lives to him, okay?"

"Wait up, Chelsea!" Luke called across the school parking lot."I heard you prayed with Hannah and Tawni last night."

"Yeah! Luke, it was really cool. They became Christians before the evening even started. They both wanna come back tonight, too!"

"That's great, Chels! I've invited some of the guys from the basketball team."

"Pastor Steve said we could be pushing close to 450 tonight. Everyone's been inviting friends like crazy."

"Well, ya gotta admit—nothing's more important than making sure our friends know Christ."

"You can say that again! What's Pastor Steve talking about tonight?"

"I think he's still on how to know for sure if you'll end up in heaven," Luke said.

"Good. I need that. Even though I know I'm forgiven, I still have a few doubts. I'll see you there, Luke."

• • •

"Many of you have asked me if it's possible to know beyond a doubt that you'll go to heaven after you die," Pastor Steve said. "Jesus gives us a sure strategy for knowing if we're ready to meet him. It's sort of a three-part game play, and it's found in Matthew 25."

Luke flipped open his Bible and winked at Chelsea a few rows over as she reached to share her New Testament with Hannah and Tawni.

"We find three incredible stories in this chapter of Matthew," Pastor Steve said. "The first story is about 10 bridesmaids waiting for the bridegroom. Jesus tells this story to illustrate the kingdom of heaven," he continued.

"Each of the 10 bridesmaids had a lamp—more like a lantern—which ran on oil. Five of the bridesmaids filled their lamps with oil, and the other five put it off.

"When they heard that the bridegroom was arriving, the five without oil had to leave and fill their lamps. The five who were prepared met the bridegroom and went inside to celebrate with him.

"The other five returned with oil in their lamps only to find the door locked. They banged on the door and begged to be let inside, but the bridegroom said they were too late. They weren't permitted inside."

Know It!

Throughout the Bible, oil symbolizes life. It's reflective of the Holy Spirit living within us. It means we have an active, growing relationship with the bridegroom—Jesus Christ.

Read It!

Matthew 25:1-13; Luke 3:7-8

Pray It!

Don't let your relationship with God grow stale. Ask God to renew your thirst for him.

Investing the Resources

Know It!
Jesus has blessed each one of us with specific gifts, abilities, and talents. He expects us to use those gifts to bring glory to him, the Giver. Ever wonder why some Christians seem to ooze with talent? It's because they're using what they have for God's glory, and he continues to multiply and bless it. But when we don't use what we've been given, we're insulting our heavenly Father.

Read It!
Matthew 25:14-30; 1 Corinthians 12

Pray It!
Ask God to forgive you for the times you don't use the gifts and abilities God has given you. Commit to using your gifts to bring glory to God!

"So the first thing you need to do to make sure you're ready to meet Jesus," Pastor Steve continued, "is to make sure you have an active, growing relationship with him. That's the first key to the entrance of heaven.

"Some of you have recently accepted Christ as your personal Lord and Savior. I'd encourage you to develop that relationship by joining a Bible study and spending time every day praying and reading God's Word."

Chelsea grinned at Hannah and Tawni and noticed they were listening carefully.

"That's the first step. And you *can* know beyond doubt that you'll spend eternity in heaven with Christ," he continued.

"But Jesus is calling our attention to a three-phase game plan in Matthew 25. So let's continue to go through the plan. You'll notice in this particular chapter, Jesus is describing the kingdom of heaven. The second way he describes it is in a parable of a wealthy man with three servants. The man decided to go on an international trip and called his servants in for last-minute instructions. He entrusted $5,000 of his estate to his head servant and told him to make wise investments during his absence.

"He entrusted $2,000 to another servant and $1,000 to the last servant. The master left on his trip, and his head servant immediately began buying and selling in order to increase the $5,000. He had soon doubled it to $10,000 and knew his master would be pleased.

"The second servant also went right to work and doubled the $2,000 for his master. But the third servant simply set the $1,000 aside and waited for the master's return."

Luke underlined the story Pastor Steve was talking about. He wanted to read it again later.

"When the master returned," Pastor Steve continued, "he called his servants together. His head servant proudly handed over $10,000–double what he had been entrusted with. The master affirmed him and smiled as the second servant also handed over the money he had doubled. But when the third servant simply gave the master what he started with–the $1,000–the master became angry because the servant had been lazy and had hoarded the money. Then he took the $1,000 away from him and gave it to the head servant. The lazy servant was cast into darkness."

"So let's do a quick recap," Pastor Steve said. "In Matthew 25, Jesus gives us three ways to make sure we're ready to meet him." Tawni grabbed her pen as Pastor Steve's PowerPoint presentation flashed behind him.

#1: Do you have an active, growing relationship with Jesus Christ? "This doesn't mean simply knowing about God," Pastor Steve said. "It means just what it says–having a real, growing, active relationship with the creator of the universe."

Hannah nudged Chelsea for another sheet of paper.

#2: Are you consistently and wisely using what he's blessed you with to bring glory to him? "God blesses you with gifts and abilities for a reason," Steve continued. "It's so you can bring glory to his name. If you've been a Christian for a while and you're not using what he's given you, something's wrong in your relationship with Christ. The disciple who has an active, growing relationship with Jesus is consistently using his God-given gifts with excitement."

Chelsea glanced at Luke. He had invited several friends to Explosion, and one had come. Luke was sharing his Bible with Taylor, and Taylor seemed genuinely interested.

"But there's a third section to this chapter," Pastor Steve said. "Let's take a look at it. So far, Jesus has been talking about the kingdom of heaven, and he continues to do that through the rest of the chapter. He describes the thousands who will approach the gates of heaven. He compares them to sheep and goats. He welcomes the sheep into heaven and turns away the goats. When those who are turned away ask why they are denied entrance, Jesus explains it's because they never reached out. They never offered water to him, never clothed him, never fed him.

"They're confused. They argue they never saw him needing help, being thirsty, naked, or hungry. And Jesus tells them whenever they refused to help someone in need, they in essence, refused to help him."

Know It!

Since Jesus is no longer walking the earth in his flesh, he expects you to be his hands and feet to those in need. Anytime you help someone holding a sign by the roadside advertising, "Work wanted. Homeless," you're actually helping Jesus. Whenever you go out of your way to sit with someone who's known as an outcast on your campus, you're actually sitting with Jesus. Anytime you go the extra mile, you're walking for Christ.

Read It!

Matthew 25:31-46; Luke 10:30-37

Pray It!

How often do you truly go out of your way to help someone? Ask God to give you the desire to reach out, to leave your comfort zone, and to get your hands dirty for him.

Three-Step Strategy

Know It!
If you've met the game plan outlined in Matthew 25, you should be confident in your relationship with Christ. If you *do* have doubts, ask God to identify the source of doubt. If he pinpoints one of these three areas, ask him to help you correct and strengthen that area. If he doesn't, know the doubts are from Satan and ask God to help you ignore them and to give you assurance in your salvation.

Read It!
Isaiah 55; Matthew 25

Pray It!
Tell the Lord you want to activate those three areas in your relationship with him that he outlined in Matthew 25. Ask him to help you make sure your walk with him is active and growing. Ask him to teach you how to use the gifts he's blessed you with and to give you specific ways to minister to those around you.

"There you have it," Pastor Steve said. "Three essential check points to evaluate your relationship with Christ. Are you ready to meet Jesus? Let's do a quick recap."

Chelsea loved the animation on Pastor Steve's PowerPoint presentation and was glad it held the attention of the crowded room of teens.

#1: Do you have an active, growing relationship with Jesus Christ? "If you don't," Steve continued, "you're not ready to meet Jesus. If you don't have an actual relationship with the King of kings, you won't spend eternity in heaven with him."

#2: Are you consistently and wisely using what he's blessed you with to bring glory to him? "If you are, you're living out the active, growing relationship you have with Christ. Your lifestyle proves you know him," Pastor Steve said. "You see, someone who's deeply in love with Jesus excitedly shares what Jesus has given him because he wants to bring glory to the Father. To do that, think about the things you're good at and find ways you can use those to glorify God. Can you sing? Join the church choir and lead a congregation in praising God. Are you great with little kids? Consider helping with Vacation Bible School."

#3: Are you involved in a ministry? "A vibrant ministry is reflective of an active, growing relationship with Christ. Some of you are just starting out your Christian life, and you'll get to this point. But if you're not a new Christian and you're not ministering, I question your relationship with Christ. You're not ready to meet him. And don't think ministry is just becoming a missionary. Hey, if that's the direction God is leading you, great! But your ministry may simply be offering free baby-sitting for the single parent down the street. It might be sending note cards to encourage those who are discouraged or organizing a Bible club at your school. All you need to do is ask God to give you a ministry, and he will.

"And guess what! If you have an active, growing relationship with Christ, if you're consistently using what he's given you, and if you're intentionally reaching out with the love of God to those around you, you're ready to meet Jesus! There should be no doubt in your mind where you'll spend eternity."

Being a ***Christian***
a. means I read the Bible every now and then.
b. is knowing a lot about God.
c. is having a personal, growing relationship with Christ.

Going to ***heaven***
a. is something I can hope for but can't be sure of.
b. is something I can know for sure.
c. can only be attained by saints.

The first key to ***entrance*** *through heaven's gates is*
a. having a wallet full of money.
b. having the right words to say at the right time.
c. having an active, growing relationship with Christ.

The second part of the ***strategy*** *Christ gives us is*
a. using people.
b. using the gifts he's given us to glorify him.
c. using our credit cards wisely.

The ***third*** *part of this strategy is*
a. wearing the right clothes to church.
b. going on lots of mission trips.
c. being involved in a ministry.

Having a ***ministry*** *means*
a. going to China to build an underground church.
b. reaching out to those around you as God directs.
c. getting your own radio show.

Why didn't ***all*** *10 bridesmaids get to* ***meet*** *the bridegroom?*
a. All 10 weren't dressed properly.
b. All 10 didn't have oil for their lamps.
c. All 10 weren't well.

Jesus compares ***sheep*** *to*
a. the Roman guards.
b. those who know him personally and obey him.
c. the angels.

Jesus compares ***goats*** *to*
a. those who refuse to pay taxes.
b. the magicians.
c. those who claim to know him but don't really have a personal relationship with him.

Know It!
The person you would least expect to come to church may be the person who's simply waiting for you to ask. Dare to reach out and invite your friends to church. They need to hear the message of God's love and forgiveness.

Read It!
Proverbs 4; Matthew 25

Pray It!
Ask Jesus for confidence to know for sure that you'll get to spend eternity with him. Commit to growing closer to him every single day.

Stuff to Think About

Know It!
When faced with problems, it's tempting to take the easy way out. Satan is working overtime to convince you the easy way out is the best way out. Don't fall for his strategy. Seek God's wisdom in all you do!

Read It!
Proverbs 1–3

Pray It!
Ask God to help you stop looking for the easy way and start seeking the right way through his wisdom.

The Bible is full of stuff to think about. In fact, the book of Proverbs has an incredible amount to say about wisdom. If you truly want wisdom, you can have it. Wisdom begins with a strong foundation in Jesus Christ. It's then nurtured through the *reading* of God's Word, and multiplied through the *studying* of his Word.

Wisdom without common sense isn't worth much. And common sense minus wisdom won't get you very far. It takes both wisdom and common sense working together to comprise a smart person.

Let's check your wisdom and common sense, okay?

Sid E. Slicker had a well that was 63 feet deep. A squirrel fell inside. Each day the squirrel climbed seven feet up the well but fell down four feet each night.

Question: How many days did it take the squirrel to get out of the well?

Added information: Mr. Slicker gave the squirrel food and water each day so it wouldn't die.

You may be thinking, *The squirrel gained 3 feet each day, so it took 21 days to get out of the well. After all 63 divided by 3 equals 21. That's the obvious answer.*

Jesus said, "Wide is the gate and broad is the road that leads to destruction, and many enter through it. But small is the gate and narrow the road that leads to life, and only a few find it" (Matthew 7:13-14).

You can discover the solution to life's problems by turning to the Bible. The person who is truly wise knows that the Word of God offers truth and guidance. It may take a little more time to study the Word and fervently seek God's will, but once you've done that and have yielded to his leading, you'll have the correct solution to life's problems.

Back to our squirrel problem. In a class of 30 students, two usually discover the correct answer. If our friendly rodent gains three feet each day, where is he on the 19th day? He's up the well at the point of 57 feet. On the 20th day, the squirrel goes up 7 feet and is out. How? Because 57 feet plus the 7 feet he goes up each day makes a total of 64 feet. Since the well is 63 feet deep, the squirrel is out on the 20th day without falling back that night.

Zak-A-Tude

You may be familiar with the story of Zacchaeus—the tax collector and short guy who climbed a tree so he could see Jesus above the crowd. You can read the entire story in Luke 19:1-10. Here's the scene: Jesus is coming through town, and practically the entire city has thronged Main Street so they can catch a glimpse of him.

There's almost a "parade feel" in the air. Lots of excitement, huge crowds, animals, children, elderly folks. Some youth group is probably selling hot dogs to earn money for their annual ski trip. A lot is happening.

Everyone has heard about Jesus of Nazareth. Some are saying he's a prophet. Others have determined he's a really good teacher. Still some others say he's a wonderful healer. Others just say he's a nice person. But Jesus had claimed that he was the Son of God—the long-awaited Messiah.

So on this particular day, when Jesus is scheduled to come through town, hundreds have thronged the streets to catch a glimpse of him and make up their own minds as to who he is. *Could it be possible? What if he really IS the Messiah?* people were thinking. You can imagine the excitement, the wonder, the anticipation, the tension in the air.

Zacchaeus, too, wanted a glimpse of Jesus. He, like everyone else, was anxiously awaiting the promised Messiah. If there was even a slight chance that Jesus of Nazareth could be the One, Zacchaeus wanted in on the action.

So he closed shop early that day. He rolled up his sleeves, loosened his necktie, and headed toward Main Street. Imagine the frustration he must have felt when he couldn't even get *through* the crowds—let alone see *over* them! Spotting a sycamore tree not too far from the street, he proceeded to climb its branches to get a glimpse of the man from Galilee.

But think about that for a second. An adult man in business attire climbing a tree? Must have been pretty embarrassing! The cool thing, though, is that Zacchaeus so desperately wanted a personal encounter with Jesus Christ that he was willing to look like a fool to do it!

That's an admirable attitude—one worth adapting to our own lifestyle. In fact, let's just go ahead and name it. We'll call it a Zak-A-Tude.

Know It!

God desires to develop that same attitude in you. He wants you to want Jesus so badly, you're willing to do anything to have a personal encounter with him.

Read It!

2 Chronicles 30:19; Luke 19:1-10

Pray It!

Tell God how much you want to have a personal encounter with him.

Short *and* Crooked

Know It!
God blesses our honesty. He wants you to live and act with such honesty that people can't help but notice you're a young man or woman of great integrity. Do others see you as a person of integrity? Or do they see you as someone who tries to cut corners and take shortcuts? Are you known for "little white lies"?

Read It!
Malachi 3:1;
Luke 19:1-10

Pray It!
Ask God to help you be a person of total integrity. Pray that he'll nudge your conscience next time you say something that's not completely true.

Okay, you already know Zacchaeus was short. But there's something else you ought to know: His shortness was more than simply being vertically challenged. The original writings of the Bible describe him as being a man in a boy's body. In other words, he was underdeveloped. This made him look odd. People stared. They made fun of him. He was often the brunt of cruel jokes.

So that's one thing Zacchaeus had against him. But there's another reason he wasn't very popular—he was a tax collector. This was kind of like being a social leper. People who were physically afflicted with leprosy were required by law to shout, "Unclean! Unclean!" so people within hearing distance could back away. No one wanted to get close to a leper.

Being a tax collector was like having social leprosy. No one wanted to be near you. No one asked you out for a cappuccino or a latte or even a hot chocolate.

Why? Because even to *become* a tax collector, you had to do some pretty crooked negotiating. You had to betray your own people. Here's how the scenario would go down: You'd approach the Roman officials and offer them a bribe to allow you to collect taxes from your own people (the Jews). If they accepted the bribe, they would then set an amount of tax for you to collect. But here's the sticky part: Let's say the Roman officials told you to tax your people one dollar. That's what you have to turn in to the officials. They'll hold you accountable for that amount.

But what you want to *charge* the people is totally up to you! So why not charge them 10 dollars? You give Rome one dollar, and you pocket the rest! That's what tax collectors did. And they weren't fooling anyone. Everyone was aware of what went down, but ordinary citizens were powerless to stop it.

It's a little easier now to understand why Zacchaeus was hated so much, isn't it? He was a traitor to his own people. But before we become 100 percent negative on Zack, let's spend the next couple of days looking at some positive things we can learn from his life.

Yes, Zack had a few strikes against him. He was dishonest, and he was known for taking advantage of others. He had swindled innocent people out of their hard-earned money. He had taken advantage of widows and the elderly. He was easy to dislike.

But we can learn a few things from his life, if we'll look closely.

He had a ZAK-A-TUDE. He so desperately wanted a personal encounter with Jesus, he was willing to go to great lengths to make sure it happened. What an attitude of determination! How determined are *you* to get as close to Jesus as possible?

He was aware of his SHORTCOMINGS and did something ABOUT THEM. When Zack realized he was too short to see above the crowds, he could have given up. He was extremely aware of his limitations, but he refused to let them stop him from doing something important. Do you find it easy to rationalize your areas of weakness? *I'm not really an outgoing person, so I'm not going to invite anyone to church,* you might think. Don't let your shortcomings get in the way of becoming all God dreams for you! Like Zacchaeus, do something about them!

He HEARD the CALL of Jesus. The Bible tells us that when Jesus walked by the tree in which Zack was sitting, he stopped, looked up, and called him by name. (We'll get more into that in a few days, but right now let's take a look at Zack's ears.) Zacchaeus *heard* Jesus call him! His ears were tuned to the voice of the Master! Think of the plethora of sounds competing for Zack's attention at that time—sheep bleating, children crying, the youth group selling hot dogs, someone asking to be healed—a lot of noise was happening around Zacchaeus. Yet when Jesus spoke his name, he *heard* and *responded.*

Know It!
God wants you to be aware of your weak areas—your shortcomings—and instead of rationalizing them away, he wants you to do something about them! He also wants you to learn the sound of his voice so you can be constantly tuned in to the Master.

Read It!
Deuteronomy 30:19-20; 1 Samuel 15:22; John 10:3

Pray It!
Do you sometimes use your shortcomings as a cop-out? Confess that to Jesus now and ask him to help you stop rationalizing and start strengthening your weak areas.

Taking Jesus Home

Know It!
It's always easier to ask God for forgiveness than to ask people, isn't it? But if you've wronged people, God wants to help you make things right. He wants you to seek their forgiveness and correct the situation.

Read It!
Exodus 22:3; Leviticus 6:5; Numbers 5:8

Pray It!
Ask God to bring to your mind anyone to whom you need to make restitution. Pray for the strength to make things right.

Imagine the frustration of the crowd! Jesus, the honored guest, was paying attention to a tax collector! People must have been furious. *Why is he even talking with that jerk?* some probably thought. *He should be paying attention to us.*

Jesus spoke the name of Zacchaeus, and Zack responded. What a Zak-A-Tude! Let's take a quick recap of his positive characteristics:

He had a ZAK-A-TUDE. He was willing to do anything to have a personal encounter with Christ.

He was aware of his SHORTCOMINGS and did something ABOUT THEM. This is part of having a Zak-A-Tude—he wasn't willing to sell himself short (pardon the pun).

He HEARD the CALL of Jesus. (Another element of a Zak-A-Tude. His ears were tuned in to the voice of the Master.)

He TOOK Jesus HOME. (This is the most essential part of a Zak-A-Tude.) Sure, we go to church with Jesus, we talk about him with our Christian friends, but are we willing to take him *home?* Are we willing to allow him inside the very private areas of our lives? Zacchaeus knew that once Jesus entered his home, there would be no more hiding. Everything about Zack would be out in the open for Christ to see. His closets, his office, his receipts—proof of the crooked way he had run his business—things he hoped no one would ever find out about . . . Zack allowed Jesus full access.

Guess what? God wants full access to *your* home, too. He wants to invade every area of your life with love . . . and with truth. You see, Jesus loved Zacchaeus too much to let him stay trapped in deceit and hypocrisy. And he loves *you* too much to allow things to stay the same in your life.

When you invite Jesus into your home (into the innermost depths of your being), he'll make changes. Are you willing to allow him the freedom to do that?

He was WILLING to make RESTITUTION. Big word. Simple definition. Restitution means to go back and make things right. Zacchaeus stood in front of the crowd that had gathered around his home and publicly stated that he would make right the wrong he had done by overcharging folks. He pledged to pay back those he had swindled *four times* what he had cheated them!

Zacchaeus didn't develop a Zak-A-Tude in his own strength. God Almighty was working in his heart. As Jesus approached the sycamore tree that memorable day in Jericho, he acted on his Father's prompting to help develop the Zak-A-Tude in Zacchaeus.

Now that we've taken a look at what Zacchaeus did, let's scoot a little closer for a peek at what Jesus did.

He CHOSE the OUTCAST. As we study the Bible, we see that God has never chosen only the most popular, the most talented, or the most beautiful. Throughout history, he has specifically selected the unwanted, untalented, and the outcast. He has the miraculous ability to take an ordinary person and do extraordinary things through his or her life. That's because Jesus sees the potential of what someone can become with his help.

Everyone—at one time or another—feels like an outcast. Your dad leaves, you experience a breakup, someone makes fun of you, people spread rumors. It's easy to feel unwanted and unloved. But you can take comfort in the fact that God has chosen *you*!

He CALLED Zacchaeus by NAME. Zacchaeus had been called a lot of things in life—shorty, jerk, thief, traitor. It must have felt *great* to be called by his *name . . .* and to have it spoken by someone so important!

Jesus calls you by your name, too! He'll never address you as, "Hey, Big Nose!" or "Slow Stuff." He'll always call you in the most personal way imaginable—by your name. Think about it: The creator of the universe knows your name! How does it make you feel to be on a first-name basis with the King of kings?

He went AGAINST THE FLOW. The crowds complained when Jesus went to Zack's house. "He's hanging out with sinners!" they jeered. Though Jesus was constantly pressured by the masses to hang out with the "pretty people" and the "important ones," he dared to go against the flow. He was more concerned about leading Zacchaeus to receive forgiveness for sins and inherit eternal life than he was in what the crowds had to say.

Know It!

Jesus went against the flow for *you,* too. If you were the only one in the entire world, he still would have chosen to suffer the horrendous death it took to pay for your sins. He has chosen you, he calls you by your name, and he goes against the flow for you. He looks beyond what others say about you and chooses to see your highest potential.

Read It!

Luke 19:1-10;
1 Thessalonians 2:12; 5:24

Pray It!

Thank God for choosing you, for calling you, and for believing in all you can become.

Quiz Time

Know It!
God has an incredible plan for your life! Can you trust him to make something beautiful out of your past? He has the power and the desire to do amazing things with your mistakes . . . if you'll let him.

Read It!
Romans 8:28; 12:1-2; 1 Corinthians 1:7-9

Pray It!
Thank God for going against the flow for you, and ask him to help you not take that for granted.

*Zacchaeus **worked** as*
a. an animal trainer.
b. a tax collector.
c. a hair stylist.

*People **disliked** him because*
a. he dated more than one girl at once.
b. he had purple hair.
c. he swindled people out of their money.

*Zacchaeus couldn't **see Jesus** from the street because*
a. he was too short.
b. he needed new contact lenses.
c. he was blind.

*Zacchaeus wanted to see Jesus **so badly**,*
a. he shot himself out of a cannon.
b. he climbed a sycamore tree.
c. he used a pogo stick to jump above the crowd.

*When Jesus **approached** Zacchaeus,*
a. he called him by name.
b. he asked if he was building a tree house.
c. he pretended he didn't see him.

***Zacchaeus** took Jesus*
a. to the mall.
b. to his home.
c. to the temple.

*The **crowds** were*
a. angry because Jesus was with a sinner.
b. laughing all the way to the bank.
c. convinced the sky was falling.

*Jesus **chose Zacchaeus** even though he was*
a. an alien.
b. had six toes.
c. an outcast.

*Jesus **ignored** the pressure*
a. of Hollywood.
b. of the crowds.
c. in his tires.

Who Would Have Guessed?

Would you have ever guessed that . . .

- a Boeing 747's wingspan is longer than the distance of the Wright brothers' first flight.
- apples are more efficient than caffeine at helping you wake up in the morning.
- the "57" on the Heinz ketchup bottle represents the number of varieties of pickles the company once had.
- most dust particles in your house are from dead skin.
- dentists have recommended that a toothbrush be kept at least six feet away from a toilet to avoid airborne particles resulting from the flush.
- the first owner of the Marlboro company died of lung cancer.
- no piece of paper can be folded in half more than seven times.
- it takes 3,000 cowhides to supply the NFL with enough leather for a year's supply of footballs.
- the drink 7-UP was created in 1929. The number seven was chosen because the original containers were seven ounces. The "UP" indicated the direction of the bubbles.
- donkeys kill more people each year than airplane crashes.
- one in every four Americans has appeared on television.

Who would have guessed?

And who would have guessed that the King of kings would leave 11 ordinary men in charge of spreading the gospel to the entire world? We tend to wonder why God didn't create a super plan of evangelism and high-tech publicity to reach the masses. After all, Jesus was only on earth for 33 years . . . and God had to come up with a plan to spread the Good News to every generation across time in every part of the world. And he stuck with ordinary people!

Through the years, God's plan hasn't changed. He's still counting on ordinary people to spread the news of his saving grace and gift of eternal life. But ordinary people filled with the consuming supernatural power of the creator of the universe can accomplish extraordinary things!

What are you personally doing to spread the gospel?

The very best witness is a sold-out lifestyle. Yes, it's important to talk; people certainly listen to our words. But our actions and reactions can shout even louder than words. When you think no one's looking, someone is watching your life. Is your lifestyle a witness to Jesus Christ?

Know It!

Ever heard the phrase, "you're the only Bible some people ever read"? It's true. Your lifestyle is a book of words. How you live and interact with those around you is either a witness *for* Christ or a witness *against* Christ.

Read It!

Matthew 5:13-16; 10:27-33; Luke 9:57-62; Colossians 1:28-29

Pray It!

Ask God to help you live a life of integrity even when no one's looking.

Dear Diary

Know It!

A kind word goes a long way. In fact, you can make or break someone's day by the words you choose to share with him. Take stock of your relationships. Are you nurturing your friendships or taking them for granted?

Read It!

Proverbs 12:25; 15:4; 16:24; 17:22

Pray It!

Ask God to help you care more about those around you.

Hey, Diary. Yeah, me again. I know you're surprised to hear from me. After all, it's been since . . . March 17! But I need to spill my thoughts somewhere, and you're available, so here goes.

Why are relationships so hard? Beth told me I don't encourage her enough. When I talked to Mark about it, he said it's because I'm insecure.

Gimme a break!

Nathan says I don't really compliment others. Rebekah says I'm a great friend—I just need to work on establishing better communication with my friends.

Ugh!

You'd think it wouldn't be so hard to be involved in my friends' lives . . . but I'm beginning to realize that friendship—real friendship—takes a lot of work.

So I guess I have to ask, "Is it worth it?"

I already know the answer, Diary.

Yeah, my friends are important.

And I really do want to be the best friend I can be to them. I want them to see Jesus in my life. I want to be an encouragement to each one of them. I guess . . . I don't know . . . I just get busy and caught up in my own little world. And I tend to take it for granted that they know I appreciate them.

Pastor Steve says we can never tell people too much how loved they are. Hmmm.

Come to think of it . . . I hardly ever tell people how much I appreciate them. Okay, enough! I'm gonna make a list right now of people in my life I can send an e-mail or a note to and just remind them that I'm grateful for each of them. And after this list, Diary, I'm going downstairs for some Rocky Road ice cream!

Mom and Dad
My friends
Youth pastor
My two favorite teachers
Coach Wilson
Mr. Sanders for giving me that part-time job last summer
My Sunday school teacher
Our senior pastor at church

Ever wonder why some people have tons of friends and seem to be able to make any relationship a great one? It's probably because they've learned the secrets of relationship strategies.

The truth is, Jesus knew the art of good relationships, and he wants us to have solid relationships too. So let's look at a few strategies that will help us do that.

The Power of Words. If you've ever said something you immediately wished you hadn't, you know the power of thoughtless words. They can crush, demean, and intimidate in a matter of seconds, can't they? On the other hand, positive words can affirm, encourage, and motivate. People who have good relationships know the power of their words. They have realized those around them can never receive too much encouragement. Think about it: Have you ever grown tired of someone affirming *you*? We love positive affirmation!

We're warned in James 3:1 about the power of our words. We're told that not many of us should be teachers—or people who give instruction—simply because of the potential damage we're able to do with our words.

People all around you are dying for encouragement. If you truly desire to have good relationships with others, you'll learn how to become a genuine encourager. Why is it sometimes difficult to encourage others?

1. *Because of intimacy.* To affirm those around you requires an intimate exchange of words. Often times our own personal insecurity keeps our mouth shut. *What will he think if I affirm him? I don't feel good enough about myself to encourage someone else. If I try to encourage her, I'll come off sounding stupid.* All of these thoughts often invade our minds.
2. *Because of inability.* Are you harboring anger in your life? If so, it will be tough to encourage others. Think about it: What comes out of your mouth reveals what's in your heart. Ask God to help you resolve any anger and bitterness you may be holding inside.

If you've been encouraged by someone, you know the results genuine affirmation can produce. First, *affirmation brings change into a life.* What an amazing challenge—to be able to build someone's self-esteem and change her life by *your* encouraging words! Second, *affirmation brings confidence.* "I believe in you" are four extremely powerful words! Use them to make a positive difference. Exercise them to provoke change.

Know It!
God wants to perform heart surgery on you! He wants to soften your heart to be more sensitive to others and give them the encouragement they need. This will automatically make your relationships more genuine.

Read It!
Matthew 12:35; James 3:2-12

Pray It!
Ask God to bring to your attention people who need a special word of encouragement from you.

Identification Station

Know It!
God created you in his image, and he wants to shine through your life. Your true identity will always be found in him.

Read It!
Psalm 139

Pray It!
If you've struggled with your identity, admit that to God. Ask for his guidance in finding your identity in him.

He calls himself CatMan, and he's spent thousands of dollars transforming his physical appearance to look like a tiger. And if you've seen photos of him, you have to admit he really *does* look half man and half feline. CatMan's body is covered with tiger-striped tattoos. He's also undergone countless surgical procedures. Implants have been placed in his eyebrows and in the bridge of his nose. His ears have been cut so they're pointed, and his earlobes have been relocated to give his ears a more catlike appearance.

CatMan's septum has also been relocated to stretch out and flatten his nose, and his lip has been cleffed—all so he appears more catlike. He's had silicone implanted in his cheeks, upper lip, and chin in order to change his profile. He wears contact lenses that make his eyes appear more catlike and has had his teeth cut and reshaped. His front teeth are split in the middle, and he has long pointed fangs.

Is that all? Not by a long shot! His upper lip sports labret-type piercing—six on each side—that his "whiskers" thread into. You can imagine what his fingernails look like: They're a few inches long and curl downward near the end . . . yes, just like a tiger's. When he has the money and has found the right surgeon, he'll have fur sewn on to his skin.

Sound like someone's having an identity crisis? What would motivate someone to spend thousands of dollars to look a way most of society considers freakish? We may think that's weird, but think again. Hmmm. What motivates *us* to spend big bucks just to have the latest Nikes laced up our feet or to wear Tommy Hilfiger's newest creation? It's all about identity, isn't it?

Not only do we desire to know ourselves; we also want to be noticed for who we are. You may be known as the best trumpet player on your campus, the most popular student in the hallway, the girl with the golden voice, the guy who makes everyone laugh, the girl who could actually make professional basketball her profession, or the one who's headed for Hollywood.

Maybe that's what others are telling you, but what is God telling you? Who does he say you are? (Hint: It has nothing to do with your talents, skills, or gifts.)

Looking beyond Appearance (Part 1)

It was the stuff movies are made of. Handsome, strong, athletic, 19-year-old Brian Sakultarawattn (pronounced skoon-tra-WATT) hiked the mountains with his best friend, 18-year-old Haley Havlik. She had packed their lunch, and the two were excited to be breathing in the fresh Oregon air. They laughed, panted, and half-ran to the very top of the mountain, then paused to thank God for the beauty he'd created.

While Haley packed the remains of their lunch back into the basket, Brian reached into his backpack and pulled out a miniscule box. When Haley turned around, he was on one knee and had opened the box.

"I always want to take care of you," he said. "Will you marry me?"

Brian had already cleared his intentions with Haley's parents and promised he and Haley wouldn't set an immediate date for the wedding. After Haley said yes, she and Brian talked about a year-and-a-half engagement. They hiked down the mountain as happy as any two people in love with God and each other could be. Little did they know their world was about to change forever.

Tuesday, December 26, 1995—a day Brian and Haley would never forget.

Brian was working at Teen Trees International, a tree farm near his home in St. Helens, Oregon. He had been learning forestry management skills there for the past two years. Brian and his supervisor tossed a few loads of discarded paper into a burn barrel in the parking lot and watched it burn. Dan left for lunch, and Brian guarded the fire alone.

When the flames shot above the barrel's rim, Brian glanced around the shop for a bucket of water to dowse the fire. But as soon as he tossed the contents of the bucket onto the flames, the fire erupted with a mighty *BOOM.*

Brian had mistakenly grabbed a bucket of gasoline instead of water.

Hours later, Haley, her family, and Brian's family listened as the surgeon approached them with the news that Brian had miraculously survived. Even though 94 percent of his body had been grotesquely burned, Brian was alive. But the handsome, dark-skinned, athletic young man was no longer even recognizable.

Brian learned fast that true identity *cannot* be established on anything other than a close relationship with Jesus Christ.

Know It!
Resist the temptation to place your identity in things that can change quickly. If your identity is founded on talent, physical appearance, or the reactions of those around you, it can be demolished in a matter of seconds.

Read It!
Genesis 1:26-27, 31; Romans 12:2-5

Pray It!
Pray that you won't base your identity on outward appearance.

Looking beyond Appearance (Part 2)

Know It!
God can use you just the way you are! He wants to help you discover your true identity in him, and he yearns to guide you into developing a positive self-image. He wants your identity to come from the fact that you have incredible value to him!

Read It!
Genesis 2:7;
Romans 13:9

Pray It!
Thank God for the privilege of being made in his image. Ask him to help you accept yourself just as you are.

During the next several months, the burn staff had to reconstruct Brian's exterior shell. Using skin from cadavers and grafts from what little skin Brian had left, surgeons stapled together an intricate quilt of skin.

This blanket of cadaver skin was just temporary; it bought the physicians enough time to have Brian's own skin grown in a lab from a small graft. When his new skin arrived, cut into squares the size of mini Post-It notes, doctors repeated the grueling process of scraping off the old skin and stitching on the new.

To keep Brian alive, surgeons had to sacrifice his infected limbs. His forearms were amputated, part of his left leg was gone, and he was still in danger of losing his right foot. He endured 19 surgeries during the several months he was at the Oregon Burn Center. Three weeks after the accident, Brian regained consciousness.

He later lost his vision.

What about the engagement? Haley had a big decision to make. When she promised to spend the rest of her life with Brian, he was everything she'd ever dreamed of—physically, emotionally, and spiritually. Things were different now.

But Haley's response? "It just doesn't matter to me how Brian looks on the outside," she said. "He's still the same on the inside. I still see that boyish smile. I still share the dream of someday raising a family."

Two years after the accident, Brian and Haley were married. Brian wears his wedding ring on a chain around his neck, and the doctors say he can father a child. "I thank God every day for another chance to live," he says. "I especially thank him for Haley. Someday we'll have kids!"

The community rallied around the young couple and collected enough funds to build them a special home with ramps for Brian's wheelchair. And today, seven years after the accident, Haley still doesn't question her commitment to Brian. She knows true beauty comes from the soul and real identity comes from a solid relationship with the Creator.

"So," Latasha said after the youth meeting, "how do I know who I am?"

"Ah, you've asked a great question," Pastor Steve responded. "People have been asking that same question for centuries."

"Okay. So how do I find my identity?"

"It all begins with a strong relationship in Jesus Christ," he answered.

"Yeah, I've heard you say that before," Latasha said. "But I don't get what that has to do with anything."

"Latasha, God created you. He knows everything about you—your fears, what makes you happy, when you sit or stand, why you procrastinate on your homework. . . . He knows it all."

"Yeah, I believe that. But I still don't understand how that can help in my search for identity."

"Let's say you invented something, Latasha. You're on the track team, aren't you?"

"Yeah, but what's that got to do—"

"Let's say you created a special running shoe that enabled you to run the mile in one minute. Not only will this shoe give runners greater speed, it will also help them jump long distances. Get this: From a stationary position, you'd be able to jump 10 feet."

Latasha couldn't help but laugh.

"But there's something special about these shoes," Pastor Steve continued. "They have to be laced a certain way. They need to be kept at exactly 34 degrees for eight hours before you wear them, and you have to rub baby oil on the soles. If you do all this before you wear the shoes, you'll be able to set new records in running and jumping."

"That's wild! If it were true, my shoes would definitely be a hit worldwide!" Latasha said.

"They sure would. And the media would be hounding you for interviews. But other sports companies would soon start copying your shoe, and the media would begin interviewing them as well."

"Yeah, but I created the original. So what I say holds more weight than those other guys, right?" Latasha asked.

"Exactly," Pastor Steve said. "And guess what—it works the same way in your relationship with Jesus Christ. Since he created you and knows you better than anyone else, doesn't it make sense that if you really want to find out how you work and who you are, that you should go directly to the Creator?"

"Ahh," Latasha said. "I think I'm starting to get it. Keep going."

Know It!

Jesus Christ wants to lead you in your search for identity. Since he knows you better than anyone else, doesn't it make sense to trust his guidance?

Read It!

Psalm 139; Ecclesiastes 7:13

Pray It!

Read Psalm 139 as a prayer. Let yourself be amazed by how well God knows you.

Going to the Source (Part 2)

Know It!
Instead of searching for your identity in temporary things such as relationships, activities, or talent, base it on a firm foundation in Christ. He is unshakable and can't be defeated or swayed. He is eternal.

Read It!
Psalm 139;
Hebrews 12:28

Pray It!
Tell God that you want to know him better and better. Ask him to help you discipline yourself to know him more each day.

"Pastor Steve, I'm really glad you've been doing this series on finding our identity," Latasha said. "I really *do* want to find my identity."

"You're not alone, Latasha! Every human in the world wants to know himself. Think about this: There will always be other voices who surround you proclaiming that *they* can tell you who you are, how you work, and what you're made of. Some of your friends will offer *their* take on your identity, and I'm guessing your school friends will say your ability on the track is who you are."

"That's exactly what they'd say," Latasha admitted. "But they don't know how tired I am of competing. In fact, I think this will be my last year on the team."

"So their assessment is incorrect. They don't really know you at the core of your being, right?"

"Yeah."

"And I'm guessing your church friends would say your identity is in your voice. After all, Latasha, no one can sing 'America the Beautiful' like you!"

"That's exactly what my church girls tell me!"

"But if you developed nodules on your vocal chords in the next few weeks, chances are good that you'd never sing again. So music really isn't your identity. Your church friends don't actually know you at the core of your being, do they?"

"Wow. Guess not."

"But there's Someone who *does* know you, and he knows you much better than you'll ever even know yourself. And that's your Creator. Just as you would want the media coming to *you* to find out about your creation–your shoes–so your heavenly Father wants you coming to *him* to find your identity."

"I get it. That makes sense!"

"So Latasha, the more you get to know Jesus Christ, the better you know yourself. You learn your identity through the only One who can *give* you identity!"

"Yeah! I'm with you. If I want to know myself better, I need to spend more time with Jesus. And the closer I grow to him, the more whole I'll become."

"Exactly. Now I've got the munchies. How about a burger and fries?"

"No thanks, Pastor Steve. I've got an idea for some athletic shoes I wanna sketch out."

"Ha! Get real."

"And then I'm gonna start a prayer journal."

"Now you're talking!"

Being Content with Who You Are

What's the bottom line on finding your identity? Get to know the source of your identity, Jesus Christ. Here are some practical tips on discovering who you are.

1. Determine to be real. Pretending to be something you're not will only harm your search for identity. In the classic children's book *The Velveteen Rabbit* by Margery Williams, a toy rabbit longs to become real. Let's eavesdrop on his conversation with another toy in the nursery:

"What is REAL?" asked the Rabbit one day. "Does it mean having things that buzz inside you and a stick-out handle?"

"Real isn't how you are made," said the Skin Horse. "It's a thing that happens to you. When a child loves you for a long, long time, not just to play with, but REALLY loves you, then you become Real. It doesn't happen all at once. You become. It takes a long time. Generally, by the time you are Real, most of your hair has been loved off, and your eyes drop out and you get loose in the joints and very shabby. But these things don't matter at all, because once you are Real you can't be ugly, except to people who don't understand."

2. Understand the risks. Being real means being vulnerable. And being vulnerable means being honest. Jesus was extremely real. He never pretended to be something he wasn't. When he felt anger, he showed it and explained the source. When he was moved by pity, he expressed it and taught his disciples to do the same.

But with being real comes the risk of being rejected. Jesus was willing to take that risk, and he wants to empower you to take the same risks he did.

3. Don't argue with your Creator. Ask God to give you contentment in who you are. Instead of questioning why you're not good at this or don't look like so-and-so, simply trust your heavenly Father in knowing that his plan is absolutely perfect! Brian and Haley Sakultarawattn found the strength to accept without understanding. God desires the same of you!

Know It!

You may not understand God's reasoning for making you tall, shy, stocky, or impulsive, but his plan is perfect! The mature disciple will accept God's ways, even though she doesn't fully understand them.

Read It!

Psalm 40:8-10, 16-17; Isaiah 45:9-12

Pray It!

Admit to God that you have questioned his ways. Ask him to help you become content with the way things are, and ask for strength to accept his ways without understanding.

How's Your Commitment?

Know It!
God's not into playing games. He's made it very clear that we're living on earth on borrowed time. He needs sold-out Christians who are fully committed to him to spread the gospel, love their neighbors, and make a difference in people's lives that will last eternally.

Read It!
2 Chronicles 16:9; Psalm 37:5-6; Proverbs 16:3

Pray It!
Tell Jesus of your desire to make a difference in the world. Place yourself in his hands and ask him to reshape you in his image.

In 1776, 50 colonists signed their names to a declaration that would change the world. In unison, they pledged a higher standard for themselves and all who would come after them. "We mutually pledge to each other our lives, our sacred honor . . ." Wow! Our lives and our sacred honor?? To say they risked a lot would be quite an understatement. They truly knew the meaning of commitment!

History teaches us again and again that it doesn't take a lot of people to change the world—it just takes a lot of commitment. To what and to whom are you truly committed? Are your commitments making a genuine difference in your life? In the world?

Are you aware of the fact that you can make a difference by the kind of commitments you make? You see, your commitments define who you are. Strong people make a commitment and stick to it through good times and bad. And God is looking for people who are willing to make a genuine difference in their world. There's only one requirement: We must be fully committed to him.

There's a huge difference between "fully" and "almost." There's a big space between "casually following" and "sold-out obedience." During the next few days, let's take a closer look at how you can make a genuine difference in your world . . . by your commitments.

Can I Really Make a Difference?

But I'm just one person, you may be thinking. *Can anything I do really matter to the world around me?*

One person really can make a difference! In fact, if you'll take a look at history, you'll see that "ones" have made a huge difference! For instance, did you know:

- Just one vote caused King Charles I of England to be beheaded in 1649.
- One vote made Adolf Hitler head of the Nazi Party in 1923.
- Just one vote in 1776 determined that Americans would speak English rather than German.
- One vote elected Thomas Jefferson president in 1800.
- Just one man, Noah, heard and obeyed God's voice. The ark he built saved the entire animal kingdom and allowed the earth to be repopulated.
- She was just one woman, but Phoebe volunteered to deliver Paul's letter to the Romans. And that book has influenced millions of Christians through the ages!
- Just one man—the Son of God, the greatest gift of all—offers eternal life to you and your friends. And Jesus Christ makes the biggest difference ever!

Are you ready to make a difference? It all happens through your commitment. Let's take a look at the secrets. To be fully committed to making a difference, I must . . .

Secret #1: Commit my life fully to Jesus Christ. Your purpose on earth is to be fully committed to your Creator. He made you with the capacity to know him. And through his holy Word, the Bible, he has made this very easy to understand. No one can use the excuse, "I just don't get it. It's too difficult to comprehend." He made it simple. God wants to be the director of your life, because he has an incredible plan for you.

Secret #2: Commit to being a member of God's family. God doesn't expect you to make it on your own. He places other believers in your path to encourage you, help solidify your faith, and affirm your relationship with him. Are you plugged in to a church? A youth group? Are you a part of a Bible study? Being an integral part of God's family will provide the support you need to make a genuine difference in the world. Being inside God's family is what will get you through the tough times.

Know It!

There are Christians all over the world! So don't settle for being a spiritual orphan. Determine to make yourself accountable to other believers, and bask in their fellowship.

Read It!

Romans 10:9; 12:9-11; 1 Peter 1:3

Pray It!

Tell God you don't want to settle for being a spiritual orphan. Commit yourself to him and his family. Ask him to remind you of this commitment when you're going through tough times and start to back away from Christians who care about you.

Continuing with Commitment

Know It!

God knows you need some downtime, and many people relax by watching TV. But God also yearns to bring balance to your life. Ask him to help you assess your time spent in leisure activities and your time spent with him.

Read It!

Proverbs 2; 23:12; Ephesians 5:1

Pray It!

Tell God that you want to become more like him and you're willing to spend the daily time necessary to get to know him on a deeper level.

To be fully committed to making a difference, I must . . .

Secret #1: Commit my life fully to Jesus Christ.

Secret #2: Commit to being a member of God's family.

Secret #3: Commit to being a model of Christlikeness. Has anyone accused you of being like Christ? If not . . . why? Shouldn't others notice the difference he's making in your life? The apostle Paul tells us to be imitators of God. If we're truly doing that, people will have to notice!

Determine that WWJD won't simply be a fad for you, but you'll live your life asking, "Really . . . what would Jesus do?" Think about it: What would he say? How would he act and react? When God shines through your life, people can't help but see!

God wants you to grow up spiritually! *That sounds good,* you may be thinking. *But how? How do I actually become more spiritually mature?*

It's a decision and a lifelong process of conforming to Christlikeness. The secret to becoming more like him is in the Bible. Commit to read the Word on a daily basis! If you've never read the Bible all the way through, decide to do it! (Flip back to February 26 for a quick recipe on how to do this.)

The more you get the Bible into your heart and mind, the more you'll become like Jesus. As you read it and absorb it, you'll begin to understand it. Think of the Bible as your friend—it feeds you!

We're told in Proverbs to commit ourselves to instruction and knowledge. How are you responding to that? The answer, more than likely, is found in how you spend your time. Do you believe answers to life can be found in the Bible . . . or TV? It all comes down to priorities. How much time are you spending reading and absorbing God's Word, and how much time do you spend watching TV? How can you be a model of Christlikeness if you don't know what he looks like? His lifestyle, his profile, and his character are all found inside the pages of the Bible . . . not on TV or in the movies.

Checking Your Commitment

To be fully committed to making a difference, I must . . .

Secret #1: Commit my life fully to Jesus Christ.

Secret #2: Commit to being a member of God's family.

Secret #3: Commit to being a model of Christlikeness.

Secret #4: Commit to being a messenger of his love. You don't want nonbelievers watching your life and thinking, *If that's what being a Christian is, I don't want it.* Give them every reason in the world to want what you have—by the way you live your life!

Secret #5: Commit to be a minister of his grace. How are you using the gifts God has given you? Do you know what ministry is? It's using your gifts unselfishly to help others. If Jesus Christ, the King of kings, served others, so must we. Our attitude must be like his. And as we serve those around us, we become ministers of his grace.

If you've made these five commitments, you're fully devoted to him. And he will use your commitment to make a genuine difference in the world around you. Imagine the positive and life-changing way those around you will be touched, when they see in you . . . a sold-out commitment to Jesus Christ, involvement in his family, Christlikeness, and God's love and grace. That *can't help* but make a difference in your world! But the best difference of all . . . is the growing difference in your own heart!

Know It!

Your response to this will be one of the following: (a) I need to become fully committed to Jesus Christ; (b) I've asked Jesus to forgive my sins, but I've settled for simply being an attendee to his family instead of a member of his family; (c) He is making a difference through my life and my total commitment to him.

Read It!

Matthew 20:25-28;
2 Corinthians 5:19-20

Pray It!

Tell God that you don't want to settle for simply hanging out at his family functions but you want to be a member of his actual family. Thank him for helping you see the difference.

Quiz Time

Know It!
God can and will use you to make a difference in your world, but he's going to work through your commitment to him. So the deeper your commitment, the more he's able to use you in a positive and eternal way!

Read It!
Proverbs 4:23-27; 11:30; Isaiah 42:5-6

Pray It!
Thank God for his desire to use you to make a difference in the lives of others. Ask him to help you become a world changer.

***One** person really*
a. can't make a difference. It's impossible.
b. can make a difference when he or she is totally dependent on God.
c. is extremely insignificant.

*A **mature** Christian will make*
a. waves.
b. a huge batch of brownies with extra frosting.
c. a commitment and stick to it through good times and bad.

*To make a **genuine difference** in the world, I must first commit*
a. my life to Jesus Christ.
b. myself to work.
c. random acts of kindness.

*To become a **model** of Christlikeness*
a. I must stand very still in a storefront window.
b. is totally impossible.
c. I must commit to reading and absorbing the Bible.

*If I use my **spiritual gifts** unselfishly, I'll be*
a. the most popular kid in Sunday school.
b. the center of attention at school.
c. a minister of his grace.

*To be a **fully devoted** follower of Christ, I must also commit*
a. my little brother to a psychiatric ward.
b. to being a messenger of his love.
c. myself to read only Christian books and magazines.

Computer Conversations

Jamie headed to the den and flipped on the family computer. *Hope Ashley is online,* she thought. *I need a good buddy chat right now.*

Jamie always looked forward to chatting with her cousin and enjoyed her perspective on things as a college student.

Jamie17: Hey, Cuz! What's happening?
20ash: Got that part-time job on campus I was hoping for. What's goin' on with you?
Jamie17: Remember that guy in my science class I told you about?
20ash: Tim, right?
Jamie17: Yeah. What a jerk! He's constantly picking on me. I'm so fed up with it, I can't stand it! This guy hates everyone! He'd just as soon spit on you as say hi to you.
20ash: Whoa! Have you invited him to youth group?
Jamie17: You're kidding, right?
20ash: Nope.
Jamie17: You couldn't pay me to invite this guy to church!
20ash: Whoa, Cuz! Even though he's a jerk, he's also someone Christ died for!
Jamie17: Well, someone else can invite him. I can't stand the guy.
20ash: But, Jamie, think of it this way: If no one shares the gospel with Tim, he could end up in hell-forever separated from God.
Jamie17: Okay, I know this sounds terrible . . . but I'm just being honest. Ashley, Tim deserves hell.
20ash: So do you, Ash. So do I. We were all born with sin, remember?
Jamie17: You don't understand, Ashley! If Tim hears the gospel, who knows? There's a chance he may actually decide to give his life to Christ. I don't want that to happen! I don't want him in church . . . or even in heaven.
20ash: Okay, now *I'm* being honest, Jamie! You're dealing with a major attitude problem. In fact, let's call it what it really is: Sin!
Jamie17: But I'm just being honest, Ashley. I don't want to pray for him, I don't want to see him get saved, and I don't want anyone reaching out to him.
20ash: Girl, we got to do some heavy prayin'. But before we do, I want you to read the story of Jonah.
Jamie17: What's that got to do with anything?
20ash: Believe it or not, Jamie, *you're* Jonah!

Know It!

Jesus wants everyone in the entire world to be saved! The Bible tells us the reason he's delaying his return to earth is simply so more people will hear the gospel and have the opportunity to come to him.

Read It!

Isaiah 48:1-11;
Joel 2:12;
1 Corinthians 9:16

Pray It!

Ask God to bring the people to your mind with whom you have attitude problems. Seek God's forgiveness.

A Whale of a Tale

Know It!
Jonah was a real, living, breathing person, and we can accept his story as true.

Read It!
Jonah 1; 2 Kings 14:25; Matthew 12:38-41

Pray It!
Ask God to open your heart to the lessons he wants to teach you through the story of Jonah.

Let's take the next few days and put the story of Jonah under a microscope. It's a story about a rebellious prophet, a wicked city, and the God of the second chance. If we were to set Jonah's experience on stage, we'd script it in two acts:

ACT I
SETTING: THE GREAT SEA—MEDITERRANEAN
PLOT: JONAH FORSAKING HIS MISSION

ACT II
SETTING: THE GREAT CITY—NINEVEH
PLOT: JONAH FULFILLING HIS MISSION

CAST
STAR: GOD
Supporting Actor: Jonah
Cameo Appearance: The Great Fish

Many people find the book of Jonah hard to believe, so some critics have suggested different ways it should be interpreted: (1) *Mythologically.* It's a fascinating story, but it's not supposed to be taken literally. Like *Moby-Dick* or *Robinson Crusoe,* it's interesting, but it's fiction. (2) *Allegorically.* Jonah represents the Jews. The Great Sea represents the nations of the world. The whale symbolizes the Babylonians who held the Jews captive for 70 years. The entire story is simply an allegory filled with symbolism.

If you believe the holy Word of God is absolute truth (and I do, wholeheartedly!), then the story of Jonah should be interpreted (3) *Historically.* It's not a myth. It's not an allegory. It's an actual event in history. It truly happened.

How can we know? Two reasons:

1. Jonah is referred to in the Old Testament (2 Kings 14:25). He's referred to as an actual person, he's named as a prophet, and his hometown is identified—making him an actual, literal, historical person.
2. Jonah is referred to in the New Testament by Jesus himself. In Matthew 12 and 16, and also in Luke 11, Christ validates and verifies this Old Testament account.

Nineveh: Not a Family-Friendly Place

As we begin this short book of Jonah, we quickly learn that God has called this prophet to share the gospel with the city of Nineveh . . . and Jonah refuses. Let's pretend we're able to travel back in time and visit the city of Nineveh to gain a better understanding of this story.

As we enter the city gates, we're tempted to flip on the camcorder because this great city is truly magnificent to behold! As our tour bus guides us through the streets, we notice 1,200 towers filling the city limits. Any one of these 200-foot buildings would make a great postcard! The foundation of each 200-foot tower is made of polished stone, and each one is wide enough that three chariots can drive on top of it side-by-side. What a vacation spot!

Our tour continues and we're captivated by hanging gardens that fill the city with rich plants. There are designated areas for rare and exotic animals. We're guided through the temples, libraries, arsenals, and palaces, and we continue to snap photos and secure footage on our video cameras. Then our tour guide makes an announcement through the bus microphone that we're not comfortable with. "All this incredible beauty was built with slave labor."

There are knots in our stomachs. As we go farther, we learn that the Ninevites—the Assyrians—are a cruel and sadistic people. We'd like to stop the tour and head back to our hotel, but the bus continues. We drive past furniture made of human skin. We see pyramids constructed of human skulls. It's tough to swallow as we learn the Assyrians have perfected the word *torture.*

Flash back to the present now. Is it a little easier to understand why Jonah didn't want to go to Nineveh? He was scared! But before you begin to develop a big soft spot for this reluctant prophet, take a deeper look at what frightened him. It wasn't the cruelty of the Ninevites he feared!

Know It!

God loves every single person in the entire world. He hates sin, but he loves the sinner. He'll go to great lengths to bring a sinner to him.

Read It!

Jonah 1

Pray It!

Tell God you want to go anywhere and do anything at any time he asks you.

Something Fishy

Know It!

There's no place we can go to hide from God. Unless we're running from him, we can take great comfort in the fact that he always knows where we are!

Read It!

Jonah 1–2

Pray It!

Seek God's forgiveness for the times you've tried to escape his leading. Ask him to help you be more sensitive to his guidance in your life.

Throughout world history, the Assyrians have been known as some of the most sadistic people who ever lived. And though Jonah was scared to go to Nineveh (one city where the Assyrians lived), he wasn't afraid of their cruelty. He was afraid of the mercy of God!

You see, Jonah knew God would be quick to forgive and offer mercy to the citizens of Nineveh. That was the last thing Jonah wanted to see! He didn't want them blessed; he wanted them blasted! Yes, he definitely needed an attitude check.

But before we're quick to judge Jonah as being heartless, let's search our own hearts. Do you ever find it tough to forgive someone who's been mean to you? Are you willing to go out of your way for someone who's been a jerk to you or your friends?

As we read the first chapter of Jonah, we see that after he got his mission from God, he caught a ship and headed toward Tarshish—the opposite direction from Nineveh. Guess what? When you're running from God, Satan will always have a "ship" ready to take you the opposite direction. In other words, the devil will always tempt you with a means of escape.

The Bible tells us that Jonah went down to the port of Joppa. Jonah boarded the ship, went to a downstairs cabin, and fell asleep. But when a horrendous storm began to threaten the ship's safety, the sailors were terrified.

They began tossing things overboard in order to lighten the ship, and someone remembered Jonah, who was asleep in the bowels of the boat. Don't think for a second that he was sleeping because he was at peace. He was sleeping out of rebellion and escape. Have you ever felt so down, so confused, so angry, that you simply went to bed and pulled the covers over your head? It enables us to forget—for the time being—the heaviness that weighs on our heart.

The sailors finally woke Jonah, and they cast lots (like throwing dice) to see who had made God angry and caused the storm. When Jonah lost, he admitted that he was the reason for the storm. He even told them that if they'd toss him overboard, their lives would be spared. So they did. And just as Jonah had predicted, they safely sailed on to their destination.

Hard to Swallow?

Today we get to the part of Jonah's story you've probably heard about—the part where he's swallowed by a huge fish!

The sailors tossed Jonah overboard. They might have thought he'd seen his last days, but God wasn't finished with him. God caused a giant fish to approach Jonah and actually swallow the prophet alive.

Now this is where many people grow skeptical. "How are we supposed to believe a fish swallowed a man, and he lived through it?" they chide.

Check out the following account by M. de Parvelle, a French scientist and editor of the journal *Des Debats:*

> In February 1891, the whaling ship *Star of the East* was in the vicinity of the Falkland Islands when the lookout sighted a large sperm whale three miles away. Two boats were lowered and in short time, one of the harpooners was able to spear the creature. The second boat also attacked the whale but was upset by a lash of its tail, causing the crew to fall into the sea. One of them drowned. But the other, James Bartley, simply disappeared without a trace.
>
> After the whale was killed, the crew set to work with axes and spades to remove the blubber. They worked all day and into the night. The next day, they attached tackle to the stomach in order to hoist it to the deck. In doing so, the sailors were startled by something in the stomach which gave spasmodic signs of life. Inside was found the missing sailor, doubled up and unconscious. He was laid on the deck and treated to a bath of sea water which soon revived him.
>
> At the end of the third week, he had entirely recovered from the shock and resumed his duties on the ship. Although his face, neck and hands were bleached to a deadly whiteness and he took on the appearance of parchment, Bartley affirms that he probably would have lived inside his house of flesh until he starved, for he lost his senses through fright and not through lack of air.

That's only one of several records of men surviving inside whales. Also, some types of whales have been known to swallow other unusually large objects whole, including a 15-foot shark and a 400-pound squid! Again, Jonah's story is not a fairy tale. It's an historical event that actually happened!

Know It!

God has no problem at all making the seemingly impossible become reality. If he created a world out of nothing, a man from dust, and raised the dead to life, he could certainly enable a man to survive in the belly of a fish for three days!

Read It!

Jonah 1–3

Pray It!

Ask God to deepen your faith and to erase the doubts about everything he wants you to believe.

Gone Fishing

Know It!
God can work through anyone and anything to accomplish his purposes. He can use Christians, non-Christians, the weather, and even mammals. God's plans *will* survive and thrive!

Read It!
Jonah 1–4

Pray It!
Tell God you don't want a reputation of having a lousy attitude. Ask him to help you be sensitive to the leading of his Spirit in your life.

Okay, so Jonah's vacation dwellings aren't the most desirable in the world! Can you even imagine? Ugh! He was definitely in a tight spot! And tight spots are interesting, because they either make us bitter or better. Think of it this way: The same boiling water that hardens an egg softens a potato. We always have a choice about our attitude!

The second chapter of Jonah begins with the fact that Jonah began praying. But it wasn't right when he was swallowed. He waited until he truly felt he had no other choice. Jonah waited for three days and three nights before he finally turned to God.

He must have been totally miserable! What can one do inside the belly of a whale? Untangle the intestines? Sort through the menagerie of other things the whale has swallowed?

With seaweed wrapped around his head and fish slapping him in the face, Jonah sweated through a stifling 98.6 degree temperature inside the belly of that great fish. And three days later, when he could absolutely not stand it any longer, he began to pray.

Can you identify with that? Is it easy for you to wait until your back is against the wall before you turn to God? Do you sometimes try all your other options, working hard to fix the problem, and finally—when nothing else has worked—turn to your heavenly Father?

God heard his prayer. The fish suddenly felt the urge to regurgitate, and Jonah was vomited onto the beach. He might have felt that he had been going nowhere for the past three days and nights, but the whale was always moving. And he moved right to the beach where God wanted Jonah all along.

Now we get to the part of the story where we see God as a God of second chances. He didn't give up on Jonah. He had an incredible plan for an amazing revival in Nineveh, and he wanted to use Jonah to usher it in. So God gave him a second chance.

Jonah obeyed this time, but he still had a rotten attitude. Even though he shared the gospel with the Assyrians and told them to repent in three days or God would destroy them, he secretly wanted to see them destroyed.

A Whale of a Tale Comes to an End

In spite of Jonah's rotten attitude, the people of Nineveh listened. They'd never heard the message before. They had no idea God loved them and wanted to grant them forgiveness. A great revival broke out, and the entire city—including the government leaders—repented and turned from their wicked ways.

Why were they so quick to believe? Two reasons:

1. *The message was simple.* The gospel—when preached in pure form—is always simple. It's easy to understand. Reverend Billy Graham is known for preaching the gospel in a simple and easy-to-understand manner. And that's why thousands of people have come to know Jesus over the years through his crusades. If we'll keep it simple and just share the Word of God, people will respond!
2. *The messenger was real.* Can you imagine what Jonah must have looked like when he was vomited up on the beach? In the three documented cases of men being swallowed by whales, all three men emerged in the same condition: Due to the gastric juices in the whale's stomach, they looked like hairless albinos—pure white with not even an eyelash or eyebrow to be found. Jonah was a living testimony! How could people *not* believe him?

That's encouraging, because it proves we don't have to be perfect to be used by God. Jonah was able to testify, "Hey! I've been in the pit of a fish for three days and three nights. Yeah, I'm bleached, but I'm alive! God has been merciful and gracious to me, and he wants to offer grace to you as well."

You'd think Jonah would have felt privileged to have been used by God in such a mighty way. But instead of rejoicing over what God had done in a wicked city, Jonah was angry at God. We can imagine a conversation something like this:

"See, God! This is exactly why I didn't want to preach forgiveness to those people. I knew if they repented, you'd forgive them and save them from their sins. And what about the destruction I predicted? Now it's not gonna happen, because they've turned from their wicked ways. I look like a fool talking about something that didn't happen!"

Not exactly an attitude of gratitude, huh?

Know It!

Even though Jonah was used to usher in one of the greatest revivals in the world, he's still known as the reluctant prophet. Determine not to be a reluctant follower of God! You don't have to come across to your unsaved friends as perfect—only perfectly forgiven. They *will* listen! Just keep it simple.

Read It!

Jonah 1–4

Pray It!

Tell God you want to follow him wholeheartedly and don't want to be a reluctant disciple. Ask him to help you fall so in love with him that you'll obey him immediately.

Quiz Time

Know It!
God wants to use *you* to tell others about his love and forgiveness. It won't always be easy, but he promises to stay with you and enable you to share his words.

Read It!
Jonah 1–4

Pray It!
Spend some time thanking God for giving second chances.

We should ***accept the story*** *of Jonah as*
a. a myth.
b. an allegory.
c. an historical event.

We know the story of ***Jonah is true*** *because*
a. it's referred to in the Old Testament and validated by Jesus in the New Testament.
b. we hear similar stories every single day.
c. we've seen the movie.

Jonah was ***afraid***
a. of God's mercy.
b. that he might end up being a sofa in an Assyrian's house.
c. that his skull would be permanently placed as a cornerstone in one of the city's pyramids.

Jonah ***ran from God*** *and set sail on a ship headed for*
a. Cancun.
b. the Bahamas.
c. Tarshish.

Once Jonah was ***on board****, God brought forth*
a. a midnight buffet for all on board.
b. a storm.
c. a shuffleboard tournament on deck two.

Jonah was tossed ***overboard*** *and*
a. soon swallowed by a large fish.
b. caught a small raft headed toward Jamaica.
c. did the butterfly stroke for three days.

Jonah ***finally turned back to God*** *after*
a. he'd had a chance to go to church.
b. he'd spent three days and nights in the belly of the fish.
c. he'd been to an Audio Adrenaline concert.

Jonah preached to Nineveh, and ***the people believed*** *because*
a. he kept the message simple.
b. he used a PowerPoint computer presentation.
c. he showed come cool videos.

Through the story of Jonah, we learn that ***God is a God*** *of second*
a. helpings.
b. innings.
c. chances.

A Holy Car???

We all know that WWJD stands for "What would Jesus do?" But let's use our imaginations. It could stand for "We want jelly donuts!" or "What would Jesus drive?"

Hmmm. What would Jesus drive? Several people have speculated, and as you can guess, there are a variety of opinions.

Some believe Jesus would tool around in an old Plymouth, because the Bible says, "God drove Adam and Eve out of the Garden of Eden in a **Fury.**"

Maybe God favors Dodge pickup trucks, because Moses' followers are warned not to go up a mountain "until the **Ram's** horn sounds a last blast."

Meanwhile, Moses rode an old British motorcycle, as proven by a Bible passage declaring that "the roar of Moses' **Triumph** is heard in the hills."

And the apostles pooled in a Honda: "The apostles were in one **Accord.**"

The real issue, of course, isn't what kind of motor vehicle Christ would use to get around town, because he has chosen to use an entirely different vehicle. He has chosen you! So think about it: How are you doing at getting Christ where he needs to go? Let's go through a quick checklist. Are any of these warning lights blinking?

- FUEL. Are you fueled up? Yes, this comes from the Bible (see Psalm 19:7-9 or Psalm 119:28). The more time you spend reading it, the more spiritual fuel you'll have in your tank. If you're going to be a vehicle Jesus uses, make sure your tank is full!
- SPEEDOMETER. Check your speed. Are you moving so slowly you're unable to get things done? Are you recklessly cutting in front of others to get ahead? Christ wants to bring balance and consistency to your life.
- VIEW. Check your windshield. How's your view? Have you allowed pollution, garbage, and things of the world to obstruct your view? Christ wants you to see him as a "wiper blade" that continually cleans and clears your vision. But you need to do your part. Don't attempt to drive through the trash thinking, *It won't affect me.* It will. Keep your view clean!
- OIL. Are your gears shifting and running smoothly? Only the Holy Spirit can make your relationships run smoothly. If you're having trouble with a specific gear, don't hesitate to make things right.

Know It!

For you to be the vehicle God uses to transport Christ, you need to be constantly in tune with the Master Mechanic.

Read It!

1 Corinthians 9:24-27; Ephesians 4:31-32; Philippians 4:8

Pray It!

Tell God you've never really thought of yourself as his vehicle, and ask him to help you keep in tune spiritually.

GO!

Know It!
If there's one thing God doesn't want you to settle for, it's mediocrity. Refuse to ride the fence, play the game, have a foot in both worlds. Give God your absolute best—100 percent. If you simply go along for the ride, you'll only go from bad to worse.

Read It!
Matthew 7:7-8;
Revelation 3:15-16

Pray It!
Tell God that you don't want a mediocre relationship with him. Ask him to help you settle for nothing less than total commitment.

Go against the grain
Go all out
Go ape
Go bananas
Go climb a tree
Go cold turkey
Go fly a kite
Go for broke
Go for it
Go for the gold
Go forth
Go from rags to riches
Go full circle
Go hand in hand
Go haywire
Go hog wild
Go like the wind
Go out on a limb
Go in peace
Go out with a bang
Go West
Go to town
Go out like a light
Go public
Go over the top
Go the extra mile
Go through a phase
Go over something with a fine-toothed comb
But don't simply
Go along for the ride!

Instructions

Have you ever wondered who writes the instructions that come with the appliances we buy? They must think without those instructions, we'd have no idea what to do with the appliance we purchased. The following are actual printed instructions:

- **On hair dryer:** *Do not use while sleeping.* (Those 1,500 watts can really lull you to sleep, you know!)
- **On a bag of Fritos:** *You could be a winner! No purchase necessary. Details inside.* (So . . . are they encouraging us to steal the chips?)
- **On a bar of Dial soap:** *Use like regular soap.* (Do they actually think we'll try to dial it?)
- **On a frozen dinner:** *Serving suggestion–defrost.* (Do you even own utensils that can cut through a side of frozen beef?)
- **On a Korean kitchen knife:** *Warning–keep out of children.* (Say "Ahhh.")
- **On an American Airlines packet of nuts:** *Open packet, eat nuts.* (So if you didn't have those instructions, you'd sit politely, holding the small packet in your lap just wondering and wondering what in the world to do with them??)
- **On a Swedish chainsaw:** *Do not attempt to stop with your hands.* (Glad we got THAT information. Without it, you probably would have been tempted to use your hand as the off switch?)
- **On children's cough medicine:** *Do not drive car or operate machinery.* (Is it really that common to see a child driving a Mercedes or operating a crane while fighting a cough?)

We laugh at the above instructions because they seem to insult our common sense. It seems obvious we'd cook a frozen dinner or dry our hair while we're awake.

God has also given us some instructions. They're called the Ten Commandments. Many people laugh at those as well and think they're silly. *Do not commit murder.* "That's common sense," some say. Is it?

There's certainly more than one kind of death. Let's take a closer look.

Know It!

God doesn't speak just to hear himself talking. When he gives us commands, instructions, and guidance, it's for a specific reason. Instead of assuming we already know it all, or thinking our common sense is all we need, discipline yourself to learning, hearing, and obeying *all* of God's instructions.

Read It!

2 Corinthians 5:9-11;
Galatians 1:10;
2 Timothy 3:16-17

Pray It!

Seek his forgiveness for sailing through your day without stopping to consider his instructions. Instead of assuming you already know what he wants, ask him to help you take his commands more seriously.

Thou Shalt Not Kill

Know It!
God gives specific commands for specific reasons, and he expects his children to obey.

Read It!
Exodus 20:13

Pray It!
Tell God you want to take his commands and instructions seriously.

"Hi, girls! How was volleyball practice?"

"Hey, Pastor Steve!" Nicole replied as she stuffed her Nikes in her duffel bag.

"Looooong. And tiring," Beth answered. "What are you doing here?"

"I thought maybe you could use a cold drink after a hard practice. Wanna head to McDonald's?"

"Sure . . . if you'll toss in some fries, too!" Nicole said.

"I'm game," Pastor Steve said, laughing.

"Hey, Pastor Steve," Beth said as they drove. "Are you really just here to treat us? Or is there something else on your mind?"

Pastor Steve laughed as he opened the door to his favorite fast-food stop. "You know me pretty well."

They grabbed drinks and food and found a table. Pastor Steve smiled, but both girls could tell his heart was heavy.

"Girls, you know I care deeply about you, but something's bothering me, and I think we need to talk about it."

Beth looked Pastor Steve in the eye. "What is it?"

"I know you've been inviting some of your non-Christian friends from the volleyball team to church."

"Yeah, and last Sunday, Annette actually took us up on it and came," Beth said.

"Yeah, I saw the three of you sitting together during the morning worship service," Pastor Steve said.

"I'm so glad Annette finally came," Nicole said. "We've been inviting her for months."

"And why have you been inviting her?" Pastor Steve asked.

"Her parents have recently gone through a divorce, and she's questioning everything," Nicole said.

"She's never had any kind of faith or gone to church her whole life," Beth added. "But she seems really interested."

"She's always asking what's different about us, and we've tried to explain our relationship with Christ," Nicole added. "But we figured if she'd actually come to church with us, she'd understand it better than we could explain."

"Oh," Pastor Steve continued. "So you're saying she needed to hear the sermon last Sunday?"

"Well, sure!" Beth said. "That's why we invited her."

"Hmmm." Pastor Steve looked sad. He stopped drinking his Coke. "Girls, I've been praying about this conversation for the past few days, and what I have to say to you isn't easy, but I need to say it. It's about last Sunday's service and your friend Annette."

"Well, I know you're just as excited as we are that Annette actually came to church with us last Sunday," Beth began.

"Girls, I applaud you for caring deeply about your friends who don't know Christ, but I'm afraid you may have aided in some spiritual destruction without realizing it."

"What?!?"

"You know we've been talking about the Ten Commandments in youth group? Next week we'll be discussing 'Thou Shalt Not Kill.' But the three of us need to talk about it first."

"Pastor Steve, you're coming from a different planet," Nicole said. "I don't get what you're saying at all!"

"Girls . . . there's more than one way to kill someone. Obviously, you're thinking of physical murder. But you can also 'kill' a person by gossip or by damaging her reputation."

"We'd never do that!" Beth said.

"I know. I wouldn't say you committed spiritual murder toward your friend Annette last Sunday, but you did instigate some spiritual destruction."

"No we didn't," Nicole stated. "She's our friend."

"But you've already told me that her parents recently split up, she's questioning everything, and she's never had any kind of religious faith or been involved in a church," Pastor Steve said.

"Yeah . . . and that's why we invited her to church!" Beth said.

"Exactly," Pastor Steve said. "She needed to hear the sermon last Sunday. Girls . . . she really needed to hear the sermon! She's spiritually hungry. She's confused. Annette is searching. And last Sunday's sermon was just what she needed."

"So I'm glad she was in church!" Beth said.

"Why?" Pastor Steve asked. "You two talked to her and passed notes the entire morning. She never heard the sermon!"

"Wait a second," Beth began.

"Annette came to church seeking answers, hope, direction," continued Pastor Steve. "God desperately wants to do a mighty healing work in her heart . . . and he wanted to start last Sunday. But because you kept her from hearing the sermon . . . you played a role in some spiritual destruction."

"You're serious, aren't you?" Beth said.

"Absolutely. 'Thou shalt not kill' isn't inclusive of physical murder only. And though you didn't 'kill' her, you kept her from experiencing what God wanted her to hear."

"Pastor Steve . . . we had no idea," Nicole said.

Know It!
God's commands are serious. Discipline yourself to knowing and obeying Him daily.

Read It!
Matthew 7:15; Matthew 9:12-13; Matthew 13:14; Matthew 19:14

Pray It!
Ask God to examine your heart and to show you if you're guilty of breaking this precious commandment.

Is There a Pulse?

Know It!
God wants you to invite your friends to church. But once they're inside, he wants to speak to them in a life-changing manner. Don't get in the way with chit-chat and note-passing. Once you enter the house of the Lord, be very aware of his holy presence.

Read It!
Hebrews 11

Pray It!
If you've committed spiritual murder, seek God's forgiveness right now. Ask him to help you take church seriously and to listen with open ears and an open heart to what your pastor has to say.

"Church isn't always about having a good time," Pastor Steve said. "Yes, it's fun to worship with our brothers and sisters in Christ. And yes, we have a great time learning about our Lord and Savior. But sometimes we simply need to be still and listen without having a good time. In other words, what we *need* to hear and what we *want* to hear aren't always the same thing."

"But I thought church was supposed to be fun," Beth said.

"It usually is," Pastor Steve continued. "But that shouldn't be the reason we come. Think about it: God doesn't simply tell us fun things. He disciplines us, corrects us, turns us around, and redirects us. That's not always fun. Sometimes hearing the truth hurts. But Christians who are serious about their relationship with God are in it for much more than simply having a good time. They're walking with Christ because they've chosen to give up their lives and love him with all their being."

"But we want our friends to think Christianity is fun," Nicole said.

"And it *is* fun to know the creator of the universe on a first-name basis," Pastor Steve said. "But we don't follow God out of the expectation we're in it for fun. Sometimes following him isn't fun at all."

"What?!?"

"Take a look at the faith chapter—Hebrews 11. These people gave their lives for the gospel," Pastor Steve explained. "It wasn't *fun* to be sawed in two, burned at a stake, or crucified. Girls, Christianity has to go much deeper than simply having fun. It's about having a genuine relationship with the King of kings, being in love with him, and obeying him because you want to—not because it's fun."

"I feel terrible," Beth began.

"Me too," Nicole said. "Let's go to Annette's and tell her we blew it by trying to make sure she had a fun time last Sunday."

"Let's pray first," Pastor Steve said. "God still wants to do a miracle in Annette's heart, and nothing is impossible for him to fix. So let's saturate this situation with prayer."

When you roll out of bed in the morning, one of the first questions you have to deal with is, "What am I going to wear today?"

We're barraged with a variety of sources that offer the latest fashion suggestions. And whether we're male or female, we often find ourselves consulting the latest fashion mags for hints on hairstyles, clothes, and what's considered "in."

But have you ever thought of consulting the Bible? God's Word actually offers some great tips on fashions that never go out of style. Check out the following suggestions:

- *A gentle and quiet spirit.* No, that doesn't mean you have to be silent. And it doesn't mean you can't voice your opinion. It does mean that you shouldn't call attention to yourself by being brazen, critical, or boisterous.
- *Contentment.* You may not have the most expensive labels in your closet or live in the biggest house on the block, but count your blessings for the things you do have and learn to be satisfied with what God has given you. Nothing wears worse than a jealous spirit. It'll never look good on you!
- *A smile.* This is always in; it will never go out of style. A smile is a reflection of something much deeper than what's spread across your face. It's actually a reflection of a joyful heart. As a Christian, you have every reason in the world to be happy. Know why? Because you have hope above all hope! (Check out John 16:22.) Those around you won't be interested in following Christ if they see you wearing a frown. So don't leave home without your smile.
- *Inner peace.* God gives you strength and peace to face any and all situations. Are you wearing your peace? Can others see it in your life?
- *Confidence.* No, not in yourself (though you will develop a healthy self-image as you draw closer to Christ), but in Jesus. Since he's on your side, who can be against you?
- *Kindness.* Get into the habit of considering the feelings of others before you react to circumstances around you. How would you feel if you were in their shoes? Treat them with gentleness and compassion.

Know It!

If you'll wear these things daily, you still may not make *People*'s best-dressed list, but you'll make Christ's list. And really . . . which is more important?

Read It!

Matthew 7:2;
John 16:22;
Romans 5:1;
Philippians 4:13;
Hebrews 13:5;
1 Peter 3:3-4

Pray It!

Ask God to help you focus more on his fashion tips rather than the world's.

Why Does God Send People to Hell?

Know It!

The only reason Christ is delaying his promised and expected return is so more people worldwide can come to know him. It's God's will that everyone would follow him and live eternally. But he gives each person the freedom to decide.

Read It!

Matthew 5:29-30; Luke 12:5; 16:19-31; 2 Peter 2:4

Pray It!

Ask God to help you view hell as a real place that exists for those who will be forever separated from him—so that it would spur you to tell your friends about Jesus.

"Hi, Pastor Steve," Lucy said in the hallway after youth group. "Um . . . there's something on my mind I'd like to talk with you about if you have a few minutes."

"Sure!" Pastor Steve said on the way into his office. "Grab a chair."

"I've been trying to share my faith at school, but sometimes my friends throw questions at me that I just can't answer. One of them is about hell."

"Let's hear it," Pastor Steve encouraged.

"Well, we always talk about how God is so good. But how can a loving God actually send people to hell?"

"Lucy, that's a great question! And a lot of nonbelievers get tripped up on it. First of all, God really *is* a God of love. He loves each one of us so much that he gave his only Son to die in our place so we wouldn't have to! But we have to accept his death as a gift."

"But still . . . since we know he loves us so much, why would he send us to hell?"

"Well, he loves us so much, he gives us freedom of choice. Would it really be genuine love if God forced us to accept his gift of eternal life?"

Lucy thought for a second. "No, I guess not," she concluded.

"Right," Pastor Steve continued. "But in giving us free choice also comes the reality that many people will choose not to serve Christ. They'll follow the world and do their own thing."

"And those are the people who will spend eternity in hell?"

"All people who have not repented of their sins and accepted Christ as their personal Savior. And Lucy, that's not just murderers and drug pushers. That's me, too!"

"What are you talking about, Pastor Steve?"

"We're all in the same boat," he explained. "Every single one of us was born with sin. So if I had never repented and asked Christ to forgive me, I'd be headed for hell, too."

"So what you're saying is that a lot good people—not necessarily criminals—will go to hell if they choose to ignore God."

"Exactly," Pastor Steve said.

"So it's not that God is deliberately sending people to hell," Lucy summed up. "He has clearly provided a way to escape hell by simply following him."

"Right, Lucy. God doesn't send anyone to hell. We send ourselves there."

What *Is* Hell?

"I really want my non-Christian friends to get to know Christ," Lucy told Pastor Steve, "but I keep getting tripped up on these tough questions they're throwing at me."

"They're asking you questions because they're curious about your faith. Take it as a compliment."

"I still have a few more questions about hell," she said. "Is it a real place?"

"Yes, hell is a physical place," Pastor Steve said. "The Bible tells us that our bodies will be raised on Judgment Day and will join our souls. Those physical bodies will have to be in a physical place. The Christians will spend eternity in heaven (a physical place), and the non-Christians will spend eternity in hell—which has to be a physical place to accommodate those bodies."

"Some of my friends say that hell will be one big party," Lucy said. "I know that's not true, but I don't know what to say."

"Think of it this way: Every time hell is talked about in the Bible, it's described as a place of great torment and pain. It's also described as total separation from God. That means love will not exist in hell. Neither will laughter or meaningful relationships. Every single person in hell will be there because he rejected Jesus Christ. Hell will be comprised of hate, selfishness, and all that is evil."

"It seems too easy to just accept Christ, live for him, and get to spend eternity in heaven," Lucy said. "So why don't more people accept his gift and avoid going to hell?"

"Lots of reasons," Pastor Steve said, "but let's just chat about two. One reason is that many people still haven't heard the wonderful news. And that's why it's so important to support missions through our local church, give in the offering, and participate on mission trips. And another reason is that many people simply don't trust God."

"So just because they can't see him, they choose not to trust him?"

"Lack of faith keeps a lot of people from coming to know Christ," Pastor Steve said. "But we can actually ask God to *give* us faith, and he will! And it doesn't take a ton of faith to come to Christ. The Bible says all it takes is a small amount—the size of a mustard seed."

"What a gift we have!" Lucy said smiling from ear to ear.

Know It!

God is going completely out of his way to make sure people know about his gift of eternal life. He gave his Son, he provided his holy Word, and he's sending missionaries all over the world to spread the gospel. Are you participating in the Great Commission?

Read It!

Genesis 18:25;
Matthew 28:19-20;
Acts 1:8;
2 Timothy 4:2

Pray It!

Ask God to help you bring your non-Christian friends into a relationship with his Son, Jesus, so they won't have to experience hell.

How to Raise Your Parents

You're probably well aware of the fact that the Bible tells you to honor and obey your parents. Sometimes it's tough. But look at it this way: God never said you have to *agree* with them. He knows they're human. And he also knows there will be times when they'll make mistakes. It's okay to disagree with your folks . . . you just need to do it the right way.

Here are– the top 10 ways NOT to disagree with your parents:

1. Whine.
2. Stomp your feet.
3. Slam your door.
4. Turn your music up really loud.
5. Ignore them for three days until they give in.
6. Refuse to take a shower.
7. Tell them all your other friends have it better than you.
8. When they try to talk to you, turn away and pretend they're not even there.
9. Squint your eyes and look mean when they're trying to reason with you.
10. Go ahead and do what you want. It's your life anyway.

Not a good strategy. If you need to disagree with your folks, use some common sense! When your mom is coming through the door trying to balance four bags of groceries in her arms at the end of the day, don't approach her with, "You're so unfair! Everyone else is going to the party!" You'll be lucky if you get supper.

When you *do* approach your parents, don't throw everything at them at once. Simply ask for a time the three of you can get together to discuss some stuff you're having trouble understanding. Offer to make dinner the following evening, and suggest you talk then. And when you *do* talk, keep your voice on an even tone.

After you've talked things out, your parents still may not give in. You still may disagree. Now it's time to practice honoring them in spite of how you feel. God has an incredible promise for those who honor their folks. Know what it is? A long life! That's a pretty good reward. And if you're having trouble honoring them, try making a list of all the things you appreciate about them. Then start praying for them. It's hard not to honor someone you're consistently lifting in prayer.

Know It!

It's not easy to raise your parents these days. It takes staying plugged into God's power and consistently asking for his discernment, patience, and wisdom. Try to see your parents as God's gift to you. He has placed them in authority over you, just as Jesus is in authority over them, and God is in authority over Christ. It's a system of balance and accountability.

Read It!

Proverbs 17:6; Ephesians 6:1-4; Colossians 3:20; 2 Timothy 3:1-2

Pray It!

Ask God to help you see your parents through his eyes. Tell him you want to learn how to honor them—even when you disagree.

Don't Be a Cheater!

Know It!
To be a young man or woman of character means that you're interested in living a lifestyle of integrity. And people notice those who have integrity. Usually people with integrity are respected and trusted more than anyone else.

Read It!
1 Chronicles 29:17; Nehemiah 7:2; Job 2:3; Psalm 25:21

Pray It!
Ask God to use his Holy Spirit to work through your conscience and remind you that it's wrong when you're tempted to cheat. And at the moment you're tempted, stop and pray. Claim God's strength not to yield to the temptation you're facing.

Some people cheat and get away with it. But you've already noticed this, right? Students cheat in school all the time. Maybe *you've* even done it and have gotten away with it. Since it didn't really hurt anyone, you may be tempted to keep it up. Others in school certainly do, right?

Those who start young and cheat in the little things usually continue cheating later in life, but this time in bigger things. Some are in jail because of it. Most aren't. They took shortcuts to get through their education, they "borrow" from the company, and they fudge a little on their income taxes. They think that whatever advantage they can get that doesn't directly hurt someone else is okay. Where did this line of thinking start? When they were kids, of course.

It's important that you strive to see the bigger picture. If you start young with anything–good or bad–you're likely to continue that habit as you progress through life.

Cheating is occurring all around you by people of weak character who can't face the consequences of their own actions.

Don't be weak!

Have a strong character.

Face the consequences of your actions like a Christian soldier. If you've been caught cheating, don't do something worse to try and cover it up . . . like lie. Admit you cheated. Seek forgiveness.

Realize you do have limitations. Don't try to overcome them by cheating. Just work a little harder. In the end, you'll be glad you did.

Tonight, before you go to bed, grab a notebook and jot down all the areas in which you're tempted to cheat. Schoolwork may be the most common area, but if you'll give it some thought you'll think of other areas as well. Examples: Cutting short your piano practice, doing a half-hearted job with your chores or at your job, driving over the speed limit, receiving too much change from the cashier and not returning it, etc.

Next to each item in your notebook, jot down a Scripture verse that will help you overcome the temptation to cheat in each area you've listed.

What Are You Afraid Of?

Everyone's afraid of something. I'm afraid of being on a train that derails. And bugs—yeeecch! I'm also frightened of being captured by aliens and being forced to do math homework for years on end, forgetting to brush my teeth and having bad breath all day, falling out of a Ferris wheel, and being run over while I'm riding my motor scooter. I'm scared of lots of stuff!

While it's okay to be afraid once in a while, it's not okay to let our fears take the best of us. For instance, if you don't have many friends because you're afraid to make friends, then fear is robbing you of an important part of life. Determine to overcome!

When a fear grows bigger and larger in our minds, we become obsessed with it. And when an obsessive fear gets out of control, it becomes a phobia.

Well-known author and public Christian speaker Patsy Clairmont admits she used to be *agoraphobic*—she was afraid to leave her home and go out in public. She was allowing her fear to rob her of many blessings, as well as keeping her from the adventure of meeting new people and traveling to new places. With God's help, she overcame it and now travels all across the United States communicating his love to large groups of people.

Here are a few phobias you may not be aware of: *hematophobia* (sight of blood), *monophobia* (being alone), *ombrophobia* (rain), *erythrophobia* (blushing in public), *anthophobia* (flowers), *phonophobia* (sound), *toxophobia* (being poisoned), *trichophobia* (hair).

While you probably don't suffer from any of the above, you might be allowing fear to rob you of something terrific. For instance, could it be that the reason you're not growing spiritually is because you're afraid of what God *might* ask of you? Do you avoid opposite-sex friendships because you're scared of not knowing what to say or how to act? What about witnessing? Are you afraid that others will make fun of you?

Why not take a few minutes right now and ask God to reveal to you any fears that are holding you back from becoming all he wants you to be. Once you've identified what you're afraid of, commit those fears to God. Refuse to let *any* fear stand between you and your Creator.

Know It!

Did you know there are 365 "fear nots" in the Bible? Hmmm. What could God be trying to tell us?

Read It!

Psalm 34:4;
Isaiah 44:2;
2 Corinthians 7:5;
1 John 4:18

Pray It!

Tell God you want ALL he has in store for you. Ask him to replace your fear with solid faith.

The Trouble with Lies

Know It!
God is a God of absolute truth, and he expects his children to live lives of truth as well. Think about Jesus and his disciples. They were persecuted for their faith. It would have been easy to rationalize and lie their way out, but they didn't. They continued to tell the truth even when their honesty cost them their lives. They knew their reward was in heaven.

Read It!
Psalms 5:6; 34:13; Proverbs 30:8; Acts 5:1-11

Pray It!
Ask God to search your heart and bring to your mind any lies you've told recently. Ask him to forgive you, and be willing to make things right with the person you lied to.

Never lie to your mom and dad.

Why? Because:

- It's wrong.
- You break one of the Ten Commandments when you lie.
- You lose your parents' trust.
- When people lie, they often continue to lie to cover up the past lie, and life becomes a vicious circle of lies. (Hey, after the 14th lie, it's tough to remember what exactly you said two weeks ago that you're still trying to cover up.)
- It's a bad habit to fall into. And once you pick up one bad habit, it's easier to add others.

  For instance, if you lie to your folks, you're probably also disobeying them and will break curfew and only pretend to go to your harp lessons and forget to feed the pet goldfish (hey, is it really your responsibility?). And when that happens, the fish dies and you'll flush it down the toilet and buy another one so your parents won't figure out the first one died. But when you don't feed the new fish, it dies. So you flush it down the toilet. And this goes on and on and on until the city sewer has an abnormal amount of goldfish floating in the system. And when the evening news picks up the story, your mom casually asks over dinner, "Honey, don't you think it's odd that there are so many dead goldfish in our city's sewage plant?" And since you've fallen into the nasty habit of lying, you'll get really defensive and probably lie again, "Hey! I always wanted a horse anyway. If you'd have just given me a *horse* for Christmas instead of a *fish*, we wouldn't even have this problem. I mean, who could ever flush a horse down the toilet? Not that I know anything about pets going down the toilet . . . but . . ." (See what lies people get into? After a while, NOTHING makes sense!)

So go ahead. Just determine to be a young man or woman of truth. Build a trustworthy reputation so people know that you're a person of your word. Let them know that you mean what you say. And if you blow it? Instead of lying, try asking others for forgiveness. They'll think even *more* of you! And your trustworthy reputation will continue to soar.

Three Tight Buds

Jesus placed great value on friendships during his time on earth. He knows how important friends are. They're the spice of life. They make our victories worth celebrating, and they help make our defeats bearable. We gain perspective, loyalty, and camaraderie from our friends. Yet even the best of friendships are often tested through tough times. If the bonds of love are strong enough, the difficult times make the friendship even deeper.

Three guys who knew this all too well were Shadrach, Meshach, and Abednego. They were Jewish teens who were deported from their hometown to the city of Babylon under the rule of King Nebuchadnezzar. They were tight. They'd been through a lot together. But as close as they were, they didn't allow their friendship to come before God's ultimate place of authority in their lives.

It's often easy to let our friends creep into the number one spot in our lives. We usually don't do this intentionally, but ever so gradually they become more important to us than our relationship with Christ. If God is to be LORD of our lives, he must always be our top priority—even higher than friends, family, and dating relationships.

It's been said that during times of turmoil, our true character surfaces. The same can be said about our friendships. With Shadrach, Meshach, and Abednego, their friendship faced a crucial moment of truth. Although they had been accused of being disloyal to King Nebuchadnezzar because they refused to worship his statue, they stood true to God and to each other when faced with the threat of being tossed into a fiery furnace.

It would have been easy for them to renounce their faith, save their friendship, and continue to enjoy each other's company. But because their friendship was centered on their deep bond with God, they chose not to compromise. They stood tall while those around them bowed low. They placed their trust—and their lives—in the hands of God. They were ready to die for the Lord!

You probably know the rest of the story: They were thrown into a fiery furnace, but God sent his angel to protect and save them from death. What an incredible victory! And what solid, God-centered friendships!

Know It!

God wants you to have friendships, but he wants to be the center of those relationships. When your friendships are founded on him, they're not only stronger . . . they're eternal. There's a lot of strength in godly friendships! It's important to stand with our Christian friends with whom we share convictions. But it's also important to evaluate our friendships from time to time. Are you placing more importance on your pals than on Christ?

Read It!

Daniel 1–3.

Pray It!

Ask God's help in choosing close friends. Seek to make a strong foundation in him as your common denominator.

Are You Serious?

Know It!
God will never call you stupid or laugh at you for doing something ridiculous. He loves you more than you can imagine, and he wants to make your life better by enabling you to fulfill your greatest potential.

Read It!
Proverbs 3:5-6; 10:17-25

Pray It!
Seek God's forgiveness for trying to work things out on your own. Thank him for having the answers ahead of time for each trial you'll encounter.

In October 2000, a ranger for the Yellowstone National Park noticed a crowd of people, cars, and trucks gathered closely together to view a nearby bear. As he approached the crowd, he noticed a woman smearing something all over her little boy's face.

When the ranger approached her, he asked what she was doing. She stopped smearing the substance on the boy's face momentarily to answer the ranger's question. "I'm putting honey on him."

The ranger, still confused, asked why she was coating her son's face with honey.

Her response? "I want to take a photo of the bear licking it off his face!"

Fortunately, the ranger put an end to the woman's photographic dream and sent her on her way.

It's easy to read this true story and think, *Wow! She was certainly a couple of sandwiches short of a full picnic!*

But before you start to think she's an isolated case, read on.

A man who was drunk and out of cash stopped at a gas station in Ionia, Michigan, and demanded that the two service station attendants hand over their cash. When they refused, the drunk threatened to call the cops on them! The attendants could see the robber was extremely intoxicated and stood their ground, refusing to give him any money. The robber, obviously not thinking clearly, called the police and waited for them to arrive at the gas station.

As the police approached the scene, the drunk complained that the attendants wouldn't give him cash, and of course, he was immediately arrested!

We have no trouble agreeing how ridiculous these stories are, yet it's often much harder to admit how ridiculous it is for us to take matters into our own hands instead of allowing God complete control.

Think about it: Any time you try to "fix" something in your own strength, you are operating with an incomplete roll of film! God doesn't ask you to figure it out, make it work, fix it, or control it. He asks you to give it up, lay it down, place it in his hands. And even though we probably look stupid from his perspective, he loves us so much, he continues to see the good in us. He sees your potential and all you can be in his power.

Can You Believe *This*?

Check out these bizarre true stories from travel agents!

- I had someone ask for an aisle seat on the plane so her hair wouldn't get messed up by being near the window.
- I received a call from a man who asked, "Is it possible to see England from Canada?" I said, "No." He said, "But they look so close on the map!"
- Another man called and asked if he could rent a car in Dallas. When I pulled up the reservation, I noticed he only had a one-hour layover in Dallas. When I asked him why he wanted to rent a car, he said, "I heard the Dallas airport is huge, and I'm thinking I'll probably need a car to drive between the gates to save time."
- A nice woman just called our office. She needed to know how it was possible that her flight from Detroit left at 8:20 A.M. and arrived in Chicago at 8:33 A.M.

  I tried to explain that Michigan was an hour ahead of Illinois, but she couldn't understand the concept of time zones. Finally I told her that the plane just went very fast. She believed me.
- A woman called and said, "I need to fly to Pepsi-Cola on one of those computer planes." I asked if she meant to fly to Pensacola on a commuter plane. She said, "Yeah, whatever."
- A woman called to make reservations. "I want to go from Chicago to Hippopotamus, New York," she said.

  The agent said, "Are you sure that's the name of the town?"

  "Yes. What flights do you have?" replied the customer.

  After some searching, the agent came back with, "I'm sorry, ma'am. I've looked up every airport code in the country and can't find a Hippopotamus anywhere."

  The customer retorted, "Oh, don't be silly. Everyone knows where it is. Check your map!"

  The agent scoured a map of the state of New York and finally asked, "You don't mean Buffalo, do you?"

  "That's it!" she said. "I knew it was a big animal!"

Know It!

God is the source of all wisdom, and he wants to help you become wise. Instead of blurting out what you *think* or *assume* is correct, ask him to help you seek his truth before you announce your opinion, belief, or viewpoint.

Read It!

Proverbs 1–3

Pray It!

Ask God to forgive you for the times you speak without thinking. Instead of simply blurting out an incorrect viewpoint, ask him to teach you his wisdom and to help you think and evaluate before you speak.

I've Had It!

Know It!
Bullies are tough to categorize. A bully may be outgoing and aggressive—the kind who gets her way through force or obvious teasing. On the other hand, a bully can appear reserved on the surface, but may try to manipulate people in more subtle, deceptive ways, like anonymously starting a damaging rumor about someone just to see what happens. But all bullies are focused on themselves and struggling with insecurity.

Read It!
2 Corinthians 4:7-9; 1 Peter 5:10-11

Pray It!
Tell God how you feel when you're being bullied. Now ask for his help in seeing that person through his eyes.

"Nate! How's it goin'?" Pastor Steve asked after youth group.

"Okay, I guess."

"You don't sound too convincing. What gives?"

"I feel stupid even telling someone this, but I'm totally fed up with this guy in my gym class," Nate admitted. "Okay, so I'm short. And scrawny. And so I've had some physical problems and a few surgeries. I know I'm not as strong or tall or athletic or cool as the other guys. But I'm okay with it."

"You seem pretty confident to me, Nate," Pastor Steve said.

"I'm okay with it, but Conner's not. And I've had it! I mean, I finally think I understand why some kids bring a gun to school and threaten to use it! I'm so angry I could spit!"

"Okay, so spit! But you and I both know a gun is never the answer. So keep talking, Nate."

"I feel like such a kid saying all this. I'm 16! It's not like I'm trying to hide from the big kid on the playground. But you know—in a way, it is kinda like that. This guy harasses me in PE; when he sees me in the hall, he knocks my books outta my hands; he shoves me into my locker; he hides my clothes when I'm taking a shower after gym; he trips me; he cusses me out—"

"Why?"

"I think it's just because I'm small and have a few physical problems."

"Nate, you're being bullied. And when we think of bullies, we tend to think of kids on a playground—as you said. But really . . . bullying continues to happen throughout our entire lives."

"You're kidding!"

"Nope. Just yesterday, a guy cut me off when I was trying to change lanes. And if that wasn't enough, he rolled down his window, cussed me out, and made an obscene gesture at me! He's an angry man full of rage. And that's what's going on with Conner. He's angry, insecure, and wants to exert power. And unfortunately, it's always easier to feel more powerful with someone who's smaller, weaker, younger, or nicer. That's why he's picking on you, Nate."

"So what do I do?"

"Let's spend some time praying for Conner," Pastor Steve said.

"Nate, let's think about Conner for a second. Most people who bully others are trying to make themselves feel more confident or powerful. So they put someone else down. Do you see any insecurities in Conner?" Pastor Steve asked.

"Well, I never thought about it till now, but teachers are usually yelling at him for something. And I've heard a few kids call him stupid."

"Maybe his grades are low. Who knows? He may have a reading problem or a learning disability that prevents him from catching on as quickly as other students.

"And Nate, sometimes people become bullies because they've been bullied by others. We don't know what Conner's home life is like. Maybe he's been abused."

"Yeah, I never thought about that," Nate said.

"Okay, so you're being bullied. I know it's frustrating, but it's not the end of the world. Let's create a strategy," Pastor Steve suggested. "In fact, let's get it down on paper."

Bravin' a Bully

- *It's okay to be a tattletale.* Even if you've already shared the situation with one adult, if that person doesn't help you, share it with someone else.
- *Walk away.* It may seem like a coward's response to ignore the bully and leave, but it's really not. Bullies thrive on the reaction they get, and if you walk away, the message is that you just don't care. Sooner or later, the bully will probably get bored with trying to bother you.
- *Be confident.* Walk tall and hold your head high. Use your body language to show that you're not vulnerable.
- *Try humor.* If you can learn to laugh at yourself, you won't give the bully the response he's looking for.
- *Avoid violence.* Don't use physical force. Violence never solves a problem, and you can't be sure of what the bully will do in response.

Know It!

Research shows that 30 percent of sixth- through tenth-graders are involved in bullying at school. Don't be a statistic. If you're being bullied, do something about it. Seek help and ask God for direction. Most people who bully are lonelier than most teens and don't have good relationships with their peers. Pray for them, and ask God to use you to be a positive influence for them.

Also, think carefully about the way you interact with others. Could the things you say or do—even if you mean it as teasing—be interpreted as bullying? If so, apologize to that person and make a commitment to treat everyone with respect.

Read It!

Matthew 5:39; Colossians 4:2; Hebrews 12:14-16; 1 John 3:18

Pray It!

Ask God to give you compassion for the people in your life who give you a hard time. Tell him you realize he died for them, too.

Thinking Ahead about Temptation

Know It!
God will not allow you to be tempted beyond what you can bear. When you're in the middle of fighting temptation, don't fight it alone—seek his help!

Read It!
1 Corinthians 10:13; Hebrews 12:1-4

Pray It!
If you're giving in to temptation more than you'd like to admit . . . go ahead and admit it to God right now. Ask for his strength not to yield to temptation.

No one's immune. Every Christian who has ever lived has faced temptation. Before we go any further, it's important to remember that being tempted isn't a sin. It's when we act on temptation—when we give in to it—it becomes sin.

Sometimes temptation may seem so strong, you find yourself wondering if you can truly be victorious. You can win the battle of temptation! The Bible gives us a clear pathway to freedom. Let's take a peek at some specific things you can do:

1. *Predetermine Your Pattern of Temptation*
Do you realize that you have a unique fingerprint, palm print, voice print, and heartbeat? It's true! There are patterns in your life representative only of you. Temptation works in a similar way. There are some things that entice you; others don't. Satan knows exactly what your areas of temptation are. Do you?

If you can identify the specific things that tempt you, you can become proactive. In other words, you can make wise choices to prevent giving in to temptation. If you're not sure in which areas you're vulnerable, ask these questions to find out:

- *When am I most tempted?* Is there a certain time of day or day of the week that you're most tempted? Is it while you're home alone, at night, in the afternoon? Nail down the time.
- *Where am I most tempted?* Is it when you're standing next to the magazine rack, sitting in front of a computer, in the kitchen, in your bedroom? Discern the place of your temptation.
- *Who's with me when I'm most tempted?* Which friends am I with? Is it when I'm alone? In a crowd of strangers? Identify who.
- *What temporary benefit do I receive when I give in?* Think about it: If sin was never fun, you'd never give in! The Bible tells us that sin is fun for a season. But it's always temporary and short-lived. So you may get a kick out of it, but there's a huge kickback. The fun doesn't go on. Try to figure out why you continually give in instead of resist. Is it relief? Is it exhilaration?
- *How do I feel right before I'm tempted?* Are you frustrated? Feeling unloved? Physically exhausted? Mentally drained? Worried? Are you lonely?

Answering the above questions will help you understand the pattern of temptation in your life.

No Footholds

Let's continue with our victory plan to win the battle of temptation:

2. *Protect the Condition of Your Heart*
Ever heard the phrase "garbage in/garbage out"? It's true that whatever we allow to collect in our heart will affect everything we do! So what condition is *your* heart in? The psalmist asked God to *search* his heart—to see if there was anything that displeased God—and to help him surrender it. God will do the same for you, if you'll ask him.

You see, the HEART affects everything you do. It's the holding tank for your emotions and feelings. The condition of your heart will determine your ability to withstand temptation. So be certain your heart is truly and totally in God's hands.

We're told in Ephesians not to give the devil a foothold. What does that mean? Satan has the ability to carve out the tiniest space in your life. It's unnoticeable at first. But he holds on so he can eventually grab more and more. That's what a foothold is. If an alligator bites someone's foot and can hold on long enough, he'll eventually have the entire person.

When soldiers want to take possession of an island, their strategy is to first get a beachhead—an area on shore that's secured to make way for safe landing of more troops and supplies. After they have control of the beachhead, they push and push until finally the entire island is theirs.

Know this: All Satan wants right now is a tiny foothold in your life. And how does he get a foothold? Any negative emotion can be a start. It may be a tiny portion of your heart. But two or three tiny portions make you an easy target. Frustration in itself won't do you in. But frustration, worry, and anger all together becomes a powerful combination, and it sets you up for temptation.

Know It!

Guard your heart! Protect it as you would a gold mine—because it really is! Don't allow negative thoughts and bitter feelings to collect there. Like the psalmist, approach God and ask him to search your heart. There's no one who can help you protect it better than the One who created it!

Read It!

Psalms 9:1; 19:14;
Proverbs 4:23;
Ephesians 4:26-27

Pray It!

Confess the negative feelings, bitterness, and grudges you've held. Tell God that you don't want your heart simply to become a holding tank for things that can give Satan a foothold. Ask God for a pure heart—one that belongs totally to him.

Letting It Go

Know It!
You'll never be the person God wants you to be by holding on to sin in your life. So go ahead. Release it. Give up that grudge. Give him your anger. Be willing to walk away from your hurt. Quit living in the past. Let go of your failures. Allow him to help you become all he wants you to be!

Read It!
Psalm 50:15;
Matthew 26:41;
Hebrews 4:14-16;
James 1:14-15

Pray It!
Tell God that you're realizing your area of weakness is not giving him your temptations immediately. When something enters your mind that shouldn't be there, seek his help to surrender it quickly!

Let's do a quick recap! To win the battle over temptation:

1. *Predetermine Your Pattern of Temptation*
2. *Protect the Condition of Your Heart*
3. *Pray for God's Help!*

Prayer gives you an inner strength to overcome. We're told in Matthew 26:41 that the consequence of not praying is that temptation will overpower us!

Prayer is the strongest defense you have against temptation. It's your ammunition in the battle! Throughout the Bible, we're shown time after time how God definitely answers prayer: Shadrach, Meshach, and Abednego in the fiery furnace; Daniel in the lions' den; Jonah in the whale. God provides help when you call on him. So when you're tempted, PRAY! Hebrews 4:15-16 tells us that he not only *understands* your temptation, he's already been *through* your temptation!

Repeat: he knows and understands what you're going through! Hebrews 4:15 says he was tempted "in every way, just as we are." He was tempted to hold a grudge. He was tempted sexually. He was tempted to disobey. He was tempted to take the easy way out. He was tempted to get ahead and exert his power and gossip and get angry for the wrong reasons. But he overcame temptation . . . and so can you!

Sometimes we don't pray because we're not sure we want to end the battle! If you talk to him about your anger, you can't continue to be angry. He'll ask you to release it. He's going to tell you to forgive. He'll want to bring healing to your heart.

4. *Point Your Attention Elsewhere*

Temptation always begins in the mind . . . with a thought. It never begins with an action. The very moment a tempting thought enters your mind, give it to God. Pray. Read Scripture. Doing this automatically points your attention in the opposite direction of temptation. Realize that whatever gets your attention gets *you*!

The more you think about something, the stronger a grip it has on your life. When you're upset, you think about it. And the longer you turn it over in your mind, the more upset you become. Next thing you know, you're not simply upset, you're angry! So instead of focusing on the temptation, switch your concentration to WWJD (What Would Jesus Do?). And what *would* Jesus do? He'd pray. It's hard to hold a grudge against someone when you're praying for him!

To divert your attention away from temptation, it's important to know the different stages of temptation:

- *Attention* (This involves what you see, hear, think about, and read.)
- *Arousal* (Your emotions kick in at this stage. You begin to play out the tempting thought and action in your mind.)
- *Action* (This is the final stage of temptation—the point where you give in. This is when temptation actually becomes sin.)

The key to winning temptation is not to fight it. *Hey, wait a sec,* you're probably thinking. *Whaddya mean, not fight it?*

Fighting temptation isn't scriptural. The Bible never tells us to fight temptation. It always tells us to FLEE it! We're told to resist the devil, but we're told to flee temptation. And again, we're able to flee it by capturing the tempting thought and giving it immediately to Christ.

The power of Jesus Christ is able to transform you. His power can actually renew your mind and make you holy. Therefore, it simply makes good sense to surrender to the power and authority of the Holy Spirit.

You can't control what temptations pop into your mind, but you *can* control how you react—what you do with the temptation.

5. *Participate in a Small Group*

Accountability is a great piece of ammunition in fighting the battle of temptation. It helps to have godly Christians praying for us and even asking us about the weak and vulnerable areas in our lives. We're reminded in Ecclesiastes that we need each other. But often times we don't want support or accountability. It's much easier to simply rationalize and say, "Next time I won't give in" than to actually make yourself vulner-able to others about your weak areas.

"Next time I won't give in" isn't a solid plan! You need to do more than simply hope to do better the next time around. You need the indwelling power of the Holy Spirit. The most spiritually mature people are those who allow themselves to be held accountable. They're willing to be asked hard questions, and they submit themselves to the Holy Spirit's leading.

Know It!

No one is exempt from temptation, but God can empower you to overcome! You *can* win the battle. Are you willing to become accountable to other Christians? Will you allow the Holy Spirit to have complete control of your life?

Read It!

Ecclesiastes 4:9-10;
1 Corinthians 10:13;
James 5:16

Pray It!

Tell God that you know you can't be victorious in the battle of temptation without his help. Right now would be a great time to surrender ALL to him. Pledge to make yourself accountable to other Christians and to give his Holy Spirit supreme control in your life.

Quiz Time

Know It!

You don't serve a God of frustration; you serve a God of promise and victory. He doesn't say, "Run from temptation, and I'll check up on you next week to see how you're doing." He promises that he'll be *with* you and empower you and equip you to be victorious *over* temptation.

Read It!

Hebrews 13:5; James 4:7-8

Pray It!

Tell God that you want to be a victorious Christian—not a defeated one. Ask him to give you a hunger for his Word and to help you thirst for him.

*To **predetermine** your areas of temptation means to know*
a. how long your temptation will last.
b. when, where, and with whom you're most tempted.
c. that you'll be tempted.

*The **Bible** tells us that sin is*
a. contained in a hot-fudge sundae.
b. okay if you're lonely.
c. fun for a season.

*Giving the devil a **foothold** means*
a. he knows your shoe size.
b. he has control of a small area of your life.
c. Satan will cripple your feet.

*The Bible tells us the **consequence** of not praying is*
a. that we'll be overcome by temptation.
b. that we'll have to go to the dentist more often.
c. that we won't recognize temptation.

*Jesus truly **knows and understands** what you're going through because*
a. he read the book.
b. he wrote the book.
c. he, too, was tempted.

*Temptation **always** begins*
a. on a date.
b. in the mind.
c. in Texas.

*The **stages** of temptation*
a. are contagious.
b. are action, regret, guilt.
c. are attention, arousal, action.

*The key to **winning** the battle of temptation*
a. is to fight it as hard as you can.
b. is not to fight it.
c. is always to have music on.

*The **most spiritually mature** people are those*
a. who allow themselves to be held accountable.
b. who never miss church.
c. who can quote an entire chapter of the Bible.

This or That?

Life is full of choices. Take a few seconds to decide between the following:

Would you rather

a. do three push-ups every time someone older speaks to you OR

b. do three sit-ups every time someone younger speaks to you?

Would you rather

a. be three feet tall OR

b. be ten feet tall?

Would you rather

a. remind people of the latest pop music/dance star when they see you OR

b. reflect the character of Jesus Christ when they're around you?

Again, life is full of choices! You make hundreds every single day—many without even thinking twice. For instance, you probably don't spend a lot of time choosing between Captain Crunch or Honeycomb when getting your breakfast. You may not think twice about climbing into the shower or the tub, or whether to apply deodorant. We make several choices so quickly, they really don't even seem like choices.

But there is a choice you make every day that does deserve some thought and attention. And that's the choice of clothing you wear. Modesty may not be a hot topic, but reflecting Jesus Christ will always be a hot topic with your Creator. And one of the best ways to do that (or to fail at it) is in how you dress.

Mind if we get a little personal? Guys, when you're not wearing a shirt in the summer, is there a reason for it? If you're mowing the lawn, working out, or swimming, it makes a lot of sense not to have a shirt on. But are there other times you're not wearing a shirt simply to catch the attention of the opposite sex? Is there a reason to make sure everyone can see the waistband on your underwear by wearing your pants so low?

Girls, how low is that spaghetti-strap shirt cut? How much of your tummy does it show? What message are you sending when you wear this specific piece of clothing? Are your shorts so short that someone can see up your legs when you sit cross-legged on the ground?

If you knew you planted impure thoughts in someone's mind because of your attire, wouldn't it be worth praying about?

Know It!

God wants you to look and feel your best, but he also wants you to take the responsibility of how you dress *seriously.*

Read It!

1 Corinthians 12:22-23.

Pray It!

Ask God to help you spend more time thinking about and evaluating what you wear. Tell him you truly want to reflect his holy character in how you look.

What God Hates

Though we tend to think of God as a God of love, we're clearly told in the book of Proverbs that there are seven things he hates. Know what tops the list? Haughtiness. It means DISDAINFUL PRIDE. And *disdainful* means to feel scornful; as if someone or something is beneath you. Arrogance, self-exaltation, conceit, loftiness–all these words describe what it means to be haughty.

And we're told that God hates haughtiness. Wow. Pretty strong, huh? He doesn't just dislike it. More than simply disgusting him, pride (or haughtiness) brings forth the emotion of hate in a God of love. Wanna tick God off? Act with pride. Be haughty. Treat others as though they're beneath you. Be full of yourself.

What's the big deal about being prideful? Well, wounded pride makes us want to lash out (Numbers 22:29). Pride causes us to want and seek recognition (Judges 8:1-3). Pride causes us to take too much of the credit (Judges 15:14-17). Haughtiness makes us want to take credit for the deeds of others (1 Samuel 13:3-4). A haughty spirit is what caused the death of Absalom (2 Samuel 17:11). Pride leads to corruption (2 Chronicles 26:15-16).

Prejudice grows out of pride (Esther 3:5-6). God's presence is not compatible with a haughty attitude (Psalm 138:6). There's even a link between pride and sexual sin (Proverbs 2:16-17). It's the ingredient in every argument (Proverbs 13:10). Satan attacks us in our areas of pride (Matthew 4:1, 4). It affects our values (Mark 9:34).

Pride can be a barrier to believing in and accepting Christ (Mark 6:5, John 5:45). Oftentimes, haughtiness is a result of wealth (Mark 10:17-23). It blinds us to our faults (Ephesians 2:11-13), and it affects our relationships (1 Peter 5:5).

Know It!

But can't pride sometimes be good? Pride sometimes can; haughtiness can't. Since we're using the two words interchangeably, you can find out if your pride is selfish or good by checking out Romans 15:17. What are you proud about? And by the way, haughtiness vanishes when we realize who we are in relation to who Jesus is (John 1:26-27). God hates haughtiness. It's disdainful, ruins friendships, and separates you from knowing true spiritual intimacy.

Read It!

All the Scriptures cited in today's devotional.

Pray It!

Tell God that you don't want to exhibit anything that saddens or angers him. Seek his forgiveness for a prideful spirit and haughty attitudes. Ask him to help you to see others—not as being beneath you—but as valued people he chose to die for.

The next thing on God's hate list from Proverbs 6:16-19, is lying. We know the definition all too well, don't we? Lying is purposefully deceiving. Not being honest. Skirting the truth.

Based on the above description, let's take a little quiz about lying, okay?

Which of the following statements in the given situations are lies?

1. Your curfew is midnight. You come in at 12:30 A.M. The next morning at breakfast, Dad says, "Did you come in late last night?" Your response: "Are you kidding? I know what a big deal curfew is!"
2. You totally spaced on the homework assignment. Your teacher asks, "Did you complete the assignment?" You respond, "I forgot to bring it with me."
3. Your coach has mandated that during track season no one is to consume any caffeine. You scarfed down two chocolate bars after lunch. Your coach looks you in the eye before the meet and says, "Have you had any caffeine?" Your response? "Coach, I haven't had a Coke or coffee since the season began!"

You might classify the above as "white" lies. But if a lie means to deceive, there are no white lies. Notice when God lists lying in Proverbs 6:17, he doesn't say he hates black, brown, and gray lies but overlooks white, orange, and yellow ones. When it comes to being dishonest, there are no colors! Dishonesty is dishonesty, plain and simple.

Throughout Scripture, history shows us time and again that when people tried to deceive God, it always backfired. We can't hide the truth from the One who knows all. God desires . . . and ever yearns for your honesty!

If lying and deceit cause our loving heavenly Father to hate it, it must be a big deal. Let's take a closer look.

Dishonesty dulls our sense of right versus wrong (1 Samuel 15:10-14) and is destructive to the church (Acts 5:1-11). God hates lying (Proverbs 20:23). Dishonesty only compounds our problems (Genesis 12:10-20). It's dangerous to unity (Ephesians 4:25) and is forbidden by God (Exodus 20:16).

People sometimes lie to make themselves look good (2 Chronicles 18:5-15). And sometimes lying is caused by fear (Genesis 18:15).

Know It!

Lying is like digging a hole and burying yourself in it. After you've told one lie, you usually have to tell another one to cover it up. And then another one. And another. As you do, the hole you're burying yourself in simply gets deeper and deeper. Deceit and dishonesty act as a bondage that keeps you from becoming intimate with God. Ask him to free you from the bondage of deceit.

Read It!

All the Scriptures cited in today's devotional.

Pray It!

If you sometimes struggle with honesty, admit that to him right now. Tell him you now realize that a lie is a lie in his eyes and that you don't want to be deceptive any longer. Ask his help to be as honest and truthful as he is.

Is Murder *Always* Bad?

Know It!

Of course, there's more than one way to commit murder. (Flip back to May 25-28 and reread those devotions on murder.) We can murder someone's reputation, kill his character, and slay his name. Those things make God angry, too! He hates anything connected with murder, because it removes a life he created and died for.

Read It!

All the Scriptures cited in today's devotional.

Pray It!

Tell God that you've killed some people by the words you've used. Seek his forgiveness. Tell him you don't want anything to do with murder—physical, emotional, or verbal. Ask him to help you glorify him with your life.

Guess what's next on God's hate list—murder! We're not told these items are in any specific order, and I believe God hates one just as much as he hates all of them. So it really doesn't matter if murder is number one on the list or number seven. The real issue is that it's on the list! And even though it's listed as third from the top, we're told God hates it with a passion.

We'd probably all agree that a drive-by shoot-to-kill is insane and wrong. But is murder always wrong? For instance, if we know ahead of time that an unborn baby will have birth defects, is it wrong to end his life before he enters the world?

In *The Living Bible,* it's interesting to note that murder on God's hate list is termed as "hands that shed innocent blood." That leads us to believe that whether a baby is inside the womb or outside the womb, it's an innocent being. To abort that life would be to "shed innocent blood."

Abortion has been a hot debate for years, and the issue just keeps getting hotter. The most frequent argument from those who support abortion is that until the baby is outside of the womb, it's not really a life. Yet we're told in Psalm 139 that God knew us when we were being conceived! He looked upon us as life at the very moment a sperm fertilized an egg. And since we know the embryo's heart starts beating just days after conception, fingerprints are formed, and DNA develops—all before birth—we know that life inside the womb is still life.

To abort—to murder that innocent life—makes God angry. He hates it! That life means no less to him if it's deformed; he still died for it. And there are literally thousands of people standing in line waiting to adopt healthy and unhealthy children. Who are we to decide when a life will end? God hates it when we make that decision our responsibility. It's not our responsibility, and it never will be!

Let's take a closer look at murder as discussed in Scripture. Cain committed the first murder (Genesis 4:8-10). We're capable of murder in our hearts (Matthew 5:21-22). See Genesis 9:5-6 on why murder is wrong.

We'd expect God to hate evil, so it should come as no surprise to find it on the list of seven things he hates. The New International Version phrases it as "a heart that devises wicked schemes." Osama Bin Laden viewed his September 11, 2001 plan as a religious justification, but God saw it for what it was—100 percent evil. To plot and scheme evil of any kind angers the King of kings!

Let's take a closer look. Evil is defined as "something that brings sorrow, distress, or calamity. The fact of suffering. Not good morally. Arising from bad character or conduct."

Ready for another quiz? Which of these statements are characteristic of evil?

1. Jayme and Nick are both running for student body president. You've been friends with Nick since kindergarten, and you know he'd be a great leader. You want Nick to win the election so badly, you devise a scheme that will cause students to question Jayme's character.
2. Terry really hurt your feelings when your dating relationship ended. You can't stop thinking about it. You talk your best friend into helping you get even. You'll show Terry!

Evil, anger, and deceit almost always go together. It's impossible to plot an evil scheme that God is proud of. He hates all kinds of evil.

After I spoke at a youth retreat, a high school girl approached me and said, "I'm a Christian, but I love Satan." When I asked her to explain, she said, "I think it's a sin to hate anyone and anything, therefore I refuse to hate Satan. I have hope that someday he'll change his mind, accept Jesus as his Savior, and spend eternity in heaven."

We can't love God and evil both. We must love one and hate the other. God is extremely bold about hating evil, and he wants us to hate evil as well. And if we claim we have feelings for evil other than hate, we haven't totally surrendered to Jesus Christ. Evil hung Christ on the cross. It was part of God's plan, and love caused him to stay there, but evil was responsible for his torture. Evil separates families, dissolves friendships, and can cause us to spend forever in an eternal environment of evil—hell itself. The cure for evil? Forgiveness from Jesus Christ.

Know It!
We were all born with evil hearts, but God wants to transform our hearts and replace the evil nature with his Holy Spirit. The evidence of our evil nature plays itself out in bitterness, jealousy, anger, wrong motives, and plotting to harm others. But the evidence of being filled with God's Holy Spirit reflects joy, peace, self-discipline, and love.

Read It!
Romans 6:6-8, 11-14; 12:1-2; Galatians 5:19-23

Pray It!
Be honest with God and tell him that you sometimes struggle with the temptation to do evil. Ask him to help you remember that temptation itself isn't a sin, but that acting on temptation is. Ask God to transform your heart to be more like his.

Be Careful, Little Hands

Know It!
Destroy evil in your life (Numbers 33:50-53). There is no evil too great for repentance (1 Kings 21:28-29), but you must admit your evil potential (Psalm 51:3). For guidance on how to pray to God about evil, see 1 Chronicles 4:10 or Matthew 6:9-13.

Read It!
All the Scriptures cited in today's devotional.

Pray It!
Tell God that you don't want to be associated with evil. Ask his help in teaching you to flee from evil. Seek his empowerment to walk away from temptation and to deepen your trust in him.

You may remember singing a little song as a child in Sunday school or Vacation Bible School that went something like this:

"Be careful, little hands, what you do. Be careful, little hands, what you do." There were a few more lines to the song, but each verse used a different word:

"Be careful, little feet, where you go."

"Be careful, little mouth, what you say."

"Be careful, little eyes, what you see."

We have a huge responsibility to refrain from evil. The good news is that God doesn't expect us to do that alone. He wants to fill our lives with his Spirit and enable our hands, feet, eyes, ears, and mouth to glorify him.

The next item on God's hate list is an "eagerness to do wrong" (TLB) or "feet that are quick to rush into evil" (NIV). So God not only hates evil, but he also hates an eagerness or excitement about doing evil. Understand the connection? We don't commit acts of evil dragging our feet. When we do evil, it's because we've decided to act in an evil way.

Let's take a closer peek at evil. Without God, you are capable of any evil (Judges 21:25). It's wrong to return evil with evil (Genesis 34:1-31). All of the occult is rooted in evil (Leviticus 19:31). Holiness separates us from evil (Leviticus 11:44-45). People usually slip into an evil lifestyle gradually (Numbers 33:55-56).

God doesn't want us to become curious about evil practices (Deuteronomy 12:29-31). We're never alone in our battle against evil (Psalm 12:1), and we can't get away with evil forever (Psalm 37:1-2). Evil acts begin with evil desires (Psalm 141:4), and planning evil is just as bad as doing evil (Proverbs 24:8).

A small amount of evil can affect many (Matthew 16:5-12). The church won't shelter you from evil (Luke 4:33-34), and there are powerful evil forces at work against us (Ephesians 6:12).

A False Witness

Isn't it interesting how the seven things that God hates all intertwine with each other? The next item on the list is "bearing false witness." This is connected with lying. And lying is connected with evil, which is connected with an eagerness to do evil. Murder is evil, and so is a haughty, prideful spirit.

Could one reason for God's hatred of these seven things be that once we've adapted one of them to our lifestyle, it's only a matter of time before we embrace the others? Can one even exist for an extended amount of time without the others?

Ted Bundy, a noted serial killer who probably murdered more than 100 women, admitted before his death sentence was carried out that he had become addicted to pornography as a teen. Sex crimes and porn often go hand in hand. Statistics show that men who commit sex crimes have also been exposed to porn.

Could it also be said that someone who's a habitual liar will eventually be led to other evil habits?

It's against the law to give a false testimony in court. It's called perjury. One can go to jail for committing this crime. Is it any wonder that God hates it? A false witness is a lie. And again, lies–hiding the truth–have a foundation of evil.

God's Word gives us several warnings about falsehood. We're told not to give a false testimony (Exodus 20:16), not to spread false reports (Exodus 23:1), and to have nothing to do with a false charge (Exodus 23:7).

On June 19, we looked at passages that tell us to hate evil. The proof of that is found in Proverbs 13:5. We see that a false witness is deceitful in Proverbs 14:25, we're assured that a false witness won't go unpunished in Proverbs 19:5 and 19:9.

Matthew 7:15 commands us to watch out for false prophets, and Matthew 15:19 advises us to be on guard against theft, false testimony, and slander.

In 1 Peter 2:1 we see grave consequences for those who teach false doctrines.

Know It!

God hates lies, and obviously he hates a false witness or testimony. Will you make time to evaluate your testimony? Is it genuine? Do you truly reflect the character of God? Or are your actions, conversations, and lifestyle a false witness of the King of kings?

Read It!

All the Scriptures cited in today's devotional.

Pray It!

Tell Jesus that you don't want to be a false witness, a false Christian, or be taken in by false prophets. Ask for his wisdom and discernment to know truth and to live your life by it.

Wanna Fight about It?

Know It!

God calls us to be peacemakers. Yes, there's a time to speak out in boldness—but those times usually need to be reserved for speaking against immorality, injustice, or evil. When taste or personal opinion is at play, it's best to quietly make your thoughts known but to remain unified when others don't agree.

Read It!

Psalm 34:14; Proverbs 12:20; Romans 12:17-18; James 3:17-18

Pray It!

Ask God to help you develop a lifestyle of peacemaking and not an argumentative spirit.

The last item on God's hate list (Proverbs 6:16-19) is to cause dissension . . . to sow discord among brothers. In other words, God hates it when we pick a fight. Some folks thrive on conflict so much that if there's *not* a conflict, they'll create one!

Well, God hates that. He despises it when we purposely stir things up just to get an argument going. And people who thrive on that are usually insecure. Talking loudly, quarreling with those around them, and enjoying the heat of an argument makes them feel powerful.

Now, God's not talking about debate. Nor is he against being a lawyer or arguing a court case. This last item on his hate list is about Christians stirring up trouble with other Christians in the church.

"United we stand; divided we fall." It's really true. The body of Christ has to be united to grow and thrive. The entire purpose of the body is to glorify God and bring others to him. As soon as we start arguing, quarreling, and causing dissension among the believers, the church is in danger of splitting or completely falling apart.

So does that mean we have to agree with everyone in our church? No. But we need to understand the difference between disagreeing and being united. We can disagree and still be as one. Someone who thrives on looking for something he knows will stir everyone up, however, is someone who's sowing discord. And God hates that.

Let's imagine your church has voted on building an addition to its already-existing complex. There are 25 of you on the building committee that will decide issues such as size of addition, color of carpet, expenses, etc. Imagine that 20 people on the committee feel strongly that the carpet should be forest green. You and four others really want beige, but the five of you decide to vote for green simply because you understand the importance of being united.

That doesn't mean you agree with the color choice. It's not your pick, but you'll go along with it because you're determined not to be a stumbling block to the process as a whole. That's spiritual maturity.

But if you were to leave the meeting and talk others in the church into being on your side, you'd be sowing discord. That's spiritual immaturity.

Checkin' Out . . . Forever

JUNE 23

Sure hope Ashley's in her dorm room, Jamie thought. *I need a good chat with my cousin right now!* She flipped on the computer and logged on.

Jamie17: Hey, Ash! I need to talk.
20ash: What's up, Cuz?
Jamie17: Ashley, it's terrible. This kid at my school—Troy—he committed suicide. He shot himself.
20ash: Oh, Jamie! I'm so sorry.
Jamie17: The whole school's in shock.
20ash: Did you know him?
Jamie17: Yeah. I didn't know him real well, but we had math together.
20ash: Does anyone have any idea why he did it?
Jamie17: Well . . . not exactly. But he did leave a note.
20ash: Do you know what it said?
Jamie17: Something about he just couldn't go on, and he was sorry.
20ash: Wow. That's hard to accept.
Jamie17: Ashley, I think he was a Christian. I know what church he went to, and I saw him lead the team in prayer once before a football game.
20ash: Hmmm. That's interesting.
Jamie17: So . . . if he really was a Christian . . . do you think he went to heaven?
20ash: Wow. That's a tough question, Ash. And it's one thousands of others have asked over the years.
Jamie17: So what's the answer? Can you go to heaven if you commit suicide?
20ash: We discussed this just last week in Bible class. My professor had some interesting things to say.
Jamie17: Well, fill me in!
20ash: First of all, we've gotta remember that God hates murder, and he's extremely clear when he says, "Thou shalt not kill."
Jamie17: Yeah, but maybe that's talking about killing someone else.
20ash: Second, we need to remember that when someone takes his life, it means he's usurping God's role. It's as if he's saying, "God, I don't trust you to know what's best for my life. I'm going to take your place and determine when I'll quit living." Jamie, none of us have the right to make that decision.

Know It!

God understands confusion and irrational thinking. If you ever struggle with desperate thoughts that concern suicide, talk to your heavenly Father, and talk with a trusted adult. DON'T push those thoughts inside. Let your parents, your youth pastor, or a counselor help you deal with them!

Read It!

Exodus 20:13;
Proverbs 28:17;
1 Timothy 1:8-9

Pray It!

Ask God to help you be sensitive to those around you who may be confused, despairing, and searching. Think about it: you have what they need! So seek his help in sharing Christ with them. Ask for the right words and the right timing.

Suicide . . . Not an Option!

Know It!

When we take the place of God's authority in our lives, we're sinning. Make time to evaluate your own relationship with Christ. Where do you stand? Is everything in order? Is he truly Lord?

Read It!

Proverbs 7:1-4; 28:14; Jeremiah 10:6-7; John 11:26-27

Pray It!

Ask God to keep you from getting wrapped up in issues that you don't need to be involved in. Seek more faith to simply trust in him and to keep your spiritual life in order. Tell him that you don't ever want to take his place in your heart.

Jamie17: Yeah, I realize that someone who commits suicide is basically playing God in his life. But if someone's desperate enough to take his life, he's not thinking straight, right?

20ash: That's true. And I believe God understands an unbalanced mind. But again, taking a life—whether it's your own or someone else's—is sin.

Jamie17: Yeah, I agree with that. Murder is sin. But what about the question? Can a Christian who commits suicide go to heaven?

20ash: Look at it this way, Jamie: We can be grateful God understands an unbalanced mind and irrational thinking. You and I can't imagine what would be so bad that we'd wanna end our life because of it.

Jamie17: No kidding!

20ash: But at the same time, when someone takes his life, he's sinning. So this makes me question the sincerity of Troy's faith. It seems as though someone who chooses suicide lacks faith in God's omnipotence and providence.

Jamie17: So the answer is . . . ?

20ash: I know this isn't what you wanna hear . . . but I don't know the answer. I do know this, however. It's too big of a risk to take. To assume the role of God is sin. I'm glad I don't have to judge.

Jamie17: Me, too.

20ash: God knows each heart. He understands the hurt, the depth of the pain, and the irrational thinking. But at the same time, he expects Christians to follow his commands.

Jamie17: Yeah, I see both sides.

20ash: The issue really isn't that we need to know if Troy went to heaven. That's between him and God. Our priority is to make sure our own lives are in order and that we don't take such a huge risk ourselves.

Jamie17: Yeah, that makes sense, Ashley. Thanks for listening.

20ash: I'm really sorry, Jamie. But it makes you think twice about how valuable life is, doesn't it?

Jamie17: Sure does! And it makes me wanna evaluate my spiritual life—just to make sure everything's in order.

20ash: I think that's exactly what Jesus would want you to do right now.

Jamie17: Hey, hurry up and finish summer school and come home. I miss you!

Dear Diary:

Okay, it's about this Christianity stuff. I'm a good person! I've gone to church all my life. My parents go to church. I got a Bible in Vacation Bible School the summer after my second-grade year.

But this Sunday, Pastor Steve said something I can't forget. He goes, "God has no grandchildren."

Now I like Pastor Steve. I think he's a great youth pastor. He's always shown up at my B-ball games, and I know he cares about us. But I think he's missed the boat this time around.

What's he talking about? "God has no grandchildren"??? I can't stop thinking about that. And that's why I'm so ticked off right now. I want that phrase outta my head. "God has no grandchildren."

Hey, God loves everybody. We're all one big happy family, right? That's what I've always believed. And since I go to church, read my Bible every now and then, and do stuff with the youth group, I figure I'm part of the "family."

"God has no grandchildren."

"God has no grandchildren."

"God has no grandchildren."

Sigh. I'm really tired.

Till next time, Diary. (And you know that could be a while, right?)

No one makes it into heaven on his parents' relationship with Christ. Each and every Christian has to have his very own, intimate, personal, growing relationship with Jesus. The fact that "God has no grandchildren" means you aren't a Christian simply because your friends and family are. God only has children—not extended family or relatives.

If you've never asked Christ to forgive your sins and come into your heart, you're not a Christian. You may be a good person doing good things, and you may even read your Bible on a regular basis. But Christianity is all about having an actual relationship with the living King of kings.

Know It!

You can be a part of God's family right now! Eternal life with Jesus is a gift—and it's free for the asking.

Read It!

Romans 3:22-26; Revelation 3:20

Pray It!

Admit to Jesus that you're a sinner. Tell him you're sorry for trying to run your own life, and ask him to forgive your sins. Pledge that from this very day, your life will no longer be your own. Commit that your life is in his hands to be done with as he wills.

All because of Hollywood

Know It!
Christianity can handle every doubt and question you toss its way, or it wouldn't have lasted more than 2,000 years. It's okay to doubt, as long as you give those doubts to God and let him replace them with solid faith.

Read It!
Psalm 19;
Ecclesiastes 3:11; 12:13-14;
Matthew 4:10

Pray It!
Ask God to help you know beyond all doubt that Christianity is genuine and true. Ask for courage to "dial the number" and check it out for yourself. Seek his guidance on your search for truth.

What if we had to learn everything we know from TV and movies? If that were the case, then we'd automatically assume the following is true:

- All phone numbers in America begin with 555.
- All grocery shopping bags have at least one stick of French bread in them.
- When paying for a taxi, there's no need to look at your wallet as you take out a bill. Just grab one at random and give it to the driver. It will always be the exact fare.
- Anyone waking from a nightmare will bolt upright in bed and pant.
- Even when driving on a perfectly straight road, it's necessary to turn the steering wheel vigorously from left to right every few seconds.
- The Eiffel Tower can be seen from any window in Paris.
- All bombs are fitted with electronic timing devices with large red readouts so you know exactly when they're going to explode.
- Any lock can be picked with a credit card or a paper clip in seconds . . . unless it's the door to a burning building with a child trapped inside.
- It's always possible to park directly outside the building you want to enter.
- Cars that crash will almost always burst into flames.

If Hollywood were our only teacher, we'd have a false view of life, wouldn't we? Maybe we'd never know a phone number doesn't actually begin with the digits 555 until we tried to place a call starting with those numbers. (The entertainment industry decided to use 555 as the beginning digits for all phone numbers several years ago, because viewers were memorizing the phone numbers actors used during filming and calling them. No actual phone numbers in the U.S. begin with 555.) We'd know the truth, however, after trying to make a call and not getting through.

What about Christianity? Can we assume it's the embodiment of truth? Have you tried "dialing the number"? If you've actually tried it, you know it's not a fairy tale or a myth. You recognize it as truth. But if you've never "dialed the number," go ahead. Do a little research. Compare it with other world beliefs and see how it stacks up.

More things we'd assume were true if Hollywood were our only teacher:

- TV news bulletins always contain a story that affects you personally at that precise moment.
- Anyone can land a plane if there's someone in the control tower to talk the person down.
- There are no light switches in kitchens. When entering a kitchen at night, you should open the fridge door and use that light instead.
- A detective can only solve a case after he's been suspended from duty.
- It doesn't matter if you're heavily outnumbered in a fight involving martial arts. Your enemies will wait patiently to attack you one by one by dancing around in a threatening manner until you've knocked out their predecessors.

Again, we'd assume the above was true . . . unless we actually tried and failed . . . or did our own research. Instead of simply assuming Christianity is true, let's see how it stacks up against other world religions.

Buddhism
View of Christ: He was a good teacher, but he wasn't divine or as important as Buddha. There is no personal God.
How Can One Be Saved? The original teachings of Buddha say you're the only one who can save yourself, through controlling your actions, speech, and thoughts. But Mahayana (another form of Buddhism) teaches there are many savior gods called *Bodhitsattvas.* The Bodhitsattvas can be called on to help you achieve nirvana (the highest degree of God-consciousness that involves denying oneself of desire).
View of Sin: Sin is lust. The way to get rid of lustful desires is by working really hard at it or by relying on Bodhitsattvas.
Life after Death: Buddhists believe in reincarnation, and that people can be reborn as an animal, a demon, a human, or a god.

Christianity
View of Christ: He's the Son of God and died for man's sin. God is personal, omniscient, and omnipotent.
How Can One Be Saved? You can be saved by placing your faith in Jesus Christ and seeking his forgiveness for your sins.
View of Sin: All have sinned, but Christ will forgive our sin and transform us through the power of the Holy Spirit.
Life after Death: Everyone spends eternity in heaven or hell.

Know It!
Does Christianity seem simple when stacked next to Buddhism? It is!

Read It!
Matthew 19:26;
John 1:29-34;
Acts 4:8-12;
Romans 5:6-8;
Ephesians 2:8-10

Pray It!
Tell God how grateful you are that you don't have to try to earn salvation.

Christianity vs. Hinduism

Know It!
One major difference between Christianity and all other world religions is that Jesus Christ—the One whom Christians follow—left an empty tomb. The leaders of all other religions are still in their graves. Christians serve a living God. Believers of other religions serve a dead man.

Read It!
Matthew 28:18-19; John 1:1, 14; 14:6; Hebrews 9:27-28; 1 John 5:11-12

Pray It!
Ask God to help you reach out to those whose religious beliefs differ from yours. Tell him you desire to show your friends that he truly is the Way, the Truth, and the Life.

Since we're taking a closer look at how Christianity stacks up against other religions, let's take a peek at the comparison with Hinduism.

Hinduism
The Soul: Hinduism teaches that the soul is uncreated and eternal. It's also perfect, free, and unlimited. No matter how many lives it takes, eventually each soul will reach its divine nature.
Reincarnation: A person's actions from his past lives determine his identity and status in the next life. This is due to karma, which is a law of retribution and justice.
View of Christ: Hindus don't believe in a personal, loving God. They believe instead, in Brahma–an abstract eternal being with no attributes who was the beginning of all things. They don't believe that Jesus is God, but they have hundreds of deities.
View of Sin: Sin is referred to as "illusion." Hindus seek deliverance from it through the endless cycle of death and rebirth, and through union with Brahma, which is achieved through meditation, self-control, good works, and devotion.
Salvation: Achieved through works. Brahma–the Hindus' god–is found by seeking within one's self, because everyone is part god.

Christianity
The Soul: The Bible teaches that all people are created by God.
Reincarnation: Each of us has only one life to live. We die and face judgment.
View of Christ: He's the Son of God and died for man's sin. God is personal, omniscient, and omnipotent.
View of Sin: Sin leads to eternal separation from God. But we can have forgiveness of our sins, if we confess, repent, and allow God to be the authority of our life (one life–not many).
Salvation: Is not achieved through good works but by faith in Jesus Christ. Christians believe people can't earn salvation; neither do they deserve it. But because God loves people so much, he offers salvation as a free gift.

Other Contrasts:
Hinduism: We are all divine.
Christianity: We are all born in sin.
Hinduism: Promotes a rigid caste system (social hierarchy).
Christianity: Teaches that all people are equal and cherished in God's eyes.

Since the terrorist attacks on September 11, 2001, the interest in Islam has grown. People are curious about Muslim beliefs. Let's scoot a little closer for a clearer view.

Islam

View of Christ: He was only a prophet.

Sacred Scriptures: The Koran. This book of writing teaches that Allah is God, and God is one. There are no other "partners" to Allah, the way Jesus and the Holy Spirit are part of Jehovah God. The Koran teaches that Allah is impersonal. He is called by 99 different names, but "Father" is not one of them. The Koran also teaches that Jesus never died on the cross. The teaching says that Allah took Jesus to heaven before the crucifixion because a prophet of God wouldn't have had to face such torment. Islam promotes that either Simon of Cyrene (who carried the cross for Jesus when he fell) or Judas Iscariot were made up to look like Christ and died on the cross.

Judgment and Eternity: Allah will judge humanity, and each individual will be sent to either heaven or hell. Heaven is a place of sensual pleasure. Hell is where everyone else lives who opposed Allah and his prophet Muhammad.

Christianity

View of Christ: The only Son of God Almighty.

Sacred Scriptures: The Holy Bible. The Bible was inspired by God himself and written in obedience to his guidance. It teaches that God is the head of the Trinity–which is also comprised of Jesus Christ (God's Son) and the Holy Spirit. Though God existed before anything else, Jesus Christ and the Holy Spirit are part of God. The Bible teaches that Jesus actually died on the cross for our sins and rose from the dead three days later.

Judgment and Eternity: God will judge humanity, and each individual will spend eternity in either heaven or hell. Heaven is living with God forever in celebration, peace, joy, and praise. There will be no sickness and no death in heaven. Hell is eternal separation from God and is described in the Bible as a place of great torment. Everyone who has not accepted Jesus as his personal Savior will live forever in hell.

Know It!

Jehovah is a loving and personal God. He has several names and all of them are descriptive of his love and care for humanity.

Read It!

Psalm 77:11-15;
Isaiah 43:13;
Jeremiah 31:3;
John 1:12-14;
1 Corinthians 15:3-4;
1 Peter 3:18

Pray It!

Tell God how grateful you are for Christianity and the free gift of eternal life.

Christianity vs. Islam (Part 2)

Know It!
God is crazy about you! He loves you more than you can comprehend. And because of that love, he sent his only Son, Jesus Christ, to die for your sins. You can't earn it, and you don't deserve it. But you can accept it —for free!

Read It!
Matthew 17:5;
Luke 1:26-38;
John 10:30;
Colossians 1:15-17

Pray It!
Thank God for loving you more than you'll ever deserve or fully comprehend. Seek his help in loving him with your very life.

Let's continue with our comparative look at Christianity and Islam.

Islam

Sin: Muslims believe that people are born without sin. If they do sin, they can earn forgiveness to overcome their sins.

Salvation: To become a Muslim, one must publicly repeat "There is no god but Allah, and Muhammad is the prophet of Allah." One must also pray five times a day while kneeling and bowing toward the direction of the holy city, Mecca. Muslims must also give 2.5 percent of their earnings, called alms, to orphans, sick people, and widows. Muslims must fast an entire month during the ninth month of the Islamic lunar year, Ramadan. Food, sex, smoking, and drinking are all off-limits–but only during daylight. Muslims must also make a pilgrimage to Mecca at least once in their lives.

Holy Scripture: The Koran is only one of four books Muslims believe are God-inspired. The Torah (Genesis through Deuteronomy in our Bible), the Zabur, and the Injeel are also viewed as holy Scriptures.

Allah: Islam teaches that Allah doesn't love those who sin. Each human being has to earn his own salvation.

Christianity

Sin: Christians believe that all are born with sin and are separated from God until they accept forgiveness for their sins from Jesus Christ. Jesus then becomes the mediator between man and God.

Salvation: Christians accept forgiveness for one's sins through faith in Jesus Christ. After repentance, Christians then develop a relationship with Jesus. They pray often, but they don't have to pray a specific number of times a day. Christians pray not because they have to, but because they're in love with Christ and enjoy talking with him and listening to him. Sometimes Christians fast for a specific time, but it's not a requirement for salvation. When Christians fast, it's so they can focus more intently on a specific prayer request or facet of their lives.

Holy Scripture: Christians believe there is only one holy book of inspired words from God–the Holy Bible.

God: Christians believe that God loves man in the midst of his sin. And because of this great love, he provided forgiveness for sin through his only Son, Jesus.

Christianity vs. Jehovah's Witnesses

Maybe they've knocked on your door—a couple of well-dressed young men who want to tell you about God. Chances are they were Jehovah's Witnesses.

Jehovah's Witnesses

View of Christ's Return: They believe Christ was supposed to have returned in 1874. When he didn't, JWs moved the date to 1914, then 1918, 1920, and 1925. New dates were assigned to the years of 1975 and 1979. So many JWs were disillusioned by this time that approximately 750,000 left the church in 1979.

View of Jesus Christ: Christ is not God. He's God's Son, but he's inferior to God.

Who Goes to Heaven: Only 144,000 people will get to live in heaven with God for eternity. These are God's anointed. Earth will become paradise, and it's for all the other good people who simply weren't anointed.

View of Salvation: JWs believe that Christ's death (on a stake—not a cross) provides the chance for people to work for their salvation.

About Authority: JWs aren't allowed independent spiritual thinking. They must adhere to the decisions and scriptural understanding of the Watch Tower Society.

Man's Immortality: JWs claim that humans don't have immortal souls. When humans die, their spirit also dies.

More Facts About JWs:

- They don't believe in hell.
- They don't celebrate Christmas, Easter, Thanksgiving, or birthdays.
- They don't believe in the Trinity (Father, Son, Holy Spirit).

Christianity

View of Christ's Return: Christians believe that no one knows the time, day, or year when Christ will return except for God himself.

View of Jesus Christ: He is the Son of God and part of God. Christians believe Christ's words: "Anyone who has seen me has seen the Father" (John 14:9).

Who Goes to Heaven: All who have repented of their sin and accepted Christ as their Savior will spend eternity in heaven with God.

View of Salvation: Christians believe that Christ's death (on the cross) paid for all sins and that those who accept him as their personal Savior are forgiven by God's grace.

About Authority: Christians trust the Holy Spirit to guide them as they read the Scriptures and obey God—not man.

Man's Immortality: Man has an immortal, eternal soul that, at death, awaits judgment or goes to be with Christ.

Know It!

If you have accepted Christ as your personal Savior and are living according to his will, you'll spend eternity with him in heaven. If you choose not to accept Christ as your personal Savior, you'll spend eternity in hell—forever separated from God.

Read It!

Matthew 24:36;
John 14:9;
Romans 5:12-19;
2 Corinthians 5:8;
Philippians 1:22-23

Pray It!

Thank Jesus for how easy it is to become a Christian.

Christianity vs. Other Beliefs (Part 1)

Know It!
A mature Christian will know *what* he believes and *why* he believes it. For further study on Christianity and its differences with other religious beliefs, check out *Why So Many Gods,* K. Etue, general editor (Nelson Publishing) and *So What's the Difference?* by Fritz Ridenour (Regal Publishing).

Read It!
Isaiah 43:10; Malachi 3:6; Mark 7:14-23; Romans 5:12; 2 Timothy 3:16

Pray It!
Ask the Lord to keep you from being confused by other religious beliefs and to solidify and deepen your understanding of his holy Word.

Wicca–a popular subject matter for books, TV, and movies–is growing rapidly among teens who seek power and share a desire to get closer to nature. Casting spells and controlling nature is the big attraction to Wicca.

Wicca is grounded in reverence for planet Earth. It's a nature religion. Those who follow Wicca are called Wiccans or witches, and they practice some or all of the following: divination, magic, sorcery, psychic abilities, and spiritism (interaction with spirits–demons). Many involved in Wicca today claim they only practice "good magic."

Witches don't believe Jesus is God or that he created the universe. Most Wiccans believe that Christ was the great white witch. Christians believe that one of Jesus' names is Emmanuel, which means "God with us."

Wiccans believe everyone is divine in nature; Christians believe everyone was born with sin. Most witches believe in reincarnation; Christians believe we have one earthly life and will then spend eternity with God or without him.

Wiccans see sex as something to be enjoyed at any time with two consenting adults. Christians believe sex is a gift to be enjoyed between a man and wife in marriage only. Witches meet in groups called covens; Christians meet in groups called churches.

The code of conduct for Wiccans is: "An ye harm none, do as ye will." In other words, as long as you don't hurt yourself or others, do whatever you want. Christians believe in the Ten Commandments and living according to God's holy will. Christians only adhere to the Bible–the holy Word of God. Christians believe in the Trinity–God is one being with three distinct revealed personalities or parts.

Take a few minutes to examine your relationship with Christ. Are you vigorously working with the Holy Spirit to consistently become more like Christ? Is the Bible your standard for living? If so, you're headed in the right direction!

Actors Tom Cruise, John Travolta, and Jenna Elfman have made Scientology a popular religious belief. Scientologists believe that humans are spiritual beings and basically good. In simple terms, it's a self-help set of religious beliefs.

They believe there are eight channels to achieving eternal life. They also believe your mind and body are separate from your spiritual side. Your mind keeps track of all your past lives–including good, bad, and problems you weren't even aware you had. These repressed memories are viewed as *engrams*–spiritual blockages. The people who can help you find and understand these memories are called auditors. They believe, once you're rid of these blockages, you'll be more fulfilled.

Jesus is seen as only one of many good teachers. Your main goal in life is to understand yourself and others and to make the world a nicer place to live.

Christian Science is an entirely different religious belief than Scientology. It was founded in 1879 by Mary Baker Eddy, who claimed she was healed while reading Scripture. Actor Val Kilmer is a Christian Scientist. This group believes that people can't sin, Jesus wasn't God, and you become saved by believing sin doesn't exist. God isn't personal, but he's present in all things. God is all, and all is God. Heaven and hell aren't actual physical places; they're only an aspect of one's mental state. Christian Scientists don't believe in seeking a physician's help when ill.

The Unification church (also known as the Moonies, because this group was founded by Sun Myung Moon) believes the Bible has some truth in it, but it's not "the truth." The *Divine Principle,* by Rev. Sun Myung Moon, is believed to hold the absolute truth.

Moonies believe that people are physically and spiritually corrupt and are under Satan's rule. So how does one become saved? Well, because Jesus didn't marry before he died, he can only save man spiritually. But Rev. Moon, the Second Messiah, can save men physically. It's this physical redemption that will bring about the kingdom of heaven on earth.

Rev. Moon is the one who decides who you can marry, and at one time he performed a wedding ceremony for 6,516 couples at once.

Know It!

It's okay to know about other religions, but God wants you to be so grounded in his truth—the Bible—that you'll never be swayed to the false teachings found in other religions.

Read It!

Genesis 1:31; Matthew 7:22-23; Romans 3:10-23; 6:23

Pray It!

Spend some time thanking Christ for being the only way to heaven and for making the plan of salvation a simple one.

Bored with Nothing to Do?

Know It!
God has a million resources for a bored mind. He wants you to glorify him in all you do. Determine to make the most of your free time this summer.

Read It!
Psalm 119

Pray It!
Ask God to help you use your time productively and to enhance your creativity for his glory.

Know what the cool thing to do in Leyden, Italy, in the late 1600s was? Get all dressed up and take your friends to an anatomy theater to watch surgeons dissect corpses. The anatomy theater in Leyden, Italy had hundreds of seats for accommodating large crowds, and often still had standing-room only.

Okay, so maybe you're not into watching someone operate on a dead body. It's easy to get bored during the summer. Let's create a list of boredom-busters to jolt you out of the vacation-time blahs. I'll start you off; you finish the list.

- Read a biography.
- Write your own biography. (If it's about yourself, it'll be an autobiography; if it's about someone else, you better ask permission before you start writing.)
- Create a brand-new board game and send it to Milton Bradley.
- Plant a garden (veggies, flowers, fruit—your pick).
- Learn a new sport.
- Go to the library and get a book on a specific musical instrument you've always wanted to play. Rent the instrument and teach yourself.
- Invent a new color.
- Set up a backyard volleyball set and invite your friends over. After a couple of games, grab a deflated volleyball and fill it with helium. The ball won't fly away, but it will go higher and take longer to come down. After a few games of helium v-ball, place the sprinkler underneath the middle of the net. Switch sides and start a new game—in the water!
- If you have a dog, check into getting it certified as a "therapy dog" so you can take it to retirement centers and hospitals.
- Create the world's largest Popsicle, using a brand-new (and cleaned) trash can with a two-by-four in the middle for the stick. (You'll probably have to check with an ice company or restaurant with a huge freezer to freeze your creation.)
- Try to convince your youth group to help you break one of the records from the Guinness Book of World Records.
- Memorize an entire chapter from the Bible.
- Create your own Web site.
- Volunteer at your local library to read for children's story hour.
- Plan the perfect vacation—then start saving for it!

Inside Out or Outside In?

Cindy Jackson (no relation to Michael) has quite a record of elective plastic surgery. She's had 27 operations in nine years. No, she wasn't in an accident or born with any kind of disfigurement. She has had three full face-lifts, thigh liposuction, two nose jobs, abdomen work, breast reduction and augmentation, jawline surgery, knee work, and permanent makeup. Cindy has spent approximately $100,000 changing her looks and trying to feel better about herself.

Erik Sprague has spent 450 hours getting tattooed, has pierced several parts of his body, and has placed himself on a strict diet of bugs and pizza. He's also had his tongue surgically split to give a forked look and has had horned ridges implanted above his eyes. His teeth have been filed into fangs, and his tattoos are green to give him the appearance of a lizard. He calls himself Lizard Man and slithers around the country performing a live stomach-pumping routine on himself at various sideshows.

It's obvious that Erik Sprague and Cindy Jackson are determined to change who they are by altering their outer appearance. Too bad they've never heard that real change comes from the inside. Genuine change doesn't happen outside in. It always occurs inside out.

Once you've experienced a change on the inside, it will eventually be reflected on the outside. There's a legend about a popular clown named Grimaldi. Each night he brought laughter to hundreds of people who came to see his performances at the town circus. A physician had taken his family to see the show, and they were ecstatic. Their trip home was filled with laughter as they recalled what the clown had done on stage.

The next day, a stranger came to see the physician in his office. "Doctor, I need help," the man said. "I'm falling apart inside. I can't sleep, I have no reason to live, and I haven't laughed in months."

The physician quickly recommended the man attend that evening's circus performance. "It will do you wonders!" he said. "In fact, I'm making that my prescription for you. Go to the circus and be entertained by the wonderful Grimaldi. He'll make you forget your troubles as you laugh the night away."

The man left the physician's office even more devastated than when he entered . . . for you see, that man *was* Grimaldi!

Know It!

God dreams BIG dreams for you! He offers you a life of fulfillment, joy, and peace. And a smaller nose, bigger muscles, tattoos, jokes, laughter, or popularity won't bring happiness. Allow Christ to transform your heart and your mind. Those around you will definitely notice the difference!

Read It!

Proverbs 14:13; Romans 12:1-2; Ephesians 3:20-21; Philippians 4:6-7

Pray It!

Ask God to change you from the inside out. Seek his help in refusing to believe the lie that your worth comes from your outward appearance.

Checked or Carry-On?

Know It!
God wants your baggage. So go ahead—check it! Place it in his lap and experience victory as you run the course he has set for you.

Read It!
1 Corinthians 9:24-27; Galatians 5:7-9; Hebrews 12:1

Pray It!
Ask God to reveal any baggage in your life that you're holding on to. When he brings it to your mind, surrender it to him.

Airport customs agents have recently seized some interesting "luggage" from passengers.

At Chicago's O'Hare International Airport, an African passenger was detained because of what he had in his carry-on luggage: A monkey head and carcass on a stick.

In Malta, investigators stopped four men carrying the skins of 100 protected birds, including tooth eagles, eagle owls, and kingfishers.

From Costa Rica, officials nabbed 490 sea-turtle eggs, eight turtle flippers, and 30 pounds of smoked turtle meat.

In Melbourne, Australia, a man heading to Vienna was separated from his travel companions: 31 live Australian geckos, including 11 leaf-tail, 13 knob-tail, and seven beaked. (Wildlife export can bring up to 10 years in jail and/or a $110,000 fine.)

Most of us have no problem seeing all of the above as unnecessary luggage.

But lots of people carry unnecessary luggage to places other than airports. Some of your friends carry baggage on their dates, to their part-time jobs, and even to church. What about you?

Are you carrying some unnecessary baggage? If so, there's good news! You can check it. That's right. God wants you to check your baggage with him. No fines. No prison sentence. He's willing to take it so you can travel without being weighted down.

So how is your travel? In your walk with Christ, are you traveling freely and productively? Or are you hindered by baggage that's slowing you down? The apostle Paul compares the Christian life to a race. You wouldn't think of making your way to the starting block encumbered with ankle weights. If you wanted to win the race, you'd wear light shorts, light track shoes, and a lightweight shirt.

Serious male swimmers shave their legs, because they don't want to be slowed down even by a millisecond by the hair on their legs. A determined athlete does everything he can to eliminate anything that could prevent winning the competition.

What things are slowing you down and keeping you from becoming all God wants you to be? If you're trying to run the Christian race with carry-on baggage, you're not going to win. In tomorrow's devotional we'll talk about some types of baggage you might have.

Is Your Baggage Labeled?

Just as you'd never consider running a race while wearing an overcoat or entering a swimming event wearing sweats, hopefully you won't carry unnecessary baggage in your relationship with Christ. What kinds of luggage do Christians hold onto that affects their walk with Jesus?

Go through the following packing list and mark any items you may have in your baggage collection.

- ❑ Bundle of bitterness. Someone hurt you, and you're holding on to the hurt. It's packed deep inside your heart, and it's keeping you from experiencing the joy God wants you to have.
- ❑ Bag of anger. Something happened, and you're so angry you can't think straight. Instead of living out God's love, you're trapped within a cave of paralyzing anger.
- ❑ Box of jealousy. Someone else has what you want. You're feeling insecure and jealous. It's preventing you from sharing laughter, smiles, and happiness.
- ❑ Briefcase of inferiority. You're self-conscious about your weight, your face, your hair, your grades, etc. Instead of living with confidence, you're battling self-esteem issues and having trouble believing you're valuable.
- ❑ Bunches of unforgiveness. Let it go. You're right–it shouldn't have happened, but it did. Dad left the family. Someone broke up with you. Rumors were spread. Whatever the situation, you feel rejected . . . and you've become spiritually crippled because you haven't forgiven. Release it. (As in right now!)
- ❑ Batches of the past. You blew it. Failed big time. You feel terrible about it and have never gotten over it. If only you'd never . . . but you did, and you'd give anything in the world to walk without this cloud over your life. Guess what! God will gladly trade you the sun for your cloud. And his Sonshine is brighter than any other sun in the galaxy. Know that he's forgiven your past; he died for it. Accept his forgiveness and move on.

But I'm not sure what baggage you're carrying. God knows. So instead of trying to read the labels yourself, ask him to identify your baggage for you. And when he does? Thank him. Seek his forgiveness. And get rid of your luggage by checking it with him forever!

Know It!

God wants you to experience spiritual victory—not spiritual depression. You can be victorious and remain victorious by refusing to carry baggage that gets in the way of your relationship with him.

Read It!

Galatians 5:19-23; Colossians 3:1-5; 1 Thessalonians 4:1-5; 2 Peter 1:2-11

Pray It!

Ask God to remove anything in your life that's slowing you down in becoming all he wants for you.

That's Hard to Believe!

Know It!
None of us can be "good enough" to earn forgiveness for our sins. The payment is too high. That's why God paid it for you.

Read It!
Matthew 23:33; 25:31-46; John 12:48; Acts 10:42

Pray It!
Ask God to help you understand the reality of spending eternity in heaven or hell.

A few years ago Stella Liebeck from Albuquerque, New Mexico, spilled a cup of McDonald's coffee in her lap. She claimed the coffee was so hot it caused her undue physical pain, and she sued McDonald's. She won the suit and became an instant millionaire.

Ever since that publicized lawsuit, attorneys decided to begin the annual "Stella" awards—giving recognition to the most outlandish lawsuits of the year. Check out the following candidates:

- June 1998: Nineteen-year-old Carl Truman of Los Angeles won $74,000 and medical expenses when his neighbor ran over Carl's hand with a Honda Accord. Carl apparently didn't notice there was someone at the wheel of the Honda when he was trying to steal his neighbor's hubcaps.
- January 2000: Kathleen Robertson of Austin, Texas, was awarded $780,000 by a jury after breaking her ankle tripping over a toddler who was running wild inside a furniture store. The store's owners were surprised at the verdict since the misbehaving little boy was Kathleen's own son.

Though all of the above accounts are true, you may be thinking, *That's really hard to believe!* It may also be hard to believe that not all good people will go to heaven. Even harder to believe is that good people will spend eternity in hell.

But God is crystal-clear about who will spend eternity with him and who won't. Good people are fun! And nice. And considerate. And cool. So why would a loving God really send good people to hell?

The answer: He doesn't. Good people send themselves to hell. God loves good people—as well as bad people—so incredibly much that he gave himself (in the form of his only Son, Jesus Christ) to die a horrendous, excruciating death. Why? Because the punishment for sin is death (see Romans 6:23). Since we've all sinned, we're all doomed to die. Unless . . . someone else would volunteer to take our place on death row.

That someone was Jesus Christ. He died so you wouldn't have to. If you want to accept him as your Lord and Savior and live according to his will, you'll get to spend eternity in heaven with him. If you choose *not* to seek forgiveness for your sins and to ignore Christ, you'll spend forever in hell after you die—even if you're a good person.

Are You Really Listening?

During their formative years, children sometimes hear phrases from popular songs incorrectly. Do any of the following sound familiar?

- "Olive, the other reindeer . . ."
- "Oh beautiful, for spaceship guys . . ."
- "He is exhausted; the King is exhausted on high . . ."
- "On the first day of Christmas, my tulip gave to me . . ."

It's understandable why children would misunderstand the above phrases. If a child hasn't yet learned to read, all he has to rely on for learning is his hearing. As we get older, we learn by reading and hearing. Still, we often listen with one ear and don't truly hear what's being said.

In our relationship with Christ, it's important that we read his love letter to us (the Bible), and that we listen with both ears, our heart, and our mind. If we fail to listen to God's leading in our lives, we soon find ourselves living in disobedience to him.

The Bible tells us that one quick way to measure our love for Christ is to examine our obedience to him. If we really love him, we'll obey him. And to obey him requires listening very carefully.

Do you remember the story of Samuel? He was a young boy living with Eli, an elderly priest. One night after Samuel had gone to bed, he was awakened by a voice calling his name. He rushed into Eli's room, asking what the priest wanted. But Eli said he hadn't called Samuel, so Samuel assumed he must have dreamed it.

After he crawled back into bed and fell asleep, he was again awakened by a voice calling, "Samuel!" The boy rushed back to Eli's side only to learn that Eli had also been asleep and hadn't called him. This happened a third time. The priest was a wise man, though, and he knew Samuel had been anointed by God. So he instructed the boy that if he heard the voice again, he should respond with these words: "Yes, Lord, your servant is listening."

Sure enough, Samuel was awakened again by the voice. He knew it was God and responded in obedience.

Are you hearing God's voice when he speaks to you? Or, like a child, are you confusing God's conversation with bits and pieces of the world's conversation around you?

Know It!

God has important stuff to tell you. So make time to read some of his letter to you on a daily basis. You'll hear his voice through Scripture, and you'll also hear his voice through your prayers, your spiritual leaders (pastor, Sunday school teacher, youth minister, parents), and your heart.

Read It!

1 Samuel 3;
John 14:15, 23-24; 15:10

Pray It!

Ask God for sensitive spiritual ears to hear and recognize his voice. And as you hear his voice, commit to responding in immediate obedience to what he says.

What Kind of Tator Are You?

Know It!

God wants to use *you* to be a positive influence at your school, in your community, at your part-time job, in your family. He can do BIG things through a willing spirit. Are you willing to forget sitting on the sidelines? Ready to hang up a critical spirit? Will you be a "Sweet Tator"?

Read It!

Proverbs 17:22; Romans 15:5; Philippians 2:1-2; Colossians 3:14

Pray It!

Tell God you're willing to be molded in his image. Allow him to break you and reshape you . . . into a "Sweet Tator"!

If we compared human nature to vegetables—potatoes in particular—we might be able to categorize people this way:

- People who are bossy and enjoy telling others what to do but don't do much work themselves are called "Dick Tators."
- And there are always a few people who say they'll help. They *intend* to get involved. But they never actually get around to doing anything. They're called "Hezzie Tators."
- Some people seem to love conflict. If there's not any current controversy happening, they'll create something! They're called "Aggie Tators."
- Other people never seem motivated to get involved. They're content to simply watch while others do the work. They're called "Speck Tators."
- Some people try to act like someone they're not by putting on a front. They're called "Emma Tators."
- Some people never actually offer a helping hand, but they constantly find fault with how others do things. They're called "Comment Tators."
- And then there are the people who are really genuine. They're willing to get involved. They help others in need. They make a conscious effort to be a positive influence on those around them. They're called "Sweet Tators."

Which kind of tator are you? Are you known for having a critical spirit, or do people truly enjoy being around you? Think about that person everyone loves hanging out with. Chances are, that person knows how to make others feel good about themselves. He is an encourager and affirms others easily. That person isn't a troublemaker; rather, he enjoys bringing unity and consensus to problems and tense situations. No wonder everyone loves being around him. This person is a "Sweet Tator"!

The Bible talks a lot about unity. Interestingly, the apostle Paul tells us in Galatians 5:9 that it only takes one wrong person to affect an entire group. God doesn't spread a spirit of discord and argument. Instead, he is the Author of peace and harmony. Think about your reputation. Are you known as a peacemaker? Someone who enjoys people and has a positive attitude? Or do others see you as a complainer, one who doesn't keep his word, or someone who's trying to be something he's not?

Undercover Christian?

The first time we meet Nicodemus is when the Scriptures show him coming to Jesus at night. Nick was a Pharisee, which means he was one of the respected religious leaders of Israel. Jesus didn't have a lot of good things to say about this specific group of people who seemed more concerned about keeping petty man-made rules than they were about genuine worship.

The Pharisees were the ones always questioning the people Jesus healed. When they noticed the paralyzed man by the pool (John 5) had been healed, they didn't rejoice in his healing. They were angry because he was carrying his mat—which qualified as "working on the Sabbath"—and demanded to know who gave him permission to do that!

The Pharisees talked the talk, but they didn't walk the walk. In other words, they quoted Scripture, dressed nicely, and went to church, but they weren't genuinely concerned with the well-being of those who were less fortunate.

Nick was one of these guys. So it's really no surprise that he came to Jesus during the night when no one would see him. He knew a lot was at stake. He'd heard Jesus preach, seen his miracles, and believed he truly was who he claimed to be—the Messiah.

The Bible doesn't tell us exactly when Nicodemus committed his life to Christ, but if we study the Scriptures we can see definite signs of spiritual growth. The next time we see Nicodemus in Scripture, he was part of a group of chief priests and Pharisees trying to decide how to get rid of Jesus. Nicodemus stuck his neck out and spoke for justice. Even though he was ignored, it took boldness for him to speak out. Quite a difference from when he approached Christ during the night!

The last time Nicodemus is shown in Scripture is after Jesus has been crucified. Nicodemus, along with Joseph of Arimathea, took a huge risk and asked if he could give Jesus a proper burial in a special tomb. Nicodemus was no longer an undercover Christian. His spiritual boldness was shining brightly.

Though Nick began as a shy Christian afraid to be known for his association with Christ, he definitely made great spiritual strides. God isn't concerned with how *fast* you grow spiritually. But he *does* want to produce steady growth in your relationship with him.

Know It!

Make time to evaluate your own spiritual growth. Are you growing steadily in Christ, or are you simply standing still? A Christian who stands still for an extended period of time is in danger of falling backward in his relationship with Christ.

Read It!

John 3:1-21; 7:5-52; 19:30-40

Pray It!

Tell God you want to grow closer to him. Ask him to deepen your faith and to help you become more bold in your witness.

He Knew All the Words

Know It!
Head knowledge is great, but it won't get you into the kingdom of God. You need heart knowledge to have eternal life with Christ.

Read It!
Luke 1:77; Acts 4:12; Romans 1:16; 2 Corinthians 7:10

Pray It!
Ask God to help you evaluate your relationship with him. Are you where you need to be spiritually? Or are you merely "talking the talk" without "walking the walk"?

When Nicodemus came to talk with Jesus at night, he wanted more information on being a Christian. Actually, the term "Christian" wasn't in use yet; it was coined after Jesus died and the church was organized. But Jesus spoke boldly and publicly about the necessity of being born again and experiencing the forgiveness of sins.

As a Pharisee—an important religious leader—Nicodemus thought he'd heard it all. He knew the Scriptures. He obeyed the rules. He went to the temple regularly. He gave offerings and was a kind and considerate man. Yet, as Jesus spoke about eternal life, Nicodemus realized he was missing something.

So he made an appointment to talk with Jesus. He wanted more information. Jesus told him that in order to enter heaven—to gain eternal life—he would need to be born again. Nicodemus didn't get it. He asked Jesus how it would be possible for a grown man to become a baby again and be born of his mother a second time.

But Jesus wasn't talking about a physical rebirth. He was talking about a spiritual birth. Though Nicodemus knew a lot about God, he didn't actually know God personally. Jesus was telling Nicodemus that he needed to come to God in humility, admit his need for a Savior, and seek forgiveness for his sins.

Nicodemus finally understood and became a follower of Christ. Though it was slow, his lifestyle eventually began to reflect his newfound faith. What about you? Do you actually have a personal, growing relationship with the creator of the universe? Or do you simply know a lot about him? It can become easy to settle into a good reputation and develop a good habit of church attendance. But if that's all our Christianity consists of, we're lacking a great deal!

What's Missing?

The following announcements were found in church bulletins.

- Miss Charlene Mason sang "I Will Not Pass This Way Again," giving much pleasure to the congregation.
- Ladies, don't forget the rummage sale. It's a chance to get rid of those things not worth keeping around the house. Don't forget your husbands.
- The sermon this morning: "Jesus Walks on the Water." The sermon tonight: "Searching for Jesus."
- For those of you who have children and don't know it, we have a nursery downstairs.
- Potluck supper Sunday at 5 P.M. Prayer and medication to follow.

Isn't it interesting how misplaced or missing punctuation, spelling errors, or a simple rewording of a sentence can change the entire meaning? It's obvious that something's missing in the above statements. But what may *not* be so obvious is what's missing in your relationship with Christ.

If Christianity is starting to feel boring to you, or if you think something may be lacking, it may be time to take a spiritual examination. Answer the following questions:

1. Do I have a daily quiet time with my Savior?
2. Am I involved in church and plugged into a youth group?
3. Am I growing in a Bible study?
4. Is Jesus Christ as real to me as my hands and feet?
5. Do I know the sound of God's voice?

If you can't answer yes to all of the above questions, you may need to get more serious about the time you spend with God. If you've never disciplined yourself to having a daily devotional time with God, now's the time to make some changes! Let's take the next few days and chat more in-depth about how to establish a quiet time.

Know It!

Jesus Christ holds all the treasures of wisdom and knowledge. Does that sound like something you need? If you'll make time to meet with him on a daily basis—have fellowship with him, learn from him, and allow him to guide you—he'll share that wisdom and knowledge with you!

Read It!

Colossians 2:3;
1 Thessalonians 3:12-13;
Titus 3:14; 1 Peter 3:12

Pray It!

Ask God to share his wisdom and knowledge with you, and let him know how excited you are about meeting with him on a daily basis.

Meeting with God 101

Know It!
God wants to help you develop strong spiritual muscles. But that's hard to do without having a consistent spiritual workout. Reading your Bible daily, reading a devotional book (like this one!) daily, and spending time in prayer will help you develop a strong spiritual physique.

Read It!
Psalm 107; Mark 1:35; Hebrews 6:12; 2 Peter 1:5-9

Pray It!
Tell God about your desire to grow spiritually stronger and ask him to help you carry through on your pledge to spend daily time with him.

Imagine that computer genius and billionaire Bill Gates said he wanted to meet with you tomorrow morning at 6:30. Chances are, you'd clear your schedule, set your alarm a little early, and show up. Why? Because Bill Gates is important. You'd *want* to meet with him. You'd care about what he had to say.

The King of kings is much more important than any human! And he has incredible things to say to you. He wants to meet with you every single day. And the best part? He doesn't want to do all the talking; he wants you to take an active part in the conversation!

Knowing that God really wants to meet with you on a daily basis *should* make you excited! If not, maybe it's because you're afraid to get close with him or are juggling too many other things. Having a personal quiet time (some people call this devotions) is really important. It's *so* important that it's almost impossible to grow spiritually stronger without it.

If you've never disciplined yourself for a daily time with God, let's create a strategy that will help you get started.

#1: Make a pledge. Decide that your quiet time with God will be a daily priority, and tell him so. Be aware that as soon as you make this pledge, you'll probably find yourself thinking, *As soon as this TV show is over, I'll have my quiet time.* Or *When I've finished e-mailing friends, I'll begin my quiet time.* Part of your pledge to have a daily quiet time should include the decision to avoid these kinds of excuses.

#2: Make a plan. Deciding to have a quiet time is great, but you need a practical plan to turn your good intentions into action. This is where your plan comes in! Set aside a specific time each day to spend time with God. Lots of people like to do this in the morning, because it helps them get a jump start on their day. Others like to do it in the evening so they can review their day with God.

Decide what time works best for you, and then decide on a specific place to have it. Jot these two decisions on a sheet of notebook paper and put it inside your Bible so you'll have it as a constant reminder.

Finding the Time

Okay, you've decided you want to grow closer to Christ, so you've made a commitment to spend time with him daily. You've even come up with a plan that includes when and where you'll carry out that pledge. But what happens if you miss a day? Do you throw in the towel? No. To succeed, you've gotta keep on keeping on!

What happens if you miss lunch one day? Do you quit eating lunch altogether? No. If you miss your quiet time one day, pick it up the next day and keep going! The more consistent you become at having a daily quiet time with God, the easier it will be and the more you'll start to depend on it. You eventually get to the point where you truly miss it if you don't spend time with God every day.

If you do skip your quiet time, stop and think about why you didn't have it. Was it too hard to get up early? Are you going to bed early enough the night before? Is there anything you need to change in your daily schedule to better accommodate your quiet time? If it's too hard to get out of bed, put one foot on the floor and go from there!

Or if you know you're not a morning person and wouldn't understand a thing you read even if you did get up when your alarm went off at 6 A.M., consider rescheduling your devotions for another time that works better: right after school or right before bed, for example.

Realize that some quiet times will be more meaningful than others. Don't expect every single quiet time to be a spiritual high. Try to recruit a couple of prayer partners who will encourage you and hold you accountable. Determine to be honest with them. When you miss a day, let them know.

The Bible shows us that Jesus spent time with his heavenly Father. He sought strength, fellowship, and guidance from God. If Jesus Christ, who was God, needed time with the Father, how much more do you need time with him? Through your daily quiet time with God, you'll become more like Christ as you follow his example and as you receive his power through prayer and the Bible.

To talk with God, you have to believe he's present even though you can't see him the way you see your parents and friends. Faith isn't hoping that God will listen and speak with you; it's trusting that he's real and available for conversation.

Know It!

Check your attitudes, your motivation, and your relationships. If your prayer life is weakened by a problem in one of these areas, pray about that problem and correct it with God's help.

Read It!

Proverbs 15:8; Acts 1:14; Ephesians 6:18; Hebrews 11:6

Pray It!

Tell God about your desire to maintain a daily, disciplined time with him. Ask for his help in putting that into action. Also seek his guidance in finding a couple of prayer partners who can hold you accountable in this area.

Learning to Pray

Know It!

Have you ever known a spiritual giant? Someone who was really strong in his faith? Guess what—your public strength is gained in your private moments with God! So take your pledge of having a daily devotional time with the Lord seriously. Exciting things happen when you pray.

Read It!

Isaiah 40:31;
Acts 16:22-33;
Ephesians 6:18;
2 Thessalonians 1:3

Pray It!

Tell God how you want to be successful in having a daily quiet time with him. Seek his help in implementing these strategies into your daily routine.

Now that you've created a strategy for having a daily quiet time with God, what should you do during that time? Let's divide your quiet time into two parts and go from there.

Part One: Listening to God

Start your devotional time by reading Scripture. The book of Proverbs is a great place to start. There are 31 chapters—one for each day of the month! As you begin reading, ask God to bring to your mind any examples to follow, commands to obey, sins to confess, promises to claim, or new thoughts about God. You may want to use a small notebook to keep track of what you learn as God speaks to you through your Bible reading.

Part Two: Talking to God

As you talk to God on a daily basis, strive to cover these five areas in your conversation with him: *praise, confession, thanksgiving, intercession, petition.* Praise is very similar to thanksgiving—but there IS a difference! To praise God means to adore him for who he is—his character. Thanksgiving is thanking God for what he's done—his actions. When you praise God, you're showing love to him. When you express thanksgiving, you're showing God how grateful you are.

A. *Praise:* Begin your prayer time by praising God. "I love you, Father. I praise you for being all-knowing."

B. *Confession:* Ask God to bring to your mind any sins that you haven't confessed. Ask him if there's anything in your life that's standing between you and him. Whatever he brings to your attention, confess and commit to him. Seek his help to avoid these areas of weakness in the future. Accept his forgiveness.

C. *Thanksgiving:* Be specific as you express your gratitude to God. "Father, thanks for helping me do well on today's science quiz. I'm so grateful you helped me reach out to Staci."

D. *Intercession:* To intercede for someone means to pray for them, to go to God on their behalf. Tell God about specific needs of your friends and family members.

E. *Petition:* Pray for your own needs. What should you pray for? Your spiritual growth, your needs, the desires of your heart—anything that concerns you! Remember, your heavenly Father cares about everything you care about!

Touchdown!

Drew lived alone with his mother, and he cared for her like she was a queen. When Drew entered high school, he went out for the football team. He was the smallest guy to hit the field, but he had such a positive spirit, the coach decided to put him on the team. Even though Drew sat on the bench for the next four years, his mom made every game.

When Drew entered college, he went out for the football team as a walk-on. The other athletes doubted he'd make the cut, but to everyone's surprise, he did! The coach admitted that he kept him on the roster because of the way he put his heart and soul into every practice and, at the same time, motivated the other athletes with the spirit and hustle they desperately needed.

Drew sent his mom season tickets for all the college games. She was thrilled once again to be at every game. This persistent young athlete never missed practice during his four years at college, but he repeated his high school record and never got to play in the game.

The end of his senior football season, he trotted onto the practice field shortly before the big play-off game. The coach met him with a telegram. Drew read the telegram and fought the lump in his throat to share the news with his coach. "My mother died this morning. Is it all right if I miss practice today?"

The coach stretched his arm around Drew's shoulder and said, "Take the rest of the week off, Son. And don't worry about coming back to the game on Saturday. You take all the time you need."

Saturday arrived, and Drew surprised the team by showing up for the big game. He dressed in silence and made his way to the bench. The game was one of the worst they'd ever played. In the third quarter, Drew approached the coach and begged to play. The coach, figuring he had nothing to lose since they were already so far behind, relented and sent Drew to the field.

Suddenly, the game took a turn for the better. This little unknown, who had never before played in an actual game, was doing everything right. The opposing team couldn't stop him. He ran, blocked, and tackled like a star. His team caught up, and the score was eventually tied.

In the closing seconds of the game, Drew intercepted a pass and ran for the winning touchdown. The fans broke loose. His teammates hoisted him onto their shoulders. The coach approached him soon afterward in the locker room. "Drew, you were fantastic. I don't get it! Your mom just died days ago. How did you do it?"

"Sir, my mom was a Christian. She's in heaven now. Yes, she came to all my games, but she was blind. Today was the first time she got to see me play, and I wanted to show her I could do it."

Know It!

God is your biggest cheerleader. He's at all your games, and just like a proud parent, he cheers you on whether you're on the bench or the field.

Read It!

Jeremiah 29:11; 33:3; Ephesians 1:19-20; 3:20

Pray It!

Ask God to help you do your best whether you're the star or standing in the shadows. Thank him for believing in you.

Back to the Basics

Know It!

There's a big difference between acting like a Christian and actually living a Christlike life. Where are you? If you've never confessed your sins, now would be a great time to do so!

Read It!

Psalm 51:5;
Romans 3:23-26; 4:7-25

Pray It!

If you need to ask God's forgiveness for your sins, consider praying this prayer: *Jesus, I admit I've done a lot of assuming about Christianity. But I come to you now and confess that I'm a sinner. I'm so sorry I've sinned against you and tried to run my own life. Will you forgive me? Will you come into my heart and make me a brand-new creation in you? I give you my life, Jesus. I want to live for you. Thank you for your incredible gift of forgiveness and eternal life. I accept you as my Savior. Amen.*

This guy is really getting on my nerves, Todd thought as the camp speaker continued his message.

"Some of you have been coming to this camp for years," he said, "and you may assume because you go to church camp, you're a Christian."

Todd shifted his weight on the wooden bench. *Can't wait till chapel is over so I can head to the rock-climbing wall.*

"Many of you are from Christian families, and you're involved in church and plugged in to your youth group. But that doesn't make you a Christian."

I go to church, Todd mused. *And I've got some pretty cool Christian friends. I even helped out at the soup kitchen last Thanksgiving with the youth group. I do all kinds of good stuff.*

"You may even be a good teen doing good things," the speaker continued, as if he'd somehow read Todd's thoughts. "But that doesn't make you a Christian either."

Todd glanced at his watch and looked toward the lake.

"You're not really a Christian until you've repented of your sins, asked Jesus Christ to forgive your sins, and committed yourself to live in obedience to him.

"And even that's just the beginning," the speaker said. "Being a follower of Christ isn't simply believing in his teachings; it's having an actual relationship with him that consistently grows and deepens."

Hmmm, Todd thought. *I've never really considered myself a sinner. Yeah, I've told a few lies and cheated on a couple of tests, but who hasn't?*

"The Bible says that every single one of us was born with sin, and the only way we can have a genuine relationship with Jesus Christ is to seek his forgiveness for our sin."

Todd focused on the speaker's words. *I can't remember ever actually asking forgiveness for anything,* he thought. *So does that mean I'm not really a Christian?*

"And the interesting thing about Christianity," the speaker said, "is the fact that we can't earn eternal life. None of us deserve it, but God loves us so much, he offers it as a free gift to all who seek him."

After chapel ended, Todd decided to hang around and talk with the speaker instead of heading toward the rock-climbing wall. *I sure would like to know for sure if I'm a Christian,* he decided.

Todd shared with his camp counselor that he'd given his heart to Jesus the previous day after chapel. "I guess it never really hit me that I might not be a Christian," he said. "I go to church, and I'm not a bad person, but until yesterday I'd never asked Jesus Christ to come into my life."

"I'm excited for you, pal," Brian said. "But tell me . . . what kind of changes will you need to make when you go home?"

"What do you mean?"

"I've heard you brag to a few of the other campers about your drinking escapades and about how far you've gone physically with your girlfriends."

"So?" Todd said. "I'm a guy. It's what guys do. Hey, I can't become perfect just because I asked Christ to come into my life."

"But now that you're a Christian, you'll want to please Christ and obey him, right?"

"Whoa! I don't know about *that,*" Todd said. "I'm still planning on drinking and sleeping around a little. That's just life, man!"

"Then, Todd, I question if you're really a Christian."

"Of course, I am," Todd insisted. "I prayed the prayer!"

"But Christianity is a lot more than simply praying a prayer, Todd. It's developing an actual relationship with Christ and following him."

"Look, I asked Christ into my life. I'll read the Bible some, and I'll pray some more. But I'm not ready to give up *everything,*" Todd said.

"Hmmm. Sounds as though you didn't count the cost, pal. When you prayed the prayer, you didn't think about what it would mean to your life."

"I guess we'll just have to agree to disagree on this. I think I'm a Christian."

"It doesn't really matter what *you* think, Todd."

"Oh, and it *does* matter what you think?"

"Nope. It really doesn't. The only thing that matters is what God thinks. And you can find out by reading the Bible."

Know It!

Christianity isn't a religion, it's a way of life. It's developing, maintaining, and growing intimately in a *relationship* with the creator of the universe. When we enter into a relationship with Christ, we begin to fall in love with him. And the more we grow to love him, the more we want to please him by living in obedience to him. Are you in love with Jesus? Or are you simply going through the motions?

Read It!

1 John 5:1-21

Pray It!

Tell Jesus you don't simply want to love him, you want to BE IN LOVE with him! Ask him to help you fall more and more in love with him every single day of your life.

Basic Truth

Know It!
God hates hypocrisy. Don't call yourself a Christian if you're not willing to live it every day of your life. That's why we're told to count the cost before we commit to following Jesus.

Read It!
Luke 14:25-35; Hebrews 12:14; 1 John 2:3-7

Pray It!
Aren't you glad that when Jesus counted how much it would cost to save your life and forgive your sins, he didn't walk away from the Cross? Thank him! And tell him that because he gave 100 percent for you, you want to give 100 percent to him.

"Hey, Todd!" Brian yelled across the softball field. "Today's the last day of camp, and I wanted to catch you before you left."

Todd sprinted toward his counselor.

"I'm concerned about you, Todd. I want you to understand how this whole Christianity thing works."

"Well, it sounds to me like it's just a bunch of rules."

"It may sound that way, Todd, but it's really not. The religious leaders of Jesus' day—the Pharisees—were totally into 'the rules,' and Jesus reprimanded them for it."

"Then what's the big deal about me saying I'm a Christian but still doing the stuff I wanna do with my buddies who aren't Christians?"

"Let me ask you something, Todd. I know you're starting quarterback for your high-school football team. Would you consider approaching your coach and saying, 'I don't mind suiting up and playing when there's an actual game. But I'm not gonna make practice any more.' "

"That's crazy, man! Coach would never let me play if I skipped practice. He's pretty strict. We have to maintain a passing grade average and even wear a tie on game days!"

"Hmmm," Brian continued. "Sounds to me like you're following an awful lot of rules just to be able to play football."

"Nah, it's not like that at all. I love football! I'd be miserable if I weren't playing."

"Todd, listen to yourself. That's exactly how it needs to be in your relationship with Jesus Christ," Brian said. "We don't follow him because it's the thing to do or because our parents are into it. We give our lives to him because we love him, and we'd be miserable without him."

"Yeah, but—"

"Hang on, Todd. Hear what I'm saying," Brian added. "And because we love him, we *want* to follow his plan for our lives—just like you want to do everything your coach tells you to. You trust that he's a good coach and he knows how to help you become the best player you can be. He can even prepare you for a college scholarship. And Jesus Christ can prepare you for eternity. That's the greatest 'prize' we'll ever receive!"

"Hey, Bri, I gotta pack."

"Yeah, I know. But how 'bout meeting down at the dock for a hot dog before you leave?"

"Okay. I'll see you in about 30 minutes."

"Get everything packed?" Brian asked Todd as he approached the hot-dog stand by the lake.

"Yep. I'm ready to go. My bus will be here in an hour."

"Mind if we skip a few rocks before you head home?" Brian asked as he handed Todd a couple of flat, smooth stones.

"Great." Todd watched Brian's stone skip three times across the water.

"Todd, it sounds as though you want it both ways."

"Whaddya mean?"

"Well," Brian continued, "you want to call yourself a Christian, but you still want to do your own thing."

"Yeah," Todd agreed. "Like I said before, I'm still gonna sleep around and probably go drinking with my buddies on Friday nights after the game. No big deal."

"Yeah, it *is* a big deal," Brian said.

"Why? I'm still gonna go to church. I'll still be plugged into the youth group."

"Jesus has a name for people like you, Todd. It's 'hypocrite.' "

"Whoa! You're coming down hard, Bri. Back off."

"Todd, I care enough about you to give you the truth. And you can't ride the fence forever."

"You know, Brian, I really *want* to be a Christian. I love our youth group, and I enjoy reading the Bible. I just don't want to let go of everything."

"There's a spiritual battle going on right now, Todd. Satan and God are playing tug-of-war with your soul. God wants 100 percent, and so does Satan."

"Hey, I'll never follow Satan!"

"You can't remain neutral, Todd. By not following Christ, you end up following Satan by default. There's no neutral ground. You're either *for* Christ, or you're *against* him."

"I'm for him, Brian. I really am. I prayed the prayer, remember? I know the Bible well enough to know that it says whoever believes in Jesus Christ will be saved. I believe, man. So I'm saved!"

Know It!

Yes, Jesus said if you believe in him, you'd be saved. But guess what—in the original language the Bible was written in, the word used for "believe" meant to *completely adhere to.* So when Jesus urged people to believe in him, he was passionately pleading for them to completely dedicate their lives to him.

Read It!

John 1:12-13; 3:18-21; 7:37-39

Pray It!

Tell God that you don't simply want to call him Lord, you want him to be your Lord. Give yourself, your will, and your entire life to him.

Adhering to God's Truth

Know It!
God doesn't expect you to be perfect, but he *does* expect obedience and commitment.

Read It!
1 John 1:5-6; 2:1-2; Revelation 3:15-16

Pray It!
Thank Jesus for his forgiveness and his desire to help you be all he calls you to be.

"Todd, you're leaving in just a few minutes," Brian said. "Will you listen carefully to what I'm saying?"

Todd sighed. "Sure, Bri. Go ahead."

"Look, Todd, I know you think you're a Christian because you believe . . . but believing's not enough. Even Satan believes in God! You have a heart that God wants to use. But he needs all of it."

"I just don't wanna quit having fun."

"Todd, you can still have fun—but the right kind of fun. I gotta tell you, man, I've never been more fulfilled than since I totally gave my life to Christ."

"Yeah, I've heard it all, Brian. But I'm not sure I can quit doing the stuff I know God doesn't want me to do."

"Todd, do you realize what Jesus says about those who play the game?"

"Whaddya mean?"

"Riding the fence—having a foot in the church and a foot in the world. He calls it being lukewarm."

"That's like room temperature, right?"

"Yeah, sort of. It's a combination of hot and cold. He tells us to make a decision—to be really hot, or to go ahead and just be cold. But if we're lukewarm (if we're in the middle), he'll spew us from his mouth."

"Spew?!? What . . . you mean like . . . vomit?"

"Yeah," Brian said. "That's pretty strong, huh?"

"Sure is," Todd agreed. "Okay, here's the deal, Bri. I'm scared. I'm afraid if I make a total commitment to Christ, I'll fail. I'm human, man! What if I blow it?"

"That's where forgiveness comes in. When you approach God with a repentant heart, he'll forgive."

"You mean, I won't have to start all over again?"

"No, Todd, you don't have to start over again. If you're truly repentant and genuinely desire to follow Christ with all your life, he'll forgive you when you ask. At that point, you accept his forgiveness and keep walking with him."

"That's what I want, Brian! That's what I really want!"

"Are you willing to give God *all* of your life—even the stuff you know doesn't please him?"

"Yeah, I am, Brian. I said it was fun . . . but it's also miserable at the same time. I'm tired of the guilt. If God can really equip me to live the way he wants me to live, I'm ready to give him everything."

Check out the following advertisements. Each was actually printed as is in a local newspaper.

- GEORGIA PEACHES—California grown. Eighty-nine cents a pound.
- Two wire-mesh butchering gloves: One 5-finger, one 3-finger. Pair $15.
- Nordic Track $300. Slightly used. Call Chubby.
- Snowblower for sale. Only used on snowy days.
- Nice parachute. Never opened. Used once.
- Full-sized mattress. Twenty-year warranty. Like new. Slight urine smell.
- OPEN HOUSE: Body Shapers Toning Salon. Free coffee and donuts.

The above advertisements don't really make the reader want to rush out and purchase the items for sale, do they? Have you ever stopped to think that you're a walking advertisement for Jesus Christ? If someone were to run an advertisement on you, how would it read? Maybe you've heard the saying, "If you were arrested for being a Christian, would there be enough evidence to convict you?" So . . . if you actually were arrested for being a Christian, what would the evidence say? Do people know about your relationship with Christ? Is it as obvious as your hair color? When you walk into a room full of people, do they sense there's something different about you?

Let's take this a little deeper. Do the following key areas of your life give a true advertisement of Jesus Christ living in your heart?

#1: Conversation. Is your chit-chat filled with gossip and rumors? With criticism or sarcastic remarks about others? Do you tend to spice your words with bitterness and negativity? Or are your conversations filled with words that bring glory to Christ?

#2: Clothing. Does what you wear (and how you wear it) cause others to question the depth of your relationship with Christ? Do you dress in such a way that the opposite sex has trouble keeping a pure mind when around you? Or have you learned the art of remaining modest?

#3: Character. Does your lifestyle echo WWJD? Do you base your actions on what Jesus would do? Can others trust you to keep your word? Are you dependable? On time? Honest? Do you live a life of integrity . . . or is there always that little "something" that causes others to doubt your genuineness?

Know It!
You're a walking billboard for God. Non-Christians are watching your life for clues to what makes you tick. Are you living up to the advertisement God needs you to be? He can empower you to be a glowing ad of his love!

Read It!
Proverbs 10:9; 13:6; 1 Timothy 3:7; Titus 2:7

Pray It!
Ask God to help you be the living advertisement he wants you to be—one that will glorify his holy name.

Paradise

Know It!

Heaven will be the ultimate eternal party of praise, worship, joy, and celebration. And God wants so badly for *you* to share in his lavish forever kingdom, that he sent his only Son to issue your invitation.

Read It!

Matthew 3:2; Revelation 7:9-10; 21:5

Pray It!

Spend some time thanking God for his incredible love for you. Tell him how excited you are to spend eternity with him in his perfect kingdom of heaven.

In an attempt to save money, many airlines have cut back on a lot of the "extras." They no longer allow silverware in coach class, and most airlines don't even serve a meal now—unless it's an international flight.

Here are signs that you're flying on a "No Frills" airline:

- The airline doesn't sell tickets, it sells chances.
- You're not allowed to board the plane unless you have exact change.
- The airplane has both a bathroom and a chapel.
- All the insurance machines in the terminal are sold out.
- Before you take off, the airline attendant tells you to fasten your Velcro.
- There's no movie. You don't need one. Your life keeps flashing before your eyes.
- Before the flight, the passengers get together and elect a pilot.
- The captain asks all the passengers to chip in a little for gas.
- You see a man with a gun, but he's demanding to be let off the plane.

Though airlines have certainly cut down on their frills, God hasn't cut down on his. Right now he's preparing a place for you to live eternally with him. We don't know exactly what heaven will be like, because our human minds aren't able to comprehend its splendor. But we do know that God won't be cutting back on the frills. He's going all out for his children! We know heaven will be a place of absolute perfection. There will be no sickness, no death, no sadness, no sin. Even to describe heaven as eternal happiness would be a gross understatement. We simply can't imagine how incredibly fantastic it will be!

Why will heaven be so grand? Because of God's lavish love for you! *Why will it be perfect?* Because God is perfect, his kingdom is also perfect. *But how will I get in? I'm nowhere near perfect!* That's where Jesus enters the picture! He'll stand in front of you, so when God looks at you, he's actually looking through Jesus to see you. And because Jesus paid the price for your sin—death on the cross—you're now declared not guilty. When Judgment Day arrives, and you stand before God, he'll see a perfect disciple . . . all because of Jesus standing in front of you.

It doesn't matter if you've ever been on a date or not, you still have to settle the issue of sexual purity in your life. You may wonder if you're abnormal because you've never had a boy/girlfriend. Of course, that's totally ridiculous! Many people don't date until college or after. Whether or not you date has absolutely nothing to do with being normal. Being normal means having an active, growing relationship with your Creator, Jesus Christ.

Having a boyfriend or a girlfriend isn't the most important thing in the world. In fact, there can be some real advantages to being relationship-free during your teen years:

- You can eat triple-cheese and onion pizza and not have to worry about your breath!
- No relationships means no break-ups.
- You have more time to invest in a job, a new hobby, or developing your talents.
- There are enough pressures in life as it is without having a guy or girl pressuring you to go further than you want.
- When you're at a group function, you're totally free to hang with more than just one person.
- You're able to concentrate more intently on deepening your relationship with Jesus Christ!

So if you've never been in a guy/girl relationship, don't rush it! But even if that's the case, chances are great that someday you will. And right now is the time to begin establishing your standards. Think ahead. Have you made a commitment to wait until marriage to become sexually intimate?

If not, how about doing that right now? Go ahead! Take the pledge:

THE TRUE LOVE WAITS PLEDGE

Believing that true love waits, I make a commitment to God, myself, my family, those I date, my future mate, and my future children to be sexually pure until the day I enter marriage.

____

(Signature) *(Date)*

Perhaps you've made a True Love Waits pledge but are wondering how in the world you'll be able to keep it. Great point! Let's take the next few days to unpack a strategy.

Know It!

Sex is an incredible gift created by God himself. But he has a perfect plan for sex, and he wants you to experience it within the boundaries of a lifetime of marriage.

Read It!

Exodus 22:19; Ephesians 5:3; Philippians 4:8; 1 Timothy 6:11

Pray It!

Ask God to help you maintain your pledge to remain sexually pure until marriage.

Regaining Sexual Purity

Know It!

You need God's help to maintain sexual purity—you can't do it on your own. Come to him with a repentant heart and ask him for help.

Read It!

1 Corinthians 5:9; 6:13, 18; 10:8

Pray It!

Do you need to seek God's forgiveness for being sexually intimate outside of marriage? If so, now is a great time to pray!

Now that you've made a pledge to remain sexually pure until marriage, let's look at how you can maintain that pledge. When you're with someone you really care about, and the passion is rising between the two of you, you may not feel as strongly about your commitment to purity as you do right now reading this book.

You can't do it on your own, that's for sure! This is where the power of the Holy Spirit comes into play . . . as well as good ol' accountability with Christian friends, parents, and youth leaders. Before we get into how you can *keep* the pledge you've made, let's first take a quick detour.

What if you've already gone too far sexually? Right now is the perfect time to seek God's forgiveness and ask him to grant you "spiritual virginity." Even though you may no longer be a physical virgin, with God's forgiveness you can become a "spiritual virgin." He will forgive your sexual sin and look at you as though you were a virgin. In other words, he transforms you into a "spiritual virgin" and you live in sexual purity from now until you're married.

But when you seek his forgiveness, make sure you're doing it with a repentant heart. Not the attitude of: "I'll ask God to forgive me for having sex with my boyfriend . . . even though I know I'll probably have sex with him again next week. He'll forgive me again."

Guess what–that's not a repentant heart! In Bible days, when someone saw a friend going the wrong direction, he would shout, "Repent!" meaning, "You're going the wrong way. Turn around. Change direction. Alter your course!"

If you come to God with a repentant heart and seek his forgiveness for your sexual sin with the attitude of, "Oh, Father, I don't ever plan on going down that road again. In fact, I'll go out of my way to build guardrails around my life that will keep me from moving in that direction again"–that's reflective of a repentant heart. God will forgive and completely forget, and he'll grant you "spiritual virginity."

Planning for Success

Though TV, movies, magazines, and even some of your friends will tell you it's impossible to remain sexually pure until marriage, you can be victorious at keeping your True Love Waits pledge! Let's use the word SUCCESS to outline our strategy.

S: Start establishing your dating guidelines now! What kind of person do you want to date? Hopefully, you'll decide to date only Christians (we'll get into why later). What are your guidelines and standards for dating? You'll begin with group dating? You won't be alone with someone of the opposite sex in a dark, secluded area? You won't go past holding hands? You won't go past a kiss?

U: Understand you can't get comfortable. If you let your guard down, your standards will begin to slip. In other words, if you've decided not to be alone with someone of the opposite sex inside your home, don't allow yourself to make excuses: *But it's Valentine's Day. He's just coming over for a few minutes. Mom and Dad will never know.* If you're committed to stay away from R-rated movies, don't rationalize: *But everyone says it's a great movie. And it would be such a fun date.*

C: Clarify your boundaries. You've decided not to kiss someone of the opposite sex until you're engaged? Then make that known. You're uncomfortable with the jokes he tells? Let him know. You're determined to obey your parents' curfew of being home by midnight? Make that clear.

C: Create your own success story. With God's help, you can maintain your sexual purity until marriage. Refuse to become one of the millions of statistics about teens who are sexually involved.

E: Expect flak. Know that many around you won't share your standards. You may be teased and ostracized. That's okay. Just expect it. You haven't decided to be sexually pure because it's the "in" thing to do; it's not. You're basing your decision and your actions on obedience to God's holy Word. You're in love in Jesus, and you love him so much that your heart's desire is to obey him and bring glory to his name. That's why you're remaining sexually pure.

S: State your convictions. Know what you believe and why. You don't go to dance clubs? Be ready to explain. You don't listen to specific secular artists? Get ready to defend your decision. Just believing something in your heart isn't enough. God wants to help you articulate why you believe what you do.

S: Stay tuned in to an intimate, growing relationship with Jesus. There's no way you can remain sexually pure in your own strength. But when you're plugged into a supernatural power source–Jesus Christ–you can keep his commands to remain pure!

Know It!

God wants you to be successful in maintaining your purity. He's your greatest cheerleader. When you feel weak, turn to him!

Read It!

Matthew 15:19;
Acts 15:20;
2 Corinthians 12:21;
Galatians 5:19

Pray It!

Spend some time talking with God about your dating guidelines, your convictions, your standards, and how you'll handle the flak from those around you.

Quiz Time

Know It!

Guys and girls don't think alike. They're wired completely different. Guys are sexually aroused visually. In other words, what they *see* greatly affects them! Girls are sexually aroused through romance. Your goal in a dating relationship shouldn't be to arouse the opposite sex; it should be to complement his/her relationship with Christ. What you wear, talk about, and do all revolve around this!

Read It!

1 Corinthians 5:9; Ephesians 5:3; Colossians 3:5; 1 Thessalonians 4:3

Pray It!

Ask God to point out anything you're doing in your dating life that's not right with him. Seek his forgiveness and commit this area to him today.

Okay. Let's see what you're thinking . . . regarding this subject of sexual purity.

*Does **true love** really wait?*

a. Yes, always.

b. Well . . . if we really love each other, we shouldn't have to wait.

c. Never.

*We hear the term **"sexual purity"** a lot. But what exactly is it?*

a. It means not dating.

b. It's never going past a kiss.

c. Not having intercourse.

d. Remaining single your entire life.

e. I'm not really sure what it is.

f. I think it's a bunch of rules we're supposed to follow when we're in a dating relationship.

g. It means living in holiness in everything we do–our relationships, our words, and our actions.

*God wants us to save sexual intimacy **until marriage.** It's possible to experience sexual intimacy without having intercourse. Which of the following cause you to experience sexual intimacy? (Circle all that apply.)*

a. Sitting together on the couch.

b. Resting your hand on his/her thigh.

c. Going to the movies.

d. Lying down together.

e. Sleeping in the same tent while camping together.

f. Making out. (Excessive kissing and fondling.)

g. Riding bicycles together.

h. Playfully slapping each other on the rear.

i. Cuddling on the couch together with his/her head in your lap.

Many Christians think that as long as they don't have sexual intercourse, they're sexually pure. WRONG! They may technically be virgins, but sexual purity isn't simply saying no to intercourse. Sexual purity is a lifestyle! It involves what you listen to, who you date, how you dress, and what you think about. It encompasses everything we put into our minds, how we act and react, and how we live!

Part of maintaining your commitment to sexual purity is being extremely selective about whom you'll choose to date. It's smart to set a high standard of only dating Christians who share your morality. *What's wrong with dating non-Christians? Jesus hung out with prostitutes, after all!* But Jesus' mission was to bring the world to a saving knowledge of forgiveness for sins and eternal life. Yes, he reached out to everyone; but he didn't become emotionally intimate with those who didn't share his faith.

Christ wants you to reach out to those around you—regardless of their religious beliefs—but there's a huge difference between reaching out to someone and becoming emotionally involved with someone who doesn't share your faith. If you're attracted to someone who's not a Christian, be a friend but ask God to bring someone of the same sex to witness to that person and lead him/her to Jesus.

But some of the Christians I know really aren't worth dating! They're not any more moral than non-Christians. Great point. As I said earlier, it's smart to set a high standard of only dating Christians who share your morality. If you don't go to dance clubs, don't date a Christian who does. If you're not listening to specific secular song lyrics, why go out with someone who has inundated herself with those lyrics? Again, be extremely selective about whom you choose to date.

It's okay to say no! Girls, you don't have to go out with every guy who asks you. And guys, you don't have to ask a girl out just because all your friends are dating. Remember . . . the most important thing in your life is not who you're going out with; it's your relationship with Jesus Christ! Keep it in perspective.

So if you're out with a Christian who suggests you compromise your values, guess what? You're out with the wrong person! Call it off.

Know It!
God wants to help you with the decisions you make concerning your dating life and your standards. Can you trust him with your dating life?

Read It!
1 Corinthians 6:9; Hebrews 12:16; 13:4

Pray It!
Will you give God complete control of your dating life right now?

No Regrets

Know It!

When your integrity is at stake (as it always is when moral choices come up), you'll never regret saying no! You're worth waiting for! Get it? You're WORTH waiting for! Say no to going out with someone who doesn't share your faith and your morality; you're worth more! Don't give in to the pressure of drinking; you have a higher calling on your life! Refuse to settle for a lack of convictions; God dreams bigger for you! You're worth waiting for! Repeat: *I'm worth waiting for!*

Read It!

Proverbs 2; 3:1-8

Pray It!

Ask God to help you develop a lifestyle of integrity and to give you the strength and wisdom you need to make the right decisions in the midst of a tough situation.

God desires for you to someday look back on your life and have no regrets sexually. If you become sexually intimate outside of marriage, you will regret it—because it goes against God's will for your life as outlined in his holy Word. He can help you live a life with no sexual regrets.

Check out this verse of Scripture from *The Message:* "I'll not deny my integrity even if it costs me my life. I'm holding fast to my integrity and not loosening my grip—and, believe me, I'll never regret it" (Job 27).

Wow, Job was determined, wasn't he? Are integrity and sexual purity that important to you? If so, you'll want to live your life with that same kind of determination. Job lived a life of no regrets; you can, too!

Let's unpack that thought and put it into everyday terms. How does this apply to real life?

A close friend of the opposite sex suggests you do something you're not comfortable with.

a. You'll someday regret saying no.
b. In the long run, you won't regret saying no.

You're at a party and someone brings in the beer. Everyone starts drinking. You politely refuse.

a. Years from now, you'll look back on this day and regret saying no.
b. You'll never regret saying no.

You're out with friends on a Friday evening and they suggest a specific movie. You know your parents—and God—wouldn't want you to see it. You decline. They give you a hard time.

a. You'll someday regret saying no.
b. You'll never regret saying no.

Family Altar

What is an altar, anyway? Well, in the Old Testament, people often built altars (special places or symbols of their dedication to the Lord) to pray around.

Many churches have altars. And people who attend churches with altars usually like to pray at them. It's nice to have a special place to kneel and talk to the Lord. Of course, you can actually talk to God anywhere . . . at any time. You don't have to have an altar to do it. Or . . . anywhere you pray can become an altar to the Lord.

When I was growing up, my family often had prayer time together. We called this "family altar time." We'd gather in the TV room, kneel, and pray where we were. My dad would get up from his chair, kneel in front of it, and pray for each one of us. Mom would kneel in front of the couch, Kent by the coffee table, and I'd kneel in front of the piano bench (or wherever I was sitting at the time). We'd lift our hearts to Jesus.

It was a close, special time when together we could take our concerns and problems to our heavenly Father. I have wonderful memories of our family altar time.

Does your family have a special altar time? If not, why not suggest it to your parents? Ask if there's a night each week when you can all come together, kneel, and pray with one another.

If your parents aren't too keen on the idea, try something like this, "Mom, Dad, every Thursday at 9 P.M., I'm going to kneel here by our sofa and pray for our family. If you want to join me, great! If not, that's okay. I just want you to know that's what I'll be doing when I'm here every Thursday night, okay?"

(And when you tell everyone about your altar time, you really have to be consistent in keeping it!) Maybe your folks aren't Christians. Can you imagine what the Lord could do through your prayers and in your family after one month of consistent altar time? There's something humbling about kneeling and praying as a family. Try it!

Know It!

You don't have to kneel to make sure your prayers get through. God hears every single prayer you pray. But kneeling reminds us very quickly who's in charge. When we kneel, we're humbling ourselves before our great and almighty King of kings.

Read It!

Genesis 8:20;
1 Samuel 7:17;
Proverbs 15:8;
1 Peter 3:12

Pray It!

Ask God to help you develop a family altar time. If your family won't agree to the idea, ask God to help you develop a consistent altar time to pray for the needs of your family.

To Party or Not to Party

"Hey, Joel!" TJ said as he slapped his pal on the back. "Can you give me a ride to Dustin's party Friday night?"

"Sorry, TJ. Not goin'."

"Oh, wow. Man, I was sure you'd been invited. No prob. I'll talk to Dustin. Probably just an oversight."

"It's okay, TJ. I was invited. But I'm not going."

"What? You're kidding, right?"

"Nope. I'm not going."

"Joel, what gives? This party's gonna be huge!"

"Yeah, I know. But there's also gonna be alcohol there, TJ. I've made a commitment not to go to any parties where alcohol is served."

"That's crazy, Joel! You don't have to drink it. Why miss out on a great party just because of alcohol? You can still go!"

"That's what I used to think, TJ," Joel said. "I started out going to parties just to be there. And I always told myself I wouldn't drink–and I didn't for the first few times. But the more I went, the tougher it got to say no. So I started drinking. And after talking and praying with Pastor Steve about it, I rededicated my life to Christ and am committed to staying away from alcohol completely."

"I still don't get it. I mean, what happened? Are you telling me that you became an alcoholic after a few drinks?" TJ asked.

"No, I wasn't an alcoholic," Joel explained. "But alcohol started to become important to me. My focus on God shifted to other stuff."

"So, are you saying it's wrong to drink?" TJ questioned.

"Yeah, man. That's what I'm saying. I've promised God I'll never drink again, and I'm gonna keep that commitment."

"I still don't get it, Joel. If we just drink a little now and then, what's the big deal?"

"TJ, talk to Pastor Steve. He's got some good insight on this whole thing. He can help you see the whole picture."

"Well, I'm going to the party!"

"TJ, we've been friends a long time. You know I care about you, man."

"Yeah, so what are you saying?"

"I'm asking you to talk with Pastor Steve before you go to the party. Will you do that for me? For yourself?"

"Yeah, sure. I'll talk to him. But I'm still goin' to the party."

Know It!

God desires that you not take part in any kind of evil. Seek his strength in fleeing from the very appearance of evil.

Read It!

Matthew 6:13; 26:41;
2 Timothy 2:22-23; 4:18

Pray It!

Admit to God that you're often weak when tempted with doing things that everyone else is doing. Ask for his strength to say no.

More to Think About

Know It!

God commands that you be different from the world around us. If you fit in with everything that's going on at your school, you may be a little too comfortable in your secular surroundings—and you won't be a very good witness.

Read It!

Romans 12:1-3

Pray It!

Ask God to help you see the whole picture when you're seeking his help with a decision.

"Hi, TJ," Pastor Steve said. "Wanna go upstairs and grab a Coke and play some video games while we talk?"

"Sure!" TJ said. He'd known Pastor Steve for years and enjoyed hanging out in the youth center of their church.

"So the big party's this weekend, huh?"

"Yep. And I don't see what the big deal is."

"I understand there's gonna be alcohol there."

"Well, yeah . . . but Pastor Steve, that doesn't mean I have to drink it."

"No, it doesn't," Pastor Steve agreed. "But let's look at the bigger picture. Let's say you're at the party, and you're not drinking, but probably everyone else is, right?"

"Yeah. So?"

"So on Monday morning at school, when everyone's talking about Friday night, do you really think they're gonna stop in the middle of bragging and laughing about the weekend and say, 'Oh, by the way . . . TJ Parker was there, but he didn't drink.' "

"I don't know. Who knows what they'll say?"

"Well, chances are, no one at the party is going to remember you weren't drinking. Think about it, TJ: If everyone else is drinking, they're too out of it to remember if you had one drink, eight drinks, or didn't drink at all."

"OK, so maybe no one will remember I didn't drink. What's your point?"

"What does that say about your witness, TJ? You've told me that people at school know you're a Christian. When people hear you were at the party, they may question your relationship with Christ. They expect you to be *different* because you're a Christian. If they see you're just like everyone else, what's the point of giving up their sin to follow Christ?"

"Huh. Never thought of that," TJ said. "So you're saying I shouldn't even go to the party?"

"Yep. If you really wanna be different, refuse to show up any time alcohol is served. And when people ask you about it, be ready to explain your Christian views and your morality."

"Yeah, I could do that," TJ said. "But there's one problem."

"What's that?" Pastor Steve asked.

"This whole thing about drinking. What's the big deal? I mean, I'm not so sure it *is* wrong."

"Lots of kids at my school drink," TJ said. "I'd never become an alcoholic, but I'm not so sure that a few drinks every now and then are wrong."

"TJ, how do you know you won't become an alcoholic?" Pastor Steve asked.

"I just know."

"That's not good enough, pal. Rehab centers are filled with people who said the same thing. The truth is, alcohol can be extremely addictive."

"But, Pastor Steve . . . I still don't get what the big deal is. I mean, even Jesus drank! In fact, his first miracle was multiplying the wine at someone's wedding."

"Yeah, you're right, TJ. And that's the first argument every Christian teen uses when they're trying to rationalize alcohol."

"Well, it makes sense, doesn't it?"

"No, it really doesn't. Again, you've gotta see the whole picture," Pastor Steve said. "Jesus didn't create some kind of drunken orgy at that wedding. In the Greek language–the language in which the New Testament was written–there are two words for wine. One is *sikera,* which means 'strong drink.' And the other is *oinos,* which was wine usually served diluted with water."

"I don't get it," TJ said.

"What Jesus made was not sikera," Pastor Steve explained. "What he made was oinos, which was not a strong drink. The Bible always condemns strong drink."

"I never knew that," TJ said.

"Another thing to keep in mind is the simple fact that it's illegal for you to drink when you're underage. The Bible tells us to respect government authority, which means we can't in good conscience break the law."

"Man. That puts a whole new spin on it," TJ admitted. "Look, I don't want to do stuff that God doesn't want me to do. I just wasn't sure this was that big of a deal."

"It is a big deal, TJ. Any time you mess with your witness, it's a big deal. The question you need to answer is: Do you want to be known for the fact that your relationship with Christ makes you different? Or do you want to be known for fitting in?"

"Jesus. I wanna be known for following Jesus," TJ said. "Think you could open the youth center for some hoops this Friday night? I'm gonna need an alternative to that party."

"You got it, TJ!"

Know It!
God wants to help you develop and maintain a strong, pure, and holy reputation. Will you let him?

Read It!
Romans 13:1-3;
1 Corinthians 1:2;
Ephesians 5:3;
Colossians 1:22;
Hebrews 10:10

Pray It!
Ask God to give you the courage to stand alone—if need be—for him.

The Master Clown (Part 1)

Know It!
God wants you to experience genuine joy!

Read It!
Psalms 20:5; 126:2-6; Proverbs 12:20; Galatians 5:22-23

Pray It!
Ask the Lord to help you reflect his joy with everyone around you.

Long before the era of clowns and comedians, there lived a very funny man. Everywhere he went, he made people laugh.

Crowds thronged him and held their sides as he brought laughter and joy to their dull lives. His humor was smooth. He was professional. I guess we could say he was the first clown who ever lived. He was *so* funny, people soon dubbed him the Master Clown.

He began performing in great auditoriums in front of thousands of people. He had the uncanny ability to captivate an audience as soon as he walked on stage. He was like a humor magnet; people were drawn to his laughter, his style, his life. People soon forgot their troubles when they saw the Master Clown perform. He had a unique way of bringing joy to the despondent, the hopeless, and the weary. All who went to see him came away with an entirely different outlook on life.

The Master Clown's fame grew, and it was soon hard for him to go anywhere without throngs of people following him. He loved his mission. He thrived on making people happy. His eyes danced with delight when he saw a smile light up a sullen face. There was nothing he enjoyed more than hearing the joyful sound of people laughing together and loving life. He was most fulfilled when he fulfilled others.

The Master Clown wanted to reach as many people as possible with his humor. His mission was to spread laughter and genuine joy to everyone—not simply a select few. He needed more of himself to go around. After much thought, he came up with an ingenious idea!

He decided to choose a dozen men and train them to make people laugh, so they could do exactly what he was doing. The 12 men he selected were ordinary men yearning for something more. One was a CPA. Another owned a seafood restaurant. One was an artist. They were from various backgrounds, and they all left their careers for the honor to study under the Master Clown. He assured them there was no higher calling than the privilege of doing what he would teach them to do.

For three years, the Master Clown trained his apprentices. They watched him closely and meticulously studied his every move on stage. They learned his jokes. They adapted his style. They took on his body movement, vocal variety, and delivery.

They learned his approach to each punch line, memorized each dramatic pause and took on his personality. They reflected his timing, and finally their humor became as professional as his. As they performed for each other under the Master Clown's tutelage, it was obvious they were protégés of the best.

He had indeed taught them everything they needed to know to be genuine clowns. He was proud of them and affirmed their humor.

The Master Clown (Part 2)

Before the Master Clown sent his trained clowns out to perform, he took them aside and warned them that many people would try to imitate them. "Some will pretend they, too, are clowns," he said. "Don't be taken in by them."

"Master, will we be able to tell who the phonies are?" one asked.

"Yes," the Master Clown said. "The only way a person can become a real clown is to come to me and ask me to make him a clown, just as I have done with you."

The 12 clowns were sent out in pairs to various regions to bring laughter to the hopeless. And sure enough, just as the Master Clown had predicted, one of the followers ran into someone trying to fool an audience into believing he was a clown. He had painted his face and looked like one of the real clowns, but his humor was lacking something.

Matt, one of the Master's clowns, pulled him aside and said, "Don't you realize you're not a clown?" The actor hushed him and warned him not to talk too loudly.

"But it's so easy to become a real clown," Matt continued. "I know the Master Clown personally. I trained under him. I can introduce you to him, and he'll gladly make you into the kind of clown he needs you to be."

"I don't have time today," the actor replied. "Maybe tomorrow."

Phil, another clown who had been trained by the Master, soon ran across a phony as well. This actor was dressed in a bright purple clown suit accented with huge pink polka-dots. He stood on a street corner attempting to juggle tennis balls for the small audience who had gathered.

The tiny crowd quickly grew impatient, and the actor struggled to hold their attention. Disappointed and frustrated, the handful of people finally left. Phil approached the actor.

"Why are you pretending to be something you're not?" he asked. "You don't have to pretend any longer. I know the Master Clown. Let's go talk with him right now."

"Oh, no!" the actor begged. "I could never talk to the Master! He's so professional. So famous. He'd never want to meet me!"

"That's not true," Phil insisted. "He loves people—all people. And he'd love to help you become a real clown. Just imagine—you'd never have to pretend any more!"

"I can't," the actor replied. "I'm just not good enough."

"Neither was I when I first met him, but he changed me!"

"No. Not yet," the actor said. "Some day. Some day when I've polished my act . . . then I'll seek out the Master Clown."

Know It!

God, the Master of the universe, accepts you just as you are. But he loves you too much to let you stay that way. He wants to help you become the very best you can be!

Read It!

Galatians 1:10; Ephesians 3:7, 20-21; Philippians 4:4-5

Pray It!

Ask God to help you see yourself clearly in relation to him. Have you truly come to him just as you are? Or have you been making excuses, putting off approaching the Master?

The Master Clown (Part 3)

Know It!
God knows everything about you . . . and yet he loves you more than anyone! He sees your past, your failures, and the times you've compromised, and he loves you in spite of them! He dreams BIG dreams for you. Will you allow him to wipe off your façade and genuinely make you his child?

Read It!
2 Corinthians 5:9-11; 12:9; Ephesians 1:19; Colossians 1:28-29

Pray It!
Ask God to give you the courage to bring others to him.

Pete, another clown who had studied under the Master, was performing to the masses when he noticed an actor in the distance with a small crowd around him. When Pete had completed his performance, he approached the group of onlookers and stood in the back. He winced as he heard the actor telling crude jokes and making obscene gestures. Yes, the people laughed, but when they left, their lives were just as empty as they had been before. The laughter was only temporary.

Seeing the actor alone after his lame performance, Pete approached him. "You don't have to tell those kind of jokes to get a laugh," he said.

"Sure I do. Crowds today are hard to entertain. A guy's gotta be willing to do anything to get a laugh."

"The laughter you're giving isn't real," Pete said. "It's only temporary. When your crowd leaves, they walk away with the same hurt and the same hopelessness. You're not replacing their despondency with real joy."

"I don't know how to do that," the actor admitted.

"It's impossible," Pete said, "without going to the Master."

"As in . . . the M-M-Master Clown?"

"That's right," Pete affirmed. "I'll take you to him."

The two traveled together back to the Master Clown's headquarters. After Pete introduced the actor to the Master, he slipped away. The Master Clown motioned for the actor to sit down.

"Hi, Jake."

"H-h-how did you know my name?"

"I know everything about you," the Master said. "And I'm so glad you've come."

Jake hung his head in shame. He couldn't look the Master Clown in the eyes. Tears began to fall down his cheeks. "Oh, Master! I'm so unworthy! The jokes I've told to get laughs, and the things I've done–"

The Master Clown put his fingers on Jake's lips. "I know all about it. I've heard every joke, seen each gesture."

Jake was weeping. "I-I-I'm so sorry."

"And you're forgiven." The Master Clown took a pure white towel and wiped the cheap makeup off Jake's face and reached into his own bag of professional clown-white and began to recreate Jake's face in his own image.

When he was finished, Jake truly *did* reflect the Master Clown's likeness. The Master Clown then handed Jake a big book. "These are my words," he said. "Learn my jokes. Learn my ways. Live by this book."

Everyone he met could tell Jake had been in the presence of the Master. He performed in front of masses, bringing thousands into the presence of the Master Clown. And Jake and all who knew him were never the same.

And the Winner Is . . .

Remember the Stella Awards? Every year, attorneys across North America submit outlandish lawsuits for consideration. (For more information, check out the devotion on July 8.) Here's a hard-to-believe . . . but-actually-happened nomination.

October 1998: Terrence Dickson from Bristol, Pennsylvania, had just robbed a house and was leaving through the garage. But he couldn't get the garage door to go up because the automatic door opener malfunctioned. And because the door connecting the house and garage locked when he pulled it shut, he was unable to go back inside the house.

The family who lived in this house was away on vacation, so Terrence was locked in their garage for eight days! He lived on a case of Pepsi and a large bag of dry dog food he found in the garage. Terrence sued the homeowner's insurance company, claiming the situation caused him undue mental anguish. The jury agreed to the tune of half a million dollars!

Even though Terrence won his lawsuit (and it's hard to believe he actually won!), he's only a temporary winner. The rest of society laughs at him and clearly knows this "winner" is the one to blame.

We often try to win at things that don't actually make us winners. Have you ever been in a heated argument about your faith with a friend who's not a Christian? You may win that particular argument by quoting Scripture and parts of sermons you've heard through the years, but chances are you won't win later on when you invite your friend to church or try to pray with him.

There's an old saying, "You can win the battle but lose the war." In other words, what good is it to win a small argument with a non-Christian friend if it's going to damage your ability to continue to witness to him in the future?

The next time you're tempted to put up a good fight, think long and hard about what you're trying to win. Being *labeled* a winner doesn't always mean you *are* a winner. God already sees you as a winner if you're following him.

Know It!

Do you find yourself arguing simply for argument's sake? Are you desperate to always look like a winner in the eyes of those around you? If so, your priorities are way off! Jesus sometimes spoke out boldly during conflict, and other times he remained silent. Seek his wisdom to do the same.

Read It!

Proverbs 13:3, 10; 17:14; James 3

Pray It!

Ask God for his wisdom and discernment to know when you should speak out and fight for something and when you should remain silent.

Somehow They Found the Time!

Know It!

Right now is the best time in the world to start your *pre-prayeration* for the coming school year. Will you do it? Solid spiritual growth doesn't just come from reading a devotional book (like this one)—though that's part of the process. Your growth is also determined by your prayer life, Bible study, and being plugged into a church and youth group.

Read It!

Colossians 2:6-7;
1 Thessalonians 2:12;
Hebrews 6:1; 12:12-13

Pray It!

Tell God you want to be spiritually prepared for a new school year. Ask him to teach you how to pre-prayer with him in order to develop the strong spiritual muscles you'll need.

The following famous men have made fascinating contributions to society. But besides what they're known for below, they also have something else in common. Can you guess what the common denominator is?

- G. W. A. Bonwill: Perfected the modern safety pin
- Doc Holliday: Wounded with the Earp brothers at the OK Corral
- Paul Revere: Famous for his work as a silversmith, but also known for his warning to the early colonists that the British were approaching
- Thomas Welch: Originated Welch's grape juice
- Zane Grey: Famous for the western novels he authored
- William Lowell: Invented the modern wooden golf tee

Any guesses as to what they all have in common? They were all dentists! That's right. Paul Revere did dental work between working as a silversmith. Zane Grey wrote books between seeing patients. Isn't it amazing that in the midst of each one's hectic professional schedule, he still found time to become famous for something other than his career?

Time for a tough question: In the midst of your fast-paced life, are you making time for the creator of the universe on a daily basis? Flash back to the beginning of this book. You pledged to deepen your relationship with Christ, and that involves spending time with him every day. How are you coming on that pledge?

Now flash back to July 13-16. During those days, you renewed your pledge to spend time with Jesus Christ on a daily basis. Your summer will be coming to a close soon. The best way to *prepare* yourself for a new school year is to *pre-prayer* yourself for the new school year. So . . . the tough question still stands: How are you doing with your pledge to meet with God every day in prayer, Bible reading, and devotions?

Yeah, but you don't understand! I have a job. I have relationships. I have a full schedule! Think about this: You have as much time as the president of the United States! You have as much time as the famous dentists listed above. Each one of us has a total of 24 hours in a day. So perhaps the issue isn't the amount of time we don't have, but rather how we use the time we *do* have.

But . . . How Could That Be Wrong?

AUGUST 9

Maybe you've heard about some old laws that are no longer in effect but are still recorded in the law books. Though there was a reason for their existence years ago, most of them seem ridiculous now. Consider the following:

- Maine state law rules that it's illegal to whistle on Sunday.
- In Normal, Illinois, you're breaking the law if you make faces at dogs.
- In Hartford, Connecticut, it's against the law to cross the street by walking on your hands.
- According to the law, no one is permitted to drive more than 2,000 sheep down Hollywood Boulevard at one time.
- In Urbana, Illinois, it's against the law for a monster to enter the city limits.
- In Memphis, Tennessee, it's illegal for frogs to croak past 11 P.M.
- A Chicago law won't allow people to eat in a restaurant that's on fire.
- It's illegal to get married in Cleveland while wearing a bathing suit.
- In Miami, it's against the law to imitate animals.
- Alaska law says it's illegal to look at a moose from an airplane.

Weird rules, huh? That's nothing new. When Jesus walked the earth, there were a lot of weird laws on the books too. Most of them were religious laws created by the Pharisees—the religious leaders of the day. But the most interesting thing really wasn't the law—rather it was the time, effort, and creativity people put into figuring out how to get around those laws.

A really important law stated that people couldn't work on the Sabbath, and this included just about everything—including carrying a bucket of water into one's home. So to get around this rule, people would fill their jugs with water, leave them just outside the door, walk all the way around the house, open the door from the inside, and simply pick up the jug of water from the porch and bring it over the threshold of the door. Technically, they hadn't really worked on the Sabbath, but they still got their water inside the home!

God isn't concerned about carrying water into your house. What he is concerned with is that you realize there are still 10 important laws in his book. They're called the Ten Commandments. Let's take a closer look at these important laws.

Know It!

The Ten Commandments are just as relevant now as they were when God first gave them to Moses.

Read It!

Exodus 20:1-17; 34:28; Deuteronomy 4:13; 10:4

Pray It!

Ask God to help you understand his laws and to give you the discipline to obey them.

AUGUST 10

No Other God

Know It!

You serve a jealous God. He created you, and he wants total commitment from you. Take time to evaluate your relationship with him right now. Is he truly Lord? Or have you allowed other gods to settle in your life?

Read It!

Exodus 20:1-3;
Psalm 14:1;
Matthew 4:10;
Revelation 3:16

Pray It!

Ask God to point out any idols you may have established in your life, and give them to him.

YOU SHALL HAVE NO OTHER GODS BEFORE ME.

Quick history lesson: Moses rescued the children of Israel from Pharaoh's bondage and started them on their journey to God's promised land. Since the Israelites had been mistreated slaves of Egypt for 400 years, Moses was anxious to lead them toward a land and a life filled with prosperity.

After Moses had begun the journey, God led him up to Mount Sinai and had a chat with him focusing on the fact that although these people would be blessed materially, it would ultimately be their *lifestyle* that would bring fulfillment. And their lifestyle would need to include total obedience to God. So God gave Moses ten rules for living and instructed that they were for all people of all time.

The first four commandments focus on man's relationship with God, and the last six deal with man's relationship with man. It stands to reason that if we have a right relationship with God, we'll have good relationships with each other. But until we establish a deep relationship with our Creator, we'll always struggle in our relationships with others.

The Israelites had just left Egypt—a land of many idols and gods. It wasn't that difficult for them to believe in God Almighty; they simply added him to their list of all the other gods they worshiped. But when Moses announced the first of the Ten Commandments—that they couldn't have any other gods except the Lord God Almighty—that was a different story. To live in obedience to God, they had to forsake all the other gods they had placed in their lives.

You probably don't have a shrine set up in your bedroom with a menagerie of brass idols and foreign gods. But an idol is anything we allow to become as important as (or more important than) our relationship with Jesus Christ. If winning a track scholarship is just as important to you as living in obedience to Christ, you have an idol in your life. If spending time with your boyfriend or girlfriend is more important than spending time with your Creator, you've established an idol, and that guy or girl has become a god in your life.

No Idols

YOU SHALL NOT MAKE FOR YOURSELF A CARVED IMAGE.

We usually don't think a lot about this particular commandment, but many Christians are guilty of breaking it. Let's flash back to the days of the caveman. Primitive cultures felt it was difficult to place faith in a God they couldn't see, so they made things to help their imagination bring God into their worship. That's not wrong–yet.

You may have a variety of versions of the Bible. You might have a few different devotional books. These help bring you into the presence of God. Your church may have an altar or a cross that helps you focus on who God is. None of these aids are wrong–yet.

The music, the sermon, your church building are all designed to shift your attention to God. If none of these aids are wrong, then where's the danger? They can *become* wrong if we start to worship *them* instead of God Almighty. And how can you tell if you're worshiping something? Ask yourself these questions: Do I need this thing or symbol in order to worship God? Am I unable to enter into worship without this aid? If so, you're putting too much emphasis on the symbol instead of Christ.

The Bible tells us that God created us in his image. Since we find it tough to live up to his image, we often try to make him fit *our* image. When we do this, we're making a graven image out of our Creator. We rationalize that it's much easier to make God like ourselves than for us to truly be like him. Why not simply reduce him to our size instead of changing our lifestyle and allowing him to make us godly people? After all, change may require repentance, walking away from a relationship, giving up a habit.

God calls us to become like *his* image. That's part of the process of holiness. When you think of God, what image comes to your mind? You'll eventually become like that image. So if you have the wrong image of God, you're in a dangerous place. The perfect image of God is found in his Son, Jesus Christ.

Know It!

After the famous sculptor Thorvaldsen had finished his statue of Christ, he invited a friend to view it. The arms of Jesus were outstretched, and his head was bowed between them. The friend said, "I can't see his face." The sculptor replied, "If you would see the face of Christ, you must get on your knees."

Jesus is the only true image of God. Determine to have no other!

Read It!

Genesis 1:27;
Exodus 20:4;
Matthew 16:16;
Luke 6:13

Pray It!

Ask God to give you the right image of himself and to erase all false or graven images you may have collected in your life.

Respect God's Name

Know It!
With the help of the Holy Spirit, your language, your actions, and your life can all reflect the holy character of God himself.

Read It!
Exodus 20:7;
Proverbs 23:7;
Matthew 7:24;
Philippians 4:8

Pray It!
Do you need to seek God's forgiveness for any profanity in your life? He's ready and willing to forgive.

YOU SHALL NOT TAKE THE NAME OF THE LORD YOUR GOD IN VAIN.

We hear God's name used so frequently today in sitcoms, movies, plays, and everyday conversations that it's easy to forget how serious this commandment is. God's name reflects his holy character. His name is sacred. How we use his name echoes how we feel about him. If we use his name in a curse or to get a laugh or in frustration, we're showing that we have no respect for his holiness. God wants us to use his name in ways that reflect his godliness.

So let's do a quick recap: The first commandment instructs us to put God first in our lives. The second commandment tells us to get the right picture or image of God. This third commandment instructs us to think about God in the right way and to use his name accordingly.

Whatever you think about eventually determines what you become. Your thoughts define your vocabulary and your actions. Ralph Waldo Emerson said, "A man is what he thinks about all day long." But way before Emerson was on the scene, King Solomon told us in Proverbs that whatever we think about in our hearts shows up in our character.

Ask God to help you think about things that are lovely, pure, true, and honest so you'll constantly be dwelling on the holy qualities of God himself. When you're saturated with those thoughts, it's difficult to take his name in vain.

Have you profaned God's holy name? How's your language? Does it mirror a holy God or what the culture around you screams? If you're reading and watching entertainment that profanes his name, eventually you'll become desensitized to it. And, of course, once you're desensitized, it's extremely easy to let his name slip in profane ways.

We can also profane God by not taking him seriously. To talk about God but choose not to live like him is profanity. God doesn't want your lip service; he wants your life service. We can also profane his name by rejecting his forgiveness. When we sin, there is only One who can forgive and cleanse us–Jesus Christ. To rationalize our sin and refuse to admit that we have truly sinned is profaning God's name.

Keep the Sabbath

REMEMBER THE SABBATH DAY, TO KEEP IT HOLY.

God gave us the Sabbath as a reward for our labor. The one who works deserves to rest. When we overlook this precious gift from God, we're cheating ourselves. God also gave us the Sabbath so we could become reenergized. Batteries and people are a lot alike. We both run down. We both need to be recharged.

Think of God as an eternal power outlet. When you take time to plug in to his power, you automatically receive new energy, new life, new power. Trying to run on reserve can only be temporary. A run-down person is unproductive and ineffective. These same principles are at work spiritually as well. Not only do our physical bodies need to be replenished, but our souls also need to be revived.

It's well documented that people who consistently take one day off a week to worship God, replenish themselves, and have fellowship with other believers are not only happier and more productive during their work week, but they're also more fulfilled spiritually and physically than those who don't set the Sabbath aside.

God yearns to speak with his children. But to hear his voice requires that we learn to become still before him. One of the best ways to do this is to make a good habit out of setting aside the Sabbath to focus on him, learn more about him, worship him, fellowship with other believers, and receive his replenishment for the coming week.

There's an old saying, "That really got my goat." This phrase began with the custom of placing a goat in the stall of a high-strung racehorse. Just being in the same stall with the calm goat helped the anxious racehorse to relax. Sometimes before an important race, competitors would steal the goat from a horse's stall. The horse would again become anxious and wouldn't run his best.

We too can easily become high-strung and anxious about life. That's why we need spiritual renewal and physical relaxation. God, our Creator, knows us much better than we know ourselves. So when he commanded that we set aside a day to remember him, he did it for our benefit.

Know It!

You can't go wrong by keeping this command. But overlooking it can damage your spiritual and physical well-being.

Read It!

Exodus 20:8-11;
Psalm 46:10;
1 Thessalonians 4:11-12;
Revelation 3:20

Pray It!

Ask God to reenergize you. Make time this week to focus more intently on him, his power, and his healing. Be still long enough to hear his voice.

Respect Your Parents

Know It!

When was the last time you told your parents that you love them? Do it as often as possible—every single day if you have the chance! They're not perfect, but they're God's special gift to you.

Read It!

Exodus 20:12; Proverbs 1:8-9; 3:1-10; Ephesians 6:1-3

Pray It!

Spend time thanking God for your parents and praying for their spiritual and physical health.

HONOR YOUR FATHER AND MOTHER.

This is the first commandment God gave us that deals with our relationship with other people. It's also the first commandment that ends with a promise. This commandment is so important that God made sure it not only showed up in the Old Testament, but also in the New Testament in the book of Ephesians.

What does it mean to honor your parents? Does this command mean you have to agree with them? No. God knows your parents even better than you do! He created them. He understands their frailty, their weaknesses, and their faults. He knows they'll sometimes make decisions that aren't the best. There will be days when your feelings are hurt by their actions and their words. But through it all, God still commands that you honor them.

To honor your parents means to respect the position of authority God has placed them in. The structure he has created places God at the top, parents underneath God's instruction, and children underneath parental guidance.

It's much easier to honor parents when they're honorable themselves. But sometimes they're not. When they ask you to go against God's law, you are not held responsible to obey them. If your parents ask you to do something illegal or immoral, you're still commanded to honor them by being polite and respectful, but God doesn't expect you to obey them.

The promise God gives us when we keep this command and honor our parents is that we'll have a long and fulfilling life. To honor your parents means to be polite, show kindness, and express your love to them. It's okay to disagree with them. Just do it in a godly manner, and continue to honor and obey.

It's obvious parents will make mistakes. Think about it: They never got to attend a "School of Perfect Parenting." They simply had you . . . and they're learning by doing. You'll someday make mistakes with your children. Be willing to give your parents room to fail. But continue to encourage them, honor them, and love them no matter what.

Do Not Murder

YOU SHALL NOT MURDER.

When God commands that we not kill, it's interesting he didn't simply focus on physical murder. There *are* other ways to commit murder. Flip back to May 25-28 for another peek at this topic.

Chances are, the first thing that popped into your mind when you read that, was the act of murdering another person. But this rule also applies to how we treat ourselves. Since we didn't create our life, we don't have the authority to decide when our life should end. And to commit suicide is breaking this commandment. Yes, God understands a mind and heart that are emotionally unstable and psychologically damaged. But he has also commanded that we not murder. So the person who commits suicide is willingly and knowingly breaking this important commandment of God.

This command also applies, obviously, to the taking of another's life. Again, since we were not given control of how long a creation of God lives, when we murder someone, we're stealing that control from our Creator. But there are even degrees to which we can act that eventually lead to murder.

For instance, when you speed down the interstate with friends in your car, you're taking the risk of breaking this command. When friends encourage others to drink, take ecstasy, or engage in other harmful behavior, they're playing around with this holy commandment.

And, as discussed in the devotions in May 25-28, we can also commit spiritual murder. Jotham was a king in the Old Testament who chose not to go to church. He was a good man and he had high morals, but he simply didn't want to go to church. When the people in his jurisdiction saw his example, they stopped going to church, too. The end result was that the nation eventually became corrupt. Jotham committed spiritual murder during his reign.

Through this commandment, God is talking about much more than an act. He's talking about a lifestyle. Because he created life and cherishes it, he wants us to value life as well—all of life. He wants us to cherish the unborn and to take care of the animal kingdom, the plant life, and our world at large.

Know It!

The old hymn "This Is My Father's World" by Maltbie Babcock and Franklin Sheppard helps us focus on the view God desires we have of ALL his creation: "This is my Father's world, and to my listening ears all nature sings, and round me rings the music of the spheres. This is my Father's world: I rest me in the thought of rocks and trees, of skies and seas—his hand the wonders wrought."

Read It!

Exodus 20:13;
2 Chronicles 27:2;
Matthew 5:21;
1 John 3:15

Pray It!

Ask God to help you appreciate and understand the value of life.

Stay Sexually Pure

YOU SHALL NOT COMMIT ADULTERY.

Sexual intimacy outside of marriage is considered to be adultery. Adultery is violating the marriage vows of faithfulness. If you're single and experiencing sexual intimacy, you're still violating the vows of marriage—even though you haven't yet spoken those vows in front of an audience. The vows are still there.

Here's an example: Say the speed limit on your city streets is 35 miles per hour. Even if you don't have a driver's license, the law still exists. You don't have to be 16 and of legal driving age to break this law. You *could* break the law on a motor scooter. In the same way, you don't have to be married to break the vows of marriage.

We often equate virginity with sexual purity. The truth is, just because someone is a virgin doesn't mean he or she is sexually pure. Virginity means that someone hasn't engaged in sexual intercourse. Sexual purity isn't simply refraining from intercourse; it's a lifestyle. It involves what we wear, what we listen to, what we watch, who we date, what we say.

You may have friends who have done "everything but" and claim they're sexually pure. Again, sexual purity is much more than simply refraining from intercourse. When God commands us not to commit adultery, he's commanding that we not experience sexual intimacy outside the bonds of marriage.

Why is it wrong? Because sex was created by God to act as a bonding agent—a sort of superglue that cements two people closer than anything else can. When we engage in that bonding experience outside of marriage, we're becoming closer and more intimate with another human than God intended. His gift of sex was intended for marriage and marriage only.

God not only wants to protect you physically (against sexually transmitted infections, pregnancy, AIDS), he also wants to protect you emotionally and spiritually. He's commanding you to say no now so you can have a more fulfilling yes in the future!

What if you've been sexually abused? Does God hold that against you? Absolutely not! You were a victim of a hideous crime, and when God looks at you, he sees a pure and a whole person.

Know It!

There are always consequences when God's commands are ignored. He has clearly given a bright red stoplight regarding sexual intimacy outside of marriage. Wait until you've said your vows and have been pronounced husband and wife to follow the green light.

Read It!

Exodus 20:14; Psalm 51:3; Matthew 5:27-28; Ephesians 5:3

Pray It!

Make a pledge to God to save yourself physically and emotionally for your future spouse.

Do Not Steal

YOU SHALL NOT STEAL.

Jesus once told the story of a man journeying from Jerusalem to Jericho. You might remember this as the story of the Good Samaritan. The man was robbed, beaten, and left by the side of the road. A priest and a Levite passed by the man but didn't stop to help. A Samaritan saw the man and stopped to help him. This Samaritan also made financial provision for the man and made sure he was nursed back to health.

Obviously, the robbers believed "What belongs to this guy, also belongs to me. I can take whatever I want." That's active and blatant stealing–the most common way this commandment is broken.

But there are other ways to steal that aren't quite as blatant. To carelessly go into debt without the means to pay off what you've purchased is stealing. Many people rack up huge bills on several credit cards and then simply declare bankruptcy. To purposely go into debt knowing you don't have the means to pay your bills is breaking this eighth command from God.

To be hired for a full day's work and not put in a full day is also stealing. Taking too long on a break, coming in late, leaving early—all these habits are ways of taking what's not rightfully yours.

We can also steal by taking someone's good reputation and purposely ruining it. Every time you gossip about someone and negate his character, you're stealing from him. You may have friends who have tried to steal your faith. Perhaps they've laughed at you and made fun of your belief in Christ. They're trying to rob you of something you own.

We can also steal by refusing to share with others. Jesus told of a man who was very wealthy and had much more than he needed. Instead of sharing his wealth, he simply built bigger barns and hoarded what he had. Everything you have was given to you by God himself. It's possible to hold so tightly to your material possessions that you end up losing them. God meant for you to share what he has blessed you with. To refuse to do that is stealing, because you're not giving away what God intended you to share with another in need.

Know It!

You can also steal from God by not giving him what is rightfully his. Have you given him complete control of your money, your talent, your service? Do you give generously in tithes and offerings?

Read It!

Exodus 20:15;
Malachi 3:8;
Luke 10:30-37; 12:16-21

Pray It!

Pray Mark 8:36, and tell God to make you aware of anything you've stolen. Then ask for his strength to make it right.

AUGUST 18

Do Not Lie

Know It!

There are no lies or deceit in God's kingdom, so start practicing honesty right now. Determine to live a life of integrity. Make it your goal to be known for gentle truthfulness. Let others know you can be fully trusted.

Read It!

Exodus 20:16;
Psalm 63:11;
Proverbs 19:22;
Revelation 21:8

Pray It!

Ask God to help you develop a lifestyle of pure honesty and integrity. Seek his forgiveness for any deceit that comes to your mind.

YOU SHALL NOT BEAR FALSE WITNESS AGAINST YOUR NEIGHBOR.

To bear false witness is to deceive, and to deceive is to lie. It's easy to deceive others by telling only part of the truth. That's why when we're sworn in by a court of law, we have to promise to "tell the truth, the whole truth, and nothing but the truth." In other words, a judge is commanding that we leave nothing out; that we focus intensely on all that is true and nothing else.

A far greater Judge commands the same of his children. Whether it's deceiving our neighbor, our friends, our parents, or strangers, God says it's wrong. Which of the following can be labeled as deceitful answers?

- "Josh, were you cheating on the quiz?" Mrs. Wilson asks. "Oh, come on, Mrs. Wilson! Surely you know me better than that!" he replies as he slides the cheat sheet inside his jacket.
- You've had a crush on Adam for two weeks but have recently heard he likes Tabitha. She doesn't know he likes her, and when she approaches you with, "Isn't Adam great? What a guy!" you respond with, "Don't bother. I heard he's already taken."
- Though you're not counting every piece of change the sales clerk places in your hand, you're pretty sure he gave you an extra bill. He shuts the register and looks confused. "Did I give you the right amount back?" he naively asks. "I wasn't counting," you respond. "Okay," he says with a shrug of his shoulders. "It's been really hectic today."

In each of the above situations, the person responding wasn't completely honest. Therefore deceit took place. And when we purposefully deceive someone, we're breaking this ninth commandment.

Aren't you glad God is totally honest with you? He doesn't withhold any of his truth from you, and he expects no less of you. *But what about the times when the truth will hurt someone?* you may be thinking. There are ways to tell the truth cushioned in love. For example, say you're shopping with Hillary and she tries on a dress that's way less than flattering on her. Instead of telling her you love it, you could say, "It's a nice dress, but I've seen other colors that bring out your features better."

YOU SHALL NOT COVET.

God's final rule for life is that we shouldn't covet. In other words, we shouldn't want what our neighbor has. While it's natural to admire what someone else has and even think, *I'd love to have a car like that!* it's when we become envious that we're breaking this tenth commandment. When we envy what someone else has, we become resentful of her.

To covet something means we begin thinking inwardly, focusing on ourselves and what we want and how we can get it. God wants us to forget about ourselves and become lost in him. When we do that, we naturally want to meet the needs of others instead of our own.

This final commandment from God teaches us to learn the secret of contentment—to be happy with what we have. How do we learn this secret? By allowing God to produce the fruit of his Spirit in our lives—love, joy, peace, patience, kindness, goodness, faithfulness, gentleness, and self-control. When we're truly living out these characteristics, we allow them to take the place of our sinful nature.

Since true contentment is found only in a solid, growing relationship with Jesus Christ, we need to allow him to meet all of our needs. When you become envious of someone, ask God to help you dig a little deeper to see if there's a more basic need you're lacking.

For example, if you're envious of Nathan's being elected class president, look a little deeper. Maybe you're feeling insecure, unappreciated, or lonely. Ask God to meet your basic needs, and this will help guard against covetousness.

Which statements depict an envious spirit?

- "Wow! Did you see Beth's new car? I'd love to be driving one just like it someday."
- "I can't believe Alex got the new Nikes! He doesn't even need new shoes. I really deserve them! I'll watch and see if he leaves them in his locker during P.E. If he does . . . too bad, Alex! They were meant for my feet!"
- "Hi, Sami. I heard you're moving to a new house. One with a pool. I guess you think you're pretty special now, don't you?"

Again, there's nothing wrong with admiring something that someone else has—as in the first example. It's only when that admiration becomes selfish, arrogant, and destructive that it turns into envy.

Know It!
When you allow God to be the source of your contentment, you're automatically guarding against envy.

Read It!
Exodus 20:17;
Proverbs 14:30;
Galatians 5:19-26;
Philippians 4:11-13

Pray It!
Pray for total contentment in your relationship with Jesus Christ.

Do You Understand?

Know It!
It's impossible to keep God's commands in our own strength. We need his power to live the holy life he commands we live. Realize these commands weren't given to make your life miserable; rather they were given so that you can truly live abundantly!

Read It!
Exodus 20:3-17; John 3:16; 10:10; Philippians 4:13

Pray It!
Seek God's forgiveness for any commandments you have broken, and ask him to empower you with his strength so you may live in obedience to his rules for living.

Some things are just tough to understand. For example . . .

- In medical terms, a black eye is technically a "bilateral periorbital hematoma."
- Years ago, rabies was called hydrophobia, because one of the strangest symptoms of the disease has to do with the repulsion and fear of water. Here's what happens: Once someone has been inflicted with rabies, the act of drinking water immediately causes violent throat spasms—choking, gagging, and great panic. As the disease progresses, even the sight or sound of water will trigger these reactions.
- If we could place your circulatory system in a straight line, it would measure 60,000 miles. That's enough to circle the globe two-and-a-half times!
- When searching for the healthiest place to build a hospital, doctors in ninth-century Baghdad hung pieces of meat at various locations. The site at which the meat last turned rotten was the place they would build the hospital.

It's tough to understand the intricacy of the human circulatory system, why physicians thought the way they did in ninth-century Baghdad, and why rabies and water don't get along. But thankfully, it's not important we truly understand these things. It *is* important, though, that we understand, know, and put into practice the Ten Commandments.

Aren't you glad God gave us 10 rules for living that are easy to understand? Think about it: We don't have to analyze them or interpret them. We simply need to accept them. They're black and white. There are no gray areas to complicate things. They're simple rules given by God to help us get the very most out of life.

If you've never broken one of God's commandments, you don't need a Savior. But each one of us is guilty, because each one of us is born with sin. It's only because of God's grace that we can be forgiven when we break his heart by breaking his commands.

Paying Attention?

Ready for a fun brainteaser? Okay, here goes! Read the following statement:

FINISHED FILES ARE THE RE-
SULT OF YEARS OF SCIENTIF-
IC STUDY COMBINED WITH
THE EXPERIENCE OF YEARS.

Now count the *F*s in the above statement. *Count only once!*

Guess what—there are actually six *F*s in that statement. Many people only count three; some will find four or five their second time around. But there are actually six.

It really does make a difference to pay close attention to the details, doesn't it? Flip back to the devotions on January 1-3 dealing with details. When you started this devotional book, you pledged to commit yourself to two important spiritual details: Giving God 100 percent and meeting with him on a daily basis. So how's your attention to those two details?

Are you paying close attention to what God is trying to teach you? Are you growing closer to him every day? The truth is, God dreams BIG dreams for you! But ignoring him and not paying attention to his voice can cause you to miss out on all he has in store for you.

One way to help your spiritual growth is to develop some accountability. Ask God to bring someone to your mind—someone you admire spiritually—who can ask you the tough questions to ensure you're "paying attention" spiritually.

Seek someone of the same sex. (When you try to develop an accountability relationship with a friend of the opposite sex, it can become complicated.) You may want to choose someone a little older. But it needs to be someone you *know* is spiritually grounded, someone who will keep your confidences, and someone who will daily hold you up in prayer.

After you've found an accountability partner, establish a specific time you can get together. At this first meeting, share prayer requests, struggles, and praises of what God is doing in each of your lives. Then decide how often, when, and where you'll continue to meet. You'll be surprised at how much easier it is to pay attention to God's voice when you know someone will soon be asking you what he's teaching you!

Know It!

God wants to make sure you "get it." That's why he provided the Bible, and that's why he brings spiritually mature friends into our lives.

Read It!

Romans 8:37-39; 14:9-13; 15:7-9, 13

Pray It!

Ask God to bring someone to your mind whom you can approach about becoming accountable.

Angels of Protection

Know It!

Never underestimate the power of prayer! God doesn't want you to make foolish decisions and then expect him to bail you out, but he does help those who call on his name in a sincere manner. He sends angels to protect and guide you.

Read It!

Hebrews 13:2, 5;
2 Peter 1:16; 3:18

Pray It!

Ask God daily for his supernatural protection and guidance in your life.

Diane, a young Christian college student, was home for the summer. She had spent the evening with friends sharing and laughing about their college experiences. Diane hadn't planned on staying so late, and when she looked at the clock and noticed it was past midnight, she wished she had kept better track of time. She had to walk home.

But it was a small town, and she only lived a few blocks away. As she started on her way, she silently asked God to protect her. She decided to take a shortcut–the alley–that would shave about five minutes off her walk home. But halfway down the alley, she noticed a man standing at the end of the road . . . as though he were waiting for her.

Diane grew increasingly uneasy and continued to pray for God's protection from harm and danger. As she neared the end of the alley, she felt as though a blanket of comfort and security were wrapped around her. She also had the unusual sensation that someone was walking with her! When she finally reached the end of the alley, she walked right past the man and arrived home safely.

The next day she read in the newspaper that a young girl had been raped in the same alley just 20 minutes after she had been in that same spot. Knowing it could have been her, she began to weep. After thanking the Lord for protecting her, she decided to help this young woman by going to the police station and describing the man she saw.

The police asked her to look at a line-up of suspects. She immediately pointed to the man she had seen in the alley. When the man was told he had been identified, he broke down and confessed. The officer thanked Diane for her involvement and asked if there was anything they could do for her. She replied that she wanted to ask the man a question. The officer took her question to the rapist: "Why didn't you attack the girl you saw about 20 minutes before the other girl passed down the alley?"

"Because she wasn't alone," the rapist responded. "She had two tall men standing on either side of her."

The Power of Water

We know water is important . . . after all, most of the world is made up of water. But here are some amazing facts about water you might *not* know!

- Research tells us that drinking eight to 10 glasses of water a day can significantly reduce pain for almost 80 percent of the people who suffer from back and joint pain.
- Seventy-five percent of all Americans are chronically dehydrated.
- A mere 2 percent drop in body water can trigger fuzzy short-term memory, trouble with basic math, and difficulty focusing on the computer screen or on a printed page.
- In 37 percent of Americans, the thirst mechanism is so weak that it's often mistaken for hunger.
- One glass of water shut down midnight hunger pangs for almost 100 percent of the dieters studied in a University of Washington research project.
- Even mild dehydration will slow down one's metabolism as much as 3 percent.
- Drinking just five glasses of water daily decreases the risk of colon cancer by 45 percent, plus it can slash the risk of breast cancer by 79 percent. One is also 50 percent less likely to develop bladder cancer.

It's obvious that our bodies need water—and lots of it! We can live a few days without food, but we can't live long without water. And just as important as it is to be sure we're drinking the amount of water we should each day, it's also essential that we consume *living water* every day. Jesus told the Samaritan woman at the well that he was living water. As she was drawing water from the well to her parched, dry lips, he explained that he could provide an H2O supplement that would last throughout eternity.

At first she didn't understand what he was talking about, but as he continued to look into her eyes and tell her the things about her life that no one else knew, she realized he was the Messiah. She accepted his forgiveness for her sins and began walking with the creator of the universe.

Know It!

God wants to fill your life with spiritual nourishment. To get the spiritual vitamins you need, make it a necessity to spend time with your heavenly Father every single day.

Read It!

Zechariah 14:8;
John 4:1-26; 7:38;
1 Peter 3:21

Pray It!

Ask God to give you an unquenchable thirst for his Word.

Handling Adversity

Know It!

You, and only you, can decide how you'll react to the tough times in your life. They *can* make you a better person . . . if you'll let them.

Read It!

2 Corinthians 4:8-9;
James 1:2-4;
1 Peter 1:7; 4:1-2

Pray It!

Ask God to use the adversity in your life to make you stronger.

"It's great to see you!" Pastor Steve announced to the youth group.

Amanda sighed. *Sure hope tonight's lesson is good,* she thought. *I have so much homework, it's ridiculous! Mom and Dad are fighting again, and no one knows if Joey's coming back home or if he's run away for good this time.* She sighed again. *Life reeks!*

"I understand many of you are going through some really tough times right now," Pastor Steve continued. "So tonight, we're going to get really basic."

Pastor Steve was always searching for new ways to drive home old truths to the students in his youth group. He asked them to follow him to the church kitchen. There they noticed three pots of boiling water on the stove.

"Amanda," Pastor Steve began, "I want you to toss carrots in the first pot, eggs in the second pot, and ground coffee beans in the last pot."

She did, and no one said a word as the contents boiled. Pastor Steve asked Derrick and Marci to read some specific Scriptures. About 20 minutes later, Pastor Steve fished out the carrots, eggs, and coffee and placed each in a bowl. Turning to Amanda, he said, "What do you see?"

"Carrots, eggs, and coffee," she replied flatly.

Pastor Steve brought her a little closer and asked her to feel the carrots. As she did, she noted that they were soft. He then asked her to take an egg and break it. After peeling off the shell, she observed the hard-boiled egg. Finally, he asked her to sip the coffee. "I don't get it, Pastor Steve," she said. "What does this mean?"

"Each of these faced the same adversity—boiling water—but each reacted differently. When you tossed the carrot into the pot, it went in strong, hard, and unrelenting. But after being subjected to the boiling water, it softened and became weak.

"You then placed a fragile egg into the boiling water. After sitting in the boiling water, its inside became hardened. The ground coffee beans were unique, weren't they? After they were in the boiling water, they *changed* the water."

Amanda swallowed the lump in her throat. Pastor Steve turned to the youth group. "Which are you? When tough times knock on your door, how do you respond? Are you a carrot, an egg, or a coffee bean?"

Bitter or Better?

Pastor Steve continued his lesson to the youth group, and Amanda listened carefully. "Think about how you react when tough times hit," he said. "Are you like the carrot that seems hard, but with pain and adversity you wilt and become soft and lose your strength?

"Or are you like the egg? Did you used to have a teachable heart? But maybe after a death in the family, a breakup, your parents' divorce, or trouble at school, your fluid spirit became hardened and stiff. Your shell may still look the same. But on the inside . . . are you bitter and tough with a stiff spirit and heart?"

Amanda fought back the tears. *Wow. This is exactly what I need to hear right now,* she thought. *I've become like the egg. Because of our family problems and everything that's going on at school, I'm becoming hardened.*

"Or are you like the coffee bean?" Pastor Steve continued. "The bean changes the hot water—the thing that's bringing the pain—to its peak flavor when it reaches 212 degrees Fahrenheit. When the water gets the hottest, it just tastes better."

Oh, dear God, Amanda prayed silently, *please forgive me for becoming hardened and unteachable. I want to be like the coffee bean. Help me!*

"If you're like the coffee bean," Pastor Steve said, "you get better when things are at their worst, and with God's help you can make things better around you.

"When people talk about you behind your back, does your prayer time increase? Do you continue to praise the Lord? When the hour is darkest and trials are their greatest, does your worship elevate to another level? Gang, the choice is up to you: Become bitter or better."

Amanda stopped trying to hold back her tears. Before she knew it, some of the youth leaders had surrounded her and were praying with her. Other students, also, were seeking help from the Lord.

"Amanda." She recognized Pastor Steve's voice.

"Amanda, this is what the body of Christ is all about," he said. "When you're experiencing difficulty, we want to pray with you, support you, and love you."

Know It!

You may be tempted to stay away from church and youth group when you're going through a tough time. Fight the urge to be alone and let God help you through other Christians.

Read It!

Isaiah 40:31;
Jeremiah 29:11-13;
1 Peter 5:7, 9-11

Pray It!

Ask God to help you evaluate what you are in adversity—a carrot, an egg, or a coffee bean. Ask him to help you become better instead of bitter during adversity.

Hearing the Right Directions

Know It!

By placing complete faith in the One who has died for you, conquered death for you, forgiven you, and is preparing a place for you in heaven, you'll be heeding the right directions.

Read It!

Proverbs 23:12;
2 Thessalonians 3:14;
1 Timothy 6:3;
2 Timothy 4:2

Pray It!

Ask God to help you not be taken in by the voices around you that may sound good but aren't speaking the truth.

A train was traveling through a horrendous snow storm. A woman with her baby wanted to exit the train at one of the little stations along the route. She repeatedly said, "Don't forget me!" to the brakeman who was responsible for calling out the stations they approached. The woman's husband was scheduled to meet her and their baby along the route, and she wanted to make sure they didn't miss each other in the heavy blizzard.

The train slowed to a stop, and another passenger spoke up. "Ma'am, this is your station," he said politely. The woman exited the train into the heavy storm. The train soon started again and continued its route. Almost an hour later, the brakeman came to the area where she had been sitting. "Where's the woman?" he asked as he looked around.

"She got off at the last stop," replied the passenger who had spoken to her.

"That wasn't her stop! The only reason we stopped was because there was something wrong with our engine."

The staff asked for volunteers to return to the spot and search for the woman and her child. When they found her, she was covered with ice and snow. The little boy was protected underneath her arms where she had pressed him close to her heart.

She had followed the passenger's instructions, but they were wrong. He was a fellow traveler simply trying to be helpful. But he didn't have the correct information.

Many of your friends and acquaintances will give you wrong directions—not on purpose—but simply because they don't know better. Determine right now who you're going to listen to. It doesn't matter how polite, popular, or fun someone is—if he's giving you the wrong directions, you'll be doomed if you follow them. Jesus Christ and his holy Word are our authorities. He's the only One who can tell us how to reach our final destination. And his book—the Holy Bible—is the only road map with the correct directions to heaven.

Friends who practice other religions, and people who say there are many ways to reach your eternal destination, may be articulate and convincing, but they're giving you false directions. Determine to know God's voice so well, and strive to know his holy Word so well, that you can quickly discern wrong directions from the truth.

(Source unknown)
As I was walking down life's highway, I came upon a sign that read "Heaven's Grocery Store." When I got a little closer, the doors swung open wide and I walked through the entrance. I saw a host of angels. One handed me a shopping cart and instructed me to fill it.

I headed down the aisles and noticed that everything anyone would ever need was in that store. Just when I began to wonder how I would ever carry everything, an angel approached me and said, "Whatever you can't carry, you can come back for."

I first grabbed some Patience. Then I found a huge box of Understanding. *Can't have too much of that,* I mused. So I grabbed an extra box. Then I noticed Love in the same row and put an oversized load of that in my cart.

Next I got some Wisdom and a couple of bags of Faith. I couldn't overlook Charity, so I grabbed that, too. *Oh, my goodness,* I thought, *the Holy Spirit's here! He's all over the place—plentiful as can be!* So I took a generous helping and then came upon Strength.

Realizing I'd need that to help me through the tough times ahead, I didn't hesitate to put some in my cart. And then I came upon Courage. *Gotta have that, too.*

My cart was getting full, but I remembered I needed Grace. Then I chose Salvation and rejoiced inwardly that it was free. *Wow!* I thought. *I've got everything I need to do God's will.*

But as I moved toward the cashier, I noticed Prayer. *I'll need a lot of that,* I reasoned, *because when I step outside this store, I'll be stepping right into a world of sin.* So I stocked up on Prayer and couldn't help but notice Peace and Joy. They were plentiful, so I helped myself. And right next to the cashier's counter, I noticed Praise and Worship, so I placed them on top.

Then I said to the angel working the cash register, "How much do I owe?"

But he just smiled and said, "Take them everywhere you go."

So I repeated the question: "Really. How much do I owe?"

"My child," he said, "God paid your bill a long, long time ago."

Know It!

Isn't it exciting that God gives you—for free—everything you need for living a godly life? You don't have to wonder and question how he wants you to live. He's already told you to live a holy life. And instead of frustrating you by making you guess how to do that, he simply gives you everything you need to become all he calls you to be!

Read It!

1 Corinthians 4:20;
Hebrews 12:14;
1 Peter 1:16;
Revelation 22:11

Pray It!

Spend some time thanking God for paying the bill for everything you need to live a holy life. Ask him to fill you with his Holy Spirit so that you may be empowered to be the godly person he wants you to be.

Are You Wearing the Right Label?

Know It!

A lot of people say they're Christians, but their walk doesn't match their talk. If your life doesn't match the definition of a Christian, you could actually be harming the kingdom of God by claiming to be something you're not.

Read It!

Matthew 23:27-32; Mark:12:15; Luke 12:1; Galatians 2:13

Pray It!

Tell God you want to be authentic. Ask him to help you live out your relationship with him through your everyday actions.

Jake moved to North America from a remote area in Papua New Guinea at the beginning of his junior year in high school. The village he was from was so primitive that the first time Jake ever saw a basketball game was when he saw some neighbor kids shooting hoops down the street from his new house.

He was fascinated with the game. He rented several videos, watched guys play pick-up games in the park, and decided to go out for the team at school.

Coach Weston knew Jake had never played before, so he spent extra time with him teaching him the basics, going through drills, and running up and down the court with him. But when the time came to try out for the team, Jake refused to dribble the ball. "I can get it down the court much faster if I just carry it," he explained.

"Then you should probably try out for the football team," Coach Weston said. "You can't carry the ball in basketball."

When he finally got the ball back, Jake kicked it toward the basket. Coach Weston pulled him off the court. "Jake, why don't you sit out for a while?"

"You can't pull me off the court!" Jake said. "I'm a basketball player. I belong out there!"

"No, Jake," Coach Weston responded. "You play with basketballs, but you're not a basketball player. Real basketball players go by the rules."

⁂

Okay, so the story's not true. In fact, it's really quite absurd, isn't it? Who would call himself a basketball player if he didn't actually play the game?

Unfortunately, the same thing is happening in Christianity right now. Many people are calling themselves Christians who really aren't living the life.

Being a Christian is much more than simply praying a prayer and continuing to live as you see fit. Being a Christian means you've sought forgiveness for your sins, given Christ control of your life, and are living in his will.

If you call yourself a Christian, you need to live up to the name and follow the definition. If not? Then call yourself what you really are—a hypocrite.

If Jake refuses to play basketball the way it's meant to be played, he really shouldn't call himself a basketball player.

God has a high calling on your life. He loves you more than you can imagine ... but be honest, okay? Don't identify yourself as his follower unless you're willing to live in obedience to him.

What does it mean to live in obedience to Christ? Two important things. *Number 1: You'll accept the Bible as God's holy Word—absolute truth.* There are professors in Christian colleges who tell their students that much of the Bible really isn't true. Someday they'll have to answer to God for that!

When Jesus spoke in parables, he always made sure his listeners knew it. In other words, he let them know that a specific story was only an example to explain the meaning of what he was saying.

But to choose not to believe the Garden of Eden actually existed and to doubt that Eve was tempted by Satan and ate the forbidden fruit? Then how sincere is your faith? If you can't accept the fact that the Bible *is* true and that all of it is God's truth, you're not really identifying with the Author of the Book, Jesus Christ.

Number 2: You'll obey God. Yes, that means you'll live as he wants you to live. You'll give him the ultimate control of your life. To say you're a Christian but to continue living however you want is not Christianity.

But what if I blow it? Is there room for failure in the life of a Christian? Yes, there is! God understands your humanness. But there's a huge difference between defiantly going against God's will and blowing it and approaching God with genuine sorrow. God will always forgive a repentant heart. To consistently live in utter defiance of his will, however, is not living with a repentant spirit.

When I recently spoke at a youth conference, an assistant youth leader approached me and said, "I'm a Christian, but I don't believe much of anything you're saying."

"That's interesting," I replied. "Because everything I'm saying is coming from the Bible."

"I don't believe the Bible."

"And you say you're a Christian?"

"That's right," he continued. "I'm a Christian, but I don't believe the Bible. It was just written by human men, and humans make mistakes."

Know It!

God wants to make his holy Word—which is absolute truth—come alive in and through your life. If you have doubts about the Bible, do some research to find out for yourself if it's trustworthy. Here are two books that can help you: student editions of *The Case for Christ* and *The Case for Faith* by Lee Strobel.

Read It!

2 Corinthians 5:17; 2 Timothy 3:16-17; Hebrews 6:1; James 4:4

Pray It!

Ask God to show you any areas of hypocrisy in your life. If you have any doubts regarding his holy Word, ask him to replace those doubts with solid faith.

AUGUST 30

Let's Be Blunt!

Know It!
Could it be that you've fallen into Satan's trap of making up your own religion? If so, you need to realize your own set of rules and regulations won't get you to heaven.

Read It!
Exodus 20:3-17; 1 John 2:4, 6; 4:1-3

Pray It!
Seek God's forgiveness for disregarding his rules and substituting them with your own.

"Yes, the Bible was penned by humans, but it was divinely inspired by God himself," I replied to the assistant youth leader who claimed the Word of God wasn't true.

"I don't believe it," he continued.

So I pressed a little farther: "If you don't believe the Bible . . . how does God speak to you?"

"Through my dreams."

By now I was *really* interested. "And you put more stock in what your subconscious cooks up during the night than what the apostle Paul said in the Bible?"

"Absolutely."

Whew! That's scary! There are a lot of people claiming to be Christians who are making up their own religion! And if you're one of the vast numbers of Christians who believe whatever they want, you're living dangerously. See, the bottom line is . . . it doesn't matter what you think about truth. It doesn't matter what Susie Shellenberger thinks or what your youth leader thinks. The only thing that matters is what *God* thinks. And someday we'll all be held accountable to his standard.

So here it is: If you're being sexually intimate outside of marriage, messing around with drugs or alcohol, living with hatred, and holding grudges, STOP calling yourself a Christian.

But wait a sec, Susie! You make it sound like Christianity is living by a bunch of rules, and if we can't obey the rules, we ought to get out of the game.

Though Christianity isn't ALL rules, there are 10 big ones we're expected to live by. You know them as the Ten Commandments. (Flip back to August 10-19 for a quick refresher course on the Ten Commandments.) *And if we break the rules, we're out of the game forever?* No. That's where repentance comes in. Seeking God's forgiveness.

So I can keep on sinning and doing whatever I want, because God will always forgive me? No, that's not repentance. Coming to Jesus with a repentant heart and asking his forgiveness is like saying, "Oh, Father, I'm so sorry. My sin has broken your heart, and it's breaking my heart. Will you forgive me? I don't ever plan on going down that road again. In fact, I'm going to build specific safeguards in my life to make sure I don't go that direction again."

That's repentance. God forgives a repentant heart. Always!

Excuses, Excuses

Don't be someone who always has an excuse. Face it: Sometimes you just won't have an excuse. Deal with it. Students who are constantly trying to make up excuses to explain their unacceptable behavior in school are usually a teacher's worst nightmare. As you think about starting a new school year, take a look at some excuses that *never* work.

- What? You mean the A.C.T. and the S.A.T. aren't open-book tests? I'm shocked! I never knew that.
- Well, yeah, I heard you give the homework assignment. I just didn't realize we were supposed to write out the answers. I did the work. I really did! It's just all in my head.
- Can I go to my locker? Well, you didn't *tell* us to bring our textbook every day!
- I thought semester exams were a group project. Honest, I really did!
- But I *wasn't* talking! Okay, yes, I was moving my mouth. And yes, sounds were emitted from my vocal chords. But it's not what you think! You see, I'm trying to learn ventriloquism. It's my only chance for a college scholarship.
- Well, it's not that I'm actually *late.* I'm just really time-sensitive impaired.
- The homework assignment? Well . . . yes . . . I'm aware that I didn't turn it in. You see, Mrs. Foster, this is really bizarre, but last night there was, uh, this tornado-thing that swept through our neighborhood, and uh, well, my homework assignment was completely destroyed.

  What's that? You live within a mile of my house and didn't hear anything about a tornado? Hmmm. That's interesting, Mrs. Foster. And it just goes to show that Mother Nature acts in unexplainable ways.

  What's that? You'll expect a five-page typed report with footnotes and research cards on unexplainable acts of nature to be turned in tomorrow morning? Okay, I know this may come as a total shock to you, but I was just kidding. I never even *did* the homework assignment. Can I just turn it in tomorrow? Tomorrow will be fine? Oh, thanks, Mrs. Foster! You're the best.

  What's that? Along with my five-page typed report on unexplainable acts of nature, you want a seven-page typed report on the pitfalls of procrastination? Uh, Mrs. Foster, can you give me any information on military school?

Know It!

Though it's often easy to make excuses to cover up our mistakes, God desires an honest lifestyle. If you're having trouble keeping your word, following through on your word, or using honest words, seek God's forgiveness and ask for his help. Excuses are only temporary. A righteous life lasts forever.

Read It!

Proverbs 10:9; 11:3; 12:22; 21

Pray It!

Tell God you don't want to be known as the student who's always trying to get by with an excuse. Ask him to help you develop a lifestyle of honesty and a good work ethic.

Truth or Flattery?

A teen girl approached me recently and said, "Hey, I'm only 14! I'm not going to give God all of my life right now. I'm too young. I still wanna have fun."

My heart broke for her. She calls herself a Christian, yet she knows in her heart of hearts that she's not following Jesus as Lord. And God has made it crystal clear that those who call him "Lord" but don't live according to his will aren't Christians. He also makes it clear that those who aren't Christians will spend eternity in hell.

Yeah, but I'm a good person. I can't believe that just because I don't live in obedience to God, I'll actually go to hell.

And that's Satan's biggest lie. How could good people go to hell? If you have trouble believing this, you're probably one of the people the apostle Paul is talking about in 2 Timothy when he says that people will look for pastors who will simply tell them what they want to hear.

This devotional book isn't meant to tell you only nice things you want to hear. I'm not going to say, "Well, it's okay. God understands your sin." I'm going to tell you the truth. He'll *forgive* your sin if you come to him with a repentant heart, but he expects you not to return to that sin.

If you fight with one particular sin and have to confess it over and over, that doesn't mean you're not a real Christian. Even the apostle Paul struggled with recurring sin (see Romans 7:15-25). But the key is in our attitude. God expects us to fight temptation. When we fall down, he wants us to ask for forgiveness and move forward. What he hates is an attitude that says, "God will forgive me, so I can keep sinning." In other words, don't call yourself a Christian if you're not willing to try with all your heart to live up to the definition.

We're living in a day when it's tough to believe that good people will actually spend eternity in hell if they don't know Jesus Christ. *What's wrong with their choices? They're not hurting anyone!* But again, the bottom line is: If someone hasn't sought forgiveness for his sins and doesn't have a personal relationship with Jesus Christ, he'll spend forever in hell. This is the absolute truth.

Know It!

Maybe you have given God 100 percent and are living in obedience to his will. Great! But if you're not, I invite you to surrender right now. If you're calling yourself a Christian—yet not living up to the name and definition—now's your chance to make things right with the creator of the universe.

Read It!

Matthew 7:21-23;
James 3:11-13;
2 Timothy 3:1; 4:3-4

Pray It!

Seek God's forgiveness for your hypocrisy, and ask him to give you a brand-new start. Confess your sins and accept him as your personal Savior.

Beware of Friendly Snakes!

Know It!
God is extremely faithful. You can trust him. He'll always respond to a sincere heart asking for discernment and forgiveness regarding sin.

Read It!
Hebrews 10:26;
James 4:17;
1 Peter 3:18;
Revelation 22:18

Pray It!
Rewrite Psalm 139:23-24, inserting your own name into the verse, and make it your prayer right now.

There's an old tale about a peasant who was working in his field during the spring. As the ground began to thaw, he noticed a snake. He raised his hoe to kill it, but the snake begged for compassion. "I'm too frozen to do you any harm," the snake whined. "Please don't kill me."

The old farmer took pity on the snake, picked up the half-dead reptile, and put it inside his overalls next to his chest. He continued to hoe his field, and the snake got warmer and warmer as the day progressed. Suddenly, the snake bit the farmer.

The man frantically reached inside his overalls, pulled the serpent out, and threw it to the ground.

"Why?" the peasant asked. "I believed you. I befriended you. I saved your life and trusted you."

"True!" the reptile hissed as it slid away. "But don't blame me! You knew I was a snake when you picked me up."

Many people fall into the easy trap of picking up sin, befriending it, and even holding it close to their heart. We can work overtime to dress it up or give it another name, but sin will always be sin. We can make excuses and rationalize why we carry it around with us, but again . . . sin is sin. And eventually—if we don't confess it with a repentant heart—it will kill us.

Is it possible to know if you have sin in your life? Absolutely! God will work through his Holy Spirit within you to let you know something in your life isn't right. If you ask God with a sincere heart to point out any unconfessed sin in your life, he'll do exactly that. And he'll be very specific, so you won't have to second-guess him.

But we often become so comfortable with sin in our lives, we don't bother asking God to point it out to us. That's a dangerous place for a Christian to live! It's like sleeping through a storm. When God allows the lightning to flash into your soul, don't snooze through it. Allow his Holy Spirit to wake you up and bring to your attention those things in your life that are keeping you from becoming all he wants you to be!

Too Comfy?

Dear Diary:

Yeah, it's been a while. . . . But I do have to admit . . . it feels good at times to be able to totally unload in here.

Okay, so here's the deal. Last Sunday our pastor talked about not being of the world. He said we can't help but be in the world, but we shouldn't get so caught up in the sin around us that we become part of the world.

Yeah. So I've been thinking about that the last few days, and now I'm totally confused. How can you live in the world but make sure you're not part of the world? I don't get it. I mean even when I'm driving through town, I see billboards with compromising stuff on them. At school I hear all kinds of language. And when I turn on the TV, almost everything I see is "of the world." Even the news is filled with sin.

So . . . I'm thinking it's probably close to impossible to not be affected by all this junk. And it frustrates me. I want to be everything God calls me to be, but I don't know how with everything that's going on around me.

It's not like I can wear blinders or plug my ears every time I walk out the door.

Sigh.

Okay, here's an example. Yesterday, while we were eating in the school cafeteria, Chris started talking about stuff that was way outta line. I just sat there and kept eating. But should I have left? Should I have said something?

I don't know.

I do want to live a holy life. And I don't want to get involved in things that are gonna drag me down and mess up my relationship with Christ.

Know It!

Though you can't help but be in the world, God doesn't want you to become like the world. When you hear God's name taken in vain, hopefully your stomach will twist in knots. When you see something that degrades his character, hopefully it will repulse you. God wants to help you avoid places that will damage your relationship with him. Strive, instead, to place yourself with people and in surroundings that will honor his holy name.

Read It!

Romans 12:1-2; 1 Corinthians 3:16-20; Titus 2:12; 1 John 5:3-5

Pray It!

Ask God to make you extremely uncomfortable when you hear or see things that break his heart.

What's Your Faucet Saying?

Know It!
God wants you to experience life abundantly! If dripping faucets are keeping you from clearly hearing his voice, call the Master Plumber immediately!

Read It!
Proverbs 14:10;
1 Corinthians 10:11-13;
2 Corinthians 12:20;
Ephesians 4:31

Pray It!
Ask God to make you aware of any dripping faucets in your life that need to be fixed.

Have you ever tried to concentrate on something and you couldn't . . . because of a dripping faucet? *Drip. Drip. Drip.* It's enough to drive a person nuts!

Instead of allowing a dripping faucet to annoy us, maybe we should let it teach us something. Think about it: A dripping faucet is saying, "Something's not right here. There's a leak that needs fixing." A dripping faucet is a signal that something's wrong. Most of us can't relax during the drip, because we know there's something that needs to be fixed, or we worry about the water that's being wasted.

In the same way, God sometimes allows "dripping faucets" in our lives to signal us that something is spiritually off-center. We often try to ignore those spiritual signals by cranking the volume on our CD player or flipping through a variety of channels on our TV. But the truth is, a dripping faucet won't quit on its own. We actually have to get up and do something about it.

Is God trying to signal you that something is wrong in your life? If so, listen to the drip and be willing to do whatever it takes to fix it. Is there a wall in one of your relationships? Have you not forgiven someone who hurt you? Has it become too easy to be critical, negative, and to make remarks that cause dissension among those around you? Are you jealous of a friend who got what you had your heart set on? Have you become bitter because someone rejected you?

Perhaps God is saying through your broken heart, "This isn't right. Let's fix it."

Or through a critical, negative spirit, maybe God is saying, "This can no longer continue. I love you too much to allow you to remain this way."

Could God be trying to speak through your jealousy . . . saying, "Instead of feeling insecure about what someone else has, will you refocus your attention on me? I dream BIG dreams for you!"

A dripping faucet won't fix itself. But our all-powerful, all-knowing, ever-present God can even masquerade as a Master Plumber. And he can provide exactly what you need to stop the leak.

Strength through the Struggle

The wind rushed through Joey's sandy blond hair as the 11-year-old boy made his way through the familiar neighborhood streets from school to his house. Just a couple of blocks from home, Joey found the cocoon of a butterfly. He stared at it for several minutes and made note of where it was so he could keep an eye on it during the next few days.

The following week, he noticed a small opening in the cocoon. Joey lost complete track of time as he sat and watched the insect inside struggle to force its body through the tiny hole. As the sun began to set, he hurried home but couldn't stop thinking about the cocoon. The next day, after school, Joey noticed the insect appeared to be stuck in the hole. It appeared as though it had gotten as far as it could and helplessly remained still mostly inside the cocoon.

The next morning, he took a pair of scissors and put them in his backpack. On the way to school, he stopped again to look at the cocoon. Feeling sorry for the insect, he decided to help it enter the outside world. He carefully snipped off the remaining bit of the cocoon. Joey smiled as he watched the butterfly emerge smoothly from the hole.

He was surprised, though, to notice the butterfly's swollen body and small, shriveled wings. Joey continued to watch the butterfly, because in his childlike innocence he expected at any moment its wings would enlarge and expand to be able to support the body, which would contract in time.

Neither happened! In fact, the butterfly spent the rest of its life crawling around with a swollen body and shriveled wings. It was never able to fly. What Joey didn't understand was that the restricting cocoon and the struggle required for the butterfly to get through the tiny opening were God's way of forcing fluid from the body of the insect into its wings so that it would be ready for flight once it achieved its freedom from the cocoon.

Sometimes struggles are exactly what we need in our lives. Though none of us enjoy them, God often uses them for our good. He strengthens us through the dark hours. He increases our faith when we call on him for help through the pain.

Know It!

If God allowed us to go through our lives without any obstacles, it would cripple us. We wouldn't be as strong as we could have been. We'd never fly. God wants you to soar! Can you trust him with your shaky wings and your daily struggles? Instead of growing frustrated with all that's going wrong in your life, try shifting your focus to what you'll become after the struggle has ceased.

Read It!

2 Corinthians 10:10; James 1:2-4, 12; 2 Peter 2:9

Pray It!

Ask God to change the way you view your struggles.

The World's Largest Backpacking Group

Know It!
Just as God led the children of Israel into a land promised specifically for them, he'll lead you into plans that he's creating uniquely for you!

Read It!
Exodus 13:20-22; 14–15

Pray It!
Ask God for faith to obey and follow him even when you can't see ahead.

They were sort of like a huge youth group. There were approximately 500,000 students! When *they* played "Capture the Flag," it was all-out war! And car washes? Well, let's just say the whole *city* got wet.

Their youth leader was Yo-Mo. Well, that's what the youth group called him. Everyone has a special nickname for his youth minister, right? His *real* name was Moses.

Anyway, these teens (the world's largest backpacking group) had worked *forever* (okay, three months) to earn enough money to go on the world's longest backpacking trip. They'd had the car washes, spaghetti dinners, and even tried selling M&Ms.

Now they were arriving at their weekly youth meeting, and Yo-Mo had his head buried inside the youth bank account books.

"You've done it!" he screamed. "You've finally done it!" A few of the guys murmured, "I didn't think *anyone* saw us put those goldfish in the baptistry. How'd he find out?"

Then Yo-Mo grabbed the microphone and said, "I'm so proud of you guys! You've finally earned enough money for us to go on the world's longest backpacking trip."

Boy, were they excited! They shouted and clapped and screamed so loud that the adults (who were meeting in the sanctuary) complained about how much noise the youth were making again.

Yo-Mo didn't waste any time. He quickly grabbed his travel notes and began his trip-talk. "I've already mapped out the place for our adventure," he began. "We're going to the Promised Land. They have some great deals on milk and honey there, and it *should* only take us about 40 days to backpack it."

(Well, some of you have heard this story before, and *you* know it actually took a little longer than 40 days! But that's what happens when we get sidetracked from God's path. It takes us a lot longer than it would have if we'd just continued following his direction.)

Yo-Mo then passed out parent-permission forms and continued with his instructions. "Since this *is* a backpacking trip, obviously that means we'll be carrying everything in our packs on our backs. So you know what that means, girls? No curling irons, electric rollers, or blow-dryers. Nobody bring *anything* extra."

40 Days . . . or 40 Years?

Yo-Mo continued with his instructions to the teens in his youth group. "We'll meet here at the church tomorrow morning at 5 A.M.," he announced. "And remember, it should only take us 40 days to get there. So tell your parents to be here waiting for you. Because I don't want to wait for 500,000 of you to call your parents once we get back to the church, okay?"

It just so happened that the students in Yo-Mo's youth group weren't very good travelers. They got antsy. They wanted to stop at every McDonald's they passed. They screamed stuff from the back of the bus. *Annoying* stuff like: "How many more miles?" And "When're we gonna get there?" Then their questions turned accusatory: "Hey! Yo-Mo, you *said* we'd be there in 40 days. It's been four-and-a-half *years*! So when are we gonna stop, huh?" And even derogatory remarks: "Yo-Mo! Where'd you get your license? Out of a Cracker Jack box?"

After 37 years, a kid from the very back of the bus raised his hand. "Um, Mr. Yo-Mo? Do you think maybe we could pull over and stop? I, uh, really oughta call my parents. They've been waiting for me at the church for 37 years now."

Finally, after being on the road for a little over 40 years, Yo-Mo pulled over at a rest stop. Everyone piled off the bus, and he climbed a mountain.

When Moses reached the top, the Lord began speaking to him. "Mo, squint your eyes a little. See way over there in the distance?"

Mo squinted. "Yeah. I see it!"

"That's the Promised Land," the Lord said.

"Wow!" Mo exclaimed. "That's it? That's what we've been trying to find for the past 40 years? Cool."

"And now that you've seen it, it's time for you to die."

What? Over 40 years of leading his youth group, and now he has to die? Without even getting to go *inside*?

That's right. You see, a little earlier, Mo had compromised. (He made excuses and said some things that were really wrong were okay.) As a result, God was withholding some of his blessings.

Know It!
There are always consequences when we compromise God's direction in our lives.

Read It!
Exodus 16–18

Pray It!
Tell God you don't want to be a complainer (like the children of Israel) when things don't go your way. Pray for a positive attitude.

A New Leader

Know It!
Maybe you, like the children of Israel, have lost someone significant in your life. Perhaps your youth leader moved away, your dad left the family, your friend is gone. God understands the hurt we feel when we lose someone we love and admire. But God never leaves us hanging. He always provides whom and what we need. Can you trust him to fill the vacuum in your life?

Read It!
Deuteronomy 1:19-46; Joshua 1–3

Pray It!
Thank God for his promise never to leave you. Tell him how grateful you are for his constant provision.

Meanwhile, the youth group had turned into a mumbling, grumbling bunch of complainers. "Where is he?" Brad asked. "Can we go ahead and eat, or do we have to wait for him?"

Someone sent a messenger to find Yo-Mo, who returned with the sad news that their leader had died. THEN the youth group changed its tune. They moaned, cried, refused to eat, and didn't sleep very well. "What will we do?" they asked. "We left everything to enter the Promised Land, and now we have no leader!"

Well, God never ever *ever* asks us to do something (or leads us somewhere) without providing everything we need to get the job done. He always meets our needs. And God had been consistently working behind the scenes. He'd already chosen a young man in their very own youth group. His name was Joshua.

Josh was a solid, godly young man. He didn't compromise. Didn't buckle when the pressure began to mount. Didn't bend when the tension started to rise. He just walked straight ahead and consistently obeyed the Lord.

He took over Mo's maps and called the youth group together. "I've studied the travel plans," he said. "And we're really not far from the Promised Land at all." (Everyone cheered.) "But there *is* this big city in the way. It's Jericho. And it's a very wicked city. So we're going to have to go through it and conquer it before we can enter the Promised Land."

(Back in the days before Christ died for our sins, the way God abolished evil was to destroy it. That's why there's so much killing in the Old Testament. It was the only plan at the time to clean everything up. Aren't you glad Jesus came?)

"Tell you what," Josh continued. "You've all been through a rough time. Let's just set up camp right here on the shores of the Jordan River and take a few days off. That'll give me a chance to send our undercover agents inside the city of Jericho to see where everything is."

Sounded good. So while the agents crossed the river and headed toward the big city, the world's largest backpacking group set up the volleyball nets, got out the Jet Skis, and started partying.

As soon as Josh's agents crossed the Jordan River, they were face-to-face with the largest wall they'd ever seen in their lives. It was huge. And it surrounded the entire city of Jericho.

But God always provides. (We talked about that yesterday, remember?) And the gates to the city just happened to be open. So Josh's undercover agents meandered right through. One guy pulled out his digital camera and started taking pictures so Joshua could see where everything was.

There was city square. And off to the right was Jericho High School. Across the street, he noticed Jericho Swim and Fitness. And up closer on the left were some really cool split-level condos.

Some of the king's employees noticed the agents staking out the city. They rushed to the king and told him about the strangers with the cameras. "Hmmph," the king said. "Betcha they're part of that world's largest backpacking group. I think they're headed for the Promised Land, which probably means they'll try to conquer *us* before they get there."

"Well, what should we do, O wise one?" one of the employees asked.

"We're going to lock the gates to the city so anyone who's not a citizen won't be able to get in! And if we see anyone *trying* to get in or out, we'll kill him on the spot."

But the king's employees weren't the only ones watching those undercover agents. There was a woman named Rahab who was standing on the balcony of her condo. She wanted to help these men of God, and she'd also overheard the conversation of the king's employees. So while the agents were still taking pictures, she tried to catch their attention.

"Psssst."

Click. Click. "Hey, Eric! Stand over there by that fountain and act like you're gonna fall in. That'll make a great shot."

"Oooooh, yeah. And get one with me next to this statue."

"Pssssssst."

"Ryan, did you hear something?"

"PSSSSSSSSSSSSTTTTTTT!!!"

"Eric, there's a lady up there making faces at us!"

"Uh . . . ma'am. Are you talking to us?"

"Yeah. The king's gonna kill you! If you want, you can climb up here and hide."

Hey, sounded like a plan. They didn't have any *other* options! So they hid on Rahab's roof till nightfall.

Know It!
When it seems there's no way out, God always provides an exit.

Read It!
Joshua 4–6

Pray It!
Ask God to help you respond in obedience when he shuts one door and opens another.

Moving Forward

Know It!
Are you spending precious time going over the same spiritual ground again and again when God is prompting you to move forward?

Read It!
Luke 7:9; Romans 12:12; Hebrews 11:1-3; 1 Peter 1:21

Pray It!
Ask God to solidify your faith and to stretch your dependence on him. Tell him you're ready to exercise your faith even when you can't see the outcome.

As soon as the sun had set, Rahab grabbed a rope, made a lasso, and tossed it over the wall. The agents climbed down the rope, over the wall, and headed back to Joshua's beach party.

"That place is huge!" Eric gasped. "And we have the footage to prove it."

"There's absolutely no way we could ever conquer that city," Ryan said. "It's too big, and there are too many people."

"And there's a massive wall surrounding the entire city! We'll never get inside. They have a special warrant issued for all noncitizens to be killed. We'd never get over the wall!"

"Someone hand these guys a Pepsi," Josh said, keeping his cool. "I think you've forgotten our theme."

"What's that?" Eric asked.

"The fact that God always provides! Guys, listen to me! He would never ever EVER ask us to do something (or lead us somewhere) without providing everything we need. Now remember that! In fact, *memorize* it. Because we *are* going to the Promised Land. And we're going through Jericho!"

Plans were made to head out the following morning, but by dawn the Jordan River was flooded. We're talking tidal wave material. Joshua halted his group. "Let's just spend a few days in prayer and wait on the Lord."

So they waited. And waited. And waited. Finally a couple of weeks passed. The river was still overflowing. It looked like they would drown if they even *tried* to cross. Joshua continued to seek the Lord. And as he did, God spoke back.

"Joshua, I have commanded that you cross this river, conquer Jericho, and enter the Promised Land. What are you waiting on?"

"The river, Lord. It's overflowing! How can we cross?"

"Trust me. I've already told you to cross."

"But, Lord, are you *sure* we're supposed to cross *right now*? I mean, we don't mind waiting," Josh said.

"You don't need to spend time praying about things I've already made clear, Joshua. There may be some battles in life you won't win, but I have already promised this is one you *will* win! I've already made myself clear: Cross the river, conquer Jericho, enter the Promised Land. Simply step out in faith believing that I will do what I have said."

Joshua exercised his faith, gathered the world's largest backpacking group together, and lined them up. Row after row after row. Over 500,000 of them. And his instructions probably went something like this:

"Okay, gang, we're crossing. I know, I know—the Jordan River is still flooded. I realize that. But I also have faith that the God who calls us to cross will somehow provide a way. I mean, that's our *theme,* right? Let's join hands and walk together."

So they began. Ryan's hand was sweaty, but he clung to his brother, Eric. And Eric clung to Joshua. And Joshua clung to Geoff. And Geoff clung to Mark. And Mark clung to Annette. And Annette clung to Liz. And on and on and on it went—all holding hands and walking toward that huge, powerful body of roaring, terrifying 15-foot waves.

You *know* what happened, don't you? Their feet touched the water and God split the river! Over 500,000 people walked across on dry land.

How did they do it? By holding hands and walking together. You see, God promises that there's nothing you'll face that will be too strong for you to handle—if you'll walk with your brothers and sisters in Christ. Isn't that what the Church is all about?

It's about patting someone on the shoulder and saying, "Good job!" Or looking a friend in the eye and saying, "Jamie, I sense that you're going through a tough time right now. Can I treat you to a Coke?" It's walking the second mile. Mailing a note of encouragement. Making a phone call. Giving a hug. Sending an e-mail.

Christ wants the church to be a place where you can collapse into the arms of your brothers and sisters and say, "Whew! It feels good to be out of the storm."

He wants your church to be your shelter; your place of refuge. We often get so caught up in who said what and misunderstandings that church and youth group become a place of avoidance instead of the place we rush to for support. Joshua was in the process of teaching his group an invaluable lesson: "If we walk together, there's no river too deep for us to cross. When we stop holding hands, become divided, and take our focus off of God, we'll drown."

Know It!
God wants to use *you* as a catalyst to promote spiritual wellness in your youth group and church. Will you let him?

Read It!
Romans 12:3-8;
1 Corinthians 12:4-31; 13:4-7; 14:33

Pray It!
Ask God if there's anyone in your youth group with whom you need to make amends.

Sticking to the Plan

Know It!
When God gives you a specific song to sing, there will always be those who try to change your tune. Don't compromise! God gives specific visions, certain dreams, unique messages for one reason: He wants *those* visions, *those* dreams, *those* messages . . . and those specific songs delivered. Don't succumb to the pressure of a crowd who wants to change your delivery.

Read It!
Joshua 6;
Psalms 112:6-9; 119:1-3, 101-106

Pray It!
Seek God's strength to continue living the way he wants you to live, and discipline to deliver the message he has given you to share.

As soon as the world's largest backpacking group had crossed the Jordan River, they realized they were up against the largest wall they'd ever experienced in their lives! But everyone remained calm. Josh had already gone over the game plan. He'd already rehearsed the instructions. They knew exactly what to do.

They reached behind their heads and untied their backpacks. Even though years earlier Yo-Mo had specifically said *not* to bring anything extra, everyone *had.* It just so happened that 40 years earlier, they were all members of the Egyptian High School marching band. So—even though they weren't supposed to—they all packed their band instruments!

They pulled out their horns, tubas, flutes, and other music makers and lined up. After tuning up, they marched around the great wall playing "Oh, When the Saints Go Marching In."

And the people *inside* the city of Jericho stopped. "Oh, when the saints," someone sang. "Go marching in," someone hummed. "Oh, when the saints go marching in," a soprano belted.

"Hey! I know that song."

"Where's that music coming from?"

"Did our city council decide to pipe in special music for us?"

"That's so great!"

And the next day at the same time, the world's largest backpacking group marched around the wall again and played the same tune. And the *next* day. And the *next.* And the *next.* Until finally at the end of the week, the people inside the city of Jericho were sick and tired of the same old music.

"Hey, can't you play anything besides 'The Saints'?" someone yelled.

"Yeah, we're SICK of that song!"

"How 'bout a C-scale or a minor chord or one of those augmented things—*something*!"

Josh addressed his group: "We're gonna keep playing the same song, and since this is the seventh day, we'll play it seven times. Ha!"

So they adjusted their instruments and began marching. But *this* time, as sort of a grand finale . . . at the end of the seventh rendition, they stood tall with their shoulders back and screamed as loudly as they could: "JO!"

The people inside the city of Jericho stopped. *Jo?*

Men who were coming out of the bank and placing money in their wallets stopped. *Jo?*

Women who were pushing babies in strollers down sidewalks stopped. *Jo?*

Adults who were coming out of grocery stores with bags in their arms stopped. *Jo?*

Teachers who were lecturing and giving homework assignments stopped. *Jo?*

And students who were listening and passing notes stopped. *Jo? Jo! Jo?*

Finally, the entire city, dumbfounded, stood to their feet and in unison cried out, "JO? JO WHO?"

And 500,000 on the other side screamed back: *Jo Mama! Jo Mama is a wimp! Jo Mama wears combat boots. Jo Mama! Jo Mama! Jo MAMA!*

There was so much noise, the walls began to shake. The ground quivered, and only minutes later the entire wall completely collapsed!

The world's largest backpacking group wasted no time rushing inside. The people of Jericho were in such a state of shock and confusion they were defeated on the spot!

Joshua grabbed the microphone at city square and announced the continuing plan of action. "Glory be to God," he cried, "for giving us the strength to defeat a city six times our size. Now listen carefully to the following instructions. I want you to go into every condo, home, and apartment and destroy everything except anything that's valuable."

"Like what?" Todd asked. (It had been so long since any of them had even *seen* valuable stuff that they were a little confused.)

"Jewelry," Josh said. "Bring all the jewelry out here—along with any valuable metals—turquoise, gold, silver, copper. We'll melt it all down and use it to build the temple once we get to the Promised Land. Bring the valuable stuff out to city square, destroy the rest—and NO ONE KEEP ANYTHING FOR HIMSELF!"

Know It!
Throughout history, God has equipped his people to overcome incredible odds. You may be struggling with something that appears six times your size, but if it's a battle God has called you to fight, he's in it with you and will provide everything you need.

Read It!
Psalm 20:5; Colossians 1:23; Hebrews 11; 1 Peter 1:9

Pray It!
Ask God to give you his spiritual vision so that instead of seeing insurmountable odds through your eyes, you'll learn to see with his vision.

What Are You Rationalizing?

Know It!

People can rationalize anything. Many dating couples rationalize that since they're in love—and will eventually marry each other anyway—having sex outside of marriage is permissible in their case. Other Christians rationalize pornographic fantasies, thinking, *Hey, it's just in my mind. It's not hurting anyone.* If you want to rationalize drinking, taking drugs, or even Satanism, you can find a "church" willing to endorse those very things. But remember—rationalizing with people is never the same as rationalizing with God. It just won't work. *Ever.*

Read It!

Psalms 119:43-48, 55-64, 128-133, 165

Pray It!

Ask the Lord to help you fall in love with his will even though you may not always understand it.

Joshua's instructions were crystal clear. He gave the signal, and away everyone went. All of them. Following his orders. Obeying the instructions. Well . . . not exactly. There was this *one guy.*

His name was Acorn. (Well, almost. His *real* name was Achan. Not much better, huh?)

Acorn went into a condo, cleaned it out completely, and just happened to notice a bathrobe. (True story. I promise. Read it for yourself in the seventh chapter of Joshua.) And even though he remembered Josh specifically saying no one could keep anything, he thought to himself, *Hey, it's just a bathrobe. It's not like it's valuable or anything.* And besides . . . no one was watching. *I'm so tired of these old gym shorts. I deserve a new bathrobe.* So he took the garment, folded it, wrapped his tunic around it, and went to the next home.

Again, he cleaned it out completely, but his eyes fell on a small gold bar—maybe three inches long. And even though he could hear Joshua's words echoing in his mind, he couldn't help but think, *It's so small. What's one gold bar?* So he took the gold bar, stuck it in his pocket, and went to a nearby apartment.

He did a great job cleaning it out, but as he did, he couldn't help but see a small silver coin—about the size of two quarters. And yes, he remembered the words of his leader, but different thoughts ran through Acorn's mind: *It's just a silver coin. It's been 40 years since I've had an allowance. I deserve this little bit of money. I'm working hard here! It's not like our group needs this small coin,* he thought. And true, it really wouldn't be missed, because people were hauling huge sections of golden walls and massive pieces of solid silver, turquoise, and other metals. One small coin really wouldn't be missed in the grand scheme of things.

So he took the silver coin and went back to his personal tent, dug a hole in the ground, and placed the coins and gold bar in the pocket of the bathrobe, folded the robe, buried it, placed his cot on top of the dirt, and probably put his CD player on top of that.

It was smooth. No one nearby. Nothing would be missed.

That night, the world's largest backpacking group celebrated its victory. They had been eating manna (white stuff kind of like Wonder Bread that God had sent from heaven) and quail meat for 40 years. But *this* night they grilled hot dogs over a blazing campfire, roasted marshmallows, and even made S'mores.

They were on cloud nine, and so was their leader. "God has been faithful," Josh reminded them. "We're so close to the Promised Land that we'll be there tomorrow night!" Everyone screamed and clapped, and a few guys in the back stuck their fingers in their mouths and whistled really loud.

"According to the map," Josh said, "there's one more city that stands between us and the Promised Land. It's a peanut-sized city. In fact, we don't even need to send our entire army. I'll have our top fighters leave tomorrow morning to conquer it, and they'll be done in just a couple of hours."

The next morning, the top fighters left to conquer the city of Ai. But just before noon, a messenger came back to camp. He explained to Joshua that every man had been killed in battle.

"What?!?" Josh cried. "That can't be true! Ai is such a small city."

The Bible tells us he was so distraught, he threw himself on the ground, tore his clothes, and cried out to his heavenly Father. I imagine his prayer went something like this:

"God, I don't understand! You've been so faithful until now. You've split the Jordan River, parted the Red Sea, given us water from rocks, turned a snake into a stick, led us with a pillar of light in the darkness, given us bread from heaven and quail meat, and you just gave us victory over a city six times our size!

"Now that we're *this close* to the Promised Land, you choose to walk away and leave us? How can this be? Why would you bring us this far just to tease us? *I don't understand!* Are you just gonna leave us out here to die?"

God listened to Joshua's prayer. And he also responded. In fact, his response was such a classic that Josh memorized it and then wrote it down:

"I *cannot* honor a group of people who choose to compromise."

Know It!

When God speaks, it's not simply to hear the sound of his own voice. When he speaks, he does so with reason, clarity, and purpose. And he expects his children not only to hear his message but to heed it as well.

Read It!

Isaiah 64:5;
Jeremiah 31:30;
Luke 16:1; John 8:34

Pray It!

Tell God you want to obey him with all your heart.

Disobedience Has Consequences

Know It!
There's no way to get around God's laws. When we choose to break them, there are always consequences.

Read It!
Psalm 51:4; Ecclesiastes 9:18; 2 Peter 2:4; 1 John 1:10

Pray It!
Ask God for a growing desire to do his will and obey his commands.

As soon as Joshua heard those words, he knew someone had taken something that didn't belong to him.

Of course, God knew who had disobeyed. He told the Israelites to draw lots, and he directed the process so the real perpetrator was revealed. But let's imagine the situation as a little more action-packed. Pretend you're watching this on the big screen:

Joshua gathered a search party and told them to go into every person's tent, dig through everyone's belongings, and find the stolen property.

They did. And they came up empty-handed. Acorn didn't even bat an eye. Why should he? No one had seen him.

But Joshua wouldn't give up. (He never buckled under pressure, remember?) So the search party went back again. They came to Acorn's tent. Searched it inside and out. No one found a thing. They left.

Except for one man. He stopped in the doorway of the tent, spun around, and folded his arms. His eyes darted from side to side. *What is it?* he thought. *What's this eerie feeling I have?*

He wandered back inside the tent and threw everything off the walls. Then he kicked the cot out the door. Then, standing where the cot had been, he folded his arms again and began kicking the dirt underneath his feet while scanning the tent.

And you guessed it. As he stood and kicked, you know what he saw. The corner of a brightly colored bathrobe. And as he leaned over to pick it up, a silver coin and a gold bar fell out of the pocket.

Acorn was brought to the center of the camp and stoned to death, then burned.

Wow. What started as a fun story about an exciting youth group has suddenly turned into a nightmare. All because one guy *compromised.*

You see, there are *some* things that NEVER change. And those things are God's laws. They don't rotate, alter, shift, or evolve. They're constant. Solid. Concrete. They will always be that way.

When we compromise God's standards, we're sinning. The world says, "It's not sin, it's just doing your own thing." But when God says no and you say yes, it's sin.

How Much Does It Cost?

We live in a gray world—in other words, right and wrong have fused together to create "whatever's right for the moment." And for Acorn, it seemed "right at the moment" to take some gold, silver, and a bathrobe.

It's wrong to steal. It's wrong to sin. It always has been, and it always will be. Maybe for you the issue isn't stealing . . . maybe it's going too far with your date. Or maybe it's the language you use, or the movies you're watching, or ____________ *(you* fill in the blank). But the bottom line is, if you're rationalizing (making excuses for something that's really wrong and convincing yourself it's okay), then you're living in sin.

So how much does it cost to live in sin? Well, the Bible says the cost is death. That's not changing, and that's bad news. But here's the good news! The Bible also says that God will forgive for the asking.

As Christians, God calls us to live a step above the rest of the world. He wants you to be *set apart.* When you do something the world calls permissible, but it lowers your standards or hinders your relationship with Christ, you're compromising.

Anything that compromises where you stand with God is wrong. You don't even need to spend time praying about it. For Acorn, it was taking something that didn't belong to him. It would have been a waste of time for him to pray, "Lord, you know I'm broke and need a little extra money. Thanks for helping me find this gold and silver. And thanks that no one saw me take it. Now, don't let anyone find my treasures while I bury them, okay?"

That's stupid, you may be thinking. *Who'd ever pray a prayer like that?* Well, don't we do the same thing when we drive too fast? *Lord, you know I don't want to be late for church, so I'm going to have to speed. Don't let me get stopped.*

Or possibly when you're watching something you shouldn't? *Lord, don't let Mom and Dad come home till this is over.*

You get the picture. No need to pray about anything you have to rationalize. Why? Because God has already made it clear that compromising his commands is wrong.

Know It!
If God searched through your heart, would you be embarrassed at what he'd find? Are there things in your life that you're trying to hide?

Read It!
Joshua 7–8;
Romans 6:23;
John 1:12

Pray It!
Ask God to point out anything you've been compromising in your relationship with him and seek his forgiveness.

Victory over Compromise

Know It!

God wants your happiness even more than you do! He doesn't place rules in your life to frustrate you or to rob you of a good time. He gives you boundaries to protect you and help you live life to the fullest in his glory.

Read It!

Proverbs 3:13-26; Isaiah 8:17; 12:2; 26:4

Pray It!

Thank God for helping you serve him better.

Instead of praying that God will help you not to get caught cheating, or that someone won't know you lied, pray about these things instead:

- *Wisdom to know the difference.* Maybe you're not sure if this specific thing will compromise your relationship with God or not. Seek his wisdom. He's more than ready to give you solid direction when you ask.
- *Discernment.* Discernment is honed wisdom. It allows you to be more than just "generally wise." Discernment helps you assess specific situations and know from the inside out whether or not it's right.
- *Knowledge.* If you *are* rationalizing something and it's not right in God's eyes, you want to know about it! So pray for that knowledge. That's why daily time spent with God in prayer and Bible reading is so important–it gives you a chance to *ask* God if there's anything in your life that's not right. Then it's *his* responsibility to help you know what it is. And when he brings it to your mind–when you have *knowledge* of it–seek his forgiveness and commit it to him. So go ahead. Let him look underneath your cot and inside your closet. Give him your locker and your diary. Surrender your relationships and your heart. Commit to him your will and your desires.

If you're serious about wanting to avoid compromise in your walk with God, consider praying the following:

Lord, sometimes I move so fast, I forget to stop and think about if what I'm doing is really okay in your sight. I hurry to keep up with my friends, . . . when I should be hurrying to keep myself saturated in your Word.

I don't want to compromise, Father. My desire is to live a life that's pleasing to you. I need your discernment, your wisdom, and your strength. Help me to discipline myself daily to establish those attributes in my life. Help me to work at them–practice them–until they become part of my lifestyle. I want to live with integrity, never compromising. Never rationalizing.

Help me to be like Joshua–standing strong when the pressure rises. I don't want to buckle when I feel the tension. But "as for me and my house . . . I WILL serve the Lord." Amen.

Can You Spot the Mistake?

Though people mean well, what often comes out of our mouths is just a little . . . off. Check out the following misstatements.

- "My best friend is a chronological liar."
- "Members of the Grovetown Woman's Club gave the speaker a standing ovulation."
- "He really gets my dandruff up."
- "All their meals include 8 percent tax and 17 percent gratitudes."
- "Well, at least she's getting it out of her cistern."
- "I have a photogenic memory."
- "If you take this subject, you may be able to enroll in Harvard, Yale, or Prison."
- "The loaf of bread had no adjectives and no preservatives."
- "I love academia nuts."
- "When the temperature is below zero, it may feel even colder because of the windshield factor."
- "My ancestors were pheasants who came over from France."

Though it's fun to laugh at the mistakes of others, God wants you to focus more clearly on what they do right, rather than how many times they mess up. How often in the past two days have you laughed at someone? How often in the past two days have you made time to point out someone's good qualities?

A little encouragement and consistent affirmation go a long way in helping someone feel better about himself. You have the power to make or break someone's day just by how you treat her. People who are always waiting for someone to mess up are usually people who are very insecure. Pointing out someone else's mistakes somehow makes them feel better about themselves.

Mistakes and sin are two different things. Yes, God wants you to be bold in speaking out against sin. Jesus never hesitated to call sin *sin.* But he never laughed at another person's expense. A sin is deliberately doing something against the known will of God. A mistake is forgetting the correct word to use. There's a huge difference.

Know It!

It's your choice. Would you rather be known as an encourager whom people love to be around? Or do you want the reputation of being the sarcastic person always looking for a laugh at someone else's expense? Let Jesus be your example.

Read It!

Philippians 2:1;
Colossians 3:17;
1 Thessalonians 5:11;
1 Timothy 4:12

Pray It!

Ask God to show you specific ways to encourage three different people this week.

Sometimes Love Takes Its Time

Know It!
Be willing to put aside your impatience and completely trust God for his best plans for your life. Even when his timetable is different than yours, remember that he loves you and wants what's best for you.

Read It!
Isaiah 55:10-11;
Jeremiah 32:26-27;
Habakkuk 2:3;
John 11:1-12

Pray It!
Pray for patience and understanding regarding God's timetable and your desires.

Dr. Hans Richter, a musical conductor, lived in the late 1800s and was a close friend of famous composer Richard Wagner. Toward the end of the year in 1870, Mrs. Wagner complained to her husband that it had been a long time since they had seen Dr. Richter. She wondered why he hadn't been out and about. Why wasn't he doing anything important? Why hadn't they heard from him?

Her birthday fell on Christmas Eve, and she was surprised by her husband and Dr. Richter playing a musical selection for her that they had spent the last year composing. Dr. Richter and Mr. Wagner had been rehearsing her surprise for weeks when she was wondering why Richter wasn't doing anything at all.

Mary and Martha, the sisters of Lazarus, probably wondered why Jesus wasn't doing more when their brother died. They had sent word to their Lord. Where was he? Why didn't he seem in a hurry to arrive and offer his help?

Sometimes love takes a little time. Often what appears as a delay from God is an act full of love and designed with rich blessing. Mary and Martha didn't know that although Jesus arrived when they felt it was too late, he was actually right on time to perform the miracle of raising their dead brother to life. And sometimes when God waits to answer your prayer, he's actually waiting for his perfect timing to give you an even greater blessing than you previously expected.

Writer Robert Louis Stevenson was known as a kind man with a huge heart. A story is told about an experience he had while living in Samoa. One day when his cook was away, he told his other servant not to bother with lunch, just to bring a little bread and cheese instead. Stevenson didn't want to bother the servant or make him feel obligated to do what the cook usually did.

The servant took a little longer than Stevenson expected. The writer wondered what was holding him up but was pleasantly surprised when the servant entered his room carrying a tray with an incredible lunch of an omelet, salad, and great coffee. When Stevenson asked him who prepared such a fine lunch, the servant replied that he had done it. Stevenson then complimented him on having great wisdom. Apparently he had brought one of the writer's favorite meals to him.

But the servant responded, "No, not great is my wisdom. Great is my love!"

Sharing What God Has Done

If you have a growing relationship with Jesus Christ, you're actually personal friends with the creator of the universe! Pretty exciting, huh! Naturally, you want to share your faith with those around you. But maybe you're not sure how. You need a tool. Some equipment. You need a testimony. (And before you start thinking, *I've never done drugs; I don't have a testimony!* think about this: There are rewards of living a straitlaced life. You're not haunted by memories you're dying to forget. You can actually feel proud of your past!)

So please know right up front: You don't have to have been on drugs or slept around to have a testimony! God rewards those who place him first and keep him first. It's only because of his Holy Spirit living within you that you're able to say no to the things he doesn't want you involved in. By not having a "testimony," you actually do have a testimony—an extremely powerful one!

Sometimes people get tired of hearing about all the bad. Though it's motivating to hear a testimony full of color, it's extremely refreshing to hear someone say, "I haven't done any of that. And it's not because I'm strong or cool or have my act together. It's because God gives me the strength to withstand temptation."

(And before you start thinking, *Oh, great! I've already blown it!* you need to realize that God can use your past filled with drugs, drinking, and sleeping around to show the incredible difference he has made in your life since you've given everything to him. God has the power to make beautiful things out of devastating situations.)

But beyond that, remember that obvious sins like sex and drugs are not the only things God saves us from. Even a person who has lived a life that's outwardly pure may struggle with internal sins like pride and anger. And God saves us from those sins just as much as he does the external vices!

Bottom line: Every Christian has a testimony! Yours may be filled with stuff you'd rather forget . . . or you may think your testimony is quite boring. But the fact that God forgave you, a sinner, and granted you salvation is certainly worth sharing!

But how? Let's take the next few days to chat about how to develop your own personal testimony.

Know It!
God has not only given you a testimony, he wants to teach you how to use it to bring glory to his name.

Read It!
2 Corinthians 1:1-5; Galatians 1:2; Philippians 1:1; James 1:1

Pray It!
Ask God to help you develop your own personal testimony to share with those who don't know him.

Developing Your Testimony (Part 1)

Know It!
Why is it so important to have a testimony? So you can lead others to Christ. Yes, you can share God's Word with them, but a life changed by God's Word shouts volumes! Be willing to put a lot of time and effort in developing your testimony. Again, it's the most important puzzle you'll ever piece together!

Read It!
Acts 1:8; Romans 1:16; 2 Timothy 1:8; 4:1-2

Pray It!
Ask God to give you a burden for those who don't know him and a boldness to share your testimony.

Every Christian has a testimony! The issue right now is putting it together so you can share it with others. Let's work it like a puzzle—the most important puzzle you'll ever put together in your whole life. The first four pieces deal more with how to *deliver* your testimony, and the last four pieces deal with how to *develop* your testimony.

Puzzle Piece #1: Strive to keep your testimony around three minutes. You don't want it to turn into a 30-minute sermon. Keep it concise so your friend won't daydream himself into the ozone layer while you're droning on and on.

Puzzle Piece #2: Be expressive. After all, you're sharing the most important thing in your life. So be interesting. Talk with excitement. Use your past experiences. Listeners relate well to personal stories.

Puzzle Piece #3: Share some Scripture. This is important so you can back up what you're saying. This means you may need to start reading your Bible more and memorize some key verses.

Puzzle Piece #4: Be sensitive with your language. Instead of saying, "Can I tell you about something exciting in my life?" try saying, "Can I share something exciting in my life?" There's a difference between telling and sharing. Using the word "telling" makes some people feel as though you're pointing your finger at them. But "sharing" sounds more friendly. And that's exactly what you want to create—a friendly situation. No one likes to feel stressed or trapped into listening.

The next three puzzle pieces deal specifically with the unique parts of your personal testimony. Without these pieces, you don't have a testimony. (We'll look at the first one today and the rest in the next few days.)

Puzzle Piece #5: Tell about your life BEFORE you met Christ. What was your lifestyle like? How did you think and act? Include attitude and habits. Examples: "I was selfish. I thought about using others to get ahead." "I was only interested in what I could get out of life." "I partied a lot and was always searching for something better. Anything that would make me feel good for the moment was an option."

You may not be able to develop your testimony overnight. Stretch it out over a few days and let each puzzle piece simmer in your mind. If you have trouble remembering a specific part of your testimony (such as what you were like before you accepted Christ as your Savior), ask those closest to you for their input. Your parents, your youth leader, and a close friend may be able to give valuable input.

Puzzle Piece #6: Tell about how you came to know Christ. Be specific. Don't say something like, "Then I met Christ, and everything changed for the better." How did you meet him? Share where and when, too.

Some people honestly can't remember a specific time when they became a Christian. That's okay. But it's important that you know this: No one is simply born a Christian. We all have to make a decision to follow Christ and actually ask him to forgive our sins and take control of our lives. You may remember a general time in your life rather than a specific day and year when this happened. Share that.

You also want to emphasize that your relationship with Christ is a free gift. Make sure your friend understands that he can't earn it. You may want to create an illustration of giving a present to him. It's not really his until he accepts it.

Here are a couple examples of how one could come to know Christ: "I was at a Christian concert, and the singer challenged us to let God take control of our lives. I knew I was sure tired of being in charge and going nowhere. So when he asked us to stand up if we wanted to make that decision, I stood. It was then that I prayed and accepted God's gift of forgiveness."

Or . . . "Our youth group had a winter retreat. I was really searching for some answers. Besides feeling lonely, I just lacked a purpose for living. Life didn't make much sense to me. On Saturday night our youth leader said he was going to pray out loud, and if any of us wanted to accept Christ as our Savior, we could repeat the prayer silently. So I did. That's how I met Christ. Now he lives inside me and is changing my life for the better!"

Know It!

Though you may initially feel unsure about sharing your testimony, God will bless your efforts. Each time you share about what he's done in your life, he'll use it for the good.

Read It!

Mark 8:38; Luke 9:26; 2 Timothy 1:6-8; 2:1-2

Pray It!

Ask God to bring someone specific to your mind with whom you can share the gospel.

Developing Your Testimony (Part 3)

Know It!
Now that you have the pieces to putting the puzzle of your testimony together, it's time to get started. Grab your notebook and make three sections: 1. *My Life BEFORE I Met Christ.* 2. *How I Came to Know Christ.* 3. *My Life AFTER I Met Christ.* Now begin writing! After you've put the pieces together, read your testimony out loud and time yourself to see if it's too long or too short. When you've honed it to approximately three minutes, ask your parents, your minister, or a Christian friend if you can practice on them.

Read It!
There's no time like right now to familiarize yourself with the Scriptures below that you'll want to use when sharing your faith.

Pray It!
Ask God to help you feel confident and secure about your testimony.

Grab a notebook and designate it your prayer journal. List the names of people you know who aren't Christians and begin praying for them. Also, designate this notebook as the place you'll write and hone your testimony.

Puzzle Piece #7: Tell about your life AFTER you met Christ. Share the *specific* changes that have happened as a result of making Jesus Lord of your life. Share what Christ means to you now. Talk about the excitement you experience from your relationship with him.

Be careful to avoid giving the impression that your life is now free from problems, because realistically, everyone will continue to face hardship. Share the difference: Now you have Someone to face the hard times *with* you and provide the wisdom and strength to handle them.

Examples of specific changes: "Now I have a reason to live. Everything is in perspective. He's given me a genuine concern for other people. I really *want* to help others. I'm not always thinking about myself—I'm learning how to meet the needs of those around me."

"Every day is a new day. It blows my mind that he loves me even though he knows I'm still a jerk a lot of times. Life is kind of like an adventure now. I mean, I'm walking hand-in-hand with the Master of the universe!"

Puzzle Piece #8: Share Scriptures. The following Scripture passages provide more information on how you became a Christian. You might want to use some of these in your testimony; if not, keep them handy to answer any questions your friend might have. These are also great verses to memorize!

- **John 3:16**: "For God so loved the world that he gave his one and only Son, that whoever believes in him shall not perish but have eternal life."
- **Romans 3:23**: "For all have sinned and fall short of the glory of God."
- **Romans 5:8**: "But God demonstrates his own love for us in this: While we were still sinners, Christ died for us."
- **John 1:12**: "Yet to all who received him, to those who believed in his name, he gave the right to become children of God."

Now that you have your own personal testimony, let's chat for a few seconds about how you present it.

Whaddya mean? I just give it, right?

Well . . . yes. But there are some other things worth mentioning that'll help you feel good about yourself when sharing it. You may be a bit nervous, and that's okay. You're normal. But you want to feel confident when sharing Christ, so here are a few security boosters.

Booster #1: The way you look. YOU may be the only picture of Jesus your friend has ever seen. So, naturally, you want to look your best (no broccoli between your teeth!). And when you look good, you feel good. The result? Confidence. This is really simple stuff . . . making sure your hair isn't shifting out to another galaxy, having good breath (Seriously! Bad breath can be a real turnoff!), and just looking like you're well put together.

Exception: You're in the locker room. The time is right. The friend you've been praying for suddenly seems interested in knowing more about Christ. You're in his world–go ahead and share your testimony. He'll relate. Don't jump up, run home and change clothes, come back, and give your testimony. That's silly. Use common sense.

Booster #2: The way you think. Ask God to help you zero in on little clues your friends might be dropping that hint of their interest in knowing more about your relationship. Learn to be a quick thinker. Be alert! Listen for golden opportunities in class, the hallways, your school cafeteria, the practice field. Keep your spiritual eyes and ears open!

Booster #3: The way you talk. You'll remember on September 22, I suggested using the word "share" instead of "tell." Try not to use so much "churchy sounding language" that your friend doesn't understand what you're saying. Make it a point to watch your general conversation as well. Don't tell questionable jokes to get a laugh. It's natural to want to be included by your non-Christian friends so you can eventually share Christ with them, but if you're being included at the expense of being *like* them instead of being *different,* your testimony will never be heard.

Know It!

Only God can provide the perfect timing—that golden opportunity, the exact right moment to share. If you try to force it or make it happen in your own power, you won't feel the confidence you need to be effective. The Holy Spirit will guide you. Learn to depend on him to help you discern the right time to share your testimony. When the timing is *God's timing,* you'll be much more confident in sharing him with others.

Read It!

Joshua 1:5-9, 18;
Psalm 138:3;
Proverbs 28:1

Pray It!

Ask God to reveal any changes you need to make in your outward appearance or inward attitude before you start sharing your faith.

Practice Makes Perfect

Know It!

If you ask God to give you specific opportunities to share your faith, he'll provide them! That's why it's important to do everything you can to be prepared.

Read It!

Romans 15:16; 1 Corinthians 1:17; 9:16; 15:2

Pray It!

Ask God to give you an opportunity to share your faith today.

Now that you've read about sharing your faith and have spent time developing your personal testimony, it's time to rehearse. Grab a close Christian friend and respond with some role-playing to the following situations, okay? I'll get you started with a few lines in each scenario. After that, you're on your own! (If you'd rather do this by yourself, you can use your prayer notebook to write out your responses.)

Situation One: Doug's dad has been in a car wreck. You're not super close to Doug, but he's in your third-period history class. You sit across the aisle from each other and are casual friends. Doug's not a Christian.

Doug: Wow. I really bombed this test. Guess my mind's been on Dad. I'm really worried about him.

You: I'm sorry, Doug. How bad is he?

Doug: He's not gonna die or anything. He just broke a leg and two ribs. But it's weird seeing him helpless in the hospital, you know?

You: Yeah. Hospitals give me the willies.

Doug: But, you know, hanging around during visiting hours has really made me think about death. And life. And you know . . . where you go after you die.

You:

* * *

Situation Two: Holly's family just moved to your city. She's a lot of fun to be around, and you've started to become friends. You want to invite her to church and eventually lead her to Christ. She seems interested.

Holly: So whatcha doin' this Friday night?

You: Goin' to a pizza party with our youth group.

Holly: Fun people?

You: Yep. But they'd be even more fun if they knew you! How 'bout if I pick you up at 6 P.M.?

Holly: Well . . . I do love pizza. Hey, how come you're so involved in church, anyway?

You:

Practice STILL Makes Perfect!

How'd you do with your role-playing situations yesterday? Are you gaining confidence in knowing what to say and how to slide your faith into everyday situations? Let's try two more.

Situation One: You've been friends with Jill for a long time. She's come to church with you often but has never made a decision to follow Christ. Recently, it seems like nothing has gone her way. You sense that she's finally close to accepting Christ as her Savior.

Jill: Can't believe the Wilsons are moving. They were my best baby-sitting income. Now I'll never have money to do anything!

You: Ah, come on, Jill. You'll find other baby-sitting jobs.

Jill: I don't think so. Dad grounded me from all means of making money until I bring up my science grade. That could take forever. So how come you've always got it together?

You: Me? I may be doing okay in science, but math? Well, that's another story.

Jill: Yeah, but you know what I mean. No matter how much rotten stuff gets tossed your way, you just keep on going.

You: It's my relationship with God, Jill. You know that. We've talked about this before.

Jill: Yeah, I know we have . . . but lately I've really been thinking about it. I'm tired of feeling as though my life's going nowhere fast. I want what you have.

You:

• • •

Situation Two: Seth is always in trouble, but you enjoy chatting with him in study hall. He knows you're a Christian. You've been praying for an opportunity to confront him about his lifestyle.

Seth: Another weekend gone too fast! I was wasted the entire weekend.

You: And that makes it a weekend to remember?

Seth: Maybe not; but it helps me forget.

You: Forget what?

Seth: Stuff, man. Just stuff. You wouldn't understand. You're too straight.

You: I know Someone who *does* understand—God.

Seth: Oh, yeah? Tell me about it. Tell me how God could possibly understand my life.

You:

Know It!
Trust God to help you continue developing your faith-sharing skills. He will!

Read It!
Ephesians 6:15;
Philippians 1:27;
Colossians 1:23;
1 Thessalonians 2:4

Pray It!
As you begin sharing your faith, you'll probably make a few mistakes at first. But God can use your mistakes too! Pray before, during, and after you witness, and ask him to use the words you say.

Being Different Makes a Difference

Know It!
It may often be your closest friends who try to pressure you into doing something you know God doesn't want you to participate in. Stand strong . . . in his strength . . . and say no.

Read It!
Psalms 25:1-5, 14-15, 20-21; 26:11-12

Pray It!
Ask God to help you live out your testimony through your actions.

South Oak's gymnasium was filled with a mixture of sweat and popcorn smells and uncontrolled exhilaration. Less than 20 seconds remained in the last basketball game of the season, and South Oak trailed by one. The players couldn't even hear Coach Marston blaring instructions from the sidelines; the roar of the student body was too loud.

Coach Marston called time-out and grabbed Shane. "Get the ball to Ryan as quickly as you can. We can still pull this one off!"

Shane and Ryan were a team within a team. Watching the two high school juniors on the basketball court was like watching poetry in motion. They'd pass the ball to other teammates, but it was obvious they had more ability than anyone else on the entire squad.

The buzzer sounded and the game was in motion once again. The opposing team started down the court with the ball. Shane stabbed for the ball with his lightning reflexes and miraculously stole it from the frustrated Eagle guard.

Now with just eight seconds left on the clock, Ryan raced past two defenders to the hoop. With two seconds remaining, Shane lofted a pass to the basket, and Ryan rammed the ball through the hoop as the buzzer sounded South Oak's dramatic victory!

Almost immediately the team was mobbed with friends, family members, and local newspaper sports photographers.

"Time to celebrate!" Kirk yelled to his teammates as he joined the massive celebration on the gym floor.

The locker room buzzed with plans for the night.

"Who's grabbing the brew?"

"Let's get outta here! We've got some serious partying to do!"

"Hey, Shane! Why don't you loosen up and come with us this time?" invited Kirk.

"Yeah, Shane. It's time you really became part of the team," pressed Ryan.

"C'mon, guys, you know I don't drink."

"So what? Just come and have fun with the rest of us. You don't have to drink," Ryan continued.

"I can think of better things to do than watching you guys fall all over each other," Shane laughed. "You can tell me all about it on Monday . . . the part you're able to remember, that is. Catch you later!"

Shane waited until Saturday afternoon to give Ryan a call. "How you doing, Ry?"

"Uhhh," he moaned. "Can you come over? I wanna talk."

"Sure, but it doesn't sound like you're in the best of shape right now. Are you sure this is a good time?"

"No, it's not a good time, but I want to talk to you anyway, man. Please, Shane. Just get here."

Shane placed the receiver in its cradle and headed toward Ryan's. As he heard his screen door slam, he couldn't help but remember all the great times they'd had the past five years. He smiled as he recalled their first meeting on the baseball field in the Blue Tigers Little League. Ryan had his cap on backward—his symbol of doing things "his way." They had collided during practice when both were going for a fly ball. Even though their white practice pants were covered with dirt and grass stains, the boys laughed hysterically. That day marked the beginning of a close friendship.

The following year, Ryan's family moved into a neighborhood in Shane's school district, and the two became even closer. Though Ryan sometimes accepted Shane's invitation to attend church, Shane was still praying that he'd become a Christian.

As he turned the corner to drive the last five blocks to Downing Street, he remembered how close Ryan had been to making a spiritual decision last summer when he had agreed to attend church camp. Though he was desperately interested in knowing God better, it was obvious something was still holding him back.

Now, as they were in the middle of their junior year, Shane worried that he was completely losing Ryan to the party scene. It had become a Friday night ritual for the rest of the team to get drunk after every game—whether they won or not. Ryan had fallen prey to the pressure.

As he shut the car door and climbed the porch steps, Shane wondered what he could say to his friend this time that he hadn't already said before.

Know It!

You may spend years sharing your faith with the same person. And he may continue to put you off and make excuses as to why he's not ready to accept Christ. Don't give up! Remember, Jesus didn't give up on you. It may be frustrating, but keep loving your friend, continue sharing your faith, and never stop praying!

Read It!

Psalm 37:7; 40:1; Habakkuk 3:16; Romans 8:25

Pray It!

Ask God for patience when you feel frustrated at the lack of spiritual progress from your non-Christian friends.

God's Words in Your Mouth

Know It!

You don't need to worry about what to say when God gives you a clear opportunity to share your faith. The same God who gives you the chance to witness will also place just the right words in your mouth.

Read It!

Isaiah 6:8, 11;
Jeremiah 1:6-10;
Habakkuk 3:17-18

Pray It!

Ask God to place his thoughts in your mind and his words in your mouth.

Shane found Ryan in his bedroom with the curtains drawn and the lights off, obviously experiencing a major hangover. Shane sat on the floor beside the bed and spoke softly.

"You look awful!"

"Tell me something I don't know," Ryan responded. "Someone slipped some 'X' in my drink last night. Ohhh. My insides feel like they've been ripped apart with a lawn mower."

Shane didn't know a lot about "X," other than the fact it was short for "ecstasy" and was a powerful and popular drug making the rounds at his high school. "Ry, do you really think it's worth it? I mean, look at you!"

"That's what I want to talk to you about, Shane. I've known you for a long time. No matter how many times I've screwed up, you've remained a real friend."

"Hey, listen–"

"No. You listen! I know I'm not in real good shape right now, but I do know what I'm talking about. You've always been a good guy. The only reason I started partying was because I couldn't say no to the pressure. I just wanted to be included, you know?"

"I hear you."

"But–you never gave in. Everyone knows what you stand for; they know how involved you are in your church and youth group. And most of the times I've gone with you, I've really enjoyed it. I've come real close several times to making a commitment to God, but something always holds me back."

"I know. I've sensed that."

"I want what you have, Shane. I need that strength. I don't want to keep giving in to the pressure of things that I really don't even want to do."

"Ryan, that's great!" Shane yelled. As Ryan covered his ears and winced in pain, Shane remembered he should keep the volume down.

"Hold on," Ryan continued. "I *want* to give my life to Christ . . . but I'm scared. And you can't tell anybody I said that!"

"C'mon, Ry! I'm your friend, remember?"

"Yeah, yeah. Guess I'm just scared of all I know I'll have to give up to become a Christian."

"Well, let's talk it out," Shane said as he reached for the New Testament that was crammed in his hip pocket.

"Hey, Ryan . . . listen to me," Shane began. "All the things you'll give up to follow the Lord are the very same things that are ruining your life. You really don't want to do them anyway. You said that yourself."

When Ryan didn't respond, Shane continued. "It just makes sense to give your life to God. You already said you need God's strength to say no to the things you don't want to do."

"Yeah, I know," Ryan agreed.

"But you're right in thinking about the cost," Shane continued. "Following Jesus isn't always easy. It means saying no to some attractive things everyone else seems to be doing. And they'll probably give you a hard time about it, too. But, hey, look who God's given you for a friend!"

"Get off it!" Ryan smiled as he tossed a pillow at Shane's head. "Everything you're saying makes a lot of sense. I really want to do this. I need to do this. But I'm still scared."

Shane smiled and breathed a prayer for help as he leaned forward and opened his New Testament.

Shane's life opened the door for Ryan's salvation. Within his lifestyle, he also had three important aspects of leading someone to Christ. Let's sneak a peek at Shane's secrets. Lifestyle evangelism for him meant:

Friendship. By being a friend to Ryan, Shane had earned the right to be heard. He had taken the time to establish rapport. Their friendship spanned five years. They had shared baseball, basketball, camping, and several other common interests. By simply being a friend to Ryan over the years, Shane had earned his respect and won his trust.

Consistency. Shane was consistent in his walk with Christ as well as in his friendship with Ryan. He continued to encourage him and kept the lines of communication open. He wasn't condemning, yet he clearly didn't condone Ryan's actions either.

Chances are your non-Christian friend already knows what's wrong in his life. Instead of focusing on those wrong things, continue to love him and make it clear you want him involved in your youth group. Invite him often and encourage his attendance. When he does come, make him feel loved and accepted by introducing him to your church friends and youth leader.

Know It!
Your lifestyle actually shouts a lot louder than your words. Are you being a consistent living example of Christ for those around you?

Read It!
Psalms 27:1-3, 11, 13-14

Pray It!
Ask Christ to shine clearly through your actions and be echoed in your words.

Person to Person

Know It!
What does this story tell you about evangelism? When your life is truly different, it will make a difference in those around you!

Read It!
Proverbs 15:33; Ecclesiastes 12:13-14; Isaiah 56:1-2; 64:4-8

Pray It!
Ask God to help you to remain true to him and different from the world—even when the pressure is on.

Shane took a strong stand for what he believed was right. This made it absolutely clear in Ryan's mind that compromise was not an option. Because of Shane's consistency in avoiding evil, Ryan was better able to discern the difference between Shane's life and the lives of their other friends. He eventually came to the conclusion that he wanted that difference.

Many times Christian teens rationalize and think, *It'll be a good witness to attend the party and not drink. Then everyone will know I'm a Christian and can actually see me taking a stand.* But the next day at school when the hallway gossip floats through the tiles and someone's naming off everyone who attended the party, they won't take the time to say, "Oh, yeah, but I don't think she drank anything." Your name will simply be remembered as one among many who attended the party. (For more quick thoughts on this, flip back to August 2.)

What kind of witness is that? Surprise! Your non-Christian friends see it as one big inconsistency. They don't want to see how similar you can be to them; if you're claiming to be a Christian, they want to see the difference!

Love. First Corinthians 13 tells us that love is patient. Ryan had come close to making a spiritual commitment several times. Shane might have been tempted to respond, "What is it with you, Ryan? I give up!" but he didn't. He continued to love his friend and demonstrated that love through patience.

National speaker Tony Campolo once asked a crowd of 10,000 Christians how they were won to the Lord.

When he asked how many came to know Jesus Christ through television evangelism, no one raised a hand. When he asked how many were won to the Lord through evangelistic tracts, no hands were raised. When he asked how many became Christians through radio ministry, he saw four hands go up. When he inquired as to how many were won through a great sermon, he counted 40 hands.

When he finally asked, "How many of you came to know Jesus Christ personally because someone locked on to you and wouldn't let you go?" a sea of hands all over the auditorium were raised.

Now that you've developed your personal testimony and are sharing your faith, what happens when one of your friends actually prays to receive Christ? Then what should you do?

Many times when we see someone commit her life to the Lord, we think, *Whew, I'm glad she's a Christian now. I'll start looking for someone else I can witness to.* But your friend has just made the most important decision in her life! There's a lot she doesn't understand. How can she grow? How can she learn to walk on her own?

Don't put the baby down till she's burped. Just because a baby has consumed a jar of baby food doesn't mean she's finished eating. If she doesn't burp, she'll get sick. The wise parent knows she needs to rock, hold, and gently pat the baby on her back until she burps.

Guess what? You're kind of a "spiritual parent" to your friend. You've fed her some terrific spiritual food, but you're not finished with her yet. You'll need to help her digest all the spiritual food that's inside her. There's a lot she doesn't understand. Be willing to explain and answer questions. You probably won't know it all. That's okay. Take her to your youth leader or other adults in your life who can help.

It's good to involve your new Christian friend in youth group parties, ski trips, and pizza flings. She needs to know that Christ is her very best friend. You can help her learn that he laughs with her, hurts with her, and understands her.

But that's kind of like just eating candy bars and drinking Cokes. They sure taste good! But to be healthy, we need more than just sugar in our diet. We need meat and veggies, too, or we won't grow properly.

Again, this same principle is at work spiritually. If your new Christian friend is really going to grow spiritually, she needs some meat and veggies—some Bible study, worship experience, and accountability.

So while you're helping her learn that Christianity is a blast, don't forget to involve her in other aspects of spiritual growth that are also important. Plug her into a church (possibly yours), a Sunday school class (to provide accountability), and a Bible study to help her deepen her spiritual roots.

Know It!
A brand-new Christian needs nourishment, guidance, and lots of love. Be willing to continue making the investment in your friend's life.

Read It!
Colossians 2:6-7, 11-15; Hebrews 4:12-14; 6:1

Pray It!
Ask God to give you wisdom to help your new Christian friends grow properly.

Stick with It

Know It!

Aren't you glad God didn't give up on you when you first came to know him? Chances are you made a few mistakes, struggled to let go of some old habits, and maybe even refused to break away from friends who were pulling you down. But because God stuck with you, showed you his patience, and let other Christians into your life, you continued to walk with him. Do the same for your friend.

Read It!

1 Corinthians 3:6; Colossians 1:10; 2:19; 2 Thessalonians 1:3

Pray It!

Ask God to give you wisdom to know when to speak out and when to be silent.

If you're able to plug your new Christian friend into a Bible study and church, she's probably beginning to grow spiritually. But she's still a baby Christian. So it's understandable she'll fail. That's okay. That doesn't mean she's "lost" it or just can't cut being a Christian. It's normal to make mistakes. Remember when you first learned to ride a bicycle? You fell, scraped your knees, maybe even ran into your neighbor's mailbox—but you didn't quit. You kept on until you got the hang of it.

Please don't give up on your friend when she blows it. Encourage her. Remind her to ask for God's forgiveness, accept it, then get up and keep walking.

There may be some habits in her life that she needs to get rid of. It's not your job to point out all the bad stuff you see. That's God's job. You're not his "sin monitor." Let him deal with it in his perfect timing.

But as she begins to wrestle with some of these issues (possibly drinking, smoking, cussing, her sex life), you can help her learn to see and understand what God wants and expects. When she asks you (yes, wait until you're asked) if you think she should go out with Mark (who's a heavy drinker), you can share that as a new Christian it might be too big a temptation for her. And you can explain the importance of dating those who share her newfound faith and morality.

But if she goes out with him anyway and drinks and tells you about it later, don't throw out the baby with the bathwater. It's understandable that you'll be frustrated. And it's understandable that you want her to "hurry and grow up" spiritually. But growth takes time.

Offer to pray with her. Seek God's forgiveness, then "toss out" the habit of going out with those who will tempt (just like you'd "toss out" old bathwater), and continue walking forward. Most important: Let your friend know you care about her spiritual growth! Don't abandon her. Stick close and introduce her to more Christian friends she can hang out with.

Will You Be the One?

Through the years, God's call on our lives hasn't changed. He's still calling his disciples to share their faith and spread the gospel. Throughout the course of time he has used ordinary people to impact their world. *Ordinary* people. People with few talents. People who sometimes get angry and lonely and hate practicing the piano and can't stand homework.

And through ordinary, everyday people, God defeated armies, turned a small group of slaves into a great nation, split seas, healed the sick, and melted the hardened hearts of sinners. All this and *more* through people like us . . . people who were willing to be used. That's the key. Are you willing? Would you dare to be the one who sets a new standard for your group of friends? Would you be the one who starts a Bible club at your school? Would you be the one who stands with integrity at your part-time job? Would you dare to be the one?

Daniel dared. Moses dared. Abraham dared. So did Noah, Enoch, Abel, Sarah, Jacob, Joseph, Paul, Phoebe, Peter, and a host of others. And because they dared to be influencers, the world was not the same when they departed. Just as God used each of them, he wants to use *you* to make an eternal difference in the lives of those around you.

Will you dare to be the one? To step out in faith? To stand alone if need be? Will you be willing to be made fun of? Laughed at? Mocked? Will you dare to let your lifestyle speak God's love? If so, your world will never be the same.

The 12 disciples Jesus chose to begin the church and spread the gospel were extremely ordinary men. Most had only received average schooling at best. They didn't have much money. They weren't well-known by society. But they were willing to step out on faith, and oh how God used them!

It wasn't easy. They left their families, their friends, and their vocations. They slept outside, worked long hours, and walked long distances. But because they were willing to be used, God changed people's lives through their commitment.

God isn't after the one with the ability; he's seeking the one with the availability. And if you're available, he wants to use *you*!

Know It!
So how about it? Will you dare to be the one? Will you allow God to use you to make a difference in the lives of those around you?

Read It!
Hebrews 6:12; 10:16; 11

Pray It!
Ask God to mold your heart into one that's available for his use.

God Is Depending on YOU!

Know It!
God is counting on you. He needs you. He wants to use you. Will you dare to be the one?

Read It!
1 Corinthians 1:17; 9:16; Ephesians 4:11; 2 Timothy 4:5

Pray It!
Tell God that he can depend on you to do your part in spreading his wonderful news of salvation.

There's an old tale about Jesus ascending to heaven after he'd been resurrected and met with the disciples and other believers. The tale states that Jesus entered heaven and was greeted by the angel Gabriel. "Well, you did it! You became the greatest gift of all. You gave your very life for sinners that they may be forgiven and have eternal life. Was it worth it?"

"Oh, yes," Jesus said. "It was worth every drop of blood."

"And now you've conquered death and have come here to prepare an eternal home for all those who will accept your wonderful and free gift of salvation."

"Yes," Jesus replied. "That's correct. And oh, how I yearn for everyone to accept my gift and live with me forever here in heaven."

"So what's the plan, Jesus?" Gabriel asked.

"The plan?"

"Surely you have a plan! State-of-the-art technology? Huge marketing campaign? Maybe a few celebrities to endorse your gift?"

"No, that's not the plan," Jesus said.

"Oh. Well, what *is* the plan?" Gabriel asked.

"I only have a few followers . . . and I've entrusted the entire gospel to them."

"You mean . . . that little band of Christians?" Gabriel asked.

"That's right," Jesus said.

"But how will they ever spread your wonderful gift from generation to generation? Shouldn't we come up with another plan?"

"There is no other plan, Gabriel. My Christians are all I have. And I trust them."

Something's Wrong

Check out the following announcements found in church bulletins:

- Please place your donation in the envelope along with the deceased person you want remembered.
- The ladies of the church have cast off clothing of every kind. They may be seen in the basement on Friday afternoon.
- Low Self-Esteem Support Group will meet Thursday at 7 P.M. Please use the back door.
- The church will host an evening of fine dining, superb entertainment, and gracious hostility.
- The eighth-graders will be presenting Shakespeare's *Hamlet* in the church basement Friday at 7 P.M. The congregation is invited to attend this tragedy.

And check out the following blunders found on billboards and signs:

- At a restaurant-gas station: *Eat here and get gas.*
- Found on the sign of a New Mexico dry cleaning store: *Thirty-eight years on the same spot.*
- Inside a Los Angeles dance hall: *Good clean dancing every night but Sunday.*
- On a sign in front of a New York convalescent home: *For the sick and tired of the Episcopal Church.*
- Sign in a clothing store: *Wonderful bargains for men with 16 and 17 necks.*
- On a highway in Ohio: *Drive slower when wet.*

Something's definitely wrong in all of the announcements and signs listed above. Though each was written by someone with the best intentions, we laugh at the mistakes and find humor in how the finished product reads.

The best intentions don't make something right. Even good *people* with the best intentions don't make something right. For validation of your morality and the decisions you make on a daily basis, don't look to those around you. Look only to Jesus Christ.

Know It!

God is your absolute and ultimate source of truth. With his Holy Spirit working in your life, he can help you discern what's wrong with a situation you may feel questionable about. He can help you split fantasy from reality. And he'll help you discipline your good intentions into godly plans.

Read It!

Matthew 5:18;
John 3:3; 14:6; 16:13

Pray It!

Instead of simply accepting everything you hear from someone with good intentions, pray for God's Spirit to show you real truth in all you hear.

Bought, Branded, Bonded

Know It!

Yes, it's a bizarre illustration, and you won't realize its full impact until you've finished reading the following pages. But get this: God wants there to be no doubt that you belong to him.

Read It!

John 15:19; Romans 1:6; 14:8; 1 John 3:9

Pray It!

Ask God if you're allowing his reflection to shine clearly through your life. Do people see you and know you belong to God? Are there any blockages that are standing in the way?

Don't even think about reading the next three devotions unless you're willing to stretch your mind, use your imagination, and enter into a world from which you may never want to leave.

Yeah, it's bizarre, but you were warned. Ready to travel? Okay. Close your eyes. Go ahead. As in now. (Hey! Your eyes can't be shut if you're still reading!)

Okay. With your eyes closed . . . pretend you're a cow. A beautiful golden-brown cow.

Are you hungry? Okay, let's mosey out to greener pastures. As we stroll through the thick, tall, green grass, you stop to swish your tail and show the flies who's boss. The warmth of the yellow sun on a clear day feels incredible. *Ahhh. How could life be any better?*

Your four hooves leisurely lead you through the bright green pasture, rich in a grassy buffet of your favorite vegetation. *Yep. This is the life,* you think as you chew on your favorite meal.

Suddenly, your thoughts are interrupted by the sound of horse hooves invading your territory. You turn your head to see the owner of the ranch dismounting his horse, holding a long iron rod. Almost immediately, several ranch hands join him. They start a fire, and you turn back to your lunch.

Within no time, the fire has become steady, strong flames of heat. You hear one of the ranch hands say, "It's hot enough now. Grab the iron."

You turn around just in time to see the owner of the ranch dip the iron rod in the blazing fire. What happens next is a blur.

The owner pulls the rod out of the fire, and you notice that what was once black iron is now a brightly glowing red. But in just seconds, you not only see it, you *experience* it.

The owner raises the glowing-red rod to *you*! You're too stunned to move. And in a millisecond, he's pressing the iron to your back. *What? Hey!* You don't even have time to think. All you can concentrate on is the sound of your own flesh being seared with the owner's rod.

You've been branded.

Everywhere you graze, anywhere you wander, everyone will see your owner's mark on your skin. From this point on, there will be no doubt about whom you belong to.

The time is the early 1800s. And the unthinkable has happened. You're a slave. As you stand half-naked on the auction block, you're humiliated. Men are watching your every move and eyeing you closely.

"In less than a year, I'd have her plowing," one says. "Yep. Tie her up to my yoke, attach a harness and plow to her, and I'd have 40 more acres of corn."

A human plow? You can't believe these heathens don't see your humanity. The same guy lets out an eerie sneer. "That's not all I'd use her for." The others laugh in a half-drunken stupor.

Then, from the crowd of sweaty, cursing men pushes a man who's smiling. There's something different about him. He never looks at your beaten body; he simply looks into your eyes . . . and he smiles.

Someone starts the bidding at $5. You can't bear to look. You're too humiliated. *If only I could escape,* you think. *Oh, for a warm bath and clothes to cover my nakedness.*

Another ups the price. You're worth $7.50 now. Then $10. Your head is still hung in shame. The bidding has come down between two voices. You recognize the one belonging to the man who will turn you into a human plow. The other voice? You can't place it, but you don't dare raise your head.

The human plow guy is nervous. You can tell by the sound of his voice. *Is he afraid he's going to lose?* you wonder. "I'll give $52," he screams. The other voice counters the offer. Plow Man is angry. He's not used to being outbid. The numbers continue to increase. "I'll pay $71," he screams in desperation. The other voice calmly increases his counteroffer.

Plow Man just might lose, you think. And you find yourself desperately hoping you won't have to make your home in his barn. You know if the plow guy gets you, you'll also be having his children. You'll carry the scars of his whip. You'll never feel hope again.

"I don't know who you are, mister," Plow Man snarls. "But if you know what's good for you, you'll leave now!"

The other voice–ready to end the battle–matter-of-factly states, "I will never leave. I'm here to see this thing through. I'll pay any price. She's mine. I have chosen her."

Know It!
God sent his only Son to purchase you while you were a sinner—standing naked on the auction block. Are you living out your gratitude for him through your actions?

Read It!
1 Corinthians 7:39; 15:23; Galatians 3:29; 5:24

Pray It!
Express your thankfulness to God for sending his only Son to pay the price for you.

Bought and Set Free

Know It!

How would it feel to be saved from an evil person such as the Plow Man and then to be granted your freedom? Would you choose to go? Or would you choose to remain with the master who more than adequately provides for you?

Read It!

John 8:47; Romans 6:18; Galatians 5:1; 1 Peter 2:9

Pray It!

Ask God to help you truly understand what it means to be "bought" and "set free."

You timidly glance up to see Plow Man rushing the other bidder. He violently throws him in the dust and raises a knife to the stranger's throat.

Plow Man's a maniac! Oh, God, protect me! you pray desperately. The stranger is suddenly on top of Plow Man holding the knife to *his* throat. The stranger stabs the ground. Then he stands and says, "Get this through your head. She's mine. There is no price too high for me to pay."

Plow Man raises himself to his feet and pulls his knife from the ground. "You can *have* her," he hisses, "but this isn't over. When you least expect it, I'll take her from you!" He spits at the stranger's feet and leaves.

The stranger turns around. You gasp. It's the guy with the gentle eyes and the warm smile. He pulls out a wad of bills—empties his wallet—and unchains your feet and hands. "Here," he says, "wrap yourself in this."

Flannel. My favorite. Ahhh, it feels so soft against my filthy body.

He doesn't put you in the back of his wagon. He has a place ready for you up front—with him. On your way out of town, he stops at a tailor's. "Only the best," he says. "Make her fine clothing out of your best material. Spare no expense."

Days turn into weeks. And you can't believe your good fortune. You're a slave, but you're being treated like a queen. Your master cares and provides for you more than you imagined. You're so grateful, you find yourself wanting to serve him. "What can I do for you, Master?" you ask. "Can I clean the barn? Can I plant seed?"

He smiles and takes you by the hand. "I'll show you how," he says. While you're working alongside your master, you try to concentrate on your good fortune of meeting such a wonderful friend, but you're haunted by the words of Plow Man: "When you least expect it, I'll take her from you!"

A month later, your master calls you into his office. "You've done a fine job here," he says. "But I bought you. You had no choice in the matter. I paid for you, and I brought you here as my own. I love you so much that I will not keep you against your will. You're free to go."

"But . . . I . . ." You're in shock. "I don't want to go, Master. I love you. I want to serve you."

"You're choosing to remain even though I've granted your freedom?"

"Yes, Master. I love you so much, I choose to be your slave forever."

"Are you sure?"

"Yes. There's only one thing that frightens me."

"What's that?" he asks.

"Plow Man's threat to take me from you. If he kidnaps me, no one will believe I really belong to you."

"Hmmm." The master was deep in thought. Then his eyes fasten onto yours, announcing a solution. "I will give you my mark," he declares, "so everyone will know you belong to me."

(I have to interrupt the story here. If I don't, you're gonna think, *Yikes! What's he gonna do? Brand her like a cow?* Relax. That's not going to happen. As author, I'm in control of how the story continues, and I promise there's a really cool ending. But guess what–I'm not going to end the story. You are. That's right. YOU are in control of how this story ends. Let's get back to the present so you'll know what I'm talking about.)

Remember the apostle Paul? When he wrote a letter to the folks in Rome, he began it by identifying himself as not only the author of the letter but also as someone who had chosen to be a slave of Jesus Christ.

Paul *willingly devoted* himself to being Jesus Christ's slave. He knew what Jesus had saved him from, and he was so in love with Christ, he voluntarily chose to remain bonded to him.

Back in the days of slavery, every now and then a master would grant a slave his freedom. And, though it was rare, sometimes a slave loved his master so much, he would decide to remain–bonded to him forever.

Okay, you've never had to stand on an auction block. But Jesus Christ has paid a great price for you! He wants to snatch you away from Plow Man! (Obviously, Plow Man represents Satan.) God desires to save you from cutting yourself, wasting your body away through an eating disorder, seeking false acceptance through sexual relationships–and all the other traps Plow Man tosses your way.

Know It!
Have you taken time recently to revel in the glorious realization of what Christ has actually saved you from? Think about it!

Read It!
Romans 1:1;
2 Thessalonians 2:13;
1 Peter 2:9, 16

Pray It!
Pray that God will help you never take your salvation for granted.

God's Great Love

Know It!
God is crazy about you! He loves you more than you can imagine. What are you doing with his love? How are you responding? Are you sharing it with others?

Read It!
Romans 5:6-8; 6:2-10; 14:9-15;
1 Corinthians 15:3

Pray It!
As you pray, ask God to show you specific ways you can share his love with those around you today.

It's as if Jesus opens wide the windows of heaven, parts the clouds, splits the sky right in half, and announces to all creation, "I CHOOSE YOU! I want YOU on my team."

Whew! No more standing by the fence hoping you'll be selected. He chooses you! In fact, he selected you years ago. He knew Plow Man would engage in a bitter bid of wills offering all kinds of things for you—sex, attention, popularity. So he said, "I'll just go ahead and pay the highest price anyone could ever pay. I'll give my *life.*" And he did. He paid for you with his blood.

(If this is sounding too good to be true, you can find the proof in Romans 5:8 about how God selected you when you were still a sinner!) Isn't it exciting that he didn't wait for you to get your act together before choosing you? He could have said, "Whoa! Once you get off that filthy auction block and clean yourself up . . . once you've become involved in a youth group and have become a respectable person. . . ." But he saw you at your point of greatest need and said right then, "I want you right now—just as you are!"

Wow! That's grace!

I like being chosen, you may be thinking. *It feels great to be selected—to realize that God loves me so much, he looked inside my mom's womb even before I was formed and said, "I want him!" Wow.*

But really . . . what are we talking about here?

We're talking about you being so in love with Jesus Christ that you become enslaved to him. In other words, as a slave would belong to his owner for a lifetime, you want to belong to Jesus for a lifetime and an eternity.

Yeah, I DO love Jesus, you're thinking. *And I DO want to serve him forever. But how do I become his bond slave?*

1. *Realize you've been bought.* Remember, he paid for you with his life. You are incredibly valuable to him. Don't ever take his death for granted. (If you start to think his death was no big deal, flip back to the devotions found on March 21-25 for a recap of what Jesus actually went through for *you*!)

Okay, this is starting to make sense now, you may be thinking, *and I really want to be so in love with Jesus that I become his bond slave forever. But how does that work?*

1. *Realize you've been bought.* Remember, he paid for you with his life. You are incredibly valuable to him.

2. *Realize you've been branded.* Ranchers brand their cattle. Loggers carve a symbol on their trees. Dignitaries seal important papers with their insignia on melted wax. All these are marks of ownership.

Jesus Christ also has a mark of ownership. It's his Holy Spirit. We're told in Ephesians that we were *marked* with the Holy Spirit. Having God's brand–the Holy Spirit ruling your life, energizing you, saturating you, filling you–should be as evident as a brand is on a cow. The Holy Spirit wants to make such a difference in your life that people around you *know* you're owned and energized by a supernatural power!

Imagine . . . you walk into a room and people immediately think, *Whoa! She's not her own. She's plugged into something way more powerful than I've ever been connected with!*

In other words, shouldn't your lifestyle and the reflection of the Holy Spirit within you shine brighter and shout louder than a branded scar that's been seared into your skin?

Yeah! you may be thinking. *How can the Holy Spirit make that kind of difference in my life?* Total surrender. But we'll chat more about that in a minute.

Having his brand means we take on his name. We become like him. For proof you can check out Ephesians 5:1 where we're told to be copycats of God. *What's that mean?* It means you begin to act like Jesus! You try to please him in all you do. You take on his resemblance.

You may have heard your folks say, "Don't embarrass the family! You're wearing our name." People may have told you, "You look like your mom." Guess what–as a Christian, you should be looking more and more like your heavenly Father, and as a Christian you're bearing his name.

Know It!
It's obvious you're not going to wear a burned-into-your-flesh brand, but is the Holy Spirit that obvious in your life? Just as people would no doubt notice a burned mark on your flesh, do they see God's Spirit shining clearly through your actions?

Read It!
Psalm 139:23-24; Ephesians 1:13; 5:1; 2 Peter 3:11

Pray It!
Ask God to show you anything in your life that's keeping his Spirit from shining clearly through you.

Living according to the Brand

Know It!
When you become Christ's bond slave, you're actually living out your love for him.

Read It!
1 Corinthians 1:2; 7:14; Ephesians 1:4; Colossians 1:22

Pray It!
Tell God your desire to become his bond slave forever. Ask him to take complete control of your life.

Quick recap: Are you so in love with your Master, Jesus Christ, that you're willing to become his bond slave forever? If so, here's the process for becoming enslaved to him.

1. Realize you've been bought.

2. Realize you've been branded.

3. Realize you're bonded to Christ forever. In other words, don't simply fly through these devotional pages thinking this is just one more fad. Choose, instead, to be chained to him. Not simply attached to, but a part of! Make your prayer, "I willingly take on his name and his lifestyle."

This is an ongoing process. And to become a bond slave of Jesus Christ, this needs to be your highest priority. This is your job right now: To become as close to Jesus Christ as you can. To become so tightly bonded to him that the world just can't comprehend it.

Your job really isn't to worry about how much money you can earn or how you can push your way into the most popular clique or look better than anyone else at your school. Repeat: Your job right now is to become as close to Jesus Christ as you can. To become so tightly bonded to him that the world just can't comprehend it!

If you truly want to become all God calls you to be, then this commitment to become his bond slave will affect everything in your life. From this point on, you'll have a new standard. You'll use a brand-new measuring stick for everything in your life. You'll measure all you do according to the seal, the brand, the mark of Jesus Christ—his Holy Spirit.

"Will you go to this R-rated movie with me?"

Hmmm. Does it match the brand?

"Will you go to this party?"

Does it reflect his brand?

"Come on! *Show* me how much you love me. We won't go all the way; let's just mess around. Everyone else is."

Will my behavior echo the brand?

His seal, his mark, his Holy Spirit is branded on your heart. And inside your mind. It becomes your lifestyle.

My language. The magazines I read. What I do on the Internet. Does it reflect the Holy Spirit in my life? No? Then, sorry. It's not for me. See, I have a new standard now by which I'm measuring my life!

Let's take another look at our strategy for becoming a bond slave to Christ:

1. Realize you've been bought. Remember, he paid for you with his life. You are incredibly valuable to him.

2. Realize you've been branded. God has given you his own special mark—the Holy Spirit—that should distinguish you from the world.

3. Realize you're bonded to Christ forever. This isn't a passing fad. You're making an eternal commitment!

4. Realize you've been bought. (Yeah, I know this is a repeat of number one, but it's so important, we gotta talk about it again.) To truly realize this is to say, "I don't own my life any more. I willingly accept his purchase. He's the Master. I'm merely the slave. But I love him so much, I'm saying YES to being branded and bonded to him forever."

Guess what! You're not really saying yes to living in chains. You're saying YES to kingdom living! You're saying YES to being the prince or princess of the King! So act like it. Live out your title.

Hey, you don't have to be owned by him. He won't force you. But to be a part of his forever kingdom requires much more than settling for casual Christianity. We're talking about radical obedience to the Lordship of Jesus Christ.

You have a choice: You can be owned by him (as in total surrender), or you can maintain control of your own life.

One more thing. If you become his bond slave—committed to Jesus Christ forever, wearing his mark, living through the power of the Holy Spirit—you can't be selective with his will. In other words, when the Master says, "Mow the lawn and do the laundry," you don't respond with, "I'll mow the lawn, but hey, I don't do laundry." Your life is not your own, remember?

Who would make such a commitment? Out of the thousands who are reading this devotional book right now, I have absolutely no idea who would commit to such a pledge. I don't have a clue who would make the decision to become a bond slave to Jesus, not only in this lifetime but throughout eternity. I *do,* however, know what they're called. They are known as radically obedient disciples.

Know It!

If you'd like to become a bond slave of the Messiah, you can do that right now. God is waiting to hear your prayer. And to help you keep your commitment, consider getting an accountability partner who will meet with you regularly, pray with you, and ask you the tough questions about temptation.

Read It!

1 Thessalonians 3:13; 2 Thessalonians 1:10; 2 Timothy 1:9; 2:21

Pray It!

Ask God to help you understand the seriousness of becoming a bond slave to him.

Submitting to God

Know It!

Wow. If you prayed that prayer and meant it, you're living with all kinds of supernatural holy power within you now. Think about it: The same mighty power that hung the stars in the sky, set the world in motion, and raised a dead man to life . . . is yours! So through total surrender now, live daily in his mighty power.

Read It!

Galatians 2:20; Ephesians 1:19; Titus 1:8; Revelation 22:11

Pray It!

Spend some time telling God how grateful you are for his mighty power.

Maybe you've decided to become a bond slave to Jesus Christ. And perhaps you've already asked him to take total control. But I'd still love the opportunity to pray with you. Let's do it now.

Dear Jesus:

Wow. I never thought about loving you so much that I'd consider myself a slave to you. But it makes sense. You have saved me from so much! And you've bought me with such a tremendous price! I do love you, Father. And I want your mark. I want to be branded with the seal of your Holy Spirit.

I realize this is more than a simple prayer; it's a commitment to radical obedience. So right now I ask you to forgive my sins and help me live for you. I surrender my will. I give up the right to own my life. I yield to your plan, your way, and your will for me.

Father, release the power of your Holy Spirit within me and sanctify me. Help me become one with you. Break me and reshape me in your image. I want to be bonded, marked, sealed forever with your image. I want the world to see your Holy Spirit's mark on my life.

I now submit to your authority, Father. Thank you for forgiving my sins and cleansing me. Help me to draw ever closer to you through the Bible, through a strong prayer life, and through daily fellowship with you.

I love you, Jesus. Thank you for being my Master and for saving me from all the sin that Satan desires to use to destroy me.

In your powerful name I pray,
Amen.

*Being a **bond slave** of Jesus Christ means*
a. I'll spend the rest of my life in chains.
b. I'm so in love with him that I voluntarily choose to bond with him forever.
c. I'll never be any good at auctions.

*Jesus Christ has **marked** me with*
a. a four-color glow-in-the-dark tattoo.
b. a neon-orange nose ring.
c. the seal of his Holy Spirit.

*This mark **given** to you by Christ means*
a. that I belong to him.
b. that I no longer need a passport.
c. that I can do whatever I want.

*Christ **bought** me*
a. with MasterCard.
b. on sale.
c. with his precious blood.

*To **measure** everything in my life against the **mark** Christ has given me means*
a. I count off two yards and call it even.
b. I evaluate everything next to the Holy Spirit. If it doesn't measure up to his standard, I don't participate.
c. I always use the metric system.

*Having Christ's **brand** means I*
a. never have to buy generic stuff again.
b. can use his name like a credit card.
c. take on his name.

Know It!
God desires to share himself with you intimately. That requires total surrender on your part. No more casual Christianity. No more playing games with the creator of the universe. He wants to fill you to the overflowing point with his love, his purpose, and his meaning.

Read It!
Psalm 139

Pray It!
Spend time in prayer thanking God for giving himself totally to you, and tell him you want to be totally his.

Warning Signals

Know It!
God doesn't want you simply to walk through life ignoring problems; he wants you to experience life abundantly! He wants to fill your days with meaning, purpose, and contentment. To experience life to the fullest, however, we must learn to pay attention to his warnings.

Read It!
John 10:10; 1 Corinthians 4:14; Galatians 5:21; 1 Thessalonians 5:14

Pray It!
Ask God to help you focus more intently on the two alarms he has placed in your life.

A pilot returned his flight full of passengers to the terminal because he had heard a sound that made him uncomfortable coming from the engine. The passengers weren't delayed very long, and when they taxied a second time for takeoff, one nervous woman asked if the problem had been solved.

The flight attendant smiled as she looked the woman in the eye and said, "Yes, it has. We changed pilots."

Yikes! Ignoring the warning signals can be dangerous—and even deadly. When the *Titanic* sank, it had been steaming full speed ahead. Several iceberg warnings had been issued, but the crew had completely ignored the danger signals. People were dining, couples were dancing, children were sleeping, and the bands were playing on board. No one had any idea they were headed toward disaster.

When the ship actually began to sink, the band began playing an old hymn, "Nearer My God to Thee." But it was too late. Hundreds of people had already died and many more awaited drowning.

God doesn't want his children to walk into danger. In fact, he goes to great lengths to warn us against it. He uses two mighty alarms in our lives to warn us that we're walking the wrong way.

Alarm #1: His Holy Word. By taking the Bible seriously and studying the mistakes, trials, victories, and failures of those who have come and gone before us, God teaches us what to avoid. If you'll make reading the Bible a priority in your life, God will make it a priority to speak to you through its words.

Alarm #2: His Holy Spirit. The Holy Spirit works through our minds and our hearts to lead us in the right direction. Maybe there have been times you've started to do something but felt "checked." That's the work of the Holy Spirit! Or maybe you did something you shouldn't have, and your conscience started to bother you. That's the Holy Spirit. By heeding his warnings, you can save yourself a lot of grief. By ignoring his danger signals, you'll eventually experience disaster.

How Serious Are You?

The Old Testament prophet Elijah lived an adventurous life! He was instrumental in turning many of the Israelites back to the Lord, and he defeated the 450 prophets of Baal. When his time on earth was coming to an end, God instructed him to find a young man named Elisha and to anoint him as Elijah's replacement.

Elijah found his replacement plowing a field with a pair of oxen—and with 11 more teams of oxen in front of him. Elijah went to the back of the line and tossed his coat across Elisha's shoulders.

Elisha, a man of God, knew exactly what this action meant. He understood that God was calling him to become Elijah's successor. Elisha's response was, "First let me say good-bye to my parents before I come with you." Elijah agreed.

We're told in the New Testament of another time when someone asked to say good-bye to his parents before accepting God's call, and Jesus denied the request. Christ was issuing the call for believers to follow him wholeheartedly. One young man asked to bury his father first. Jesus told him to let the dead bury their own dead.

Was Jesus being mean? No. Culturally, it was common to make excuses regarding your family to get out of things you didn't want to do. It was very likely that this man's parents were actually in excellent health. Jesus was in essence telling him to be concerned with living instead of focusing on problems he hadn't even encountered yet—his parents' future death.

Elisha's situation was different. His father expected him to fulfill his obligation of working the fields. To honor his father, Elisha wanted to explain why he was leaving. He wasn't using this as an opportunity to let his parents talk him out of following Elijah. Rather, he was actually showing respect to his parents.

To prove that he wasn't second-guessing his commitment to Elijah, Elisha told his folks good-bye, then killed his oxen and burned their plows. With his tools now gone forever, Elisha knew he couldn't return to the fields. He was serious about answering God's call on his life!

God wants total commitment from you. Those who follow Christ halfheartedly don't follow him very far. Elisha showed that he wanted to follow God's call on his life with abandon.

Know It!

Have you given your entire life to God with reckless abandon? When you do, you'll experience true freedom and the joy of total commitment and obedience.

Read It!

1 Samuel 15:22;
1 Kings 19:15-21;
Matthew 8:22;
Luke 9:59-62

Pray It!

Ask God to reveal any excuses you've been making about your commitment to following him with total abandon.

Have You Burned Your Plow?

Know It!

Following Jesus isn't always comfortable, but it's always an adventure! Where are you in this spiritual adventure? Are you waiting to get involved, weighing the cost, in the middle of the action, or looking back?

Read It!

1 Kings 19:15-21; Psalms 4:5; 9:10; 13:5

Pray It!

Ask God to reveal anything in your life that he needs you to turn away from completely . . . never to return again.

Elisha knew God was calling him to become Elijah's successor. He didn't know everything that would involve, and he certainly didn't know what the future had in store for him. But though Elisha wasn't sure what God was calling him *to,* he knew what God was calling him *from.*

God was calling Elisha from an ordinary life of daily routine to an extraordinary life of adventure. *Is it okay to live an ordinary life of routine?* Absolutely! In fact, the way we discipline ourselves to God during the ordinary days of our routine living often determines how we respond when God allows the extraordinary to cross our path. Because Elisha had been faithful and consistent in being all God called him to be while working the fields, God knew he could trust Elisha with miracles.

But God was also calling Elisha to leave the familiar behind. He knew how to work the fields. He was comfortable with the oxen and plows. But being a prophet? That was a whole new game for Elisha! And God was asking for total commitment—no more leaning on the past of what Elisha was comfortable with and knew best.

When Elisha answered God's call by burning his plows and killing his oxen, he was showing his willingness to leave his life of farming and to follow God wholeheartedly. Without his tools and animals, there was no possibility of returning to what God had called him from.

While God wants you to be faithful in the daily routine of your ordinary life, he also wants you to be willing to be stretched and removed from your comfort zone at his leading. Have you begun to lean too heavily on what's familiar instead of trusting God for the extraordinary?

Are there things in your life that God wants you to "burn"? Are there some friends you need to walk away from? Some habits you need to release? An environment you should avoid?

Following God with reckless abandon isn't always easy or comfortable. In fact, sometimes it's downright tough! The issue isn't how many miracles you'll experience or what kind of trials you'll encounter. The issue always remains *total obedience.*

It's easy to obey God when miracles are happening! When it's cool to belong to the Bible club on campus or when people compliment you for carrying your Bible to school, it doesn't take much effort to call yourself a Christian. But when people are making fun of you or spreading false rumors about you, it's not cool anymore, is it?

Because of Elisha's obedience, God did many miracles through him. But Elisha's obedience remained strong through the tough times as well. Often it's after we've experienced a spiritual "mountaintop" high that we encounter a spiritual "low valley." After healing the undrinkable waters of Jericho (high moment), Elisha was mocked and made fun of because of his baldness (low moment). Did Elisha's faith teeter during this low time? Not at all! He had learned that the God he served was not only King of the mountain but also Lord of the valley.

Elisha had just left Jericho and was headed toward Bethel. On his way, a gang of young men began verbally assaulting him. Though they laughed at his baldness, they were also mocking the fact that he was a prophet of God. And since Elisha was on a mission to speak out against immorality, it's possible they were also warning him not to speak against their own sin. By doing this, they were flaunting their disrespect for God, his call to holiness, and his chosen prophet.

There will be times you'll be mocked for your faith. Chances are high that if you participated at the annual "See You at the Pole" event on your school campus this past September, you received some teasing. When you walk through the valley of difficulty, don't allow your faith to falter. Keep your eyes focused intently on obedience to your Master.

Following Christ with reckless abandon requires great cost and sacrifice. That's why Jesus never pulled any punches when he talked with those who followed him. He let them know the cost would be high.

Know It!

Following God in total obedience may cost you some friends, some parties, and some dreams. In fact, you probably don't know the full cost yet of following him. But *do* know this: The eternal rewards will far outweigh the temporary earthly cost!

Read It!

2 Kings 2:23-25;
Matthew 8:18-20;
Luke 14:25-35;
2 Thessalonians 1:5

Pray It!

Tell God you're ready to count the cost and follow him with reckless abandon.

Giggles, Grins, and Falling Asleep

Know It!

It's a natural progression: We get comfortable; we fall asleep. Have you become too spiritually comfortable?

Read It!

Mark 13:33;
Acts 20:7-12;
Ephesians 6:18;
1 Peter 5:8

Pray It!

Ask God to wake you up from any areas in your life in which you may have fallen asleep spiritually.

To say we've come a long way in the arena of medicine is an understatement. Ancient Egyptian doctors made sure their patients were unconscious before surgery by hitting them on the head with a mallet.

In 1800 Sir Humphry Davy discovered the intoxicating results of nitrous oxide and used it for laughing gas at parties he had with his friends. It never occurred to Davy to use the drug for surgical purposes.

Flash forward half a century. The man who really put the story together was Samuel Cooley, who attended a demonstration of nitrous oxide in 1844. At the end of the lecture, the speaker released 40 gallons of NO2 into the audience. Reacting to the "laughing gas," the audience began to giggle and move about. Samuel Cooley was laughing so hard, he fell and severely injured his leg but didn't even know it! It was his story that convinced physicians to try using nitrous oxide in surgery.

A Boston dentist named Horace Wells tried to demonstrate anesthesia on one of his patients. However, Wells didn't give him enough nitrous oxide, and the patient began screaming midway through the operation. The group of doctors left unconvinced that it was possible to have surgery without pain. A year later, in 1846, Wells's partner, dentist W. T. G. Morton, gave another demonstration for a group of doctors. He anesthetized a patient who had a tumor and then stepped aside so the surgeon could operate.

Dr. J. C. Warren was the surgeon and was shocked he could actually operate on a patient who wasn't screaming in pain. As he finished the surgery, he endorsed anesthesia. The news began to spread.

Years before Sir Humphry Davy, Samuel Cooley, J. C. Warren, and W. T. G. Morton, there was another young man who fell asleep *without* laughing gas. His name was Eutychus, and he had a little trouble staying awake during the apostle Paul's sermon.

To make himself a little more comfortable, Eutychus stretched out inside an open window and started counting sheep. In a matter of minutes, he was dead. He had fallen out of the window from the tall building in which the Christians were meeting and died.

No one was laughing when the crowd of Christians rushed to Eutychus's side. But Paul, full of God's power, exerted his faith and raised the dead young man back to life. You can imagine the ripple of relieved laughter that spread through the crowd when Eutychus promised never to sleep through church again.

He had gotten just a little too comfortable, and unfortunately when we become too comfortable spiritually, there are always consequences. God wants you to live a spiritually defensive life. He knows that Satan, your greatest enemy, is just waiting and watching for a chance to trip you! If you're on the defensive, you'll be ready. If you've fallen asleep spiritually, you could be Satan's next victim.

To live out your spiritual defense strategy, put these two ideas into action:

Determine not to become cozy with the sin around you. You live in a fallen world where sin is rampant. You can't escape that. But you *can* escape embracing it! Once you become comfortable with sin, you start to relax and doze off.

When God sounds an alarm in a specific area of your life, don't push the snooze button. God won't let you fall asleep without a fight. He'll use his precious Holy Spirit to sound a spiritual alarm in your heart. When you hear God's alarm, react in obedience.

It may be relaxing to giggle and snooze in the dentist's chair, but falling asleep spiritually is no laughing matter. Unless we allow the Holy Spirit to wake us up, spiritual sleep will eventually result in spiritual death.

Know It!

God wants to teach you how to live a spiritually defensive life against Satan's sleep strategy. Allow him to wake you up spiritually.

Read It!

2 Chronicles 16:9; Psalms 73:28; 91:14-16; 1 Thessalonians 5:6

Pray It!

Pray for discernment to recognize Satan's strategy in trying to make you fail.

Wanted: More Faith!

Know It!
Bottom line: If you truly desire to grow spiritually, you will. You do what it takes to deepen and stretch your faith.

Read It!
Colossians 1:10; Hebrews 10:19-25; James 4:8; 1 Peter 2:9

Pray It!
Be open with God. Tell him your desire to draw closer to him.

You know them . . . the people who just seem to have it together spiritually. From the way they talk, you can tell they live with a deep faith. Maybe there's someone like that in your life—parents, pastor, youth leader. And sometimes you find yourself thinking, *I want a stronger faith like that.*

Some people are just naturally more trusting. For others, faith is more difficult. But guess what? You don't need a lot of faith. Jesus compares how much we need to the size of a mustard seed, which is almost microscopic.

The fact that you're a Christian and have trusted God to forgive your sins proves you have faith. And there are some things you can do to increase the little bit of faith you have.

1. Read your Bible consistently.
2. Pray daily.

If you're not used to doing these two things, start by setting a small goal for yourself—something you know you can reach. For instance, say, "I'm going to read the Bible and pray for one minute every day." You'll easily meet your goal, and after a few weeks you'll probably want to increase it to two minutes, then three or five. Be realistic and set a goal you know you can easily reach.

3. Surround yourself with other Christians.
4. Get involved in your local church.

You may be thinking, *If I surround myself with a bunch of Christians, I won't have anyone to share my faith with.* Yes, you will. God isn't going to take you out of the world. You don't have to exclude the non-Christian people in your life in order to surround yourself with Christians. But the reason it's important to be around other Christians is because they can encourage and challenge you in your spiritual walk.

And what's the big deal about going to church? A church body provides spiritual growth through preaching, teaching, and accountability. Corporate worship is essential to mature faith.

If you're already doing all these things, watch the person whose spiritual life you admire. What is she doing that you're not? Ask her. Close friends should be able to share their spiritual highs and lows. Ask her to pray with you about your concerns.

God understands the things in your life that irritate you. But sometimes it helps to write them down. So grab a pen and add to this list:

- Having to explain to six different sales people that you're just looking around.
- Reaching under the table to pick up something off the floor and banging your head on the way up.
- Losing your keys . . . for the third time in the same day.
- Hearing your favorite new song on the radio but not finding out who sings it.
- Accidentally leaving a Kleenex in your jeans pocket and having to pull the entire load covered with bits of lint out of the dryer.
- You had that pen in your hand just a second ago, and now you can't find it anywhere!
- Setting your alarm for 7 P.M. instead of 7 A.M.
- Having to listen to that one person in class who always knows the right answer.
- Putting lotion on your hands and not being able to open the bathroom door.
- Hearing people crinkle candy wrappers in the library.
- Getting interrupted in the middle of your story.
- Hearing the car behind you blast its horn just because you stopped long enough to allow someone to cross the street.
- Having your glasses slide down your nose when you get hot.
- Leaving your notes in your locker when the test is tomorrow.
- Having 13 people in one day ask you, "What's wrong?"

You can probably add at least a dozen more things to this list, and as frustrating as the little things in life can be, we can draw encouragement from the fact that God really does understand. Isn't it refreshing to know that Jesus, too, had to deal with homework, misplacing a sandal, and possibly forgetting to feed the sheep once in a while? He knew what it was like to be human, because he chose to become human and walk through the same feelings of frustration you experience today.

Know It!

Instead of becoming overwhelmed at those little irritating things in life that tend to trip us up, rejoice in the fact that you're not alone. The creator of the universe knows exactly how you feel!

Read It!

Proverbs 17:22; 24:19-20; 25:28; 27:9

Pray It!

Thank God that he knows how you feel about the irritations you face every day. Ask God to give you his perspective and help you see things through his eyes.

Wholly Whole

Know It!

Christians aren't immune to anything. Even Jesus Christ felt loneliness. And guess what—he understands when you get lonely, too! In the next couple days, let's take a closer look at loneliness and what we can do about it.

Read It!

Psalms 34:18-20; 68:6; Matthew 26:36-46, 56; Luke 5:16

Pray It!

Ask God to glorify himself through your loneliness.

Have you ever felt as though everyone around you is part of a couple except you? If you haven't dated much, maybe you've even begun to wonder, *What's wrong with me?*

Actually, being normal has absolutely nothing in the world to do with having a boyfriend or girlfriend. Being normal has everything to do with following Jesus Christ and living in total obedience to him. It's unrealistic to think that another person can make you whole. But many teens believe a dating relationship would fill that aching void of loneliness in their lives.

While a relationship can certainly enhance our lives, it can't fill the void. Is it even fair to expect anyone to accomplish a task as big and important as that?

God's ideal is for you to be whole as an individual. Then someday when you do marry, your mate will simply *add* to your life instead of *becoming* your life. When you make God the very center of your life, he brings the fulfillment and security you need.

Realistically, Jesus Christ is the only One who can fill the void in your life. Only when you're whole in Christ are you ready to join into a relationship with someone else. Never approach a relationship expecting the other person to make you whole. It won't happen, and it can't happen. And starting a relationship simply because you're lonely isn't a good enough reason to enter a relationship.

Loneliness is universal in our world. Psychologists tell us it's one of the most frequent issues they deal with in their counseling practice. Loneliness is often the root of suicide attempts, drug abuse, alcohol addiction, and many other problems–both physical and psychological.

Doctors tell us that loneliness is as significant to high blood pressure as obesity is to a lack of exercise. Medical experts also point out that loneliness–social isolation–is a greater mortality risk than smoking.

Someone once described loneliness as "sensing the spirit of one you love pulling away from you."

You may be thinking, *But I'm a Christian! Why am I lonely? Christians aren't ever supposed to get lonely . . . are they?*

Jesus knew the time for his crucifixion was drawing near. He took his disciples to a garden and told them to wait for him and to pray. Then he took Peter, James, and John a little farther and told them his heart was filled with anguish and despair. He instructed the three disciples to wait for him and to cover him with prayer while he went on ahead . . . alone.

Imagine how Jesus must have felt when he returned and found that the three disciples who were closest to him were asleep! He had trusted them with his deepest feelings. Yet they let him down. And Jesus must have felt extremely lonely—even in the company of his closest friends.

A few hours later, when Jesus was arrested and brought in for illegal trials, illegal questioning, and horrendous torture, he must have felt extremely lonely—even in the midst of a crowd.

When *we're* lonely, we can be encouraged that Jesus knows exactly how we feel. But we should also be reminded of how he feels when we drift away from him.

We can't begin to comprehend the loneliness God felt when man was eternally separated from him, the Father Creator. Out of love, he created a bridge. And that bridge is his Son, Jesus.

He became our bridge so we'll never be separated from our heavenly Father again. In other words, we don't ever need to become consumed with loneliness. We'll *experience* loneliness, but we need never again become *consumed* with it, because Jesus forever keeps us from being separated from the one who loves us most.

No one enjoys sitting at home alone feeling as though he has no friends at all. It's important that we realize that our loneliness is sometimes caused by what we do ourselves. Other times it's caused by society or by circumstances beyond our control. Loneliness can be separated into several categories. Here's the first one; we'll look at more tomorrow.

1. Loneliness caused by isolating ourselves. We become negative, sarcastic, and cynical. We complain, harbor a bitter spirit, and eventually drive others away. Do you know someone who fits into this category? Is it possible that you could be guilty of this—of creating your own loneliness?

Know It!
It's possible . . . and you may have experienced it . . . to be lonely even in a crowd. Jesus knows how you feel. He wants to help you through your loneliness. He may not change your situation, but he can change your outlook.

Read It!
Psalms 4–5; 37:25; 43:5; 66:19

Pray It!
Ask God to help you know if you're a contributor to your own loneliness by harboring negative attitudes and grudges. Be willing to commit those to him.

Handling Loneliness

Know It!

Determine not to exaggerate your loneliness by multiplying your complaints in your mind as Elijah did. Wait for God to nourish you with his strength.

Read It!

Psalms 69:1-4, 15, 33; 2 Corinthians 4:7-9

Pray It!

When you're feeling lonely, ask God to show you others around you who share your faith and values.

We've established that loneliness is normal, everyone experiences it, Jesus experienced it, and there are a variety of categories.

1. Loneliness caused by isolating ourselves.

2. Loneliness caused by circumstances beyond our control. You don't cause this loneliness–God allows it, not out of anger or spite, but because we live in a fallen world. Sometimes bad things happen to good people. In other words, a loved one dies or a best friend moves away. Or maybe you realize that you don't have much in common with one of your good friends anymore. This usually requires adjustment . . . which is never easy.

If you're experiencing this kind of loneliness, begin praying for healing. We're reminded in Psalm 34 that God is extremely close to those whose hearts are breaking. He's also promised to be our Comforter. He can begin the healing process right now if you'll trust him with the hurt.

3. Loneliness caused by spiritual or psychological isolation. You've probably heard the saying, "It's lonely at the top." If you're in a position of student leadership, you've probably experienced the struggle of working hard to make good things happen for others (planning the dance, organizing the class party, etc.) and yet not having someone special to enjoy it with you. It's easy to feel as though you're on the outside looking in.

This type of loneliness often attacks those in positions of spiritual leadership. Remember the Old Testament prophet Elijah? (Flip back to March 12 for a quick reminder.) God did incredible things through this man. He defeated the prophets of Baal (and the odds were 450 to 1!), he stood up against King Ahab, and he led thousands of Israelites to believe in and worship the Lord.

Yet after the big Baal bash, he withdrew into the mountains and asked God to let him die. He complained that he was the only godly man left in the country. The Lord opened Elijah's spiritual eyes a little wider and revealed to him that there were actually 7,000 godly people around him.

Loneliness always seems to intensify when we can't find others who share our beliefs. When you're experiencing this kind of loneliness, ask God to reveal those around you who share your standards and values.

Quick recap: Everyone in the world experiences some kind of loneliness at some point in his life. If we can learn how to handle the loneliness and respond to it in a healthy way, we can offer it as a gift to our heavenly Father. There are different categories of loneliness:

1. *Loneliness caused by isolating ourselves.*

2. *Loneliness caused by circumstances beyond our control.*

3. *Loneliness caused by spiritual or psychological isolation.*

4. *Loneliness caused by society.* We live in such a fast-paced, technological world that everyone has been reduced to a number. When you're pulled over by a police officer, he calls in your driver's license number. When you charge a new pair of shoes at the mall, it's the number off your credit card the store wants. We can feel as though we're living in a very impersonal world where no one really cares who we are.

Guess what? God cares about you more than you can imagine. We're reminded in Isaiah that he knows your name . . . and that he calls you by name! Find comfort in knowing that you serve an extremely personal God in an extremely impersonal society.

5. *Loneliness caused by a particular path we've chosen or a specific decision we've made.*

When we take a stand for purity or morality, we often feel lonely because we've decided to go against what the majority believes. We expect to get a negative reaction from the world. After all, they don't share our conscience. But what really hurts is when we're ridiculed by one another. Sometimes people in the church will criticize each other for taking a stand. Instead of causing dissension, we need to be holding each other up, supporting one another, and affirming those around us. (Flip back to September 11 for an example of what the body of Christ should look like.)

Our Lord felt this kind of loneliness in the Garden of Gethsemane. While three of his disciples stayed behind, Jesus went farther physically, emotionally, and spiritually. Only he could communicate with God at this particular point in his life.

There comes a time in all of our lives when we must choose to go further spiritually than those around us. After all, you alone will answer to God about your spiritual depth. This type of loneliness is essential in a growing Christian's life.

Know It!

Would you consider using this type of loneliness as an offering to your heavenly Father? He would love to accept your loneliness as a unique and special gift.

Read It!

Isaiah 43:1-2; 45:3; 46:3-4; 49:1

Pray It!

Ask God to stretch you spiritually—even though it may mean experiencing loneliness at times. Allow that to be your gift to him.

Trivia . . . or Not?

Know It!

Even though the world doesn't put much stock in what the Bible says, those who heed its warnings are the wise ones.

Read It!

Matthew 24:29-30, 32, 44; 25:31-33

Pray It!

Ask God to open your spiritual eyes to the important things he wants you to learn.

It's interesting what facts different people think are important. Check out the following items and decide if you think they're as interesting as other people do.

- A pair of ruby slippers that Judy Garland wore in *The Wizard of Oz* sold for $660,000 at a Christie's East auction in 2000.
- Lake Superior is the largest lake in North America. It has a surface area of 31,700 miles and is the largest freshwater lake in the world.
- In 1900, the most popular names for American girls were Mary, Helen, Margaret, Anna, Ruth, Catherine, Elizabeth, Dorothy, Marie, and Mildred.
- Hawaii, Arizona, and parts of Indiana don't use Daylight Savings times.
- The speed of light is 186,000 miles per second. A beam of light could travel around the entire earth seven and a half times in one second.
- The Dallas International Airport is the size of Manhattan.
- Bibliophobia is the fear of books.
- In 1968, the United States Navy spent more than $400,000 to study Frisbees in wind tunnels.
- The official dessert of Massachusetts is Boston cream pie.
- There are approximately 6,000 known languages in the world, and about 1,000 of them are spoken on the island of New Guinea. Nearly half of these languages have fewer than 500 people speaking them.

Chances are good that you weren't aware of most of the above facts. Most people aren't. That's why we refer to information like this as trivia. It seems trivial–unimportant. But there are some facts the world views as trivial that are actually quite important.

Important fact: Christ will return! He promised his disciples he would someday return for his children. Christians refer to this as the Second Coming. No one knows the exact time, day, or date that Christ will return to earth, but we are given several insights into his coming.

We're told that two people will be at work, and one will simply disappear and be taken to heaven. This is referred to as the Rapture. The Rapture and the Second Coming are two important facts the world labels as trivial. But someday we'll all face the judgment of God himself, and everyone will know what is and isn't trivia!

As Christians, we're very familiar with the cross. We see it on church steeples and wear it on gold chains around our neck. It symbolizes sacrifice. It represents death.

But there's another ingredient that's just as essential in our relationship with Christ as the cross, and that's the yoke. We aren't as familiar with the yoke, are we? We don't see it on church steeples or wear small yokes on gold chains around our necks. But the yoke, like the cross, is necessary to our spiritual maturity.

The yoke is an instrument of sacrifice. It symbolizes service. It represents sweat. And if we're really serious about our relationship with Christ, we're ready at any moment to pick up the cross or be fitted with the yoke. We're willing to die or to serve. We're ready to sacrifice or to sweat.

There's a legend that Jesus was known for making perfect yokes in the family carpenter's shop. The legend states that men would bring their animals from miles around just to have Jesus make the yoke for their oxen. It's important that a yoke fit perfectly. If it's too small, it grinds the neck of the animal and can rub it raw. And if the yoke is too small, even a light load will feel very heavy to the oxen.

If a yoke is too large, the oxen can't get a good grip. It rides too loosely around their necks, making it difficult to pull a load. And again, a light load will seem very heavy if the yoke is too big.

But when a yoke fits just right, one can put a heavy load on the oxen and it will feel extremely light, because everything is in exact balanced proportion.

Know It!

Jesus Christ has spent your lifetime custom-designing a yoke that will only fit you. It fits you perfectly. Will you allow him to break you, remake you, reshape you in his image, and be fitted with his yoke?

Read It!

Psalm 22:8; Isaiah 28:16; Mark 8:34; Matthew 11:28-30.

Pray It!

Ask God to help you learn the importance of total surrender in your relationship with him and what it means to pick up the cross and be fitted with the yoke.

Learning from the Yoke

When an ox was tied to a yoke, farmers used a collar made of leather with padding so it would protect the animal's neck and forequarters. The collar was made with a leather strap and buckle at the top, and it had a rounded bottom to provide comfort to the animal. When the harness was put on the collar, it was designed to put the least amount of pressure on the ox. If the equipment didn't fit properly, it often shifted, and the ox would develop a sore. The animal would then become so stiff-necked that the farmer couldn't turn him at all. The ox would become accustomed only to going one way.

We, too, sometimes become stiff-necked. God needs disciples who are teachable, flexible, and willing to allow him to reshape them for his glory—not their own. When you allow God to fit you with his yoke, it will fit perfectly. To wear the yoke God has created specifically for you requires a few things:

Submission. Are you ready to willingly submit to the authority of Jesus Christ in your life? Can you pray the prayer that Jesus prayed in the Garden of Gethsemane: "Not My will, but Thine be done"? Wearing God's yoke requires total surrender.

Obedience. A yoke is made for two. When you allow Christ to fit you with his yoke, you don't walk alone. He's in the yoke with you! Two people in the same yoke have to walk in step and in the same direction, or they don't get very far. If you're walking with Jesus, this requires watching, learning, and doing what he does. It means you begin to imitate his lifestyle through total obedience. Are you willing to stop pulling the yoke one way while Jesus gently tugs the opposite direction?

Service. The very idea of a yoke brings up mental images of pulling, working, serving. If Jesus Christ, the Son of God, was willing to come and serve, shouldn't you be all the more willing to do the same? He calls every Christian into service.

Fellowship. When you see someone else struggling to pull a load, will you join him? Will you connect yourself to his harness and help him pull the weight? This is really what the body of Christ is all about—helping, supporting, and encouraging one another.

Know It!

Have you ever thought about your purpose? Why you're here on earth? The reason for your existence is to bring glory to Jesus Christ. Are you doing that? Or, like the ox with a sore neck, have you become stiff-necked and unteachable?

Read It!

Proverbs 19:11, 20;
Matthew 11:28-30;
1 Thessalonians 3:12-13

Pray It!

Give God your willingness to submit, obey, serve, and fellowship with other Christians.

No Regrets

Know It!
God doesn't want you to live a life of missed opportunities and spiritual regrets. Stand up, take notice, and know that you're on a mission—a mission to reflect Jesus Christ to each person with whom you come in contact.

Read It!
Jeremiah 31:13; 35:13-15; Lamentations 3:22-26; Acts 8:27-39

Pray It!
Ask God to forgive you for any opportunities you let slip past you. Then ask him to prepare you to do better next time!

It was July 1863, and the armies of the North and South were clashing fiercely in the battle of Gettysburg.

Under General G. G. Meade's leadership, the northern troops were winning, so General Lee and the Confederate forces began to retreat southward on the night of July 4. Storm clouds drenched the East Coast with rain, and when Lee got to the Potomac River, he discovered it was so high that his troops couldn't cross it. The Union army was right behind him, and the river was right in front of him. The Confederate forces were trapped!

This was the perfect opportunity for General Meade to end the battle. He could have attacked immediately, destroyed General Lee's army, and ended the Civil War. President Lincoln actually ordered him to attack. But Meade didn't. He waited. Delayed. Held a council meeting. Then delayed again.

Eventually the river went down, and General Lee and the Confederate troops escaped over the Potomac. The war continued another two years. Meade never regained his lost opportunity, and it was to General Grant that Lee finally surrendered on April 9, 1865.

What a tremendous regret! What an amazingly incredible missed opportunity! Meade could have actually ended the war and saved innocent lives if he had simply acted when the timing was right.

God is in the business of providing amazingly incredible opportunities. Are you in the business of recognizing them? When you notice a classmate who's upset, do you see that as an opportunity to comfort her? When a friend is discouraged, do you recognize the opportunity to share the eternal hope you have?

Maybe you're not sure you have those opportunities. Then follow this simple strategy:

- Pray for opportunities to share your faith. God is extremely faithful! If you ask him to give you specific opportunities to share with others what he's doing in your life, he will. Make this request a part of your daily prayer life.
- Pray for wisdom to recognize the opportunities that God does bring your way. Learn to develop the habit of seeing everyone you come in contact with as either a lost soul or a saved soul. And determine to be the hands and feet of Jesus to the lost souls he brings across your path.

Think of the thousands of opportunities that would have been missed if believers hadn't been paying close attention to God.

The Feeding of the 5,000. The multitudes had gathered, Jesus had been preaching to them, and it was too late for them to return home for food. He had already met their spiritual needs, and now he was interested in meeting their physical needs. So he called his disciples to him and specifically asked about food. Eleven of the disciples missed the opportunity. They failed to recognize this moment as an amazingly incredible time for Jesus to declare his glory through a miracle. One disciple, Andrew, spoke up. "I found a little boy who has a few slices of bread and some fish," he said. Jesus took the opportunity, blessed the food, and multiplied it in front of their eyes.

Ministering to the Ethiopian Eunuch. Philip recognized this traveling visitor as someone with whom he could share his faith. The Ethiopian accepted Christ as his Savior, Philip baptized him, and he grew in his faith. What if Philip had failed to recognize this opportunity and responded, "God, I'm already traveling in a different direction. I'm on a different mission today"?

The Acceptance of Paul. Saul was traveling to Damascus when he was stopped in his tracks, blinded by God's light. God spoke to him, changed his name, and Saul (now Paul) became a Christian. Shortly after, however, he needed Christian fellowship. Many of the believers were afraid to have anything to do with him; after all, he had a known reputation for murdering Christians. But Barnabas recognized this as an opportunity to help a new Christian, and he accepted Paul with open arms.

The Healing of the Bleeding Woman. She'd seen several doctors and had spent nearly every cent she had trying to get well. And one day she noticed a crowd following Jesus of Nazareth. She had heard about him healing the blind and causing the lame to walk. She felt a spark of hope. Could he heal her? When Jesus passed her way, she seized the opportunity to join the mass and deliberately and aggressively pushed her way through the crowd until she was able to reach his gown and touch the hem of his garment. She was healed.

Know It!

God brings amazingly incredible opportunities across your path all the time. Take advantage of each opportunity. Don't let even one pass by without obeying God's direction.

Read It!

Mark 5:24-34;
John 6:1-14;
Acts 8:26–9:31

Pray It!

Ask God to help you recognize the opportunities he brings your way and be willing to share your faith in those times.

Dangerous Christian?

Know It!
People who don't know Christ are watching your life. Are you juggling so many unnecessary things that you're causing spiritual accidents? If so, it's time to slow down!

Read It!
Hebrews 12:10, 12-13; James 1:13-16; 1 Peter 5:2

Pray It!
Ask God to show you what activities are truly worthy of your time and energy. Let the others go.

More and more people are trying to eat while driving, and it's causing a lot of accidents. If your car is a stick shift and you're trying to eat, drink, answer a cell phone, *and* shift gears, you don't have enough hands to guide the steering wheel!

Insurance companies have discovered it's really more the spill than the eating that causes the problems. So that means anything that drips isn't a good idea to consume while behind the wheel of a car. The staff at Hagerty Classic Insurance decided to do a study to see which foods are the worst offenders, and here's what they found:

1. *Coffee.* It always finds a way out of the cup. And the temperature of most coffee can cause serious burns and distract drivers who are trying to drive while in pain.
2. *Soup.* Many people drink it like coffee and run the same risks.
3. *Tacos.* This food can disassemble itself without much help, leaving your car looking like a salad bar.
4. *Chili.* Lots of potential for drips and slops down the front of clothing.
5. *Hamburgers.* From the grease of the burger to ketchup and mustard, it could all end up on your hands, clothes, and the steering wheel.
6. *Barbecued food.* The sauce may be great, but if you have to lick your fingers, the sauce will end up on whatever you touch—including the controls of your car.
7. *Fried chicken.* Another food that leaves you with greasy hands, which means constantly wiping them on something. It also makes your steering wheel greasy.

Someone trying to eat, shift, and answer a phone while driving might as well hang a sign in the window that says "Dangerous Driver." But could the same thing be happening to you as a Christian? It's easy to become so involved in a variety of good things that you find yourself simply juggling nice activities instead of really making a difference. If you're going to Bible study but getting angry at your parents . . . if you're inviting non-Christian friends on your softball team to youth group but throwing the bat on the field and cussing when you strike out . . . you might as well be wearing a shirt that says "Dangerous Christian."

Off the Wire

The following are actual news clippings from around the world.

- A man from Saegertown, Pennsylvania, was tired of looking at two telephone service boxes at the edge of his property, so he ripped them up with a tractor. The state police noted that the man couldn't be reached for comment; his phone was no longer in service.
- A motorist led officers on a freeway chase until his sport-utility vehicle ran out of gas, but the pursuit didn't end there. The man jumped out of his SUV and began pushing it. California Highway Patrol officers waited until he got tired and then arrested him.
- A lawmaker seeking reelection to the Danish parliament has said the country's 11 million pigs should be given toys to play with.

Oftentimes truth really is stranger than fiction, isn't it? It's hard to believe these are actual news clippings pulled from a wire service. Have you ever wondered what would happen if Christians had a wire service? What if anyone, at any time, could tap into a wire service and pull off information about your spiritual life? What would they read?

- Seventeen-year-old Christian says God is the most important thing in his life, but he hasn't read the Bible in months. Says he can't find it.
- Nineteen-year-old female disciple was seen tailing an elderly woman driver, angry because she was going too slowly.
- Sixteen-year-old president of Fellowship of Christian Athletes received one dollar more in change than he should have at Wal-Mart. After he pocketed the money, he turned to his friends and said, "You could tell it was her first day on the job. Serves her right. What a twit!"

Or would people be able to pick up positive news about you? Clippings that tell about your integrity, your character, and your commitment to stand up for the underdog?

Though there really isn't any such wire service for Christians, isn't it enough to know that your heavenly Father sees all, hears all, and knows all?

Know It!
As a Christian, your greatest desire should be to reflect God himself.

Read It!
Mark 9:50; 16:15-20; 1 Corinthians 16–17; Ephesians 5:1

Pray It!
Ask God to point out any actions or habits in your life that misrepresent him.

Gems of Life

Know It!
Let God know he can trust you to pass out "gems" to people who have specific needs. Make it part of your lifestyle to become as close to Christ as you can.

Read It!
2 Corinthians 3:18; 9:6-8; Philippians 2:1-2; Colossians 2:6-7

Pray It!
Ask God to give you specific opportunities to spread gems of kindness to those around you.

There's an old Arabian tale of a caravan making its way across the sandy desert. As the men and their animals inched their way across the sand, the camel drivers began to notice small rocklike pebbles. Some of the drivers dismounted and gathered a few of the stones and placed them in their pouches. Others didn't want to add weight to the already burdened animals.

When evening approached, the drivers washed their pebbles in an oasis and were startled to discover that they were actually precious jewels! Early the next morning, the caravan members quickly retraced their steps, expecting to find more of the same pebbles, but the special rocks were gone. The camel drivers who had taken time to gather a few pebbles were grateful, but they were also disappointed that they hadn't gathered more when they had the opportunity.

We can look at these gems in two different ways. First, as God himself. You can have as much of God as you want. All you have to do is choose him. Like gathering pebbles, make it a point to "gather time" for God. Get alone with him. Read the Bible. Get to know him in as deep a way as possible. The saddest thing in life would be to someday think back and say with regret, *I wish I had gotten to know God better.* You can, right now! So do it.

We can also see these gems in another way—as kindness. In a sense, you've had the opportunity to scatter a few pebbles of worth during your day today. Did you speak a kind word to the lonely person in the cafeteria? In the rush of your school day, did you stop and pick up a book for someone who dropped it? Once you pass an opportunity by, you'll never have that exact same opportunity again. Are you making good use of the situations God brings your way? Or, like the drivers who were too lazy to pick up the pebbles, do you tend to think, *I'm too busy today. But maybe tomorrow I'll pick up some gems and spread them around.*

Start collecting some gems right now. Today, make time to read your Bible and pray. Set some spiritual goals for yourself. Then make a list of ways you can distribute God's gems to those around you.

Picking up where we left off yesterday, there are two more ways we can look at the gems along the road. First, we can see them as personal invitations to an eternal life with Christ. Noah was somewhat like that camel caravan in his day. He scattered pebbles of invitation to those around him, asking them to come to the safety of the ark. He desperately warned his neighbors and friends of the impending flood. But since the earth had never been watered by rain, and people didn't know what it was, they simply laughed at him. (Up to this particular time, the earth was watered with a daily dew. See Genesis 2:6.)

Many people may have helped Noah build the ark. He probably hired carpenters, laborers, and men working with pitch. They worked on the ark, around the ark, and even inside the ark. They built the rooms and cages, and filled the ark with hay, grain, and other edibles. They did a lot of great work, but because they didn't pick up the gem of Noah's invitation, they weren't saved.

Good actions won't save us. A good lifestyle won't save us. Until we accept the gem of invitation from God himself to forgive our sins and live eternally with him, we won't be saved.

We can also view the gems as God's precious fruit of the Spirit. His fruit is yours for the asking. He'll cultivate it, grow it, and multiply it in your life, if you'll do your part and tell him you desperately *want* to produce godly fruit. To all who want joy and peace and love, God will grant it—plus other fruits of the Spirit as well.

Know It!

Why stop short? Instead of simply settling for a good life, go for the best life possible—a life fully committed to Jesus Christ. Allow him to give you all he has in mind for you to receive: A full platter of the fruit of his Spirit and plenty of invitations to extend to those around you so they, too, may inherit eternal life with him.

Read It!

Proverbs 10:28; 12:20; Galatians 5:22-23; 1 Thessalonians 1:6

Pray It!

Ask God to help you distribute his invitations for eternal life to those around you. And make time on a daily basis to allow him to develop his fruit of the Spirit in your life.

A Little Bit of Heaven

Know It!
You don't need to wait until you die to experience heaven. God wants to help you experience a little bit of heaven right here on earth through your actions, your attitude, and your commitment to him.

Read It!
2 Corinthians 5:1; Philippians 3:20; Revelation 5:13; 19:1

Pray It!
Ask God for the desire and strength to do one or all of the suggestions for another person.

On Monday morning one of Pastor Smith's wealthy church members stopped him and said, "Pastor, that was a great sermon on heaven yesterday. I really enjoyed it! But you forgot to tell me where heaven is. I've never been clear on that."

"Ah," Pastor Smith responded. "I'm glad you brought that to my attention. I've just returned from the home of Mrs. Elmore. Her husband died several years ago, and she's trying to care for her two small children alone. She's very sick today, and she doesn't have any food in the house. I have an assignment for you: Buy a few groceries and take them to her in the name of Jesus. Then ask to borrow her Bible and read the 23rd Psalm to her and her children. After you do that, get on your knees and pray for her and her children. If you don't see heaven before you're finished, I'll pay the bill for the groceries."

The man stopped by the church office the next morning. "Pastor Smith, I saw heaven! Thank you so much for pointing me in the right direction. I understand now."

Every time we do something in Jesus' name—going the second mile, giving in faith, sharing our resources with someone in need—we experience a little bit of heaven. Jesus told his disciples that anytime they offered a cup of cold water to a stranger, it was as if they were giving the water to their heavenly Father.

Have you experienced heaven on earth? Strive to be the hands and feet of Jesus to those around you. Consider doing any of the following:

- Ask your pastor for the names of three older people in your congregation who have not been able to come to church in a while because of poor health. Call each one and ask if you can come and pray and read the Bible for them.
- Do something to earn a little extra money specifically for the purpose of giving it away. Baby-sit, wash cars, have a garage sale. And use all of the proceeds to buy groceries for a needy family.
- Make a list of five areas of need you'd love to see Jesus meet. For one week, fast one meal a day and spend the time you would be eating praying for these needs.

Shut the Door!

Seth stopped at a gas station to fill up his Honda. After he paid the bill, he noticed a phone booth and decided to call his buddy Tim and ask him to go to the batting cages with him. The connection was made, but Tim kept saying, "Seth? I can't hear you! Talk louder. Seth? Talk louder, man, I can't hear you!" All Tim could hear was the noise of traffic in the background. He finally screamed, "Seth! Shut the door so I can hear you!"

Many Christians mistakenly assume that God doesn't speak to them. The truth is, God speaks to you every single day. But if you're not hearing him, it could be because there are too many other noises in your life competing for your attention. How can we hear God's specific voice if we always have the TV on?

Christian music is great, but if we never turn it off, we'll have difficulty tuning in to the voice of God. There are times when we need to "shut the door" to the world and all it offers so we can intently focus on God and God alone. The Bible tells us to be still and know that he is God. It's in the quiet moments, those times when we learn to silence ourselves before our Creator, that we hear him speak.

Have you learned the sound of God's voice? Have you learned how to be completely still before the Lord? God doesn't only speak to us when we're quiet, but it's usually those times when we're able to more clearly hear his voice. It's fine to use Christian music, Christian reading, and other Christian materials to help you focus more completely on your relationship with God. But there comes a time when you'll need to put everything down, turn everything off, and shut the door so you can hear God speaking through your thoughts, your heart, your mind, and his Word.

Know It!

If you're unsure of God's voice, make it a point to seek his voice this week! Come to him in total honesty and tell him you desperately want to hear from him. Understand it may not be an audible voice. Ask him to help you learn what his voice sounds like through your heart and through Scripture. If you set aside the time to learn his voice, God will be faithful and teach you his inflection. When you make a consistent habit of shutting everything else out to focus more clearly on your heavenly Father, it will make all the difference in the world!

Read It!

Proverbs 14:16; 18:10; Isaiah 48:17-18; 56:1-2

Pray It!

Tell God you want to be extremely sure of his voice, and ask him to help you recognize it when he speaks.

Just like Sin

Know It!
Have you asked the Great Physician to treat the sin in your life?

Read It!
Isaiah 64:5;
Jeremiah 31:30;
John 1:29; 1 John 1:7

Pray It!
Ask God to reveal any unconfessed sin in your life and seek forgiveness from him. Tell him you want a tender heart that's sensitive to the prompting of his Spirit.

Can you imagine having to scream, "Unclean! Unclean!" as you crossed the street at a busy intersection so those around you would immediately distance themselves from you? In Bible times, people who had leprosy were forced to announce that whenever they went outside. Once someone contracted leprosy, they also contracted a stigma that never left them. They weren't allowed to be in public places such as markets, temples, or schools. Friends stopped associating with them, and family members often shunned them.

Leprosy is a disease that still exists today. It's commonly referred to as Hansen's disease, and there are treatment facilities in various parts of the United States. We don't hear much about it anymore because with the proper medication, it's very treatable. People tend to think having leprosy means that a foot or hand suddenly falls off. That's really not what happens.

Leprosy is caused by a bacteria called *Mycobacterium leprae,* which is from the same family as the organism that causes tuberculosis. Leprosy destroys the nerves, which makes the patient insensitive to pain. For example, if you have leprosy in your foot, you may walk barefooted over a rusty nail and not know it—even though the nail has broken through your skin, caused an open wound, and is now getting infected. If you continue to walk on that foot without realizing you're hurt, the foot will become severely infected and may eventually need to be amputated.

Can you imagine an extremely severe case of leprosy throughout the entire body? If it's untreated, eventually it can be fatal.

Sin works in a similar way. It's possible to become so accustomed to the sin in our lives that eventually it no longer bothers us. As we continue to sin, and as we allow our hearts to harden, we become desensitized to evil. It becomes difficult even to feel the pain we're causing our heavenly Father. Eventually, sin will destroy us . . . unless we turn to God with a repentant heart.

Like leprosy, sin is treatable. God is willing not only to forgive our sins but to completely remove them from his mind. But if we continue to ignore the tender prompting from the Holy Spirit, we allow our heart to harden, and the sin simply spreads through our spiritual lives.

Check out the following actual statements found in patients' hospital charts.

- Patient's medical history has been remarkably insignificant with only a 40-pound weight gain in the past three days.
- She is numb from her toes down.
- While in E.R., she was examined, X-rated, and sent home.
- Patient was alert and unresponsive.
- The patient refused autopsy.
- The patient has no previous history of suicides.
- I saw your patient today, who is still under our car for physical therapy.
- Discharge status: Alive but without my permission.
- Skin: Somewhat pale but present.
- Patient has two teenage children, but no other abnormalities.

Even though we laugh at the above statements, they can make us wonder if the medical staff dedicated the time necessary to properly assess each patient. They were probably overworked and rushed and simply made some humorous mistakes.

Spiritually, it's imperative that we make the time to "get it" and get it right. Are you getting what God is trying to teach you? Are you understanding his ways, his words, his truth?

We're told in Acts 19 that the apostle Paul entered the synagogue in Ephesus and spoke boldly for three months about the kingdom of God. Many of his listeners became obstinate. They didn't get it. So Paul took the disciples with him and left. They headed to Tyrannus and had a revival there that lasted two years! Obviously, the listeners in Tyrannus got it.

And God began doing extraordinary things through Paul. The Bible goes on to say that even when Paul's handkerchief touched people, they were healed because of God's power surging through Paul and through everything he touched. Paul got it, didn't he? He understood what God was teaching him, and he was intensely tuned in to God himself.

But it took awhile. Remember, Paul was originally Saul—the one who hated Christians and caused many of their deaths. It took temporary blindness and a name change, but Paul finally got it.

Know It!

God desperately wants you to get it. He wants you to understand, receive, and obey all that he's trying to teach you. And fortunately, he'll go to great lengths to make sure you *do* get it. Are you paying attention?

Read It!

Acts 19:1-4, 8-12, 22-29, 35-41

Pray It!

Pray that God will help you "get it" spiritually. Ask him to keep you from taking spiritual shortcuts.

Try This!

Know It!

If you've accepted Christ's forgiveness for your sins but are still living in guilt, try this strategy: (1) Memorize specific Scripture verses that prove you're forgiven. When Satan plants seeds of doubt in your mind, quote Scripture as your defense. (2) Change the immediate environment in which you feel guilty. For example, if you used to drink and have quit and are forgiven, don't go to places that serve alcohol. That will only remind you of your past.

Read It!

Isaiah 6:7; Mark 2:7-10; Hebrews 10:22; 1 John 1:9

Pray It!

Spend some time thanking God for his forgiveness and ask him to free you from the stain of guilt your past sins have caused.

Having a tough time removing a stain? Try these helpful hints!

- If you're trying to remove a permanent marker stain from appliances or counter tops, rubbing alcohol on a paper towel should do the trick.
- Need to get rid of crayon marks on walls? A damp rag dipped in baking soda works great with lots of scrubbing.
- Have a blood stain on your clothes? Pour a little peroxide on a cloth and use that to wipe off the blood. Works every time.
- If you're trying to remove a stain from the bottom of a vase, fill it with water and drop in two Alka-Seltzer tablets for amazing results.

It's interesting how we use trial and error over and over again to come up with just the right solution for removing stains on everything from toilet bowls to clothing to counter tops. Sometimes it takes years for a researcher to discover how to remove a specific stain from a certain material.

Many people search for years trying to find a way to remove their stain of guilt caused by sin. You may have a friend who's an alcoholic. Perhaps he turned to alcohol to try to forget the guilt he's carrying from his past. Others turn to drugs as an escape. Some people are in and out of relationships—seeking that certain someone who can fill the void in their lives that the stain of sin has caused.

Guess what? You weren't meant to be able to remove the stain of sin from your life. You can spend years searching for just the right product, but there's only one way to get rid of the stain of sin forever, and that's through the blood of Jesus Christ. Ironic, isn't it? The blood of Christ doesn't *cause* stains, it totally *removes* stains! And his blood doesn't simply work for the moment. When Jesus Christ forgives, it's forever.

An old preacher once said, "Jesus forgives your sins and forgets them. He tosses them in the Sea of Forgetfulness and posts a sign that reads 'No Fishing.' " In other words, Christ wants *you* to forgive yourself as well. Once he's forgiven you, he doesn't want you to wallow in guilt. He died for your guilt as well as your sins, and he desires that you live in freedom, confidence, and grace.

You Are Blessed!

It's easy to take for granted the many things God gives us. Have you recently stopped to actually thank God for his specific blessings and provision in various areas of your life? Use this checklist to get you started in the direction of gratitude.

- If you own just one Bible, you're abundantly blessed. One-third of the world doesn't even have access to one copy.
- If you awoke this morning with more health than illness, you are more blessed than the million people in our world who won't even survive this week.
- If you've never experienced the danger of battle, the loneliness of imprisonment, the agony of torture, or the pangs of starvation, you're ahead of 500 million people around the world.
- If you attend a church meeting without fear of harassment, arrest, or death, you're more blessed than almost three billion people in the world.
- If you have food in your refrigerator, clothes on your back, a roof over your head, and a place to sleep, you're richer than 75 percent of the people in this world.
- If you have money in the bank, in your wallet, and spare change in a dish someplace, you're among the top 8 percent of the world's wealthy.
- If you hold up your head with a smile on your face and are truly thankful, you're blessed because the majority of people in the world can but don't.
- If you can hold someone's hand, hug her, or touch her on the shoulder, you're blessed because you can offer God's caring touch.
- If you prayed yesterday and today, you're in the minority and are blessed because you believe in God's willingness to hear and answer prayer.
- If you believe that Jesus is truly the Son of God and the only way to heaven, you're part of a very small minority in the world.
- If you can read this devotional, you're more blessed than over two billion people in the world who can't read anything at all.

Know It!

We all have bad days. But the next time you're frustrated or angry, stop and ask the Lord to help you focus on the blessings he's so generously given you.

Read It!

Isaiah 40:22-26, 31; Isaiah 41:1-2, 13

Pray It!

Pray for a genuine attitude of gratitude.

Real Love

Know It!

God didn't simply give you a plan for eternal life; he gave his one and only Son—the biggest part of himself he could give. And Jesus didn't simply give you a prayer to memorize; he gave his blood. What are you giving to those around you?

Read It!

Leviticus 19:34; Numbers 14:18; Joshua 22:5; 1 Corinthians 13

Pray It!

Ask God to show you specific ways you can give yourself with genuine love to those around you.

Genuine love always gives a part of itself. Imagine you've ordered a thick crust pepperoni pizza with extra cheese. It's just been delivered to your door, and you're sitting at the table with the first gooey bite in your mouth. The doorbell rings, and you welcome your friend Rachel inside.

"Hi, Rachel! Great to see you. Listen, uh . . . I'm eating a pizza in the kitchen. Why don't you have a seat in the dining room, and I'll be right back."

You run down to the Chinese restaurant at the corner and bring back egg rolls, sweet and sour chicken, and egg drop soup. You then set Rachel a place at the dining-room table and put the Chinese food in front of her. "Hope you enjoy it, Rachel! I'll be in the kitchen finishing my pizza."

Even though you would have done a great job providing for your friend, you probably would hurt her feelings as well. After all, she came over to see you, but by putting her in the dining room and not offering to share your pizza with her, you've shut her out.

Real love doesn't simply give nice things or provide well; genuine love gives a part of itself. It was said of a now-deceased multimillionaire that while he lived a wild life and enjoyed all the material things he wanted, he never showed any interest in God. But once in a while, he was known to give large sums of money to religious enterprises. Even though the organizations surely appreciated his lavish gifts, he made it known he was not giving because of his personal faith; he had none. He was giving simply to be giving.

God doesn't want only your gifts. He wants you! And those around you don't really need a slice of your pizza; they need a piece of your heart. What specifically are you doing to give yourself away?

On June 1, 1945, toward the end of World War II, the crew on an American B-29 bomber suffered a direct hit from a flak shell from Tokyo. Half of the plane's nose was shot away, and the pilot, strapped in his seat, died in the air. The copilot tried to control the airplane, but blood was flowing all over his body, and his left arm hung uselessly at his side. All the plane's instruments were broken, so the copilot didn't know his speed, altitude, or direction. He was flying blind.

If he bailed out of the plane, with the enemy waiting for him below, he would certainly die. Just when his situation seemed impossible, two American P-61 Black Widow night fighters suddenly appeared on the horizon. They flew beside the damaged plane and nudged it back safely to Iwo Jima, which was occupied by American forces.

Almost 40 years later, in 1984, the crews of the three planes met for a reunion in Long Beach, California. They talked about the day they almost died and relived their safe landing.

In a spiritual sense, your non-Christian friends and family members are flying blind. Death is their destination unless someone will intervene, come along beside them, and guide them to safety. Will you dare to be that person?

What can you do specifically to help guide the non-Christians in your life to a saving knowledge of Jesus Christ?

1. Live out loud. Contemporary Christian artist Steven Curtis Chapman sings a song called "Live Out Loud." Every day that you actually live your faith through your actions, you're living out loud. Your lifestyle is one of the best ways to come alongside a nonbeliever and gently guide him or her to the truth.

2. Know your Bible. It's important not only to read your Bible, but to memorize Scripture and study it. Then you'll be prepared when the non-Christians in your life ask questions.

Know It!
God desperately wants every single person in the entire world to come to him. If you'll let him, he can use you as a guide to bring nonbelievers safely to him.

Read It!
John 8:31-47;
2 Corinthians 13:5;
Ephesians 3:7;
Colossians 1:28

Pray It!
Ask God to bring to your mind the names of five people you can begin praying for and coming alongside of.

The Simple Truth

Know It!

Never be ashamed of the gospel! Instead, share it with joy and pride knowing that it's for everyone who's willing to listen.

Read It!

Romans 1:16; 15:16, 20; 1 Thessalonians 2:4

Pray It!

Ask God to give you a burden for those who don't know him. Tell him you want to share the gospel in a confident manner.

Dr. Owen pastored an average-sized church and had come to his congregation with high credentials from a prestigious seminary. After he had been at the church for almost a year and had not seen much growth, he became concerned that his preaching might be too complicated.

So he worked extensively on his sermon for the upcoming Sunday, and on Wednesday he decided to try it out on Betty, one of the church kitchen workers who had only an eighth-grade education. She listened to about 10 minutes of his sermon before he stopped and said, "Betty, do you understand what I'm preaching?"

"No, I really don't," she responded. Dr. Owen repeated his ideas in simpler language and asked her again if she understood it. "I see it a little," she said. Again Dr. Owen simplified his sermon and repeated the question. "Take it down a little more," she said. Once again, the pastor simplified his language. Betty looked at him with a spark in her eyes he'd never seen before and said, "I get it! I understand it now!"

Dr. Owen returned to his study and rewrote his entire sermon in the most simplified language he could. He kept Betty in mind as he wrote it and imagined that he was giving the sermon only to her.

Sunday morning approached, and Dr. Owen went to church a bit apprehensive. He was nervous that his congregation might be offended at his simplistic style, but he was determined to try his experiment. He began preaching, and to his amazement, he noticed the people in the pews were paying closer attention than they ever had before. Many even had tears in their eyes. From that time on, Dr. Owen changed his style of language and watched the church grow numerically as well as spiritually.

We often think we need to "doctor" up the gospel. We assume if we simply tell it like it is, it will come across too plain, too elementary, or too boring. But guess what—the gospel is simple!

God doesn't want his message to be complicated. His desire is that everyone would hear, understand, and respond to the gospel in a positive way. If it took a rocket scientist to understand the fact that God's forgiveness of sins and eternal life is a *gift,* many of us would be excluded.

Stand Where the Fire Has Been

In the late 1800s, Thomas and Dorothy Buttering lived in a log cabin in the middle of a prairie. One evening about sundown, they stood contentedly looking out across the vast prairie in front of them. Their land seemed to stretch forever–miles and miles of long, tall grass. They loved their quiet lives and the peaceful area in which they lived.

Suddenly, out of nowhere, a dark cloud appeared on the horizon. Behind it was a fierce, fiery glare. Though it was still a long way off, Thomas knew exactly what it meant. "Dorothy! The prairie's on fire!"

This was no ordinary grass fire. Driven by the wind behind it, the fire approached the Butterings's cabin at the rate of 15 miles an hour. Animals were already starting to run from the fire. They were terror-stricken.

Thomas intently focused on the situation at hand. Then he held Dorothy close as he gently but firmly explained his plan. "Honey, we must set the grass in front of us ablaze."

"What?!? Thomas, no! Let's run. I'm frightened."

But Thomas stood his ground. "Listen to me, Dorothy. If we set fire to the grass in front of us, it will move toward the prairie fire. And when the prairie fire reaches the ground that's already burned, it will go no further. There will be nothing more for it to consume!"

Dorothy caught her husband's vision, and together they set the ground in front of them on fire. They held each other close as they watched the two fires come together and eventually die. Dorothy and Thomas stood safely on burned, blackened, charred ground. They discovered that after the fire had gone over a place once, it couldn't do so a second time. By standing where the fire had been, they were safe from the raging flames around them.

Satan will try anything to knock you over, trip you up, and get you to turn from your faith. But though turmoil may surround you, God will provide a way for you to maintain your faith in him. How do you react when the fire rages near you? Do you panic? Give up? React in anger?

Know It!
Determine to burn the knowledge of God's holy Word into your life so the storms of the world will have no effect on you.

Read It!
Colossians 2:6-7;
1 Thessalonians 1:7-8;
2 Thessalonians 3:5;
1 John 2:15-17

Pray It!
Ask God to help you hide his Word in your mind and your heart.

Trust the Master with Your Key

Know It!

You have no idea how God wants to use your gifts and abilities, but know this: He dreams BIG dreams for you! Your gifts in the hand of the Master are worth so much more than if you maintain control of them yourself. Have you given the Master the key to your life?

Read It!

Romans 12:6-8;
1 Corinthians 12:12-26;
Ephesians 3:20; 4:4-13

Pray It!

Commit your gifts, your talents, your self to the Master's control. Let him use you in ways you've never imagined.

Years ago an elderly church organist sat on his bench and played for the last time. He was a good organist and had served his church faithfully and well over the past several years. But a new organist had moved to town, and the elderly man wanted to step aside with dignity. Though he knew he'd miss playing each Sunday, he was excited to be blessed by the new young man and the gift of music he would give the congregation.

The elderly man struck the last chord, closed the organ, locked it, and carried the key to the back of the church. And in the foyer, the new young organist was waiting for him anxiously. He asked for the key, and then he literally ran through the aisles in the sanctuary to get to the organ. He excitedly unlocked and opened the great instrument and began to play.

Though the old organist had played each note with precision, this new musician played with more intensity, more depth, and more passion. His music brought tears to the elderly man's eyes as he stood in the back of the sanctuary watching the young man's hands glide gracefully over the keys.

Within just a few months, the new organist's reputation spread, and people began coming to church from miles around just to hear him play. The new organist was definitely a master of his craft; it was obvious he had more skill than anyone in that area had ever heard. The young man's name? Johann Sebastian Bach. As the elderly man left the sanctuary one day, he thought to himself, *My! What a shame if I had never given him the key!*

Your Master—Jesus Christ—wants the key to your life. He has special gifts, talents, and skills he wants to bless you with. His desire is that you'll use those gifts to glorify the Giver. But he needs the key. When you place control of your gifts in the hand of the Master, he can do extraordinary things through you!

Reverend Lucas Abernathy pastored a small congregation in southern Texas. One Sunday morning he preached vibrantly on God's final judgment. Many folks in the church didn't like what they heard. Several of them got together the next day and appointed one man to approach Rev. Abernathy and discuss the matter with him.

Russell Browning made an appointment with the pastor and began the conversation by saying, "I believe there's a small dispute between you and me, and I thought we should try to settle it."

"I see," Rev. Abernathy said. "What is it?"

"Well," Russell began, "you say that the punishment of unrepentant sinners will be eternal, and I don't think it will."

"Oh, I see," Rev. Abernathy said. "If that's all this is about, then you can rest assured there's no dispute between the two of us."

"I don't understand," Russell responded.

"If you'll turn to Matthew 25:46, you'll find that the dispute is between you and the Lord Jesus Christ. I encourage you to go immediately and settle it with him."

It's easy to become angry with the messenger when we hear something that convicts us. It's hard to be confronted with truth, isn't it? God's absolute truth shines bright like a heavenly spotlight and points out the things that are inconsistent in our lives. Instead of becoming angry, we should be grateful that God cares about us enough to show us what's wrong in our lives so we can ask him to help, guide, and forgive.

Many Christians leave their church when the pastor starts preaching messages that make them uncomfortable. It's much easier to hear a "feel-good" message than to allow the Holy Spirit to nudge our conscience, help us feel guilty about what's wrong in our lives, and lead us to God in repentance. But if you're interested in becoming all God wants you to be, you'll find a pastor, a youth leader, and other adults who will speak truth into your life instead of simply telling you what you want to hear.

Know It!
The next time you hear something that challenges you, makes you think, or causes you to change an attitude, stop and thank God for the messenger.

Read It!
Hebrews 4:12-13; 5:12-14; 6:1, 12

Pray It!
Pray for the godly leaders in your life—pastor, youth minister, Sunday-school teachers—to be filled with the boldness needed to speak truth to you and those in your congregation.

Complaints

Know It!

You can make or break someone's day simply by the language you use. Strive to lace your words with positive remarks and encouragement. Barnabas was known as "the encourager." Ask God to make you a Barnabas.

Read It!

Acts 4:36; 13:15; 2 Thessalonians 2:16-17; Hebrews 3:13; Philippians 2:14-15

Pray It!

Ask God to help you curb your complaints and to multiply your encouragement to others.

The following are actual complaints from letters sent to landlords.

- This is to let you know that there's a smell coming from the man next door.
- Our lavatory seat is broken in half and is now in three pieces.
- I am writing on behalf of my sink, which is running away from the wall.
- Will you please send someone to mend our cracked sidewalk? Yesterday my wife tripped on it and is now pregnant.

Though we laugh at the above, it's probably hard to be a landlord who has to deal with complaints throughout the day. If you're a Christian, the world is closely listening to your words, your attitudes . . . and, unfortunately, your complaints. What kind of impression are you making on those around you?

Think of that one person in your life whom everyone loves being with. He or she is probably great with encouragement. Affirming others may come naturally, or it may be something your friend has to work at, but chances are he or she has made a habit of making others feel good about themselves.

People like that are magnets. Everyone loves to be around someone who encourages but doesn't complain. Jesus was a natural at drawing out the good in those around him. He built others up, he loved genuinely, and people followed him. They wanted what he had.

If you need to break the habit of complaining, try these suggestions:

- *Practice praise.* It may feel awkward at first, but consciously decide to praise those around you for specific things. If a friend did a great job in the school play, tell her! If you see someone at youth group acting kindly, let him know you noticed.
- *Curb the complaints.* When you do start to complain, counter it with something positive. At the end of the day, ask God to help you review your language. Did you complain more or less today?
- *Count your blessings.* When you're tempted to complain, STOP! Before the negative talk even comes out of your mouth, silently thank God for three blessings in your life.
- *Ask for accountability.* Confide in a close Christian friend that you're trying to break out of the complaining habit. Allow your friend to hold you to your resolution.

Sometimes it's tough to explain to friends why specific movies, magazines, or music harm you more than they help you. And sometimes it's even hard to understand why your parents feel a particular movie would be a bad influence on you. Check out a dad who came up with a creative way of helping his teen daughter understand this dilemma.

Brooke asked permission to attend a PG-13 movie with some of her friends from school. It starred her favorite actor, and people from her church had even seen it and said it was great. Her dad listened to all her reasons for going and then asked, "Why do you think it has the 13 rating on it?"

"Well," Brooke admitted, "there is a scene where a building and several people are blown up, but the violence isn't too bad. And there are a few other minor things, but the special effects are incredible!"

Brooke's dad wouldn't give in. He simply said, "No."

A little later that same evening, he asked Brooke if she'd like some warm brownies he'd baked. He explained that he'd used the family's favorite recipe and added a little something new.

"What is it?" Brooke asked.

Her dad calmly replied that he'd added dog poop. "But it was only a little bit," he quickly added. "All the other ingredients are gourmet quality. I'm sure they'll be fantastic!"

"You're kidding, right?" Brooke asked in shock.

"No. Go ahead and try one."

Brooke wouldn't go near the brownies. Her dad acted surprised. "You'll hardly notice that one ingredient, Brooke," he said. But his daughter held firm and wouldn't give in.

Her dad then explained the meaning behind his charade. "The movie you want to see is just like these brownies. Your mind is telling you that a little bit of evil won't matter. But the truth is, even a little bit of poop makes the difference between a great treat and something disgusting and totally unacceptable."

Brooke was silent as her dad continued his explanation. "Brooke, even though the movie industry wants you to believe that most of today's movies are acceptable for adults and teens, the truth is they're not."

Now the truth is, we live in a sinful world. It's pretty hard to do anything—spend time with non-Christian friends or go out to eat—without confronting some wrong things. This story doesn't mean you should lock yourself in your bedroom and never come out! But it does mean that you need to make wise choices. You may not be able to avoid some wrong things, like being around people at school or work who take God's name in vain. But you can make careful choices to limit the amount of time you're exposed to stuff that will hurt you.

Know It!

Satan will work through movies, TV, music, and maybe even your friends to try and convince you that something questionable is really okay. Don't fall for his lies. He's the father of deceit. Keep your spiritual guard up and let the Holy Spirit guide your decisions.

Read It!

2 Corinthians 12:9; Philippians 2:13; 4:8; 1 Timothy 4:16

Pray It!

Ask God to help you feel very uncomfortable around things that aren't pleasing to him.

How to Write a Term Paper

Know It!
An intimate, growing relationship with Christ requires spending time with him. Pledge to set aside time on a daily basis to make this happen.

Read It!
Colossians 1:10; 2:19; 2 Thessalonians 1:3; 2 Peter 3:18

Pray It!
Ask God to give you a hunger for his Word. Tell him you want to get to know him in an intimate way.

Having a little trouble getting those assignments completed before the approaching Christmas holidays? Here are a few suggestions.

- Sit in a straight, comfortable chair in a well-lighted place with lots of sharpened pencils.
- Read over your notes about the assignment very carefully, just to make sure you really understand it.
- Walk into the kitchen and pour yourself a Coke to help you concentrate.
- Make a quick phone call to your best friend. If she hasn't started her paper yet, you can both grab a hamburger first to discuss ideas.
- When you return home, sit in a straight, comfortable chair in a well-lighted place with lots of sharpened pencils.
- Go check your nose in the bathroom mirror. You think you feel a zit starting to grow. Better put something on it now while it's still in the beginning stages.
- Listen to your favorite CD—just to relax your mind—so you can jump right into starting your term paper.
- Alphabetize your CD collection.
- Check the TV guide to make sure you're not really missing anything truly important. Catch the last part of a Mary Tyler Moore rerun.
- Phone your best friend to see if she's watching. Discuss the plot.
- Sit in a straight, comfortable chair in a well-lighted place with lots of sharpened pencils.
- Read over the notes for your assignment one more time, just to make sure you really, truly, definitely understand it.
- Call your best friend to make sure she truly understands the assignment as well. Offer to answer any questions she may have.
- Scoot your chair close to the window and watch the sun set. Scream!

When you're not really into something, it's easy to put it off. If you've never really disciplined yourself to spend daily time in prayer and Bible reading, it can be tempting to make excuses and fill your time with other things.

But the truth is, your spiritual strength will come from reading the Bible and praying. Without those two ingredients, your spiritual life will suffer. Other things are important as well, such as fellowship with other Christians, ministry involvement, and sharing your faith. But without making time for a daily infusion from the Lord Jesus Christ, you'll never feel very close to him.

The place that Beethoven lived is called the House at Bonn, and the piano he used is still preserved inside. This is the piano the master used to create his great musical compositions. Many visitors enjoy touring the shrine and discovering more about one of the world's greatest musicians.

Years ago, an American girl visited the House at Bonn. She skipped airily to the piano, sat on the bench, and began playing a careless tune. She then turned to the custodian and struck up a conversation. "I guess you get quite a few visitors here, huh?"

"Yes, we do. Every year," the janitor said without emotion.

"Any famous people ever visit?" she asked.

"Yes, Paderewski was recently here."

"And he probably played this very piano," she said as her fingers carelessly thumped the keys.

"Oh, no," said the custodian. "He didn't consider himself worthy."

It's easy to adapt a flippant attitude when we enter a hallowed place such as church. If you're plugged into a growing church with a youth group, it's probably a fun place you love and enjoy. Church may be home to some of your best pizza parties, hide-and-seek games, and close relationships. And because of that, it's easy to forget that when we enter the church for worship, we're entering a sacred and holy environment.

Jesus Christ wants to be your best friend, the One you share your secrets with. But he also wants—and deserves—so much more. He also needs to be your holy Savior, your reverenced Father, and your almighty God. When we overlook that aspect of him, we're like a flippant teen approaching a great instrument and carelessly plunking the keys.

How can you learn to reverence and worship God? Try the following strategy:

Pray before entering. Before you walk inside your church building, spend some time in prayer. Ask God to remind you that you're already in his holy presence. And while he wants you to enjoy worship and have fun in church, he also wants you to remember that he's much more than a buddy.

Be still. It's natural to want to talk with your friends when you're in church, but if you'll make a point to stop chatting and learn to quiet your heart before God, it will help place your mind into a proper frame of worship.

Carry your Bible. Many churches provide Bibles in the pews, and it's not really necessary to actually bring your own Bible to church. But if you'll make a point to carry your own Bible with you and arrive a few minutes early, you can spend some time meditating on favorite Scripture passages. Having your own Bible serves as a reminder that your relationship with Christ is extremely personal. This, too, will move you into a reverent frame of mind.

Know It!
As your relationship with Christ deepens, you'll not only *feel* closer to him as your ultimate friend, you'll also grow in your reverence for his holiness.

Read It!
Nehemiah 5:15; Hosea 10:3; Malachi 4:2; Revelation 11:18

Pray It!
Tell God you want to see him not only as your best Friend but also as your holy and sacred heavenly Father.

God Wants to Be Your Security

Know It!

Other people can certainly *enhance* our life, but they shouldn't *become* our life. God wants our security, our hope, and our purpose for living to be anchored firmly in him instead of in things or people.

Read It!

Job 31:24; Psalm 16:9; Jeremiah 17:10; Hebrews 6:19

Pray It!

Ask God to bring to your mind anyone or anything in which you're placing your security. Be willing to commit that to his control.

Several years ago, police pulled the body of a suicide victim out of the North River in New York. The dead man was a graphic artist, linguist, and musician. He was 57 years old when he jumped to his death.

After he had graduated from a German university, he moved to Puerto Rico to seek his fortune. He was quite successful in business and sent letters home telling his friends and family about the printing business he had started and that was now booming. As his business grew, he eventually met a beautiful young woman. They fell in love and were married. Life seemed perfect. They lived in a beautiful country with a warm climate. They owned a majestic home, and his business was extremely successful.

Eight years after they had married, however, the woman died. The man was heartbroken. His zest for life vanished. He became careless with his business and didn't seem to care about friendships or success any longer. His business eventually folded, and he lost much of his fortune.

Two years later he moved to New York and was encouraged by a friend to teach languages. He spoke fluent German, English, French, Spanish, and Italian. Though he would have been an excellent professor, he simply didn't have the desire to keep going. Finally, with no money and without hope, he filled his pockets full of stones and leaped into the North River.

His heart had been anchored in his love for his wife. When she died, he had no hope. He lacked the security, hope, and meaning he could have found in a personal relationship with Jesus Christ. If he had been anchored in Christ, he could have gone on without his wife. Yes, he would have still grieved, but God would have brought him through the grieving process and cared for his needs.

A professional architect has many clients approach him and ask him to design a home. After he accepts the work and begins the plans, he discovers that the client has practically designed the house himself—down to the staircases and closets—and is merely coming to the architect for sanction of the plans. The professional architect complains, "The client isn't open to my ideas and expertise. He really just wants the satisfaction of seeing me draw on paper what he already has in mind."

We often approach God the same way. Instead of seeking his direction and his plans for our life, we tend to approach him with our plans already made, merely wanting him to bless them. That's not reflective of a spiritually mature disciple. The mature Christian wants to be where God is working.

Since the Bible tells us that God never leaves us and never fails us, it's easy to rationalize that he's simply following us everywhere we go . . . kind of like a puppy. But God doesn't work that way. Yes, he's committed to being with us. And no, he's not going to leave us hanging. But it's not his job to follow us around and "magically" bless our actions.

When we refuse to slow down enough to sincerely seek his will for our lives, we're in essence coming to the Master Architect with our own plans and saying, "Ready, Jesus? Okay, let's go! Follow me here, then follow me there. This is where I'm headed, and this is what I'll be doing . . . in your name, of course. So bless it all, okay?"

The wise Christian approaches life in the opposite manner. A spiritually mature disciple will say, "God, where are you working? What are you in the midst of doing? Because wherever that is . . . I want to be in the center of it. I want to be where you are."

Think about your goals, your dreams, and your plans. Have you actually sought the will of your heavenly Father, or have you made your own plans and are merely asking him to bless them? If you're a good person, doing good things, it can be difficult to discern between your own good plans and the will of your Father.

Know It!
God wants to do more than just bless your efforts. He wants to instill his plans in your life. He wants to guide your every step. Will you trust him?

Read It!
Jeremiah 29:11-14; 31:10, 33; 32:17

Pray It!
Spend some time in prayer seeking God's direction for your future. Be willing to give up your plans if they're not truly from him.

The Master Designer

Know It!

God doesn't simply want to live in your life; he wants to *be* your life. He wants your happiness and fulfillment even more than you do, and he's committed to producing joy and peace in your life. But he needs total control.

Read It!

Exodus 20:1-4;
1 Kings 8:61; 15:14;
2 Chronicles 16:9

Pray It!

Is there anything in your life you haven't given the Master Architect control of? If so, commit that area to him right now.

Let's imagine that you moved into a giant mansion and lived there alone. You're having a great time in the indoor pool, and you've invited all your friends to view the latest movies in your state-of-the-art home theater. But after a while, you become discouraged. The mansion is filled with the latest technology, but you've never learned to work it. You quickly realize you're not getting as much out of the house as you could be.

So you approach the designer and say, "Sir, you did an incredible job of designing my home. But it's so wonderfully complicated, I'm not really getting the most out of it. Would you mind moving in with me and showing me how to operate all the special features?"

The designer moves in, and you immediately begin giving instructions: "You can have the guest room. I don't mind you using the kitchen, but I really don't want you in the study. Oh, and I have a specific way I want the lawn mowed, so check with me before doing that. Otherwise, make yourself at home."

He begins to show you how to get more out of your home, and you notice a difference right away. You're learning how to operate some of the complicated technology that makes your home the envy of everyone else. But a few months later, you approach him again: "I'm really glad you're living here," you say. "But I still feel like something is missing."

He looks at you tenderly and says, "I designed this home and know it better than anyone. I know it inside and out. I really *can* show you how to get the most out of it, but to do that I have to have total control."

You hesitate but finally give in. The first thing he does is put you in the guest room, and he takes over the master bedroom. Then he goes through your personal movie collection and suggests you throw out all the ones with bad language or lots of violence. He has suggestions for the rooms you use, the books you read, and ways you can share the space with other people. Gradually, you make the changes he suggests and notice that you're happier than you've ever been before.

Extraordinary Value

A few years ago, an issue of *Coin World* carried exciting news for coin collectors: The Philadelphia mint had a printing problem on a number of 1995 pennies. The result? The words "Liberty" and "In God" are out of focus. Surprisingly, this mistake makes the coins more valuable than their street worth. Early estimates reported each penny could be worth somewhere between $175 and $225!

Think of the above illustration in light of the way God views you. Instead of getting frustrated the next time you have a bad hair day, try to focus on your value instead. Maybe there are more serious problems on which to focus your attention. Is there someone in your church, youth group, or school with serious health problems? For the teen girl or guy who has the rare disease alopecia (which involves losing one's hair), a bad hair day would be a welcome event. Even having hair would be a tremendous blessing!

Maybe your friend has a rebellious brother, an unwed pregnant sister, or an uncle who's battling cancer. It's hard to help others see that these trials and hardships can actually have positive value. It's especially hard when you fail to see the value in your own hard times or blunders. But when you focus on the positive, your friends will be more inclined to do the same.

Will you allow God to transform the mistakes and failures in your life into something valuable? You see, God has the divine power to make good things happen out of your mistakes. He can turn a disaster into a blessing . . . if you'll let him. He wants to use your hurt, your past, and your failures to help someone else who may be struggling with the same thing.

If your heart has been broken, you'll never laugh at someone else in pain. If you've ever failed at something important to you, you'll never be happy about a disaster in someone else's life. If you've ever been wrong about something, you realize you don't have the right to gloat about an error you see in someone else's thinking. If you've ever realized how serious your personal sin is, you'll find it impossible to be arrogant and judgmental about another's sin. And if you've received God's forgiveness, you'll be gracious to those around you.

Know It!

Surrendering every situation to the Lord is the only way to turn lead into gold, pain into joy, and defeat into victory. Let him transform your weaknesses into his strengths.

Read It!

2 Corinthians 10:17-18; 11:24-30; 12:9; Ephesians 1:17-19

Pray It!

Ask God to help you see the positive value in your mistakes.

Ownership

Know It!
If your life truly belongs totally to God, you'll give up your status, your position, and your rights.

Read It!
Luke 15:11-32;
Galatians 5:1, 7-9;
James 4:7-8

Pray It!
Thank God for loving you so much that he wants to saturate your life with himself.

Imagine you own a brand-new shiny apple-red Volkswagen Bug. You take it to the local auto mechanic to have some minor repairs done. And while your car is in his possession, he uses it to pick up his kids from school and haul groceries home. You'd probably be a little angry when you came for your car and found lettuce leaves and shoe prints on the backseat.

Let's suppose your dry cleaner wears your new suit to a fancy dinner he's attending. You happen to see him at the restaurant. He stutters and makes a few excuses, but there really is no excuse! He's wearing the suit that you own. And he's doing it without your permission!

Try to look at your life in the same manner. The gifts, talents, skills, and abilities you have were given to you by God. He actually owns them; he's merely letting you use them for the time being. When you give your life totally to Jesus Christ, you automatically yield your rights to him. So it's no longer, "My way! My will! My rights!" Your heart's cry becomes, "Your way, Lord. I want your will. My rights are no longer my own. They belong to you. I don't own my life anymore. I am totally yours."

So doesn't it make sense that when you're about to decide how to use this opportunity or that talent, that you should seek direction from the Owner? Just as you would want your mechanic to ask permission to drive your car, God wants you to seek his guidance for every area of your life.

Think of the Prodigal Son. The story begins as he approaches his father demanding his rights: "Give me!" The father sadly gives him what he wants, and the son quickly squanders all he has. In his poverty, the son realizes that when his father owned his rights, he was actually happier than when he had demanded ownership himself. The end of the story shows the son approaching his father with a much different request: "Make me." Note the attitude change? The son went from a vain "Give me!" to a humble request–"Make me." He asked that his father make him only a servant. He realized he had given up his rights as a son.

You may be familiar with the Old Testament story of Daniel. The part most people remember was that he was thrown into a den of hungry lions, yet God spared his life. But let's take a closer peek at Daniel. There are other memorable things in his life that are often overlooked.

King Nebuchadnezzar, king of Babylon, besieged Daniel's hometown of Jerusalem and took captives. But he didn't take just any captives; he wanted the best young men he could find. He was specifically looking for quality men he could train in his own political methods who would eventually reflect his leadership and character.

When Daniel and several other young men were brought into Nebuchadnezzar's palace, they were given a specific diet of food. The king had ordered the very best for them and wanted to make sure they continued to develop into strong, healthy men. Daniel was probably in his mid-teen years at this time.

It didn't take this godly young man long to realize that King Nebuchadnezzar was involved in all kinds of things that were displeasing to God. So Daniel refused to eat the special foods and drink the wine that was served to him. He was determined to maintain a godly lifestyle in the midst of a heathen court.

Later, Nebuchadnezzar began to have disturbing dreams. God gave Daniel special wisdom to discern and interpret the dreams, so he was able to tell the king what they meant in great detail. This helped the king place a huge amount of trust in Daniel.

Daniel's wisdom was so respected that he served as an adviser to three kings—and that made some of the other advisers jealous. During the reign of King Darius, these advisers talked the king into making a special decree that ruled no one was allowed to pray unless they wanted to pray to him. And if someone was caught praying, he would be immediately thrown to the lions.

Even in the midst of this incredible pressure, Daniel continued his daily prayer time with God. You probably know the rest of the story: He was tossed into the lions' pit, but God locked the jaws of the animals, and they didn't harm him. The next morning, Darius pulled Daniel out of the pit and listened with respect as he told about his faithful God.

Know It!

God understands the world you live in; he created it! Though he doesn't approve of the sin around you, he understands the pressures and temptations you face. He wants to empower you with his Holy Spirit to help you live the godly life he calls you to live.

Read It!

Daniel 1–2, 6–7

Pray It!

Ask God to give you a pure heart and to help you stand out in the midst of a heathen world.

Dan the Man

Know It!

It helps to surround ourselves with people who share our faith and our morals. If you're giving in to temptation, maybe you need to consider changing friends.

Read It!

Romans 12:1-2; Philippians 2:14-16; James 1:13-16; 3:17-18

Pray It!

Ask God to help you seek his power when you face temptation. Learn to lean on his mighty power so you can keep from yielding to sin.

Daniel truly was an incredible young man! Let's focus even more closely on a few special things he had going for him:

1. *Daniel had a pure heart.* It wasn't easy. Daniel had everything imaginable at his disposal—wealth, rich food, power. But he said no to the things that would have broken God's heart, and he said yes to the things of the Lord. It's never easy to say no to things that look enticing and are tempting. But God will never allow us to be tempted beyond what we can bear. We *can* lean on him to say no to evil.

2. *Daniel maintained a godly lifestyle in the midst of a heathen court.* You, too, are living in a world that doesn't follow God's ways. God wants to help you maintain a holy lifestyle even though you're surrounded by people who may not have high morals and even though you're bombarded with temptation. In the dark world in which you live, God wants to help you shine as a star, reflecting his purity and his holiness.

3. *Daniel set himself apart by living a life of integrity.* King Nebuchadnezzar took special notice of Daniel and admired his character and trustworthiness. In fact, Nebuchadnezzar put Daniel in a distinguished position of leadership.

4. *Daniel chose godly friends.* Even though he was surrounded by people who didn't believe in God, he chose to become very close with three other young men who shared his faith, his values, and his morality. You know those three men as Shadrach, Meshach, and Abednego. They were Daniel's best friends and they drew strength from one another.

5. *Daniel was consistent in prayer and in his actions.* When threatened with death, he remained consistent. When threatened by jealousy of those around him, he remained consistent. God desires the same of you!

Focus on the Truth

Stores waste no time in putting out Christmas decorations. Many don't even wait until Thanksgiving has passed to start the process of guiding their customers toward thinking about Christmas. As you move into the Christmas spirit this month, don't simply enjoy what looks good. Keep listening and keep looking beyond what you see and hear until you get to the very truth of Christmas.

Imagine that you've just arrived on planet earth and don't know anything about the approaching Christmas season. What if you based your view of Christmas on the following fractured carols children have mistakenly sung?

- "Deck the halls with Buddy Holly . . ."
- "We three kings of porridge and tar . . ."
- "Later on we'll perspire, as we dream by the fire . . ."
- "He's makin' a list, chicken and rice . . ."
- "Noel, Noel, Barney's the king of Israel . . ."
- "With the jelly toast proclaim . . ."
- "Frosty the snowman is a ferret elf, I say . . ."
- "Sleep in heavenly peas . . ."
- "Oh, what fun it is to ride with one horse, soap, and hay . . ."
- "Good tidings we bring to you and your kid . . ."
- "O come, froggy faithful . . ."

If all we knew about Christmas was what we saw in stores and on TV, or what we heard, we'd have a skewed and surface view of the season. God wants to move you beyond the surface into the very heart of Christmas this year.

Make a list of what you can do–beginning today–that will keep your focus on Jesus Christ rather than on tinsel, store sales, sprinkled sugar cookies, and midnight shopping sprees. Is there someone in your class or your youth group who's feeling desperate and alone? Do you have a friend who's upset because his parents are newly divorced and he can only spend Christmas with one of them? Make time to look around you and focus on the needs of others.

Know It!

God wants you to have a fantastic Christmas, but he also wants to teach you to give in ways you've never thought of before. Let him teach you how to give from your heart.

Read It!

Matthew 1

Pray It!

Ask God to begin *now*—on the very first day of December—preparing your heart in a brand-new way for this most special of seasons.

Are You Reading Your Mail?

Know It!
This month, as you're approaching Christ's birthday, pledge to take your Bible reading more seriously. Expect him to teach you things about the coming Christmas season you've never thought about before.

Read It!
Psalm 107:4-16;
Isaiah 1:18;
Jeremiah 42:5-6;
Habakkuk 2:3

Pray It!
Ask God for a genuine hunger for his Word.

Six-year-old Ashley couldn't wait to get to the mall. Her mom had promised since Thanksgiving that they'd hit the mall around the first of December so Ashley could sit in Santa's lap. Today was the big day! The curly-haired little girl waited patiently for 45 minutes as the long line finally dwindled to the last few children.

Grinning from ear to ear, she jumped into Santa's lap and hugged him tightly. Santa returned her smile, and with his big arm of velvet around her shoulders, he looked into her brown eyes and asked, "What do you want for Christmas?"

Ashley's smile faded. She stared at Santa and said, "Didn't you get my e-mail?"

Ashley felt as though her world had crumbled in front of her. She climbed off Santa's lap and ran back into the arms of her mother. "Never mind. He didn't even read my letter," she said through her tears.

What's the point of having mail if you don't make the time to read it? When we don't make reading God's "mail" a high priority in our lives, it breaks his heart. The Holy Bible is his love letter to you. It's not simply pages filled with meaningless words; rather, it's a book of hope, instruction, how-tos, cautions, road maps, promises, blessings, surprises, and fulfillment.

You've been reading this devotional book for almost one solid year. But if it hasn't caused you to delve more deeply into God's Word, it's meaningless. A devotional book should never take the place of the Bible; it merely serves to pique your interest and draw you inside the Bible. A good devotional will complement–not replace–the Word of God in your life.

Everyone in Toby's second-grade Sunday school class was busy. Each student was drawing a picture of the Nativity. Mrs. Johnson stood over Toby's shoulder admiring his work. He had done quite well with Mary, Joseph, and the baby Jesus. But there was a fat man standing in the corner of the stable that just didn't seem to fit. When she asked Toby about it, he responded, "Oh, that's Round John Virgin."

Another reason it's important to keep digesting the Word of God is because it straightens out the things in our lives we've become confused about. It helps us separate truth from myths and misunderstandings.

The Weight of Prayer

A tired woman entered a small-town grocery store shortly after World War I. It was the week before Christmas. She approached the owner of the store and asked for enough food to make a Christmas dinner for her children. The grocer asked her how much money she had to spend.

Fighting back her tears, she explained that her husband had been killed in the war. "I have nothing to offer," she said, "but a little prayer."

The store owner sarcastically responded, "Well, write it on some paper, and I'll weigh it. We'll find out how much it's worth."

He was shocked when the woman pulled a slip of paper from her purse and handed it to him. "I've already written my prayer," she said.

The man rolled his eyes and took the little slip of paper. Other shoppers were watching and had heard his sarcastic remarks. He had to do something! So he placed the piece of paper on the weight side of the old-fashioned scales. Then he began to pile food on the other side, but the scale wouldn't go down. He piled more and more food on top, but it still wouldn't budge.

Angry and impatient, he didn't even look at the woman as he said, "The scale won't hold any more. Put the food in a bag yourself. I have work to do."

Now fighting back tears of gratitude, the woman filled the bag, thanked the owner, and left.

When the grocer went to examine the scales, he discovered they were broken. And apparently they had broken just in time for God to answer a faithful woman of prayer.

As the years passed, however, the man often thought about his encounter with the woman. From time to time, he still unfolds the piece of paper the prayer was written on and reads, "Please, Lord, give us this day our daily bread."

As you approach the Christmas season, give God the concerns of your heart and know that he will hear. Perhaps you're worried about where you'll get the money to buy the gift you've had your eye on for your parents. Or maybe you're wondering how your family will afford groceries this season. Or maybe your concerns aren't about you at all. Perhaps God has brought someone else to your mind who's in great need this month.

Know It!

Ask your pastor or youth leader if there's a needy family in your church who's struggling to make ends meet right now. Is there something you can do? First, make it a matter of prayer. Then follow God's lead as he directs. And remember . . . nothing can outweigh a prayer!

Read It!

1 Chronicles 5:20; John 14:12-14; Ephesians 6:18; 1 Peter 3:7

Pray It!

Seek God's direction on whom you should pray for and how you should pray this Christmas season.

DECEMBER 4

What a Gift!

Know It!
As silly as it would be for us to take that line of thought, we sometimes fall into that mode of thinking without even realizing it. Subconsciously, we know that investing ourselves in the lives of others is going to take . . . time. And more time. And more time. And do we really want to do that? Guess what? That's not the right question. God calls all of us to give ourselves to those around us. And he set the extreme example by giving himself to us in the form of his only Son.

Read It!
John 10:17-18; 13:4-5; 1 Corinthians 13

Pray It!
Ask God to bring someone to your mind today who needs your love and attention.

Have you ever read the children's book *If You Give a Mouse a Cookie* by Laura Joffe Numeroff? The author tells us if we give the rodent a cookie, he'll want some milk to go with it. And then he'll have to look in a mirror to make sure he doesn't have a milk mustache. Then he'll notice his hair needs a trim, so he'll probably ask for a pair of scissors. The story goes on and on and on in creative detail about the demands a mouse could make.

After you've read the book for the first time, you'll probably close the cover with a grin on your face and think, *Okay. Enough said. The moral of the story is to never ever give a mouse a cookie!*

And you'd be exactly right. But what if we took the thought a lot farther? God could have adapted the same moral. He could have said, "Never give any of my children a cookie." Okay, God didn't really give us a sugar snack, but he did give us the greatest gift in all the world—his only Son.

If our heavenly Father could give his own flesh and blood, how much more should we be willing to give our lives to those around us! It's not easy, though, is it? After all, when we give a mouse a cookie, he'll ask for a glass of milk . . . and a million other things.

When we invest our time and ourselves in people, we can assume they're going to ask for more. If you invite your neighbor to church, you may have to let him ride with you. Then you'll have to sit with him because he won't know anyone.

Then after Sunday school, you'll have to walk him into the sanctuary. And after church is over, you'll probably have to take him to dinner. And if he enjoys your church, you'll have to bring him again. And again. And again.

And if he gives his life to the Lord, you might have to disciple him. Or go to Bible study with him. So maybe you should just stay away completely.

We can rejoice that God doesn't see his children as mice who don't deserve a cookie! He asks us to give our time, our energy, and ourselves to those around us, because that's exactly what he did. He could have said, "I'd better not leave heaven and invade their world with love. If I do, they'll probably ask me to help them. Then I'll have to do a few miracles. Heal some people. Pass out some 20/20 to a few blind men. Feed the hungry. Help the poor. And those who don't like me will probably hurt me. They may even kill me. Then I'll have to raise myself from the dead and send my Spirit to live within them. And I'll have to prepare a home for them to live in eternally. It'll never end!"

Whew! Aren't you glad our heavenly Father didn't take that kind of attitude? Instead, he chose to invade our lives with purpose, meaning, drive, and power. In return, he calls us to give away some cookies. To spread a little love. To be his hands and feet to a lost and dying world.

And if we do? We tend to forget about our problems. We don't feel as lonely or misunderstood. Having a boyfriend or girlfriend just doesn't seem as important any more. We begin to realize that life really isn't about us. How can we be giving cookies away if we're so concerned about our own refreshments? Life isn't about having our needs met. Rather, our focus should shift to meeting the needs of others. And when it does, people around us become a significant priority.

God is calling you to go the extra mile. Why?

- Because he did.
- Because in order to find yourself, you have to give away your life.
- Because giving, loving, and going the extra mile causes you to forget about yourself for a while.
- Because you grow by sacrificing.
- Because love always wins.

Know It!

Wouldn't it be exciting to celebrate this Christmas by concentrating more on giving than getting?

Read It!

John 13:14-17; 15:12-14, 17; 1 Corinthians 14:1

Pray It!

Ask God to show you how to make this Christmas season significantly different from those you've celebrated in the past by focusing on what you can give to others.

Jesus Is Always Better than Santa

Know It!
Have fun with gifts and decorations and Santa at the mall this Christmas, but never forget the real meaning behind December 25. And go the extra mile this year to keep Christ in Christmas!

Read It!
John 3:16; 15:26; 17:21-23; Acts 1:9-11

Pray It!
Pray for a godly focus on the true gift of Christmas this year.

As we approach the Christmas season, you're no doubt bombarded with advertisements featuring one of history's most loved imaginary characters—Santa Claus. And as Santas appear in shopping malls, on street corners, and in decorations, you may find yourself falling into the easy trap of forgetting the real meaning of Christmas. So spend a few minutes recapping some important details, okay?

Jesus Christ is definitely the reason for the season. And to help you keep that fact in balance, remind yourself of the following:

Jesus is always better than Santa because . . .

- Santa lives at the North Pole. But Jesus is everywhere.
- Santa rides in a sleigh. But Jesus rides on the wind and walks on the water.
- Santa comes only once a year. But Jesus is an ever-present help.
- Santa fills your stockings with goodies. But Jesus supplies all your needs.
- Santa gives you a few fun things that may last a year. But Jesus gives you life that will last forever.
- Santa comes down your chimney uninvited. But Jesus stands at your door and knocks.
- You have to wait in line to see Santa. But Jesus is as close as the mention of his name.
- Santa lets you sit on his lap in a crowded shopping mall. But Jesus lets you rest in his arms in a beautifully created eternal home.
- Santa doesn't know your name unless you tell him. But Jesus knew your name before you were even born. (Not only does he know your name, he also knows your address, your nickname, and even how many hairs are on your head!)
- Santa has a belly like a bowl full of jelly. But Jesus has a heart full of love.
- Santa says, "You better not cry." But Jesus says, "Cast all your anxiety on me, for I care for you."
- Santa makes you chuckle. But Jesus gives you joy that becomes your very strength.
- Santa puts gifts under a tree. But Jesus became our gift and died on a tree—the cross.

The Gift That Keeps On Giving

Roy Collette and his brother-in-law Larry Kunkel exchanged the same pair of pants as a Christmas present for 23 years—and each year the package became harder to open. In 1988 the pants came wrapped in a car mashed into a three-foot cube. The trousers were in the glove compartment of a 1974 Gremlin.

It all began when Larry gave Roy a pair of moleskin pants. Roy wore them three times, then wrapped them up and gave them back to Larry for Christmas the next year.

The annual friendly exchange continued routinely until one year when Roy twisted the pants, stuffed them into a three-foot-long, one-inch-wide tube, and gave them back to Larry. The following Christmas, Larry compressed the pants into a seven-inch square, wrapped them with wire, and gave the "bale" to Roy. Entering into the spirit, the next year Roy put the pants into a two-foot-square crate filled with stones, nailed it shut, banded it with steel, and gave the trousers back to Larry.

Larry had the pants mounted inside an insulated window that had a 20-year guarantee and shipped them to Roy. Roy broke the glass, recovered the trousers, stuffed them into a five-inch coffee can, and soldered it shut. The can was put in a five-gallon container filled with concrete and reinforcing rods and given to Larry the following Christmas. Next, Larry installed the pants in a 225-pound homemade steel ashtray made from eight-inch steel casings and etched Roy's name on the side. Roy had some trouble retrieving the treasured trousers, but he succeeded (without burning them!) by using a cutting torch.

Roy found a 600-pound safe and hauled it to a shipping department. They decorated it with red and green stripes, put the pants inside, and welded the safe shut. The safe was then shipped to Larry.

That December the pants were trucked in the drab green, three-foot cube that was once a car with 95,000 miles on it. A note attached to the 2,000-pound scrunched car advised Roy that the pants were inside the glove compartment.

The pants finally met their demise one year when Roy tried to have the pants shipped in the midst of 10,000 pounds of jagged glass. Unfortunately a chunk of molten glass shattered, reducing the pants to a pile of ashes. The brothers-in-law buried the pants with a special marker to attest to their years of creative gift exchanges.

Know It!

Material gifts eventually break or wear out. As you approach this Christmas, focus on the one gift that will never get old, never wear out, and isn't complicated to open. That's the gift of eternal life that Jesus Christ wants to give you for Christmas.

Read It!

Psalms 27:1; 35:3; 37:39; 71:15

Pray It!

In faith, accept God's precious Christmas gift of eternal life this year. Thank him for the fact that it will last forever!

Want Some Wisdom?

Know It!
It's great to want wisdom, but it's important that you search for it in the right place. "Wisdom" from the world is only temporary. God's wisdom is eternal.

Read It!
Proverbs 1–4

Pray It!
Ask God to guide you in your search for wisdom.

Everyone's looking for a little wisdom. Maybe you're wishing you had the wisdom to figure out a problem you're struggling with, or more wisdom to apply to your schoolwork. Oftentimes when we search for wisdom, we look in the wrong places. Our culture, celebrities, or our friends aren't the right source. Check out the following actual quotes by supermodels sharing "wisdom" on a variety of topics.

- *On poverty:* "Everyone should have enough money to get plastic surgery."–Beverly Johnson
- *On priorities:* "I would rather exercise than read a newspaper."–Kim Alexis
- *On inner strength:* "I love the confidence that makeup gives me."–Tyra Banks
- *On the basics:* "It's very important to have the right clothing to exercise in. If you throw on an old T-shirt or sweats, it's not inspiring for your workout."–Cheryl Tiegs
- *On introductions:* "I think most people are curious about what it would be like to be able to meet yourself. It's eerie."–Christy Turlington
- *On the conservation of matter:* "I've looked in the mirror every day for 20 years. It's the same face."–Claudia Schiffer
- *On thinking:* "When I model, I pretty much blank. You can't think too much or it doesn't work."–Paulina Porizkova
- *On body parts:* "I don't know what to do with my arms. It just makes me feel weird and I feel like people are looking at me and that makes me nervous."–Tyra Banks
- *On economics:* "I don't wake up for less than $10,000 a day."–Linda Evangelista

When you need wisdom, where do you go? Do you seek advice from people who will tell you what you want to hear? Do you listen to the latest rock star's philosophy or what your friends are saying? It's obvious the above "logic" won't last long. If you're searching for true wisdom, God has already provided it for you. It's found in his holy Word. The book of Proverbs is full of wisdom, and the exciting thing about this particular book is that it has 31 chapters. That's enough to read one every day for a month!

Who Qualifies?

Throughout history, God has chosen ordinary people to do his work. He has consistently used men and women with flaws, failures, and lack of talent. If we took a closer look at some of our Bible heroes—as if they had applied to pastor our church and we were considering their resumes—we might have slim pickings.

- *Noah:* Former pastorate of 120 years with not even one convert. He's prone to unrealistic building projects.
- *Solomon:* Excellent preacher, but the church parsonage would never hold all his wives.
- *John:* Claims he's a Baptist, but he doesn't dress like one. He's slept in the outdoors for months on end, has a weird diet, and provokes denominational leaders.
- *Timothy:* Too young.
- *Methuselah:* Too old.
- *Jeremiah:* Emotionally unstable. Alarmist. Negative. Always lamenting things. It's been reported that he took a long trip to bury stones at the entrance to a palace.
- *Joseph:* A big thinker and a braggart. He believes in interpreting dreams and has a prison record.
- *David:* Looked promising until it was discovered that he had an affair with his neighbor's wife.
- *Elijah:* Prone to depression. Collapses under pressure.
- *Elisha:* Reported to have lived with a widow at his former church.
- *Isaiah:* On the fringe. Claims to have seen angels in church.
- *Peter:* Too blue-collar. Has a bad temper and has been known to curse. Had a big run-in with Paul in Antioch. Aggressive, but a loose cannon.
- *Paul:* Powerful CEO type of leader and fascinating preacher. However, short on tact, harsh, and has been known to preach all night.

If we looked at the above in light of their faults, we'd probably never select any of them for God's work. But isn't it comforting to know that God doesn't look at our faults? He looks at our potential! He doesn't keep count of how many times we've blown it. He sees everything that we can become in his power! God wants to use *you.* He has chosen you to be on his team. And if you'll let him have complete control of your life, he'll do extraordinary things with you!

Know It!

Since God overlooks our weaknesses and sees our potential, shouldn't we do the same for others? Instead of focusing your attention on what others have done wrong, ask God to help you see all that they can become.

Read It!

Ephesians 1:19; 3:20; Hebrews 10:39; James 1:19-22

Pray It!

Spend some time thanking God for dreaming big dreams for you—in spite of your humanness.

DECEMBER 10

Don't Get Disconnected

Know It!

For you to experience spiritual maturity, it's important that you stay deeply rooted and connected in Christ. It's also important that you allow faith—not feelings—to pull your relationship full steam ahead.

Read It!

John 14:6;
Romans 1:17; 4:5-20; 9:30

Pray It!

Ask God to help you keep your faith and your feelings in the proper perspective.

Mr. Wrigley, the chewing gum magnate, was riding a train to Chicago, where his headquarters were located. A passenger sitting beside him said, "Mr. Wrigley, your gum in known all over the world. Why do you bother to continue advertising?"

Mr. Wrigley looked the passenger in the eyes and asked, "How fast is this train going?"

"I don't know. Maybe 60 miles an hour."

"Well, since it's already on a good run, why don't they just go ahead and disconnect the engine?"

The answer was obvious: Advertising was the "engine" that pulled Wrigley's products through the market.

Lots of people will tell you there are several ways to get to heaven. Some religions will brag that good deeds will earn you salvation. Others say you must be reincarnated and try again. But Jesus said that he alone is the Way, the Truth, and the Life. He went on to say that *no one* could get to heaven except through him. Jesus Christ is our connection to God Almighty. So it's important that we get connected and stay connected.

In our day-to-day living, faith is the engine that pulls us through life. Martin Luther caught the significance when he discovered in Romans 1:17 that "the just shall live by faith" (NKJV). This is the principle on which he formulated the Protestant Reformation.

By *faith* we are *justified.* You can put that in simple terms and think of it as "just as if I'd never sinned." That means we have been justified before God. Forgiven. Cleansed. Made whole. We are seen as pure before him.

If *faith* is the engine, what are the cars on the track that faith is pulling? Faith is pulling the cars of fact, feeling, and joy. And they're always in that order! The coal car doesn't pull the train; it comes right after the engine (at least it did before electric trains!) and provides fuel so the engine can run. Likewise, the caboose doesn't pull the train; it's always at the tail end. While freight cars or passenger cars may be interchanged, the engine, coal car, and caboose are never interchanged because they affect the destination of the train.

What's Pulling Your Train?

If we compare our relationship with Christ to a train, we have to allow faith to pull us down the track into a deeper relationship with God. Faith pulls the cars of fact, feeling, joy, discouragement, loneliness–whatever makes up your train of life. But it's important to remember that faith and fact are like the engine and the coal car; they are never disconnected or interchanged.

Jesus announced that he was standing at the door of our hearts and knocking. He went on to say that if anyone would answer the door and let him come in and reside in his home, he would come in and share a meal as a friend. The *fact* is: When you have repented of your sins, Christ has forgiven you of your sins and wants a relationship with you. And by *faith,* you believe in him. The just shall live by faith.

There is no other engine that pulls the train, and no other coal car that feeds the engine except the *fact* that you have been forgiven. The other cars in your train may come and go. There will be days when you experience feelings of joy. You may be overwhelmed by his presence. There may be other days when you have feelings of loneliness or discouragement, or you may be sick and not feel a thing.

You may think your train has been derailed because you can't feel God. During those times, Satan will work like crazy to make you think you're not a Christian. He'll tell you that you never were saved in the first place. Or he may bring up a sin from your past and try to make you think that God couldn't possibly forgive you for that. Don't believe Satan . . . even for a second!

Instead, keep doing what you've always done: Continue reading your Bible. Keep praying to your heavenly Father. And no matter what the weather is on the outside, keep the Son shining in your heart by steadily growing in his grace.

Know It!

Don't allow Satan or anyone else to get your cars mixed up. Remember, joy doesn't pull the train. Feelings don't empower the train. Faith pulls the train. Don't disconnect your faith in Jesus. He alone is the One who pulls you to your final (and eternal) destination.

Read It!

1 Corinthians 16:13; 2 Corinthians 1:24; Galatians 2:16; Revelation 3:20

Pray It!

Ask God to help you remain firmly connected to him with a deep, growing faith.

Hearing God's Voice

Know It!
You can know God's voice just as well as Elijah did. He speaks to us in a variety of ways. Sometimes he speaks in your life through trusted adults who are close to him. Other times he'll speak to you through the Bible. And sometimes he'll talk to you through your mind and heart by using his Holy Spirit.

Read It!
1 Kings 17–19

Pray It!
Ask God to help you tune in to his voice and to respond in obedience when you hear him.

When you know the voice of God, big things happen. Elijah knew God's voice, and he defeated 450 prophets of Baal. Let's put his story in modern language and take a closer peek.

Elijah was the guy who challenged King Ahab and his prophets of Baal over a dead bull. If you've ever been discouraged because your youth group isn't as big as you wish it was, Elijah could relate. You see, whenever his youth group had a pizza fling, he was the only teen who showed up.

When they organized fund-raising projects (like a chariot wash or selling tickets to the church chili supper), he was the only one who participated. Not only that, but when his church had their once-a-month potluck dinner . . . you guessed it, he was the only one who brought fried chicken. In fact, he was the only one in attendance!

That's because Elijah was from a really small church. It was so small, he was the only member. And it seemed to him as though he was the only person in the country who served the Lord. (There were actually a few more, but he couldn't find them. Maybe you can relate, feeling like you're the only Christian at your school.)

But Elijah's strength was in knowing the voice of God. When God spoke, Elijah acted! Well, God spoke. He told Elijah to tell King Ahab that he was doing a lousy job of running the country, and if he didn't shape up, God would punish the people by withholding the rain. (Bad news because the crops would wither and die and everyone's stomach would growl and no one would be able to buy Honeycomb or Trix or even Pop-Tarts. So this was serious stuff!)

Now think about it: How would *you* respond if God told you to go to the White House and tell the president a thing or two? You might tend to think, *Hmmm. Was that God speaking to me? Or was it Satan trying to mess me up and get me to do something really stupid? Or are those just my own thoughts because I want to do something important?*

Elijah didn't have to wonder if it was God speaking to him, because he knew the voice of God extremely well. And he responded immediately!

When God spoke, Elijah didn't hesitate to obey. So Elijah confronted King Ahab and told him that God wasn't too pleased with the way things were going, and if he didn't take a turn for the better (and get the people to start worshiping God instead of the idol of Baal), he'd be mighty sorry because there wouldn't be any rain and a famine would sweep the country.

But King Ahab didn't listen. Next move? God told Elijah to hit the wilderness, a place called Kerith Brook. Now while you may tend to think being banished by a brook could get boring, the Bible tells us that God provided for every one of Elijah's needs. The Lord sent ravens to bring him food every day. (Not bad room service, huh?)

A few years passed, and God spoke again. This time he told Elijah to go talk to King Ahab again. And he didn't think, *Wait a minute. That can't be God's voice, because he's the One who told me to come here in the first place. Hmmm. Must be Satan. Or maybe it's just my own thoughts. It would be kind of nice to be with people again.* Elijah didn't have to guess; he knew God's voice. And when God spoke, he responded.

You can probably imagine how King Ahab reacted when he saw Elijah heading for the palace. He shook his bony royal finger at God's man and screamed, "You! You're the one who's responsible for this mess!"

And it really was a mess. Just as Elijah had predicted, God had withheld the rains for three years, people were dying, the crops had withered . . . the country was a disaster.

But Elijah stood his ground. "*I'm* not the reason for this famine; *you* are! I told you this would happen. God has allowed our country to suffer because of the way you have chosen to rule."

"But . . . but . . . but, I . . ." (Be glad Ahab never spoke for one of your school assemblies. He stammered so much it would've taken forever to get his point across!)

"Listen, Ahab! Almost the entire country is worshiping Baal, but people think they can worship the Lord too. That's not right. God wants to turn the hearts of his people completely back to him."

Know It!
God wants his children to be totally committed to him. We're told in the book of Revelation to be either hot or cold, but lukewarm won't get us anywhere. Many of the Israelites were trying to be lukewarm.

Read It!
2 Peter 1:3;
1 John 5:3-5;
Jude 1:24-25;
Revelation 3:16

Pray It!
Ask God to help you stay "hot"—totally committed to him.

Making the Commitment

Know It!
If you haven't made an all-out decision to follow Christ with all your heart, now's the time to do it! Instead of trying to put God to some kind of test, accept his forgiveness and eternal life through faith in Jesus Christ and what he has done for you.

Read It!
1 Kings 18; Hosea 6:3; Joel 2:11-12, 32

Pray It!
Ask God to give you a brand-new life through his Son, Jesus Christ.

Elijah confronted King Ahab with confidence. When you truly know the voice of God, you can respond in boldness and confidence to whatever he asks. "Let's have a little contest," Elijah said. "You get all the people of Israel plus the 450 prophets of Baal, and we'll have a showdown between Baal and the Lord."

Settled. First Church of Baal got really excited. They had a humongous youth group—more than 5,000 teens. They decided this would be a great way to earn money for their surf 'n' swim trip to Jamaica, so they had special T-shirts printed that read "THE CONTEST" and sold them for 15 dollars each. They also took charge of the concession stand.

The big day arrived and the arena was literally packed out. Elijah got up and spoke to all the people. "If there's one thing God can't stand, it's a lukewarm commitment. Be hot or cold, but don't stand in the middle. Serve God or serve Baal, but you can't remain neutral. If the Lord is really God, follow him! But if Baal is god, follow him."

Serena Williams had a break in her tennis tour, and she was hired to commentate. She began by going through the rules:

"Since there are more people on the Baal team, we're going to let them go first. They'll drag their dead bull out here and pray to their god to burn it up. And guys . . . you're aware that you can't use kerosene or charcoal bits, right? Okay, good.

"Then, after they've had a chance to prove the existence of their god, we'll give Elijah a shot with his dead bull. Let the games begin!"

The team of Baal pulled their carcass onstage. They danced around their bull and prayed loudly to their god. People watched closely. Reporters were crouched on the edge of their seats in the press box. Cameras zoomed in extra-close. But nothing happened. The crowd grew restless.

Finally Elijah himself grew impatient and began to sarcastically mock the prophets of Baal. The prophets stepped up the intensity and began cutting themselves to show their false god how serious they were. They danced on stage all day long, but nothing happened.

Elijah approached the stage and told the contest helpers to clear the platform. As they dragged Elijah's dead bull to center stage, he gave them some interesting instructions.

"Dig a trench all the way around the stage," he said. So they did. "Pour water over the bull and the wood," he instructed. So they did. "And again," he continued. "And one more time." This time the water even overflowed the trench. The audience began to wonder why Elijah was drenching the stage before he began to pray for fire. Then Elijah stepped away from the microphone so no one could hear him. I like to imagine he prayed something like this:

"God, I *know* you're God. I have absolutely no doubt at all that you created this entire universe and you have more power than anything or anyone anywhere.

"I'm not asking you to burn this bull to prove your power to me, because–like I said–I'm already convinced of your power. Those doubts were settled a long time ago when I gave my life to you.

"I'm asking you to burn this bull, though, so these thousands of doubting, questioning, lost people can be convinced that you are the only true God."

Then I imagine a hush fell across the stadium. And stepping in front of the microphone, Elijah probably boomed in his deepest and loudest voice, "Father God of heaven and earth, *burn this bull*!"

Instantly that dead animal was ablaze. It was incredible! People all over the arena began to realize they'd been duped into believing in a false god. They saw this power, and they wanted what they saw. They began committing themselves to the one true God–Jehovah.

Elijah wasted no time. Microphone still in hand, he grabbed some of the new believers and convinced them to help him slaughter the prophets of Baal. (Before Jesus came to die for our sins, God abolished evil through death. So Elijah knew he had to wipe out the Baal gang, or they'd travel to the next town and start the same old thing all over again.)

After all the prophets of Baal were killed, God spoke to Elijah and told him to head back to the mountains. And Elijah didn't question whether it was God's voice, Satan's voice, or his own thinking. He responded immediately because he knew the voice of the Lord. Elijah went to the mountains and waited for God to speak to him. (To find out more about Elijah's experience on the mountain, flip over to March 12.)

Know It!
Though God doesn't want us to test him, he *is* faithful in showing his power through his children when they need him.

Read It!
1 Kings 18;
Psalms 63:2; 66:3; 77:14

Pray It!
Is God's power evident in your life? Ask him to reveal anything that may be blocking his power through you.

Hearing God's Voice

Know It!

Look what happened to Lazarus when he recognized God's voice! He was raised to life through Jesus Christ. The most important voice you'll ever respond to is the voice of God on your life. Learn to listen carefully!

Read It!

Deuteronomy 30:20; John 5:28; 10:3; Revelation 3:20

Pray It!

Spend some time in prayer just listening to God instead of talking to him.

Do you, like Elijah, know the sound of God's voice? God desires not only that you know it, but also that you obey it when you hear him speak. It takes discipline to learn what God's voice sounds like. It means making time daily to shut everything else out—even the stereo and the TV—to focus on his still, small voice that comes from within.

Everyone in the Bible who accomplished great things for God did so because he or she knew the sound of his voice. King Jehoshaphat knew God's voice and was able to stand up to King Ahab. (See the devotions on December 19-20). It took temporarily blinding Paul for the Lord to get through, but when he did, Paul didn't doubt the sound of his Father's voice, and God used him in astonishing ways. The disciples knew the sound of the Master. Even Jesus said that sheep know the sound of their shepherd's voice. It pays to tune in to the right voice! And the voice of God is a voice that wants to guide you, support you, and protect you.

When *you* have truly learned to tune in to the sound of his voice, big things happen! The better you know God's voice, the deeper your relationship with him will grow. Why? Because the more you know his voice, the more you'll respond to his voice. The better you know God, the more confident a Christian you'll be.

A disciple who knows God's voice equals a disciple who responds when God speaks. That in turn equals God working through your life to impact those around you!

A Christian who knows God's voice equals a Christian who is confident. A confident Christian equals one who will dare to take a stand in her school, at work, and in her non-Christian home.

Got the Joy of the Season?

Christmas is only eight days away. Have you caught the spirit? Are you spreading the joy? Here are a few Christmas laughs to get you in the mood.

- What are Santa's helpers called? *Subordinate Clauses.*
- Which one of Santa's reindeers needs to learn his manners? *"Rude" olph.*
- Ever thought about what Santa says when he gets sick? *"OH, OH, NO!"*
- Can Santa take pictures? *Yes, with his North Pole-aroid.*
- What can we call a cat at the beach during Christmas? *Sandy Claws.*
- Know which reindeer has the cleanest antlers? *Comet.*
- Who sings "Love Me Tender" and makes Christmas toys? *Santa's little Elvis.*
- What do we call Santa Clause after he's fallen into a fireplace? *Krisp Kringle.*
- How does a cow greet people at Christmas? *Moooooory Christmas*!
- What's Santa's favorite snack? *A jolly roll.*
- Where does Santa take his reindeer for lunch? *Deery Queen.*

If jokes don't get you into the Christmas spirit, maybe some random acts of kindness will. Try the following:

- Take a thermos of hot chocolate to school today and give a cup to each one of your teachers before school starts.
- Volunteer to go grocery shopping for an elderly person in your neighborhood or church.
- Ask your youth leader if your group can visit a retirement home this Christmas and spread cheer to some senior citizens who may not have family in town.
- Bake cookies for your youth pastor, Sunday school teacher, or church staff.
- Surprise your folks with some hot apple cider this evening.

Know It!

Be willing to go the extra mile this Christmas season. No one enjoys being around a Scrooge. But with long lines, hectic traffic, and little money, it can be very easy to show your frustration. Determine to spread Christmas cheer in spite of your personal circumstances. When it gets difficult, stop and count your blessings. That will quickly put things into perspective.

Read It!

Ephesians 4:31-32; Philippians 4:4-5

Pray It!

Ask God to help you reflect his love through your actions this Christmas season.

Collision Course

Know It!

God can do extraordinary things through someone who's teachable. But the one who thinks he's always right and is out to show everyone that he's in charge, is on dangerous ground.

Read It!

Acts 10;
Galatians 2:11-12, 14-15, 17-21

Pray It!

Ask God to give you a teachable spirit and to point out any attitudes or actions in your life that point the opposite.

This is the transcript of the actual radio conversation of a U.S. naval ship with Canadian authorities off the coast of Newfoundland.

Canadians: Please divert your course 15 degrees to the south to avoid a collision.

Americans: Recommend you divert your course 15 degrees to the north to avoid a collision.

Canadians: Negative. You will have to divert your course 15 degrees to the south to avoid a collision.

Americans: This is the Captain of a U.S. Navy ship. I say again, divert *your* course.

Canadians: No, I say again, you divert *your* course.

Americans: This is the aircraft carrier USS *Lincoln*, the second largest ship in the United States Atlantic Fleet. We are accompanied by three destroyers, three cruisers, and numerous support vessels. I demand that you change your course 15 degrees north. I say again, that's one five degrees north, or countermeasures will be undertaken to ensure the safety of this ship.

Canadians: This is a lighthouse. Your call.

Oftentimes Christians are seen as unbending and inflexible. While it's important to be sure of your beliefs and to stand firmly, it's also important to remain teachable. You may know a lot about the Bible, and you may belong to a great church, but you still have a lot to learn from your heavenly Father.

A Christian with a pliable heart is the one God uses to do extraordinary things. He can work through someone who isn't convinced that he's always right.

The apostles Paul and Peter had similar personalities. They were both bold, confident, direct, and intently focused on their God-given mission. Yet when Paul pointed out a mistake that Peter had made with the Gentiles, Peter displayed a teachable spirit and succumbed to Paul's truthful and constructive criticism. It would have been extremely easy for Peter to say, "Hey! I've been a Christian a lot longer than you have, Paul. I was even a disciple and followed Jesus for three years. Look at your past! How many Christians were you instrumental in killing before you asked God to forgive you?"

Peter even denied Jesus three times, but because he had a teachable spirit, he humbled himself, sought forgiveness, and was made right with God. Judas only denied Christ once, but because he didn't have a pliable spirit, he couldn't humble himself to seek forgiveness and was lost forever.

King Ahab was mad! The city Ramoth-gilead belonged to his people, yet it was not in their possession. So he called a meeting with King Jehoshaphat of Judah and asked if he'd be willing to join forces with him and fight for Ramoth-gilead. Jehoshaphat told Ahab that he was willing to help, but he also said he wanted to seek the direction of God first.

Ahab brought his 400 heathen prophets before Jehoshaphat and asked them if it was God's will they go to war. The prophets assured the king it was and that he would be victorious. That's exactly what Ahab wanted to hear. He turned to Jehoshaphat, expecting his support, but he was shocked instead.

Jehoshaphat didn't know these prophets. He didn't know their lifestyle or their motives. But he *did* know God. And he knew when he listened to those 400 prophets that he didn't hear God's voice. So he turned to King Ahab and surprised him by asking, "Don't you have a godly prophet we can talk to?"

You see, it wasn't enough that Jehoshaphat listened to good voices and positive messages. He knew he hadn't heard the right voice yet; he was waiting for God's message—be it positive or negative. You may assume that as long as you're listening to good people say good things, you're hearing what God wants you to hear. Do you realize there are Christians saying exactly the opposite of what God wants them to say? Be sure you're listening to the *right* voice—not simply a good voice.

King Ahab responded that there was one prophet of the Lord left. He explained that he didn't like to use him much, because he usually said things that Ahab didn't want to hear. But Ahab knew this prophet was a godly man. So he called for Micaiah.

There are Christian speakers, preachers, and leaders who tell an audience exactly what they want to hear. They make them laugh and feel good about themselves. And there are others who cut right to the chase and tell their audience what God wants them to hear. This usually makes people angry. We're living in a day and age where most Christians don't want to hear the truth. We simply want to hear what makes us feel good.

Know It!

Are you listening to people who make you feel good? Or are you listening to people who challenge you and make you think?

Read It!

1 Kings 22;
Jeremiah 26:18-19;
Micah 1:1;
2 Timothy 4:3-4

Pray It!

Be honest with God. Ask him to wake you up if you've been sleeping through feel-good messages.

Whose Voice Are You Listening To?

Know It!

We're in danger today of being surrounded by good people saying good things. But good things aren't necessarily godly things. God doesn't always have good things to say! Oftentimes what he has to say makes us uncomfortable. Whose voice will you choose to listen to?

Read It!

1 Kings 22;
2 Timothy 4:5, 18;
Titus 1:16

Pray It!

Tell God you're committed to hearing his truth. Ask him to help you discern when you're not hearing his voice. Tell him you want to be as discerning as Jehoshaphat; even when hearing 400 people saying good things, you want to know if the message isn't from God.

A messenger for the 400 heathen prophets got to Micaiah before King Ahab did. "Hey, look, Micaiah. All the prophets are promising Ahab he'll be victorious in battle. You'd better say the same thing." Talk about pressure! Four hundred to one!

But Micaiah responded that he would say only what God told him to say. He approached King Jehoshaphat and King Ahab and told them to proceed into battle. *Why did he say that after he had just promised to give them the Lord's message?*

Before Micaiah gave the kings God's message, he first let the kings know he was mocking the heathen prophets, acting in sarcasm and telling Ahab only what he wanted to hear. Ahab caught on immediately and asked Micaiah again what God's message was.

So Micaiah gave it to him straight. He told Ahab that he would die in battle. Ahab didn't really believe it. He was determined to conquer Ramoth-gilead, so he decided to disguise himself in battle. He was trying to escape God's judgment.

Many people today are trying to escape reality by having plastic surgery, moving to a different part of the country, even changing husbands or wives. And many are also trying to escape God's judgment by filling their lives with good things—volunteering in charities, making financial donations, or organizing neighborhood gatherings. But filling your life with good things isn't the same as filling your life with the power of the Holy Spirit. When he controls our lives, we begin to live in radical obedience to his Lordship.

Sure enough, King Ahab was killed in battle. That's a strong reminder to all of us that it doesn't pay to do things our way. Whose voice are you listening to? Your friends may tell you what you want to hear. Your parents may give great advice. Your teachers and counselors may share their wisdom. And your youth pastor may even make you think. But guess what! If they don't have the voice of the Lord, you're not listening to the right voice! And just as Ahab's 400 wrong voices eventually led him to ruin, the wrong voices you tune in to will eventually lead you to ruin as well.

Have you ever stopped to think that Mary was the one human being who was with Jesus Christ from his birth until his death? She got to know him in a way that few others did. She held the King of kings as a baby, rocked him to sleep, and nursed him when he was hungry.

She watched him grow into a teenager, listened to his jokes, and saw him hustle through his chores. As a young adult, she noticed his humble yet winning personality, the articulate way he spoke, and the determination in which he moved. She saw the Son of God preach to thousands, heal blind men, and raise the dead. She also watched him die a horrendous death, yet she rejoiced and celebrated when he rose from the dead. Mary was with Jesus during each phase of his earthly life.

Christmas is only a few days away. This year, determine to have a MARY type of Christmas by living out the following truths.

- *Mary trusted God for the impossible.* When the angel announced she would deliver the Messiah, she didn't understand it. It seemed ridiculous, but her response was, "I believe. It is as you say." This Christmas will you, too, trust God for the impossible? Is he calling you to do something that seems ridiculous? Even though you don't understand and can't see what's ahead, you have the opportunity–like Mary–to respond in simple faith: "I believe. It is as you say."
- *Mary was obedient.* Her obedience to God required her to risk disaster. In her culture, an unmarried pregnant woman was shunned. And unless the father of the child agreed to marry her, she would probably remain unmarried for life. If her own father rejected her, she could be forced into begging or prostitution in order to earn her living. And with her story about the Holy Spirit impregnating her, she risked being labeled crazy as well. It must have seemed as though everything was against her.

  But in spite of the risks, Mary still responded in obedience: *"I am willing."* In spite of the possible costs, will you be obedient this Christmas? Will you ask God to help you overlook the risks and simply say yes to his holy will?

Know It!
God wants to help you have a Mary Christmas this year—full of hope, blessing, and assurance that he is with you!

Read It!
Lamentations 3:22-23; Luke 1–2; Hebrews 11:1

Pray It!
Be honest with God. If you're scared, tell him. If you're full of doubts, let him know. If you don't understand, ask for faith to know his will in spite of your questions.

Have a *MARY* Christmas! (Part 2)

Know It!
God doesn't always reveal his plans right away. Often, when it seems as though everything is going wrong, he is quietly working behind the scenes. Can you trust him when you can't see what's ahead?

Read It!
Lamentations 3:25-26;
Micah 5:2;
Matthew 1:18-24; 2

Pray It!
Ask God to deepen your faith this Christmas.

When Mary said, "I am willing," she didn't know about the tremendous blessing she'd receive. She only knew that God was asking her to serve him, and she willingly obeyed. Will you react the same way? Don't wait to see the bottom line before obeying God. Offer yourself as a willing servant—even when the results of doing so look disastrous.

- *Mary allowed herself to be accountable.* She made herself accountable to her spiritually wise and older cousin, Elizabeth. We can imagine these two women praying and rejoicing together in their godly obedience. Make it a point to share your deepest questions, needs, requests, and victories with another Christian who is solid enough to ask appropriate questions and who is willing to pray with you.
- *Mary never lost faith that God was in control.* When Caesar Augustus, the Roman emperor, decreed that a census must be taken throughout the nation, it meant that Joseph and a pregnant Mary would have to make the trip from Nazareth to Bethlehem. Mary knew the 70-mile trip wouldn't be easy, and she could have easily begun questioning God's plans. But she trusted that God was in complete control. Can you trust that God controls all of history—even when you don't understand it?

  Because of the decree of Caesar Augustus, Jesus was born in the very town prophesied for his birth (Micah 5:2), even though his parents didn't live there. God was quietly working behind the scenes, even though Mary and Joseph couldn't see his hand.
- *Mary trusted in the midst of discomfort.* In Bethlehem, Joseph and Mary soon discovered the inns were filled with other travelers who had reached the destination much earlier. Mary was reduced to giving birth to her first child in a cold, dark, damp cave. No medical staff. No medicine or sterile environment. Just a frightened young girl, her frightened husband, and a few noisy animals.

  When we don't understand to begin with, and when our situation becomes uncomfortable on top of that, we often tend to question whether we heard God correctly, or maybe we question God himself. Mary simply continued to trust. If you can learn to trust in the midst of hardship and discomfort, God will bless you by teaching you things you couldn't have learned otherwise.

Imagine the letdown after traveling for 70 miles in the condition Mary was in, only to find out there were no more rooms available and she would have to give birth to her first child in a cave. Do you really want to have a Mary-type Christmas this year? Then realize that when you do God's will, you're not guaranteed a comfortable life. You're promised only that even your discomfort has meaning in God's plan.

We like to think that Mary was comfortable, because most of the popular Christmas scenes picture her kneeling serenely by a manger with a baby who's glowing. Chances are good that the King of kings was crying and uncomfortable himself. Stables were often crude caves with feeding troughs (mangers) carved into rock walls.

Though Christmas cards picture a clean atmosphere with happy animals in the background, the truth was that Jesus was born in an extremely unsterile and filthy environment. This certainly wasn't the atmosphere the Jews expected as the birthplace of the Messiah. They thought their promised Messiah would be born into royalty. But Mary didn't limit God by her expectations, and neither should we. God is at work wherever he's needed in our sin-darkened and dirty world.

That night, the world's greatest birth announcement took place. The greatest event in history had just happened—the Messiah had been born! For ages the Jews had waited for this, and when it finally happened, the announcement came to some humble shepherds. They were terrified, but their fear soon turned to joy. First they ran to see the baby, then they spread the word. Jesus Christ is *your* Messiah, *your* Savior. Do you look forward to meeting him in prayer and in his Word each day? Is your relationship so special that you can't help sharing this joy with your friends?

Know It!

Do you still picture Jesus Christ as a baby in a manger—or is he your Lord? Make sure you don't underestimate Jesus Christ. Let him grow up in your life! One of the best ways to do this is by exercising a mature faith in his plan . . . even in the midst of an uncomfortable situation. Jesus may not meet the specific expectations you have for your life. He may want to move you beyond your own dreams. Again, can you trust him?

Read It!

Isaiah 53:1-6; 54:17; Luke 2:8-14; 2 John 1:3

Pray It!

Give God your human expectations and ask him to replace them with his dreams, plans, and vision for your life. They may not be more comfortable, but they will always be better!

Are You like Mary?

Know It!
God's best servants are often plain people who are available to him. Mary was available. Are you? God's plans involve extraordinary events in ordinary people. This Christmas, will you let him use you in a way he's never used you before?

Read It!
Isaiah 59:17; 65:24-25; Luke 1:38; 2:41

Pray It!
Give God a merry Christmas by asking him to help you celebrate a Mary-type Christmas. And if you're wondering what to give the King of kings on his birthday . . . the very best gift is always yourself!

Are you discovering how *you* can have a Mary-type of Christmas this year? Let's recap! To have a blessed Christmas like Mary, the mother of Jesus, had:

- *Trust God for the impossible.* Even when you don't understand God's ways, maintain your faith in his wisdom.
- *Be obedient.* Display a willing spirit in spite of the risks.
- *Make yourself accountable.* Find a wise and older Christian who's willing to invest time and prayers into your life this year.
- *Remember that God is in control.* Even when it doesn't appear that God is working, have faith that he IS in control. When you can't see his hand, trust his heart.
- *Continue to trust in the midst of an uncomfortable situation.* Your faith may not cause your situation to suddenly become better. In fact, you may become even more uncomfortable. But God can and will change your heart if you'll maintain your trust in his perfect will.
- *Allow God to make good things from your mistakes.* Twelve years after Christ was born, Mary lost him! She and Joseph thought Jesus was somewhere in the caravan of family and friends they were traveling with, but she soon discovered he was missing. Yet Jesus was exactly where he was supposed to be—at the temple. Mary maintained a teachable spirit and learned more about her son from this incident.
- *Ponder some things this Christmas.* Instead of doing all the talking, consider being quiet for a while and thinking about Christ's birth and all it means. Be willing to ponder some things as Mary did. Learn to become comfortable with silence. Start a journal. Memorize some Scripture. Learn to truly meditate on God's holy Word this Christmas.

Mary was the ***one human*** *who*
a. could bake really good banana bread on a wood stove.
b. started the whole Christmas gift exchange.
c. was with Jesus from birth to death.

Mary ***trusted*** *God*
a. for a really strong donkey.
b. for the impossible.
c. for a voucher when the first Holiday Inn opened.

Mary ***dared*** *to be*
a. seen in the latest gunny-sack maternity clothes.
b. accountable.
c. pleasant even though the church didn't give her a baby shower.

God ***controls*** *all*
a. of history.
b. the hairs on your head.
c. the gifts you'll get this season.

When we ***do God's will***
a. we'll probably end up on *Who Wants to Be a Millionaire?*
b. we'll eventually get what we want.
c. we are not guaranteed a comfortable life; we are promised only that our discomfort has meaning in God's plan.

The ***greatest event in history*** *happened*
a. when Krispy Kreme donuts came to Bethlehem.
b. when the Messiah King of kings chose to leave heaven and invade our world with love.
c. no homework was given over Christmas holidays.

I can have a ***Mary Christmas*** *by*
a. trusting God for the impossible.
b. being obedient.
c. making myself accountable.
d. remembering that God really is in control.
e. maintaining a strong faith in uncomfortable situations.
f. pondering quietly instead of always talking.
g. allowing God to make good things out of my mistakes.
h. all of the above.

Know It!
A person's character is revealed by his or her response to the unexpected. When something doesn't go as you wanted it to today, how will you respond?

Read It!
Matthew 1:18-25; 2; Luke 1–2

Pray It!
Ask God to help you keep your focus on him this Christmas.

Is It Tough to Be a Christian? (Part 1)

Know It!
Being made fun of because of your Christian faith? Being made fun of by other Christians? Good news! You're on the right track.

Read It!
1 John 2:20-22; 4:1-6; 3 John 1:11; Jude 1:5-7

Pray It!
Ask God to strengthen you and help you continue to stand in boldness against sin—no matter how difficult it gets.

Is it becoming more and more difficult for you to be a sold-out, 100-percent-committed Christian? If so, you're on the right track! The apostle Paul warned his young mentor, Timothy, that in the last days it would be very difficult to live a Christian life. Was Paul trying to discourage his young Christian friend? No. He was being truthful.

If you're truly living in radical obedience to the lordship of Jesus Christ, you're well aware of the fact that it's . . . tough! It's not easy to take a stand against abortion when the entire class is saying it's simply a woman's choice. It's hard to express why you're saving sexual intimacy until marriage when you're surrounded by friends who are playing around sexually. And it's difficult to say no to a certain movie you know God doesn't want you to see—especially when all your church friends are seeing it!

When you take a bold stand against sin, it's likely you'll be labeled judgmental. But it's important for you to know that those who call you that don't really understand the concept of judgment. Do you realize the Bible says there are times when we *should* be judgmental? Many Christians have the mistaken idea that tolerance is always a virtue. Guess what—it's not! There are times when God expects you—just like Jesus—to take a bold stand against sin. Jesus never had an open mind toward sin. He called it for what it was—SIN. He loved sinners, but he never made excuses for the wrong in their lives.

God doesn't want you to be tolerant of sin. He wants you to tolerate *people* but not sin. There's a huge difference. And when you speak out against sexual intimacy outside of marriage, bisexuality, abortion, or any other sin, people will point fingers at you and call you judgmental. Some Christians will even accuse you of judging others.

But labeling sin for what it is isn't being judgmental; it's being factual. When you point to an apple tree and say, "Look at those apples," are you being judgmental? No, you're just stating what has already been proved. "That's an apple tree. It bears apples."

When you call sin *sin,* you're simply stating what God has already declared as Truth in his Holy Word. That's not judgment. That's reality.

Many Christians want to focus only on God's grace. "God will forgive," they say. And yes, God *will* forgive a truly repentant heart. (For a reminder on what true repentance is, flip back to August 30.) But God is also a God of wrath. There are two sides to our heavenly Father. If there weren't, he would be imbalanced. And we serve a perfect God. It's much easier to simply overlook his wrath and focus only on his grace, isn't it? But to do so isn't living a spiritually mature life.

Is It Tough to Be a Christian? (Part 2)

Most people want to hear about the benefits of Christianity—what they'll gain—but don't want to hear about what they may need to give up to follow Christ. The rich young ruler who approached Jesus fell into this category. He was a good person doing good things, and he was interested in following Jesus. But when Jesus told him it would cost him 100 percent, the young man walked away sadly. Jesus drew the line. It was as if he were saying, "You asked the question; I'm giving you absolute truth. Will you accept it and follow me?"

But the man didn't want truth. He wanted a "feel good" answer. He wanted Jesus to say, "I understand that your money is really important to you. You're a good person. Tell you what. Go ahead and keep living the way you want to, continue to let your wealth consume you, and I'll still let you call me Lord."

The truth made the young man so uncomfortable that he couldn't remain in the presence of Christ any longer. Jesus doesn't always tell us what we want to hear. But he *is* faithful to tell us what we *need* to hear.

Christianity isn't really about what we want. It *is* about total surrender and accepting God's Word as absolute truth.

Is it tough to be a Christian? Yes, if you give it your all. Was it tough for Jesus to obey his heavenly Father? Yes. It cost him his life. Was it worth it? Absolutely. Will it be worth it for you to give God your all in total obedience? Absolutely.

But that's going to be tough! I mean . . . I might have to walk away from some friends. Stay away from some parties. Quit gossiping and keep a hold on my temper. Yes, total obedience to the lordship of Jesus Christ is radical. It means saying no to some things so you can say a huge yes to Jesus.

Many people find it difficult to believe if they don't say yes to Christ, they'll actually be separated from him forever in hell. This isn't anything new. It all started in the Garden of Eden. Satan planted doubt in Eve's mind. *Do you really think eating one piece of fruit could separate you from your Father?*

Know It!

Satan is the father of lies. He's the master of deceit, and he'll work overtime to convince you that being a Christian really isn't difficult at all; that you can continue to do your own thing and call your own shots. Don't fall for his lies! If you listen to him, you're listening to the wrong voice.

Read It!

Genesis 3;
Matthew 19:16-30;
1 Peter 5:8

Pray It!

Ask God to help you live in radical obedience to his lordship.

Is It Tough to Be a Christian? (Part 3)

Know It!

The Bible tells us that everyone who wants to live a godly life will be persecuted. In other words . . . if it's tough for you to be a Christian, you're doing something right! If those around you are making fun of your morality, you're on the right track. Rest assured that God will never allow you to experience more than you and he together can handle.

Read It!

Matthew 7:13-14;
1 Corinthians 6:18;
1 Timothy 3:13;
Revelation 21:8

Pray It!

Ask God to strengthen you and mold you into the dynamic disciple he needs you to be.

Satan has been playing the same deceptive game ever since he deceived Adam and Eve in the Garden of Eden. *Oh, come on! How could it be wrong to make love to someone if you really care about him? Bisexuality? What's the big deal? People are just trying to express themselves in different and creative ways. Do you really believe that could separate you from your heavenly Father? Is that really sin?*

Do you realize the Bible says that no other sin affects a person as sexual sin does? Every time sexual sin is mentioned in the Bible, it's connected with a death sentence. God has given us some important rules to live by. They're known as the Ten Commandments. (For a quick refresher on those laws, flip back to August 10-19.) He expects us to live by those laws, and when we don't, it's considered sin.

As this year comes to a close, maybe it would be a good idea for you to ask God to help you get back to the basics. To take his laws seriously. To commit yourself to living in radical obedience to his lordship. And when you do? Know it will be tough to be a Christian.

Count on people giving you a hard time. Sometimes even other Christians may give you a hard time. They'll call you straight and narrow-minded. That's okay. You're walking a straight and narrow road! And yes, it's tough. It would be much easier to walk the wide road filled with thousands of other travelers. But you have a much higher calling on your life. God calls *you* to be a dynamic sold-out disciple living in radical obedience to his lordship.

Hey, Christian!

I saw you yesterday as you climbed out of bed and started your daily routine. You began the day without praying. I kept watching you—expecting you at least to pray for your meals—but you didn't. I like the fact that you're so ungrateful.

You stupid idiot! You're mine . . . and you don't even know it! You think you're a Christian because you go to church, but you've never committed your life to Christ. You've never let your "Christianity" affect choices you make. Ha! But I have you believing you're his. I've fooled you!

You and I go way back. We've been going steady for years . . . and I hate you! Do you realize that? I hate you, because I hate God. I'm only using you to get even with him. He kicked me out of heaven, and I'm going to use you as long as possible to pay him back.

You're so stupid! You don't even realize how much God loves you; that he has great plans in store for you. Ha! You've yielded your life to me, and I'm going to make your life a living hell.

And the best part about this relationship is that you don't even realize you've yielded to me. You don't get it, do you? That by not giving your all to Jesus Christ, you end up following me by default. And you know what's really funny? Most of the time I have you convinced that I don't even exist!

Thanks to you, I'm showing God who's really boss in your life. We've been having some great times, haven't we? I love watching those dirty movies with you, cussing people out when they cut in front of you on the road, lying, being hypocritical, messing around sexually, gossiping, telling off-color jokes, stabbing people in the back, disrespecting stupid adults and moronic leaders.

I'm relieved that you don't want to give this up. We're having a great time, aren't we? And what's really funny is the fact that you don't have a clue I'm doing all this to destroy you! Ha! You think we're just having fun. But I have eternal plans for you!

Know It!
Satan will do anything to get your attention off of Christ. Remember . . . you can't be spiritually neutral. You're either living for God or you're following Satan by default.

Read It!
Luke 10:18;
2 Corinthians 11:14;
Ephesians 6:10-18;
1 Peter 5:8-9

Pray It!
In the name of Jesus Christ, pray that Satan will leave you alone. Ask God to give you the strength to overcome temptation.

Letter from Satan (Part 2)

Know It!
Satan will try to convince you that wrong is right and right is stupid. Don't listen to him. Keep your eyes focused on Jesus and your ears tuned in to the Holy Spirit.

Read It!
Zechariah 3:2;
Mark 4:15;
Romans 16:20;
James 4:7-8

Pray It!
Ask God to help you memorize Scripture, so when you're tempted by Satan you can use the Bible as ammunition.

Hey, Christian!

Yeah, I'll go ahead and call you that. I know you like it, but you have no clue what Christianity is really about. If you did, you wouldn't be hanging out with me and listening to the lies I've so carefully crafted. Ha! You're such an idiot.

Do you have any idea how much I loathe you? Do you know I'm working overtime to make sure you spend eternity with me in hell? Yeah, you've heard about hell. I talk it up as the big eternity party place. And you know what's funny? You've believed me! I heard you telling someone last week, "Maybe hell won't be so bad; I mean, I'll finally get to do what I want."

You moron! That's what I want you to believe. But I have a big surprise for you. Hell will be nothing like that! It will be eternal damnation. People will be in physical, emotional, spiritual, and mental torment forever. And I'll be laughing my head off! Party time? No way. You won't even want to open your eyes to see who's standing next to you. The demons will surround you in fear and torment and mockery.

Why am I even bothering to write you? I'm sending you a sarcastic letter of thanks for letting me use you for most of your foolish life. You are so gullible. You have no idea how much I laugh at you throughout every day. When I tempt you to sin, you give in. HA! HA! HA! You make me sick. You're so stinking weak!

Sin is beginning to take its toll on your life. You're angry. Bitter. Obsessed with stupid things . . . like your weight and people liking you. If you had any idea how temporary that stuff is! But I've got you convinced it's really important. I am so good at what I do.

Of course, morons like you make my job really easy. If you were smart, you'd run somewhere, confess your sins, and live for God with what little time you have left. What a stupid jerk you are! I HATE YOU!

My dear, dear Child,

Oh, how I love you! I long for you to spend eternity with me. I've been diligently preparing a place for you in my perfect Kingdom. You'll love it. You don't have the capacity to even imagine what it's like, but someday you'll be living here with me in person. That is . . . if you let me have total control of your life.

I know you can't comprehend how very much I love you, but I'm hoping you'll know that my death was specifically for *you.* That's right. Even though you've heard that I died for the world at large, I want you to understand it was really for you! You see . . . if you had been the only person in all the world, I still would have chosen to leave the glory and splendor of heaven to come to earth and experience the torture I endured . . . just for you. I love you that much.

You are my pride and joy! I dream such big dreams for you! I want to do extraordinary things with your life. But, my child, I need *all* of you. I won't force you to give me your life. I love you too much to control your decisions, but I yearn for you to trust me with your all.

My child, I am perfect, and my Kingdom is perfect. Therefore I cannot allow sin into my Kingdom. Knowing, however, that you were born with sin, I gave myself—in the form of my Son—to pay the price for you, so you could spend eternity with me. It's my ultimate gift to you. You can't earn it, and you can't buy it. I simply want to give it to you. But again . . . I won't force you to accept it. You have to make that decision on your own.

Please choose to follow me, my child. I love you more than life itself. And I'm working diligently on our eternal home.

Your heavenly Father,
God

Know It!
God is crazy about you and has gone to great lengths to let you know it. How will you respond?

Read It!
Psalm 19:1; Jeremiah 31:35-37; 32:17; John 3:16

Pray It!
Give God your all and ask him to help you begin living in radical obedience to his lordship.